D0560207

By G. D. H. Cole

A GUIDE THROUGH WORLD CHAOS

WHAT MARX REALLY MEANT

.

By G. D. H. Cole and Margaret Cole

THE INTELLIGENT MAN'S REVIEW OF
EUROPE TODAY

A GUIDE TO MODERN POLITICS

.

Edited by G. D. H. Cole

WHAT EVERYBODY WANTS TO KNOW
ABOUT MONEY

.

These are Borzoi Books published by
ALFRED A. KNOPF

A GUIDE TO
MODERN POLITICS

A
Guide to Modern Politics

BY

G. D. H. COLE *and* MARGARET COLE

ALFRED · A · KNOPF

NEW YORK

1934

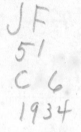

A GUIDE TO
MODERN POLITICS

PREFACE

THE DEPARTMENT OF LIFE which is called Politics is becoming, in
these days, very large and very insistent. More and more subjects
enter daily into the domain of the political State; more and more is
the politician or statesman supposed to be an expert on the most
diverse questions; more and more do politics enter into and affect
the lives of millions of people who in past generations would have
lived and died without concern with the political machine. It is true
that in Great Britain and the United States for many years the scope
of politics was far more restricted than in some continental countries; over the whole field of industry and finance, for example,
political control was long confined to the minimum. Even in these
countries, however, the situation has been steadily changing. If we
leave out of consideration for the moment the special experiences of
the war, and also any proposals which have been made by Socialist
parties, we find that the past fifty years have seen in Great Britain
an enormous expansion of the field of direct government, and latterly of State intervention in industrial and commercial questions.
Before the war, the growth of "the bureaucracy" was a frequent
theme of complaint among individualist capitalists; since the war
"the bureaucracy" has continued to grow; while the United States,
as these words are being written, seems to be in process of making
a great leap from a highly *laissez-faire* to a partly State-controlled
system.

These changes, however, pale before the much greater changes
that have taken place in Russia, Italy, and Germany. Widely as they
differ in essentials, the Communist and Fascist systems have this in
common, that in both the State is not merely omnicompetent but

also omnipresent, concerning itself positively in every walk of life. In a sense, it is idle to ask a Russian or an Italian to distinguish between politics and, say, economics, for in their countries everything is political, directed and controlled by the agents of the political State. Nor can we say rashly that this development is confined to the three countries mentioned, for Communism is avowedly an international creed, and Fascism, as we have recently seen, though anti-international, is highly infectious. At any moment, one or other of the hitherto stable countries may find its political system suddenly enlarging itself over the whole of its social life. And, whether or not that occurs, it can safely be said that the political machine is not in the least likely to retreat for many years from the positions it has seized. Anarchists, and all those who, like Herbert Spencer, think government an evil, must turn in their graves; for all present changes, and most proposed changes, tend to produce, not less government, but more.

Nor is it only that the sphere of politics has been widened to an almost incredible extent, the positive effects and the positive demands of the political system upon the individual have also enormously increased. France after the French Revolution and during the revolutionary wars was the first large-scale example of a "popular" nationalism, i.e. a nationalism which demanded, in theory at least, the direct and positive support of all the citizens; but it has been left to the twentieth century to show what fierce demands a State, even in peace-time, can make of its people. (In war, of course, we all know to what an extent "mobilisation of the forces" now means and will continue to mean "mobilisation of the population.") In Great Britain, apart from its war experiences, the positive demands of the State are still comparatively mild; but in other countries the process has gone much further. Revolutionary Russia has been the scene of one long struggle to enlist, by force if need be, the active co-operation of as many as possible of its citizens; and Nazi Germany shows clearly enough its intention, either by bludgeoning or by calls to action, deeply to affect the lives of individuals. The pure mugwump, in the modern world, will soon be as extinct as the dinosaur, or, if he survives, it will be rather in the form of an ostrich, with his head buried in the sand, hoping that the sandstorm may somehow be kind enough to pass him by. "You May

Not Think About Politics," as a recent popular pamphlet menacingly remarks; "But Politics Thinks About YOU."

For these two reasons, the growth in the scope and in the imme-
diacy of politics, the ordinary man is much more concerned with
them to-day than ever before. But there is yet a third reason—the
great political upheavals that have taken place of recent years. As
yet, the storms that have shaken one country in Europe after another have been but palely reflected here; but there is no security
that we shall escape them, that Great Britain, any more than any
other country, will be able to avoid the drastic remodelling of institutions ill-fitted to the present powers of production.

For there is nothing astonishing, though there may be much that
is alarming, in the present political struggles and earthquakes.
Struggles and changes, no less alarming and, scale for scale, no less
destructive, took place all over Europe during the sixteenth century,
and for much the same reason, because the developing powers of
production were insistently demanding a revision of out-of-date social and economic institutions. During the past century, it is now a
commonplace to say, science and exploration have so enormously
increased the productive resources at man's command that the social
and political institutions which he had previously evolved for their
control and distribution have proved patently inadequate. The recent phenomena of glut and starvation, of armies of unemployed
and of rotting wheat and burning coffee, are only the outward
symptoms of this deep inadequacy, and the social and political upheavals merely attempts, wise and unwise, to revise the institutions
before it is too late.

Somehow or other, the world must reform its institutions if it is
not to perish. But reformation can only be possible or effective if it
is based upon an adequate comprehension of three things, of which
the first is the end which has to be aimed at, viz. the reshaping of
institutions in a manner which shall enable the present productive
powers to function adequately and rationally. The second comprises
the forces and traditions, differing, certainly, among the different
countries, from and through which the necessary changes may be
produced. For no change, however revolutionary, has ever swept
away the entire tradition of the community in which the change
was made, and in the modern world, with its intense and separate

national cultures and institutions, it is more than ever necessary that the reformer should clearly understand and appreciate these various cultures and institutions. Only a political idiot would suggest that Rumania and the United States can solve their political problems by absolutely identical methods.

Finally, it is essential to have some understanding of what we may call the "technique" of political co-operation, the means and methods by which men may be induced, not merely to acquiesce, but actively to co-operate in the social institutions which are devised for their benefit. To some extent, of course, these must vary from case to case and from country to country; but since men are human, and their similarities, even in the most extreme cases, greater than their differences, there is a wide common ground, and much that one country may learn from another in the domain of political dynamic. The important thing is that it should be learned; too many ideas which were excellent on paper have perished still-born because their authors had never considered how practically they should be translated into action.

It is in this belief, that what the world desperately needs to-day is a realistic study of political dynamic, that this book has been written. It is not, and does not purport to be, a full political guide to the universe, or even a full description; for that would require many volumes at least the size of this one. What it has attempted to do is to state the underlying realities of politics and political problems to-day, to describe, for the most important countries, the forces and institutions which seem to be of the greatest strength and importance for the future, to indicate certain directions in which immediate change is most obvious and essential, and to discuss some technical problems of politics with which any government that can presently be envisaged is certain to be faced.

The authors are, as they have often stated in other works, international Socialists. That is to say, they believe that present-day economic conditions are demanding an internationally-planned Society, in which competition as we now understand it and the exploitation of communities or sections of communities for the benefit of others will eventually cease. In this belief they are at one with the bulk of the members of Socialist and Communist societies throughout the world. But they are not fatalists; they believe that only a system of this sort will ultimately solve the problem, but

they do not believe that this system is *predestined* to come, or
that it will come without the determined co-operation of men.
There are alternatives. Chaos may come again; or at the best, a
vast deal of unnecessary suffering.

Nor do they believe that they can lay down in advance and in
full detail exactly what the appropriate institutions will turn out
to be, in this or any other country. In some cases they believe that
new institutions will be evolved, in others that existing institutions
will be changed or adapted, sometimes in ways that cannot now
be foreseen. The most that they can do is to make suggestions, to
indicate the direction of change, and to describe the forces, traditions, and methods available, believing that the clearer the sense
of purpose and the wider the knowledge of those who are concerned—as we all of us are—with reshaping our political instruments to something less repugnant to common sense or common
humanity, the less of suffering, disappointment and wasted effort
there is likely to be. And if some of the suggestions, through imperfect understanding or foreknowledge of events, turn out to be
inapplicable when and where they are suggested, it may be remembered that Machiavelli, the prophet of the Nation-State, waited
three hundred years before his own State put his precepts into
action, and that Marx has come to honour in the country where
his followers least of all expected it.

A GUIDE TO
MODERN POLITICS

CONTENTS

A GUIDE TO
MODERN POLITICS

BOOK I

POLITICS IN THE TWENTIETH CENTURY

1. THE FOUNDATIONS OF MODERN POLITICS

WHATEVER the world's political systems may have come to be in thirty years' time, the one thing certain is that they will be considerably unlike the systems under which most of us have been used to living. For better or worse we are in for comprehensive changes in the fundamental structure of society; and it will depend on us and on other men and women much like ourselves what is made of the objective conditions on which the States and societies of the future will have to be built. Of this we are one and all in varying degrees aware. We cannot help seeing that if we do not take part in shaping the society of to-morrow other people will shape it for us and we shall have to submit to the results of their political activity. Whether we play an active part or not, our lives and the lives of our children are being decided for us by the contentions of those who are active in a political sense. We can, if we wish, stand aside from the struggle at any rate for the moment, though we cannot be sure it will not forcibly drag us in before long. But even if we do stand aside we can by no possibility escape its consequences. For the political battle, while it assumes many different forms from place to place, is being carried on over the whole world, and there is no spot on earth to which a man can withdraw in the confidence that there at any rate it will pass him by and leave him to live his life unaffected. We are all in this thing up to the neck, however indifferent to it we may feel or wish to feel. It may matter little enough to us which political party controls the Government as long as the rival parties are divided only on minor issues and are at one in desiring to leave the essential structure of society intact. The position is very different when the questions at issue in politics go down to the very roots of human and social relationships, and the entire basis of our living together in society comes within the area of dispute.

Ours, then, is a political age. It is so in the main not because most of us want to be politically-minded but because we are being forced up against political problems by influences which we cannot escape. We have to shape things or let them be shaped for us by forces which we have renounced all attempt to control. To a certain extent these forces are impersonal, objective, material, and there is no getting away from them. But the shaping of human life within conditions set by these forces is a work for men, and if we play no part in it others will, and what they do will affect us. If we refuse to take an interest in politics to-day we are either cynics despairing of a world gone mad or less than intelligent human beings—mere living tools who will allow our future to be settled for us without making any attempt to control our fate.

PRE-WAR POLITICS

To most of us who are old enough to remember the early years of the twentieth century, this new world of decisive political struggle still seems strange. Not that the existence of such a world is new, for in fact it is very old, but we have met with it until quite lately only in the history books and not in real life. For societies alternate between periods in which men jog along staidly, mounted upon political and social systems which it hardly occurs to most of them to question, and periods in which men swop political horses, most often in the middle of the stream. It was the fortune of the nineteenth century to live through a period which, over most of the civilised world, combined an unprecedented rapidity of technical change with a remarkable stability of political and social institutions. Between 1789 and 1917, though the material face of civilisation was changed beyond all recognition, not a single challenging new idea of primary political importance succeeded in getting itself embodied in a practical shape. This was not because no new ideas were born. Socialism, for example, both came into being as a doctrine and took shape in a world-wide propagandist movement during the nineteenth century. But up to 1917, apart from the one short-lived local adventure of the Paris Commune, Socialism was never able to express itself concretely in the institutions of any Socialist community. One idea of revolution came to practical expression in France in 1789 and the following years, and thereafter the influence of that idea spread round the whole world. Socialism had to wait till 1917 to make its practical declaration of the *droits de l'homme et du citoyen* by means of an actual Socialist revolution, and we are living to-day under the eye of that new declaration.

In effect the nineteenth century, and the twentieth up to 1917, were working out and expressing gradually in the structure of their political systems the ideas that had provided the driving force of the great French Revolution. There were no doubt startling differences between the capitalist institutions and parliamentary systems of the nineteenth century and what had been in the mind of Rousseau or of Danton or Robespierre; and the authors of the *Déclaration des Droits de l'Homme* no more imagined that they were drawing up the charter of modern Parliamentarism than that they were providing a legal foundation for the large-scale Capitalism of the machine age. But great political ideas are rare, and mankind is notably economical in their use. In the history of civilisation a new idea has to go a long way, and men put it to uses of which those who invoked it first never dreamed.

Thus it happened that the practical political precepts which the nineteenth century drew from the French Revolution were those of Nationalism and Representative Government. Out of the idea of liberty they made that of the national State, sovereign in relation to all other States and governed by its own citizens. Out of the idea of equality they made that of equal voting rights, gradually embodied in the institution of universal suffrage. Out of fraternity they made much less, regarding it perhaps as no more than a rhetorical flourish to round off a revolutionary slogan. In effect, for fraternity the nineteenth century substituted as the third member of the new trinity property, on which the revolutionary *Déclaration* had insisted as an indispensable guarantee of freedom. Indeed, this "fourth musketeer" became the D'Artagnan of the party, a knight errant for the defence not mainly of the small property-owners whom the leaders of the French Revolution had in mind, but of the great capitalists and financiers of modern industrialism, and even of the great landlords whom the Age of Revolution had failed to dispossess.

During the nineteenth century, while the wealth made possible by the new powers of science and invention was piling up in huge heaps defended by the sacred right of property, the political institutions of representative government were broadening down from precedent to precedent over the civilised world. In Western Europe and in the United States, in the British Dominions and even in the South American Republics, societies were evolving towards a system of parliamentary democracy that seemed, even to the majority of radical thinkers, the last word in political organisation and political principle. Even to India and to other subject countries outside Europe the prospect of a very gradual approach to responsible parliamentary government on the western pattern was being held out. Japan was attempting to model her political, as well as her economic system, on the great industrial countries of the West. Even China seemed destined, after the Revolution of 1912, to grow finally into a sort of parliamentary State under the influence of European ideas and European material equipment. Moreover Socialism, though it challenged the very foundations of the capitalist economic order, seemed for the most part not to challenge but to accept, through its political parties aiming at the constitutional conquest of political power, the forms and institutions of the established parliamentary State. Though Marx himself had denounced the parliamentary State quite as ferociously as the capitalist system—of which indeed he regarded it as the derivative political expression—the majority of professing Marxists "revised" on this point the doctrine of their master. The influence of the parliamentary environment in which they worked brought them round to the view that Socialism and not merely social reform could be brought about by using the instrument of representative democracy. Apart from the defenders of obsolescent forms of feudal autocracy, who clung perilously to the older doctrines, only a handful of opponents appeared to challenge the parliamentary system; and these few political heretics seemed to most people mere cranks or fanatics hardly worthy of serious refutation. The world appeared to be heading straight for the completion of the edifice of parliamentary democracy, and even the sceptics and reactionaries could see no force capable of turning the movement aside.

In the civilised world, as it was on the eve of the Great War, the opposition to parliamentary government, such as it was, came chiefly from three quarters—from the feudalists and certain reactionary capitalist elements which had joined forces with them, from some left-wing revolutionary groups, and from a handful of romantics chiefly associated with Roman Catholicism. Of these the feudalists were for the most part simply holding fast to their ancient power or giving ground as slowly as they dared before the advance of the parliamentary forces; they were definitely on the defensive, and they were being gradually driven back. Russia and Spain were their chief remaining strongholds, and to a less extent Germany and Austria-Hungary, where constitutional government had been introduced in a partial and half-hearted way. Other Constitutions, including that of Great Britain, still retained many elements from the feudal past, but these had been subordinated in actual practice to the representative elements. There was a good deal of fight left in feudalism still, but most of the feudalists had no hope of turning back the world to an autocratic system.

In the second group of opponents were ranged the Russian Bolsheviks, who nevertheless mostly expected that Russia would have to pass through a parliamentary phase in the course of her transition to Socialism, and the various schools of Anarchists and Syndicalists in Europe, together with the American Industrial Workers of the World. To the third or romantic group belonged such movements as the *Action Française,* inspired by Charles Maurras, and in Great Britain the almost solitary figure of Mr. Hilaire Belloc, with his hankerings after a return to "monarchy" and his assiduous denunciation of the "Servile State."

Russia, even before 1914, came nearest to possessing a movement which did threaten to challenge effectively the dominant conception of the sovereign State. For the Russian Marxists, having to deal with a society in which they were allowed practically no scope for constitutional agitation, were largely immune from the temptation to re-state Marxism in evolutionary terms which could be reconciled with respectable parliamentary practice. They continued to regard their mission as the overthrow and destruction and not the capture and adaptation of the Tsarist State machine. But though this was the attitude of the majority fraction of the Russian Social Democrats (Bolshevik means majority), the minority (Mensheviks) had become converts to the evolutionary Socialism of Western Europe and were prepared as a first step towards Socialism to collaborate with the Russian Liberals in building up an orthodox parliamentary State. Most people believed that, in spite of Lenin's "fanaticism," Russia would in due course follow the example of the more advanced industrial countries and abandon autocracy in favour of a constitutional parliamentary régime. In Russia Communism, as we know it now, was in embryo before 1914. It had not been actually born; and most people, even most Socialists, were hardly aware of its existence.

Far more attention was being given in those pre-war years to Syndicalism and the various movements related to it, from Industrial Unionism in America to Guild Socialism in Great Britain. The Syndicalist movement proper, born out of Anarchism by its marriage with left-wing Trade Unionism, flourished only in the Latin countries and chiefly among workers engaged in small-scale industry. In France, where it was born, it was very active in the early years of the twentieth century, but it was already ebbing fast before 1914 in face of the growth of large-scale industrialism. The French Trade Unions were turning away from revolutionary "direct action" and the myth of the "general strike" to more respectable methods of collective bargaining on the model of British and German Trade Unionism. But Syndicalism retained its importance in more backward Italy and still more backward Spain, where it remains as the ally of Anarchism, a powerful force even to-day. The Syndicalists, even more fiercely than the Bolsheviks, hated the parliamentary State; but they set out to destroy it with the aim not of setting up a new proletarian State in its place, but of eradicating centralised government altogether. Their object was to reconstitute society as a loose federation of small free communes based upon economic associations of workers and peasants who would control production under a co-operative system without the need for any form of political government. Their ideal was purely Anarchist— the abolition of all government beyond the co-operative control of economic life—and they have since shown themselves fully as hostile to Communism as they were before the war to Parliamentarism and to feudal autocracy. The Anarchists and Syndicalists had their following in Russia as well as in the Latin countries, till they were swept aside in 1917; and emigrants transplanted their doctrines across the Atlantic to America, where their ideas underwent, in the very different economic atmosphere of the United States, a significant transformation and were reborn in the revolutionary "Industrial Unionism" of the Industrial Workers of the World. In America the revolutionary Syndicalists came up against a large-scale Capitalism to which the European form of their doctrine could not be applied without substantial change; and Industrial Unionism, retaining the Syndicalist hostility to the State and to political action, came to stand for centralised economic organisation and for the construction of a new social order based on the "One Big Union." The British Guild Socialists applied Syndicalist ideas in yet another way, making a doctrine which endeavoured to reconcile them with the fundamental tenets of orthodox Socialism. The Guild Socialists did not for the most part repudiate either the State or political action. But they held that "economic power precedes political power," and that only by winning workers' control in industry through Trade Union action would workers by hand and brain place themselves in a position to control the State or to institute a Socialist system.

Extremes meet. In England the Guild Socialists found that they had something in common with Mr. Belloc, and fought side by side with him against the encroachments of the "Servile State." Later on in Italy a good many old Syndicalists went over to Fascism and took part in the building up of the Fascist Trade Unions as elements in the new Corporative State. In France M. Georges Sorel, the theorist of extreme Syndicalism, formed an alliance for a time with the Catholic Royalists of the *Action Française,* drawn to them by common hatred of the parliamentary State. More royalist than the King and far more Catholic than the Pope, who ended by repudiating them, Charles Maurras and his fellow romantics did not really want to go back to the *ancien régime,* but rather to give birth before due time to an anti-democratic movement of a type that we should now call Fascist. They were appealing from the political rationalisations of the parliamentary system to the politics of instinct and emotion, acclaiming the principle of leadership against the democratic counting of heads, and exalting the breaking of heads as a method of political controversy into a sacred gospel of national virility. They discovered, long before Mussolini and Hitler, the romantic appeal of swashbuckling nationalism; but in those far-off days not many people gave more than a literary attention to M. Maurras and M. Léon Daudet. They were amusing political *enfants terribles,* but in that seemingly stable world of the years before 1914 they did not seem dangerous.

THE PRE-WAR POLITICAL SITUATION

Thus up to 1914 most people, at any rate in Western Europe, were living in a world that seemed in its essential qualities of political and economic organisation settled and sure of itself. Politics touched, and seemed likely to touch, only a tiny fraction of most men's lives. Most people lived in a social environment which they accepted almost without question as likely to last their time, subject only to gradual and secondary changes that were in no wise likely to disturb the even tenor of their existence. The general character of political institutions seemed to have been settled; and it seemed to remain only to complete by slow stages the progressive evolution towards a thoroughly "democratic" parliamentary system. There were some who wanted to advance fast, and others who wanted to go slow along this road, and there were of course still many people who did not want to advance along it at all; but even the opponents of parliamentary democracy for the most part regarded its continued progress as inevitable, and confined their efforts to an attempt to slow down the pace of change. There was hardly any argument about the fundamentals of political structure—only about secondary questions of piecemeal reform.

Even in this situation there was of course no lack of "movements." There were reformers and reactionaries of many sorts and kinds, each aiming at the alteration of this or that particular feature of the social system. There were even revolutionaries dreaming of the "day" when at length the masses would rise from their slumbers and put an end to the capitalist system. There were Socialists, Anarchists, Syndicalists—even Communists, though in those days we did not call them by that name. Those who were politically minded could join the movement of their choice, reformist, reactionary or revolutionary, and could get as enthusiastic as they liked about their particular "cause." But to the great majority of ordinary people there appeared to be no compelling reason for taking to politics unless they had a taste for it, and even those who were active in the various movements had for the most part at the back of their minds a shrewd suspicion that, whatever they might say, nothing very sensational was really likely to happen. Most people followed the political news in the daily papers with hardly a greater sense of its importance than they accorded to the football news, and in much the same spirit, and, when they voted, did so with no more than a passing concern for the success or failure of their chosen candidate or party. They could afford to be indifferent because the advent of this or that party to power was not likely much to affect their ways of living, their relations with other people, or their pursuit of any of their varied interests. Politics was a "party game" in which it was sometimes fun to take sides. At most it tended to be a matter on which one expressed one's convictions once every few years by a vote, and left it at that. For the rest, the politicians could look after it, or, perhaps better, the Civil Servants would see to it that things went on much the same in spite of the politicians' talk. How unperturbed a Pompeii most of us lived in up to 1914; and even then how few of us knew the lava for what it was!

This attitude existed almost equally among rich and poor, but perhaps most of all among the moderately well off. The rich did not really believe that the Socialists were on the point of confiscating their property, and the poor did not believe it either. Most employers looked forward with fair confidence to being employers to the end of their days or until they chose to retire in comfort. They might grumble at rising taxes and "socialistic" legislation; but they never for a moment supposed that they were on the point of being ruined. Most workers, too, expected to go on being workers for the rest of their lives, and expected in addition that they would be able to find employers to give them jobs. They might sympathise with Socialist ideas, but they had no real belief in the imminent coming of Socialism. The same state of mind existed among the rapidly growing and highly differentiated middle classes. The grocer, the publican, the commercial traveller, the "bookie," the cashier, the accountant, the technician, the doctor, the teacher, the Civil Servant, the small *rentier,* and the maiden aunt usually accepted, almost without question, the prospect of going on in the future much as

they had gone on hitherto, and of handing over to the next generation the prospect of a very similar way of living. Even to the Socialists the capitalist system seemed to have plenty of life left in it;
and had not Marx himself said that no social system was ever flung
away until it had done its work and turned from a means of developing men's productive powers into a fetter upon them?

PRE-WAR AMERICA

What has been said so far has been conceived mainly in terms
of European opinion. But it applies with even greater force to the
condition of opinion in the United States. For the average American
citizen, while he was capable of making exceedingly loud political
noises on occasion, was as a rule even more indifferent to politics
than the peoples of Western Europe, and very much more disposed
to hold politicians in contempt. This widespread indifference was
not so much due to a sense—though that sense existed—that all the
fundamental political problems had been settled once and for all
by the framers of the American Constitution, or at any rate since
the constitution had been decisively reinterpreted as the outcome of
the Civil War, as it was to an unwillingness to be bothered with
politics when there was so much else to occupy men's minds and
energies. Business, above all the business of individual money-
making in an environment of extraordinarily rapid economic
growth, pushed American parliamentarism up a dusty corner of the
enormous American stage, and in the circumstances it is not surprising that politics came to be regarded as a special and not very
reputable sort of business, to be engaged in by professional politicians
who regarded it rather as a means of living by their wits than as
an exercise in the art of government. The art of influencing the
politicians was a recognised and important branch of the art of
business; and in this sense the Americans were politically conscious
in a high degree. They were, in other respects as well, ready enough
to clamour to the politicians when they wanted something done;
but they regarded politics as an external thing to be influenced, and
not as a means of collective political expression for themselves.
American political parties had no doubt a large and vociferous
popular following during an election campaign; but at least as much
could be said of baseball in a not very different sense. It was true
even more of the Americans than of the European peoples that

they could see no pressing need for treating their politics as a really serious part of the art of living. Accordingly it was even harder in the United States than elsewhere to say what the rival parties stood for, or over what issues they fought so furiously together during an election. An American presidential election had not a little in common with a cup final raised to the nth power.

Nor did even the events of 1914–1918 shake the Americans more than momentarily out of their political indifference. After the entry of the United States into the war there was, indeed, a great national "mobilisation," and all the arts of the propagandist were invoked to heighten the sense of national solidarity. But when the war was over the Americans promptly shed their political enthusiasms and went back to "business as usual" with even more enthusiasm than before 1914. A vista of endlessly increasing prosperity seemed to be opening up before them, and there was even less reason than before for minding much what the politicians were up to. It took the great slump of 1929 and the following years to shake the American people out of their political indifference by destroying their unquestioning faith in American prosperity. But even when they had been well shaken they did not find it at all easy to know what to do. For even more than other peoples they had forgotten the art of real political organisation. They had two huge party machines which meant next to nothing; but they had very little besides, and no background of political ideas round which new organisations could easily grow up. The American Labour Unions, with only one or two exceptions, were totally devoid of any ideas not borrowed at second-hand from the world of business. Such Socialism as existed was either an unnaturalised importation from Europe or utterly inchoate in form. Nor was there any idea round which a Fascist movement could rally; for it needs Socialism to bring Fascism into life. The Americans fell back on the strong man, and the strong man of their choice very naturally showed a marked disposition to act strongly, coupled with a considerable uncertainty about what ought to be done.

POLITICS AND THE WORLD WAR

In Europe the pre-war sense of security was shattered far sooner than in the United States, but even in Europe, though there had been long before 1914 voices crying about the imminence of a world war—imperialists calling on their own nations to arm against the others and Socialists denouncing Imperialist Capitalism as the breeding ground of war—most men were quite unable to receive into their minds the imagination of what a world war would really mean. They had no standard by which to measure the enormity of the shock to established institutions which modern war would involve. They visualised war as vaguely dreadful—which is as much as to say that they failed to visualise it at all. Even more did they fail to imagine in advance what the after-consequences of world war would be.

Even when war came, men were still slow to realise what it meant. It did indeed upset to a quite unexpected extent the routine of living, not only for the larger and larger masses of men who were drawn into it as combatants, but also for the workers behind the lines, for employers who found themselves carrying out—for the most part very profitably—the orders of the State, for women whose sphere of work and service was suddenly expanded to a tremendous extent, for children at school, now being taught to regard the Cadet Corps or the O.T.C. in quite a new light—in fact for every section of the population in every belligerent country. There was a great shaking up of the peoples, a mixing of groups and classes, a breaking down of the century-old isolation of the villages, a going to and fro over the face of the earth on an unprecedented scale, and for the amateur soldiers a strange familiarity with the notions of violence and untimely death.

Even so there were few who realised what was happening to the world. Most people regarded the war as an episode, and expected that, when it was over, things would settle down again pretty much on the old lines. The politicians had indeed made very large promises of the good times that were coming after the war, but these good times were to be essentially continuous with what had gone before. There were to be better homes for heroes, higher wages, improved social and economic conditions, but all only as a continuance of pre-war tendencies in public policy. The standard of living was to be higher all round, but it was to be the same sort of living, with the same divisions of men into groups and classes as had existed before. Where the pre-war standard had been x, the post-war standard was to be $2x$ or $x+1$, but most certainly not y. There was a great deal of talk about the return to "normalcy" and the "restoration of pre-war conditions." The soldiers coming back to "Blighty" for good expected it to be the same old "Blighty" that they had left.

This is doubtless true in the full sense only of the countries to which most of our readers will belong, of Great Britain and the British Dominions and of the United States. The French and Belgians had the war brought home to them far more drastically by the devastation of their territories; and this compelled them to think more realistically of the after-effects. But Frenchmen and Belgians, too, envisaged the post-war task chiefly as that of building up again what had been broken down, so as to re-create the means of living in much the old forms. In Germany and Austria-Hungary the situation was somewhat different, and changed dramatically towards the end of the war, when the peoples began at length to realise the imminence of defeat. The Germans, far more sharply divided in their internal politics than the British or the French, began to understand that defeat would raise the question of the very foundations of the Reich; while Austria-Hungary, made up of a medley of discontented and mutually hostile national elements, was faced with the prospect of the complete dissolution of the Dual Monarchy and the parcelling out of its territories among a number of national States, each of which would have to be built up on a basis still to be decided, and certain to give rise to serious conflicts.

Meanwhile the Russians had made their two Revolutions while the world war was still in progress, and the Bolshevik Revolution in Russia had reacted upon opinion in Western countries, making the possibility of Socialist revolution seem far more real—above all in Germany, where it combined with a sense of coming defeat to shake the foundations of the Hohenzollern Empire. The Russian peoples had suffered from the war far more heavily than any others. Theirs had been the greatest losses and the greatest physical privations; and for the vast majority no hope or sentiment of patriotism had relieved the sense of suffering. Neither the Russian workman nor the Russian peasant really cared who won the war or hoped for anything from it. Alike they only wanted it to end. That, above all else, was why both Russian Revolutions happened, for neither Tsardom nor the Provisional Government which succeeded it was able either to carry on the war or to end it. Russia was by far the weakest economically among the major combatants, and accord-

ingly she felt and began to break under the strain of warfare sooner
than the other Great Powers. Even before the first Revolution the
old political and economic system had gone far towards complete
dissolution under this strain; and for this reason it was easier for
the Russians than for others to realise to what an extent the struggle
of the nations meant the close of one epoch in the history of civilisation and the opening of another. Or, if the Russian peasants did
not realise this, but only saw that in the midst of their sufferings
their chance had come to lay hold upon the land, a large part of
the Russian proletariat did see it, and the Russian *bourgeoisie* saw
it too, and was afraid.

These ferments in Central and Eastern Europe were but dimly
understood in those countries whose social systems emerged bat-
tered but unbroken from the ordeal of war. When the fighting was
over, the British, the French, the Belgians, and the Americans—who
had felt the strain less and had less to do—set to work as speedily
as they could to restore what they still thought and spoke of as
"normal conditions." Moreover the established authorities in all
these countries were for the time powerful enough to force social
organisation back into the old forms. There were some troubles over
demobilisation, some strikes that had a faintly revolutionary temper,
some difficulties over the turning back of industry to the arts of
peace and the removal of State control. Both politically and industrially some concessions had to be made to working-class demands in very partial redemption of the large promises that had
been held out. But on the whole the pre-war structure was rein-
stated without much difficulty, and the task that remained was
only that of getting it actually to work again in the old way. The
war-time soldiers settled down again to the arts of peace. The
women were emptied out of the munition factories and the temporary hospitals and told to get married or to fend for themselves.
The Socialists were successfully beaten back wherever they attempted to advance beyond merely reformist demands. The powers
that be heaved a great sigh of relief; the "episode" was over, the
victory secured, and Capitalism still intact.

POST-WAR EUROPE

Meanwhile on the Continent of Europe the territorial map was
being remade. Germany, shorn of Alsace-Lorraine, her Polish prov-

inces and, for the time, the Saar, accommodated herself after a brief interval of revolutionary disturbance to a republican régime which most people accepted only as a compromise forced on them by defeat and the divisions of opinion within the country. The old Imperialists tolerated the Republic because they knew their impotence to keep the Empire in being; but though compelled to tolerate it they still detested it as a symbol of defeat. The great industrialists tolerated it as a bulwark against Socialism. The Social Democrats, steeped in parliamentary traditions, regarded it as a necessary instrument for the achievement of evolutionary Socialism, and as a means of keeping the extremists on their own side as well as on the other in check. Finally the non-political elements in the population looked on it without enthusiasm and with some contempt, as the instrument through which the victors intended to exact Reparations from the vanquished. The Weimar Republic, created in the image of nineteenth-century democracy, was from the first the State that nobody loved, and was soon to show itself vulnerable to attack in proportion to the weakness of the loyalties it had power to arouse.

Elsewhere the process of Constitution-making for brand-new States was soon in full swing. Poland, Czechoslovakia, Finland, Estonia, Latvia and Lithuania were all new political entities needing to equip themselves not merely with new Constitutions, but with all the essential habits for living together as members of an independent Society. Austria and Hungary had to untie themselves from their imperial partnership and re-make themselves in more humble fashion within their narrowed frontiers, subject to all the serious difficulties created by the break-up of economic as well as political unity. Rumania and Yugoslavia had been so enlarged as to be virtually new countries, with vexing new problems arising out of the existence of new national and religious minorities within their borders. Even the neutrals, who had come richer out of the war, turned to the revision of their Constitutions amid the general re-shaping of political forces and ideas. Finally, Russia, now beginning to settle down under her Communist masters, was busy Constitution-making in her own very different way; and the influence of Russia, beaten back for the time from Western Europe, was spreading eastwards into Asia and causing a fermentation of new ideas and aspirations from Turkey to Japan.

Except in Russia, the new European Constitutions were made on traditional lines. All the new States were built up, with no more than secondary differences, on the familiar parliamentary models. No alternative pattern of organisation was even considered by the builders, or found any place in the minds of those who had the making of the new Europe in their hands. The Allied statesmen had announced often enough that the war was a "war for democracy," and democracy seemed to mean completing at length the process of dividing up Europe among a number of national States each equipped with the characteristic organs of nineteenth-century democracy—a Parliament of two Chambers, a president or strictly constitutional monarch with limited powers, a Cabinet responsible to Parliament, and last but not least a party system. Almost as a matter of course the making of a new State was deemed to involve the summoning of a Constituent Assembly and the drafting for its approval of a parliamentary Constitution on these lines.

For the making of these new Constitutions the draftsmen pillaged the repertories of the older parliamentary States, borrowing a feature here from the British and there from the American Constitution, but drawing most of all on the political system of France. Most of the Socialists were as convinced as anyone else that this was the correct democratic method of going about the business, and that new States manufactured whole by this process could be trusted speedily to settle down under their synthetic Constitutions to the regular practice of parliamentary government under the party system. In this mood the German Social Democrats took the lead in creating the Weimar Republic, and in this mood every new or re-fashioned State except Russia equipped itself with a Constitution of much the same type, irrespective of its size, stage of economic development, or homogeneity of race or culture. A few short-lived attempts were made—in Hungary, in Bavaria, and to some extent in Bulgaria—to make new States on the new model of the Soviet system instead of the old parliamentary model; but the innovators were soon swept aside. It seemed as if the purpose of the war had been to complete the structure of parliamentary nationalism; and so indeed it was conceived in the most authoritative quarters, from President Wilson to Mr. Lloyd George, with Clemenceau recording a cynical assent. The League of Nations itself was conceived and instituted as a quasi-parliamentary assembly representing sovereign national States of a predominantly parliamentary character.

However, both while the war lasted and when it was over, it was impossible for most people in Continental Europe not to feel strongly political, because the settlement of their political destiny which was being made so evidently and nearly affected their daily lives. The blockaded and half-starved Germans, the new frontiersmen who were left uncertain to what country they belonged, the national minorities which had somehow to adjust themselves to living under a new State, merchants faced with uncertain and ever-shifting trade barriers, consumers unsure of the value of the money in their pockets, peasants and landowners disputing over the possession of the land—all these and many more had their political consciousness constantly stirred into active life. There was no possibility over a large part of Europe of letting things be or of carrying on with an old-established routine. Everything had to be settled afresh, and it mattered to everybody how it was settled. Almost everyone had to be some sort of a politician. The greater part of Europe underwent a tremendous process of political education during these years; but unhappily its teachers taught it for the most part only out of textbooks that were already obsolete. The questions were new, but almost everybody was still trying to make the old answers fit.

Nevertheless post-war Europe did settle down after a fashion, though men soon discovered that making a Constitution is not the same thing as making a State. In the older countries the political system is a product of long evolution, and most of these countries were States long before they became parliamentary democracies. New institutions do not work automatically according to plan, and above all improvised parties are by no means capable of working a Constitution in the same way as parties developed by a prolonged process of growth within an established political order. The difficulties would have been great enough if the new States had been internally homogeneous, and if there had been a large measure of agreement on the outstanding issues; but most of them in fact included large national minorities which felt no loyalty to the new State systems to which they were made subject. Consequently, in the formation of parties, national and racial differences almost everywhere cut across differences of class and social opinion. Religious differences and differences of cultural level further complicated the problem, and there arose in each country not two or three strong parties of Right, Left and Centre, but a medley of groups, mostly standing for distinctively sectional points of view. Parliamentary government had to be based on coalitions among these groups; but such coalitions were bound to be weak towards outsiders and often at loggerheads among themselves. Europe after the war needed strong government to face the great tasks that were before it. It got in most countries weak government, with a consequent tendency to push difficult problems aside.

THE RUSSIAN REVOLUTION

Meantime, as we have seen, the Russians were tackling their political problems in a radically different way. The prelude to the Revolutions of 1917 was the sheer collapse of the old Russia. Tsardom was not forcibly overthrown; it toppled, to the astonished embarrassment of the new leaders who were called upon to replace it. They set up as nearly as possible on the orthodox West European lines the simulacrum of a parliamentary system which lasted six months and never wielded real power. Russia was for those six months almost without government. Such authority as did exist was hopelessly divided between a frightened and helpless Provisional Government and a hesitant working-class movement organised in ceaselessly fermenting Soviets that would neither enforce nor render obedience. When the Tsar fell, all Western Europe and most even of the Russian Socialists expected that Russia would develop into a parliamentary State on the approved model, but there was no soil in which Russian Parliamentarism could grow. Even under Lvov and Kerensky real power rested with the Soviets whenever they knew what they wanted; and as soon as the Soviets had passed under Bolshevik leadership and were ready to assume the power, Kerensky's Government was overthrown as painlessly as the Tsar's, and Lenin, the architect of the new Revolution, came to authority at the head of a dictatorial proletarian régime. European statesmen found themselves suddenly confronted with a totally new kind of State, in which authority belonged neither to Parliamentary representatives elected under a constitutional franchise, nor to a hereditary autocrat, but to self-constituted organisations based directly on the factories and the army, and given form and direction by the leadership of a disciplined revolutionary party. Marx's gospel of the dictatorship of the proletariat had come to realisation not in an advanced industrial country where the proletariat was large and highly trained, but in backward Russia where the peasants far outnumbered the industrial workers and experience of any form of democratic public administration was almost totally lacking.

The Russian Revolution of October 1917 first demonstrated to the world that there was nothing inevitable about the process of parliamentary development—that experience of Parliamentary democracy was not the indispensable prelude to a Socialist victory, and that there was a hitherto unconsidered alternative to parliamentary government as the successor to feudal autocracy. But the world was slow and unwilling to learn these lessons, which went too much against the grain of contemporary thought. Most people went on for years after 1917 prophesying the imminent collapse of the Soviet Government and its replacement either by an emasculated constitutional monarchy or by an orthodox parliamentary republic, or in the alternative the break-up of Russia into a number of backward peasant States like those of Eastern Europe and South-Western Asia. Even many Socialists made haste to demonstrate that the Bolshevik Revolution had no right to have happened at all, because Russia was not "ripe" for Socialism and could be ripened only by passing through an intervening phase of development under capitalist control. Among the Bolsheviks themselves there were many who doubted right up to October the wisdom of seizing power, and clung to the view that Socialism could be established only in an advanced industrial country; and of those who did favour the seizure of power nearly all believed that the Revolution would be bound to fail unless it gave the signal for a series of revolutions in Western Europe and so turned speedily into a world proletarian revolution. For some time after the October Revolution all the Bolsheviks' hopes of success were centred upon the outbreak of revolution in the West.

The world revolution did not arrive; but, despite the boycott of Russia by the Western Powers and the aid which they furnished to a succession of counter-revolutionary attempts, the Soviet system did not collapse. Gradually the politicians of other countries had to reconcile themselves to the fact that the new system had come to stay, and that its existence as a working model of a State under Socialist control was bound to have a powerful influence on the currents of political opinion both in Europe and in the less developed countries of the East, where conditions were far more like those of Russia than in the industrial countries of the West. The civilised world had to contemplate the permanence of a new type of State and, underlying it, of a new social and economic system as different from capitalist democracy as chalk from cheese. The Communist Revolution in Russia thus took the civilised world back to fundamentals much against its will.

For of course the issue between Russia and the West was not a matter merely of rival forms of political organisation but of utterly different social systems. What was being restored in the older parliamentary countries and instituted in the new States of Europe was not democracy *sans phrase* but capitalist democracy. Behind the process of Constitution-making the struggle was being carried on to make the post-war world safe again for Capitalism, or at least as safe as it could be made in face of intensified working-class pressure. In 1918 the Germans believed, perhaps rightly, that the victorious Allies would not allow the continuance of the Hohenzollern Empire; but it is safe to say that the Allies would greatly have preferred even Kaiser Wilhelm to a Soviet Republic. The haste to equip the post-war States with parliamentary constitutions was dictated not only by the desire to eliminate autocracy, but to a far greater extent by the fear of Socialist revolution.

THE ADVENT OF FASCISM

By one means or another, the victorious States did succeed not only in putting back their old economic and political systems without any substantial change, but also in impressing their characteristic institutions on the defeated countries and on the new States created on the morrow of the war. But this process had hardly been completed over most of the countries of Europe when the restored parliamentary régime had to encounter a fresh challenge. The threat of world Socialist revolution had been successfully beaten off for the time; and Russia had been isolated from the West though not subdued. But just as the older statesmen were breathing a sigh of relief at having come so well out of an exceedingly ticklish situation, the united front of European Parliamentarism was abruptly broken in a quite unexpected place by the Revolution in Italy. Italy under Fascist leadership overthrew her weak parliamentary Government and after a brief interval of transition instituted a one-party State based on a form of dictatorship as antagonistic to Parliamentarism as the dictatorship of the proletariat in Russia. This new dictatorship, however, was not based on the working-class, and by no means aimed at the institution of a Socialist system. Fascism sought and found its active members mainly among the intermediate classes in society and the peasants, and it received the backing of the great capitalists as the determined foe of Socialism. Fascism arose and developed as an organ of struggle against Marxian Socialism, and it signalised its victory by uprooting together with parliamentary democracy every form of Socialist and independent Trade Union organisation. Its gospel was not social equality or world revolution but a nationalism which denied the primacy of class distinctions and invoked against them the collective self-interest of the nation as a whole.

Thereafter in the parliamentary countries there was no longer one alternative to the continuance of parliamentary government; there were two, between which Parliamentarism stood precariously as the upholder of things as they were against revolution and reaction alike. The character of these new Fascist movements, and their development in Europe from the rise of Fascism in Italy to the triumph of the National Socialists in Germany, we shall have to discuss in later chapters. We shall have to see how Fascism, which seemed at first to most people a peculiar product of the Italian situation, gradually strengthened its hold on other European countries as post-war disillusionment increased, and above all as economic conditions grew worse after the great collapse of 1929. It is indeed evident that the main source of the power of Fascism is to be found not so much in the mere threat of a Socialist advance as in the widespread sense of futility aroused by the great depression. Fascism was from the standpoint of the rich an instrument for fighting Socialism; but it was able to gain a large following among the poor, without whom the rich cannot successfully fight their battles, because in the years of economic depression so many of the poor were both physically and materially wretched and ready, in face of the slow advance of the Socialist forces, to clutch at any gospel that promised them a quick deliverance from their troubles.

It is true enough that in Great Britain, France, the Scandinavian countries, Holland and Belgium, the parliamentary system still remains intact to-day, though there has been in some of these countries a considerable growth of Fascist minority opinion. It is true that in the United States of America the crisis has taken shape not in Fascism but in an enormous extension of the Presidential power, and that this power has been used so far fully as much on the side of the workers as against them. But the countries in which Parliamentarism, or at any rate capitalist democracy, remains strong, are those which have not so far been compelled to face up to really fundamental problems. The European countries which are strongholds of Parliamentarism even to-day are, with few exceptions, countries which emerged from the war undamaged in their essential institutions and able to carry on to a great extent along the old lines. The neutrals, Holland and the Scandinavian countries, actually emerged the richer and accordingly the less exposed to movements based on the rival extremes of despair; and though the years of slump have shaken their complacency, they have still large reserves of wealth and strength behind their established institutions. The one country in this parliamentary group which was temporarily shattered by the war is Belgium; and the Belgians, having been on the victorious side, were able to drive a bargain which set their pre-war institutions once more upon their feet. France also suffered heavily both in loss of man-power and in the devastation of a considerable part of her territory. But she got Alsace-Lorraine and for the time the Saar, together with reparations payments for the rebuilding of the devastated areas. Though France was weakened in man-power she was enabled to restore her economic strength and to avert for the time the danger to her established system. Great Britain, though she suffered severely through the dislocation of her foreign trade, had nevertheless reserves of foreign investments and of internal productive resources so large as to see her through the perilous post-war years without so deep and widespread a distress as to threaten her strongly entrenched parliamentary system. The United States, as we have seen, enjoyed after the war a long period of unprecedented prosperity, though in the later years the prevailing impression of prosperity was chequered by a growth of distress in the agricultural areas. Not until after the Wall Street crash of 1929 did America begin to experience any serious depression, and even then, deep as the depression was, the American people was for the most part too unused to questioning its political institutions, and too unprepared with any alternative, for unrest to take shape in any practical movement for fundamental political change. President Roosevelt strained the American Constitution when he was called upon to handle the crisis of 1933, but there was not even then any question of his going outside the Constitution, or of any revolutionary change in American political institutions being seriously pressed in a practical way.

THE FAR EAST

But though parliamentary democracy remains intact in these countries its prestige throughout the world has been very greatly lowered. This can be seen most clearly of all in the reaction of the Far East to the recent development of affairs in Europe. Before 1914, as we have seen, the Far-Eastern countries seemed to be set above all else on emulating the achievements of European Parliamentarism. But to-day Japan, China and India are all in their different ways registering the decline of the prestige of Parliamentarism. In Japan, though the shadow of party government survives, the reality of power has gone back more and more into the hands of the military leaders, and there has been a marked growth of military terrorism directed against the politicians. Japanese "Fascism" is not the same thing as European Fascism, for it has its strength above all in the armed forces, and hostility to the large capitalists whom it accuses of betraying the national ideal goes deep in it. But it does stand in the same way as European Fascism for glorifying the idea of the nation, and it does uphold armed force as the embodiment of national prestige.

In China Communist ideas made great headway in the years immediately after the successful establishment of the U.S.S.R.; and though thereafter the Communists suffered a setback, and the Kuomintang became, under the control of Chiang Kai-Shek, their most determined adversary, their influence remains considerable. Substantial areas in China are to-day under a sort of Communist government inspired by the Russian example, but adapted to the conditions of a crowded peasant population and an exceedingly backward economic system. The greater part of China is indeed still subject, at any rate nominally, to the Nanking Government, which, after its break with the Communists, followed a policy of association with the capitalist Governments of Europe, and placed its faith in the League of Nations. But European prestige in China has been shattered by the failure of the League to stop Japan from seizing Manchuria, and official Chinese opinion has been showing of late a tendency to favour coming to terms with the Japanese so as to accept a subordinate place in an Asiatic group of Powers strong enough to stand up against European interference. It cannot be said that this policy has yet found any general acceptance, for hostility to and suspicion of Japan still go very deep in China; but the emergence of a pro-Japanese party among the Chinese is undoubtedly a development of the greatest significance, and, while the League's failure over Manchuria furnishes the most obvious reason for this change of attitude, a further reason is to be found in the decline of the prestige of Western institutions all over the Far East.

India too has felt the influence of the new waves of political doctrine. Until quite recently the majority of Indian Nationalist leaders appeared to envisage the liberation of India in terms of the introduction of some form of constitutional self-government on the West European model. The talk of elective assemblies based on a wide franchise with expanded legislative powers, of responsible ministers and Cabinet government and all the familiar institutions of Western democracy; and the various reports on Indian reforms drawn up by British statesmen have all been conceived along these lines. It is true that the outstanding Indian leader, Mahatma Gandhi, has always resisted assimilation to European ideas and remained an enigma to the West; but the very fact that Gandhi did not seem to be able to think in parliamentary terms, while it increased his popular influence in India, often appeared to disqualify him as a constructive political leader. He had an unrivalled power of protest and agitation, but those who had to deal with him often asked in vain what it was that he wanted in a positive and constructive sense. Nowadays Gandhi's political leadership seems to be passing away, though he retains his vast cultural and social influence. But his authority is passing less to leaders of the old westernised parliamentary type than to younger leaders such as Jawaharlal Nehru, whose most recent utterances show him to have come strongly under the influence of Socialist and Communist ideas. Jawaharlal Nehru has proclaimed himself definitely a Socialist, and has recently said that in his view the choice in India lies to-day between Fascism and some sort of Soviet system —adapted of course to meet Indian needs. Young India appears to be thinking less and less of parliamentary government as its goal, and more and more in terms of an alternative based largely on what has happened in Russia—with Italy or Germany as a possible alternative model.

THE POLITICAL OUTLOOK

This almost world-wide decline in the prestige of parliamentary institutions necessarily involves that politics must become far more a matter for ordinary people. For Parliamentarism, while as against autocracy or aristocracy it calls for popular participation in the work of government, has reconciled this demand with the practical exemption of the great mass of people from any sustained political activity. It has conceded to them the electoral rights of citizenship, but has asked from most of them nothing more than their votes. In contrast to Parliamentarism as well as to the older forms of government both Fascism and Communism call for a far higher degree of active citizenship. For they are both based on the dictatorship not of an individual or a small group or junta, but of a party with a wide basis of membership, and they demand both from the members of the party and from those who come to be associated with its fortunes not merely passive acquiescence in the new régimes which they set up, but positive and energetic participation. In Russia the members of the Communist Party are all called upon to be constantly active in political work, as leaders of opinion and practice in every sphere of social life. Nor does this demand for active citizenship stop short at the party membership; for through that omnipresent agency of Communist construction, the "collective," the same demand reappears everywhere as a claim for enthusiastic service in the common cause. The Russian Communists claim this service from the workers on the ground that the State now belongs to the workers and that accordingly they should be prepared to put all the energy they possess into building it up as the instrument of the common welfare. In Italy or Germany, on the other hand, the State emphatically does not belong to the workers or to the people in the same sense as in Russia. For in these countries private property in the means of production and class inequality remain in being. Nevertheless both Fascism and Nazism have made to their followers an appeal for active citizenship which is not wholly unlike the Communist appeal, and a large part of their success has undoubtedly been due to their ability to give their followers the sense of a "cause" to work for—a cause demanding sacrifice and loyalty in the interests of the greater whole, the nation. It remains to be seen whether this appeal to nationalist sentiment can be long sustained in face of the continuance of class divisions and of the failure to bring the economic life of society under effective social control. But whatever its fate may be in the long run, there is no doubt of its importance in bringing both the Fascists and the Nazis to power. Both these movements found an emotional appeal capable of swaying large masses of men, and found also positive work for their followers to do—not the mere voting rights which seemed to most of them all that the uninspiring institutions of Parliamentarism were willing to accord them. In both Italy and Germany as well as in Russia every member of the dominant party is called upon to play an energetic part in the creation of the new State and in the day-to-day work of its essential institutions, and a man can win a place in the privileged circle of the new dictatorship only as the reward of active citizenship in its interest. If the number of persons actively participating in political work and helping to run the political system were to be made a test of democracy, there can be no doubt that Fascism, as well as Communism, would have to be regarded as effectively more democratic than the parliamentary régime. It is true that the dominant party is in all these countries a minority of the whole people, and the dictatorship therefore in effect also that of a minority. But this does not invalidate the point that in terms of active citizenship Fascism as well as Communism goes beyond the parliamentary system.

At present, however, over a large part of the world, the political attention and activity of ordinary people are being demanded and aroused not by the nature of the political systems under which they live but by the prevailing uncertainty about the systems under which they are going to live. As soon as the issue of politics comes to be that of the very form which the social system is to take, the appeal at once lies from the professional politicians and the interested minority to the mass of the population—not merely as voters but as citizens who are called upon to act as well as vote. The political struggle comes to be a matter affecting not the secondary adjustments of social organisation, but such primary concerns as the system of property relationships and the class structure. Communists are Socialists who will stick at nothing in order to establish a classless society, and hold that it can be established only by way of a transition through class dictatorship to a new kind of democracy. Fascists are anti-Socialists who are prepared to go to any length in order to prevent the Socialists from getting their way, and, distrustful of the "freedoms" of parliamentary democracy, mean to make sure of defeating the Socialists by establishing a rival dictatorship of their own. Communists and Fascists are at one in holding that the liberal virtues of toleration and freedom of speech can have no place in the period of acute struggle which lies ahead; for how, they both ask, can men be expected to tolerate freedoms which hamper the achievement of their ideals? Freedom, they both tell us, can be allowed to exist only within a framework of accepted and strongly established institutions; and only within the limits imposed by this necessity is freedom or toleration consistent with social advance.

At this the parliamentarians hold up their hands in horror, for though parliaments have been notable persecutors in their day, and are still ready to persecute at any transgression of the parliamentary code, that code has come to include a large measure of freedom of speech and writing for those who are prepared to play the parliamentary game and keep within the limits of advocating changes only by parliamentary means. But obviously neither Communists nor Fascists will be prepared to accept these limitations. Both of them hold that Parliaments are incapable of setting the disordered world to rights, and that the appeal must be made from Parliaments to the strong right arms of men. They both appeal—not, indeed from reason to force, for both would deny the antithesis—but from a system based on assuming that it is enough to count heads, by whatever artifices those heads may be influenced, to emotions as well as reasonings that will put men into a mood to use force if force be necessary for the achievement of their purposes.

THE APPEAL TO FORCE

Force thus comes back into the political field precisely to the extent to which politics come to deal with matters about which men feel so strongly that they will use force rather than give way. Most men do not want to use force for the sake of using it, though they may on occasion be ready to glorify force when they have already made up their minds to appeal to it, and though there are always some people in any community in whom an appeal to force arouses a sadistic delight. In parliamentary countries, for force to be successfully invoked, there has to be an issue dividing men sharply enough and stirring in them emotions powerful enough to make them repudiate the parliamentary tradition. How easily they will do this depends of course largely on the hold which the tradition has over them. It will take far more to make men resort to force as a political weapon in Great Britain or even in France than it took in Germany or Italy; and in both Germany and Italy it took more than it would take in, say, Bulgaria or Yugoslavia. But apart from this a great deal depends on the opportunities for compromise which the situation presents. In the countries where the parliamentary tradition is strong, compromise has become an accepted political habit, and as long as the way of compromise remains open, force will hardly be invoked in any extreme degree. When, however, the possible area of compromise is contracted, an appeal to force becomes more likely, for neither party is prepared to yield up what it believes to be vital.

This narrowing of the area of compromise has come about to-day primarily as a consequence of economic depression. Over the past century the rapid expansion of capitalist industry has provided resources out of which it has been possible to raise almost continuously the standard of living of the mass of the people, not only without any decrease in the prosperity of the rich, but to the accompaniment of profits rising at least as fast as wages, and often faster. As long as this situation existed there was always room for compromise with the growing demands of the poor, on conditions which in no way threatened the essential institutions of Capitalism. But to-day, though the *technical* conditions for the carrying on of this policy of compromise exist more obviously than ever—for never before has the power to produce goods been advancing so rapidly—the *practical* possibility of compromise under Capitalism has grown less. National Capitalism in its latest phase of acute international competition has been losing the art of raising the workers' standard of life without endangering its own success in the competitive scramble; and during the past few years the world slump, itself the consequence of this impasse, has sharply confronted the capitalist interests in each advanced State with a situation in which they have felt the need not merely to call a halt to the advance in the standard of living, but also to cancel concessions previously made. The decline in the position of the workers, and especially the distress of the unemployed, have at the same time caused large sections of the working-class movement to assume a more militant tone, and have brought more into prominence left-wing Socialist movements directed against the capitalist order itself. The rise of these militant movements has provoked a parallel growth of protective counter-movements in the interests of the possessing classes; and these counter-movements, well supplied with resources for propaganda, have been able to suborn a section of the poorer classes to take their side, not only by promising them large immediate economic advantages, but also by appealing to their nationalist sentiments against the internationalism of the Socialist creed. If, as a result of a large measure of capitalist recovery, the area of possible compromise were again widened, both types of extremism would probably lose a good deal of their present appeal. But unless this happens both are likely to gain further ground; for the second is to a great extent the inevitable correlative of the first.

The political outlook therefore depends very largely on what happens in the economic sphere. If Capitalism can rally its forces and make its escape from the present world depression before Parliamentarism, its traditional political ally, has been everywhere broken up, economic revival may, in certain countries, give the parliamentary system a fresh lease of life. This is true in the United States, in Great Britain, in France, and in a number of the smaller States of Western Europe, as well as in the British Dominions. But even under these favouring conditions Parliamentarism is unlikely to regain its old predominance as the norm of political development for all civilised peoples. No one expects Parliamentarism to establish itself in Russia; and, if Russia stays Socialist and so provides an alternative model of political organisation, it is most unlikely that Parliamentarism will establish itself in Asia. Nor does it seem very likely to come back in either Italy or Germany; for in both these countries the destruction of all forms of constitutional opposition and the institution of the one-party State appear to leave open only the two alternatives of a further growth of the Fascist State on essentially unparliamentary lines and violent revolution leading to some form of Socialist dictatorship.

Thus the most favourable outlook for Parliamentarism seems likely to leave it in possession only in a limited group of countries. Moreover, its continuance even in these countries depends not only on capitalist recovery, but also on a further highly doubtful factor— the avoidance of world war on the grand scale. For it depends on the ability of countries which have radically different social systems to live side by side in the world without destructive conflict. As we have seen, the Russians, when they made their revolution, believed this to be impossible; and though their attitude has greatly changed of late, under the pressure of imminent danger from both East and West, the history of the past dozen years hardly serves to show that it is easy for countries whose populations are animated by vitally different political and economic ideals to live together at peace. But if world war did break out again on a scale comparable with that of the last war, it is difficult to believe that more than a vestige of Parliamentarism would survive the conflict. Far more drastically than on the last occasion, the surviving institutions of open discussion and organised opposition would be certain to be suppressed during the struggle; for in most countries there would be far stronger internal opposition to a new war than there was to the last. Whatever the military outcome might be, a new war would be likely to leave behind it a world so shattered both economically and politically as to need building up again right from the foundations, and it is hardly probable that nineteenth-century Parliamentarism would serve as a model for this colossal reconstruction of a broken world.

2. THE CHALLENGE TO PARLIAMENTARISM

THE ITALIAN REVOLUTION

As WE HAVE SEEN, the first breach in the new-made parliamentary structure of post-war Europe was made in Italy with the Fascist triumph of 1922. For some time before the Fascists won power the Italian political system had been dissolving into chaos. There was a Government purporting to rest upon a parliamentary majority, but this Government was so weak that in effect the country was hardly being governed at all. The Italian parliamentarians were weak abroad and weak at home. At Versailles their demands had been contemptuously pushed aside by their stronger Allies. Thus events abroad had undermined the prestige of the Italian Government and roused up in Italy a strong nationalist sentiment of which the Fascists were quick to take advantage. Italy, said the Fascists, had been on the side of the victors in the war, but had been wrongfully deprived of her fair share of the spoils of victory. She had been impoverished as a nation when she might have been enriched by new conquests if she had been better led. The parliamentarians had betrayed her in foreign affairs; and now they were getting ready to betray her at home. It was said that Italy was threatened by dissolution from within at the hands of the international Socialists who cared nothing for their country and whom the weak-kneed parliamentary Government was impotent to check. Down, therefore, with the Parliament and up with a power strong enough and ruthless enough to cope effectively with the Socialist menace.

Italian Parliamentarism was in truth a weak and irresolute thing with no deep roots in the sentiment of the people. Italian Socialism, affected by an unresolved mixture of Communist and Syndicalist ideas, had grown powerful enough to paralyse parliamentary government without becoming cohesive or determined enough to seize power for itself. The Italian Catholics, organised in Don Sturzo's Popular Party, were hostile to Socialism, but were attempting to bid against the Socialists by the offer of an advanced programme of social reform; and their activities, while weakening Socialism, also drew away strength from the Government. The result was an irritant condition of stalemate which roused up against parliamentarians and Socialists alike every other element in the country, from industrial employers who looked vainly to the Government to protect their property against Syndicalist violence, to impoverished peasants and unemployed soldiers who wanted somebody to blame for their distress. The Socialists, if they had been united, could probably have rallied behind them enough of the powers of discontent to make a Socialist revolution, for assuredly the Government would have been unable to stand in their way. But in 1920, after going to the length of paralysing Italian industry and defying the Government by occupying the factories, the Socialists and the Trade Unions drew back and refused to turn defiance into positive revolution. That finished their chances, and two years later Mussolini, seizing his opportunity amid the general disillusionment, led the March on Rome, and founded the Fascist State. Not long afterwards Mustapha Kemal, drawing his inspiration partly from Italy but much more from Russia, established another personal ascendancy in Turkey, and leading the restored Turkish army against the Greeks in Asia

Minor wiped out his country's defeat in the World War and created yet another new type of State to challenge the established model of government. Spain followed in 1923 with the military dictatorship of General Primo de Rivera, but the Spanish *coup d'état* takes no place beside the Italian and Turkish revolutions, in that it was designed only to reinforce the existing feudal autocracy and not to institute a new kind of State. The Spanish dictatorship, a mere shield for royal, aristocratic and ecclesiastical privilege, failed in 1931 before the united attack of the Spanish Republicans—though these have since fallen out seriously enough among themselves and for some time now Spain has been hovering on the verge of civil war between Catholics and Socialists. For a time at least the Spanish dictatorship came to an end; but Italian Fascism and Turkish Nationalism are still very much alive.

The Italian Fascists, experimenting with a new form of government, and uncertain both of their own aims and of the strength of the forces opposed to them, advanced only by tentative stages to the decisive creation of a new kind of State based on the exclusive existence and authority of a single party. Mustapha Kemal, despite the prestige accruing from his military triumph, also took time to complete his ascendancy. But both the Italian and the Turkish revolutions, and especially the Italian, which excited far more attention in the West, demonstrated very plainly that a determined party which knows its own mind and is prepared to be ruthless in its use of force can under favourable circumstances not only impose its will on the majority of the people, but utterly rout and disorganise every form of articulate opposition. This does not mean that a determined minority can, by a mere *coup d'état,* successfully defeat and thereafter permanently dominate a hostile majority, though that may in certain circumstances also be true. What it does mean is that when an established régime has become seriously enfeebled, so that the great mass of the population is in a condition of acute discontent, a determined and well-organised minority that does not shrink from force can easily defeat much larger minorities which are less determined and less disciplined, provided that it chooses to take its ground upon issues which will range the passive consent of the majority behind it and that it eschews issues likely to be unpopular with the majority. In Russia, in Turkey, and in Italy, the majority of the people did not take active sides in the course of the conflict; they accepted more or less willingly the outcome of a struggle between rival minorities. In Russia, indeed, the Bolsheviks deliberately waited till they had the majority in the Soviets on their side, and until the growth of peasant discontent had created a favourable atmosphere in the countryside. But the Bolsheviks knew that the great majority of the people would give them no more than passive support, though it was clear even before the October Revolution that they alone formed a coherent group capable of rescuing the country from chaos, and that there was a reasonable prospect that the mass would acquiesce in their forcible assumption of power under the auspices of the Soviet Congress.

The Italian Fascists were much less certain of having a majority even passively behind them. They were sure only of the irresolution and incompetence of their various rivals, and of the fact that the forces opposed to them were too sharply divided to be capable of acting together. In these circumstances they had to feel their way far more cautiously than the Russians to full seizure of power and to cloak their dictatorship at first under traditional constitutional forms, carrying with them the king, the old aristocratic parties, and the great industrialists in a "Sacred Union" against the Socialists. They waged war in the name of the nation against international Socialism; and in the name of the nation they were able to enlist powerful support from inside the structure of the Italian State. Only by stages did the real character of the new Fascist State plainly emerge, or the Fascist Party assume its exclusive position in the control of the Italian system. Twelve years after the March on Rome Fascism is still only beginning to build up the institutional structure of the Corporative State.

POLITICAL CONDITIONS IN THE NEW STATES

The Fascist revolution in Italy, happening within the circle of Western capitalist countries, struck a hard blow at the new-made parliamentary institutions of the lesser European States and of Germany. The new States, without experience of parliamentary government, or indeed for the most part of any form of government at all, without well-organised political parties, and even in some cases without any common basis of culture or national sentiment, floundered about, trying to make their manufactured Constitutions work in the same way as the gradually developed Constitutions of France and

Great Britain. It is not surprising that most of them found this task difficult, or that Governments based on party coalitions succeeded one another with bewildering rapidity. Most of the new States were unitary in structure, only little Austria being incongruously equipped with a federal Constitution designed to prevent the dominance of Vienna. Set on achieving national unification in spite of the heterogeneous racial and religious elements within their borders, the new States were acutely suspicious of all forms of decentralisation or local autonomy, because they feared that any concession of this sort might be used as a cloak for separatist movements. They tried to centralise everything in order to impress on the whole country the stamp of common administration. But they were able to do this at all only on the condition of basing their Governments more on national or racial majorities than on particular social policies, so that their Governments were mostly coalitions of elements taking very different views on economic issues. This made their handling of internal problems weak and indecisive except in the case of tariffs, which were banked up high for the purpose of developing industry on national lines. On certain issues, notably the distribution of land among the hungry peasants, the pressure of unrest was in most cases strong enough to compel the enactment of fairly drastic legislation. But even in this matter there were endless quarrels over the compensation to be allowed to the dispossessed owners. In most other matters indecision was the dominant note, for the coalitions which the multiplicity of minority parties made indispensable could be kept in being only by shelving every difficult problem which threatened to break up the Government majority.

Nevertheless the new States did to some extent shake down into political communities that were able to carry on. But under the influence of the Russian, Italian and Turkish revolutions a growing number of people in most of them began to consider that the blessings of Parliamentarism had been greatly exaggerated. Parliamentary government, it was urged, might work well enough in a strongly established State where all that was needed was to keep the existing adjustment of social relations in being, subject only to minor readjustments from time to time, and where there existed a general basis of agreement about the fundamental structure of Society. But Parliamentarism, at any rate in its traditional forms, began to seem quite inappropriate to a situation in which really deep-seated differences had to be confronted and resolved. This state of mind appeared most plainly in Poland and in certain of the Balkan countries. It was clearly that of Marshal Pilsudski, who pressed continuously for a revision of the Polish Constitution to increase the element of personal authority in the State; and it led later on to changes that reduced the parliamentary system in Yugoslavia, Rumania and Hungary to little better than a farce. There was undoubtedly substance behind the complaints against Parliamentarism; for the system of the ins and outs, of alternating party governments of varying complexion, is workable only on the condition that each incoming Government does not spend most of its time undoing its predecessor's Acts, but broadly accepts what has been done, and uses it as a foundation on which to build its own measures. Nor will the system work unless each Government has, in addition to a sufficient measure of common ground with its predecessor, a tolerably coherent policy of its own. If an incoming Government cannot accept the underlying principles on which its predecessor worked, it speedily becomes intolerable to each side that its political opponents should ever achieve power. For every change of Government threatens to involve an attempt to alter the essential character of the State. Under such conditions a parliamentary system can remain in being only as long as Governments confess their impotence and continually push vital problems aside, contenting themselves with the function of mere caretakers of whatever exists, whether it be good or bad. Within these disabling limitations it may be possible for parliamentary government to survive for a time, but it can do so only at the cost of accumulating outside Parliament a steadily growing body of active discontent. Unsolved social problems have a way of becoming more insistent and difficult the longer they are let alone. Men who have lived under a whole sequence of incompetent and ambiguous coalitions begin to hunger after the strong hand of dictatorship, and the simple authoritarianism of a State controlled either by an individual or by a monopolistic party.

REVOLUTION IN GERMANY

The Germans, equally with the smaller States, experienced to the full the disadvantages of coalition Governments drawn from elements so wide apart as to exclude all decisiveness of social or economic aim. Nor had the Weimar Republic any force of popular sentiment on which it could rely. Whereas most of the new States carried with them the prestige of nationalist triumph, the Second Reich had to bear the full stigma of imperial defeat. In its relations with other countries it was bound down by the iron hand of the Versailles Treaty, and in relation to the German people it was not only compelled to be the tax-gatherer of the victorious Allies but to embody in itself the irreconcilable antagonisms of divergent social classes. Within it Socialists and capitalists each felt strong enough to prevent the other side from getting its way, but not to get their own. Before long, indeed, the capitalist parties regained the upper hand, and post-war Germany was re-made as a definitely capitalist State. But even so, Capitalism could rule on parliamentary lines only with Socialist consent, and this was given grudgingly and subject to the condition of doles and taxes which the German capitalists felt to be oppressive and hampering to business, especially in view of the acute shortage of capital. Moreover, the old autocratic and militarist elements in the State, subdued but by no means crushed, stood sullenly aside, hating the Republic and doing all they could to hamper its work while they bided their time for a chance to restore the good old discipline of the mailed fist. They succeeded in entrenching their influence in the new standing army, the *Reichswehr;* and the *Reichswehr* was accordingly a perpetual menace to the Republic whose interests it was supposed to serve.

In this soil there was ample nourishment for a powerful Fascist movement. The premature Kapp *Putsch* of 1921 was successfully defeated by the Trade Unions by means of a General Strike, and Hitler's ill-organised Munich revolt of 1923 was also easily crushed, despite General Ludendorff's support. The memory of the war was still too fresh, and the unpopularity of Kaiserdom and militarism too great, for the Republic, weak as it was, to be overthrown. Thereafter the Dawes Plan and the vast inpouring of foreign capital which followed the stabilisation of the mark gave the Weimar Republic a further lease of life by creating a fictitious prosperity. But even in those years Hitlerism was growing and discontent piling up fast. It needed, however, a new generation that had never known German militarism in its prime to make a new German revolution. It needed also the world depression to intensify economic distress, to cut off the supply of foreign capital, and to weaken the resistance of the Republican State, before German Fascism could achieve its decisive victory.

Hitler, when his moment had come, followed the strategy of Mussolini by courting the alliance of the old aristocracy and of the great industrialists who hated the socialistic elements in the Weimar Republic. With their aid and with that of President Hindenburg, whom not long before the Socialists had helped to return to office as the guardian of the Republic, Hitler climbed to power; but once installed as Chancellor he acted far more swiftly and drastically than Mussolini had done a dozen years before. The Nazi movement at once showed itself infinitely more vindictive, barbarous and cruel than its Italian prototype. Its leaders went far beyond Mussolini in their exaltation of war and violence and in the brutality of their persecution of every political force capable of opposing them. They set out to "purge" Germany far more drastically than Fascist Italy had been "purged." Like Mussolini they set to work to uproot every vestige of the existing working-class movement, and to create in its place a new disciplined organisation under their own exclusive control for the regimentation of the "Labour Front." But they did this too with a thoroughness of violence and at a speed far beyond those of the Italian Fascists. Nor did they temporise to anything like the same extent as Mussolini had done with the existing political structure, though the task of reorganisation which confronted them was far more extensive because of the federal character of the German Reich. Within a few months Parliament had been reduced to a mere sounding-board for occasional Nazi pronouncements. The rights of the autonomous States had been completely overridden. All political parties, even that of their Nationalist allies, had been decisively broken up, and the policy of *Gleichschaltung* was in full swing in every department of German life, not excepting the powerful Lutheran and Reformed Churches. Within a year the States of the German Reich had practically disappeared as administrative units, and the complete unification of Nazi Germany had been further emphasised by the abolition of the *Reichsrat,* the federal House of the German Parliament.

German Nazism is, from the standpoint of the political rationalist, a far more alarming and horrifying phenomenon than Italian Fascism; for the Fascists rose to power on a basis that is largely capable of rational explanation. They, like the Nazis, appealed rrom a weak and crumbling parliamentary system to the powerful and familiar sentiment of nationalism and against Socialism to the self-interest of the property-owning classes; and this combination of appeals was powerful enough to ensure their victory, though it received reinforcement from a number of secondary appeals often of the most conflicting and visionary nature. There was in Italian Fascism as well as in German Nazism an element of appeal to blood-lust and love of violence. But this never reached anything like the extreme forms which it has assumed in Nazi Germany. In the main Italian Fascism was an anti-Socialist movement based on property-owning peasants and middle classes, supported by the great capitalists, and reinforcing itself with the appeal to nationalist sentiment. German Nazism was equally anti-Socialist and still more vociferously nationalist, backing up its appeal to nationalism with fantastic rhodomontades about the mission of the Nordic race. But it also built up its following far more largely than the Italian Fascists on a farrago of sheer political nonsense, which was yet so conceived and dressed up to suit all tastes as to exert a tremendously powerful influence on the thwarted and disturbed temper of the German people. For Germany, under the combined effects of the Versailles Treaty and the great depression, was in an unhealthily neurotic and pathological condition, and the persecution of the Jews and Socialists and the glorification of Nordic race superiority afforded an outlet for the pent-up complexes of the German youth.

The Weimar Republic went down in ignominy, and the German Socialists reaped in persecution and in sheer extinction as a political force the reward of their patient devotion to the patched up compromises of the parliamentary Republic. Another great country had been lost to constitutional government, and a new model of Fascist dictatorship had been brought into being with so much ruthlessness that beside Hitler and Goering Mussolini began to look like a Liberal and Italy almost to wear the aspect of a land of freedom and toleration. Moreover, Mussolini, for all his war-like speeches, never really looked very much like provoking a war with any of the greater Powers. But Hitler did and does look desperately likely to set all Europe again by the ears, even if it is perfectly true that the Germans are more intent at present on re-establishing themselves in their own national esteem and on consolidating their internal triumph than actually on embarking upon a war for which they are still imperfectly prepared.

EUROPEAN FASCISM

Meanwhile in other parts of Europe as well as Germany the new parliamentary systems installed after the war were being superseded or whittled away. Parliamentarism disappeared in Austria, where the local dictator, Dollfuss, announced his intention of establishing a Corporative State of his own on a Christian basis, with the support of Italy but in hostility to the rival attempt of Germany to make Austria Fascist under German rather than Italian influence. Turkey and Yugoslavia installed one-party Parliaments which exist only for the purpose of registering decisions already made by the party dictatorship. In both these countries all opposition parties had been suppressed, and there is no more freedom of criticism than in the States which have definitely abandoned the parliamentary system. Rumania adopted a fantastic electoral law which assures the Government in office of an enormous majority whenever it appeals to the country; and as the King has the power to appoint or dismiss the Government, the system is in effect a royal dictatorship. Bulgaria has passed in 1934 through a military *coup,* which has expelled the parliamentary government and installed a new Cabinet under a sort of Fascist leadership. Hungary also lives under a virtual dictatorship, though the semblance of a Parliament is still preserved, and some very mild criticism is still allowed. Poland, where many of the leaders of the opposition parties are in prison, is to all intents and purposes governed by a dictatorship headed by Marshal Pilsudski, and has recently been considering the adoption of a new Constitution which would place almost unlimited authority in the hands of the President acting in conjunction with a small clique of Generals and supporters of the existing régime. Latvia and Estonia have both recently made drastic moves away from Parliamentarism and towards a strengthening of the executive power; and in Latvia there has been a resort to the concentration camp and the wholesale arrest of political opponents in the German model. Spain, after two years of democratic Parliamentarism as the sequel to the Republican Revolution of 1931, is again in the melting-pot, with a Government of doubtful Republican sympathy holding office only with the support of the Right parties and under a constant threat of revolution. Almost alone among the new or reconstituted States of Europe Czechoslovakia seems to have settled down under her parliamentary system despite the multiplicity of parties based on national as well as class differences and the consequent impossibility of any Government not based on an extensive coalition. But even in Czechoslovakia exceptional laws are in force, and the stability of the parliamentary régime is by no means certain in face of Nazi threats of revolt from the German-speaking part of the country and of the existence of powerful dis-contented national minorities in both Slovakia and Ruthenia—to say nothing of a vigorous though outlawed Communist movement. Nor does the present plight of the League of Nations, conceived and founded essentially as a union of parliamentary States, augur well for the stability of parliamentary institutions over the world as a whole. For the League has been reduced, in view of the very doubt-ful allegiance of Italy, to a union of only two Great Powers, Great Britain and France, with a large number of smaller States, which cling to it more and more hesitantly and pay less and less attention to its precepts. Possibly the League will be rescued from sheer futility by the adhesion of Soviet Russia; but if this happens without the return of Germany it can be at best but a loose alliance of States, banded together for mutual security against German aggression, but impotent to institute even the beginnings of world government, or even to remove the menace of war.

Such is the tragic history of Parliamentarism in post-war Europe. Of course the play has not been acted out yet, and it is possible that despite the growth of aggressive Fascist movements over a large part of Europe, some way of accommodation will be found so as to prevent the sheer dissolution of the European State system. It is possible that countries animated by intensely nationalist ideas and intent on arming one against another will manage to stop short of actual war, and that somehow or other the territorial bound-aries of Parliamentarism and Fascism will get themselves so de-fined as to preserve a perilous balance in Europe without open conflict. It is easy to understand why, under present circumstances, the U.S.S.R., eager above all else to avoid the destruction of Socialist institutions by a plunge into war, may enter the League, or at least become the ally of the parliamentary countries in checking the am-bitions of the Fascist States. But, whether this happens or not, there is no escape from facing the fact that Europe is now divided into a series of armed camps, fully as hostile as in the years before 1914, with the additional complication that in many countries there is now the imminent threat of civil as well as international war. Such a condition is ominous for the future of democratic institutions of any kind. For the war spirit is a great breeder of authoritarian institutions, and men fly most readily to dictatorships when they are most afraid. To-day far more than in 1914 the dominant political motive is fear, and fear is in politics as in all else the inveterate enemy of reason.

3. PRESENT-DAY CURRENTS OF POLITICAL OPINION

A HABIT HAS GROWN up of late of grouping together under the name "Fascist" a large number of different movements which have in common an antipathy both to the established methods of parliamentary government and to all forms of Socialism and Communism. All these movements are grouped together as Fascist, on the ground first that they all take in some degree a revolutionary form, challenging on the one hand all the established political parties and movements which have been discredited by the experience of the post-war years and on the other hand the claim of the working class or its leaders to supersede Capitalism by some sort of equalitarian society. It can, however, be highly misleading simply to group together under this one name a large number of movements which have in common negative rather than positive qualities. It is true that all the movements that are commonly called Fascist are definitely anti-Socialist, and that they all aim at restricting if not totally superseding the powers of Parliament. But they may all share these negative characteristics and yet differ very profoundly in their positive aims, and in the nature of the social forces which lie behind them.

Sometimes, indeed, the word "Fascist" is used in an even wider sense than this. Opponents of President Roosevelt's policy in America have not been slow to call the National Recovery programme Fascist, simply on the ground that for the purpose of carrying it through President Roosevelt has been led to assume enormously wide powers which in practice both restrict very greatly the authority of the American Congress and drive a coach and four through certain constitutional principles hitherto regarded as inviolable. It is, however, quite a misnomer to call Rooseveltism a form of Fascism, though it has certain qualities in common with some of the European Fascist movements. It is bound, indeed, to have these common qualities, for both Rooseveltism and Fascism in the broadest sense are responses to a largely similar situation and enlist behind them certain of the same sentiments and ideas in men's minds. The truth is that in all the capitalist countries of the world to-day large sections of the population are in a mood which makes them open to the appeal of new political emotions or of old emotions enormously reinforced by the circumstances of the time. Fascism is one form of response to this new emotional situation; but it is by no means the only possible response, and many of the movements which are commonly called Fascist exist mainly because social classes and vested interests of many different sorts have seen their opportunity of getting popular support behind them in the imitation of those methods which were effective in bringing Italian Fascism to power.

THE CAUSES OF FASCISM

If this diagnosis of the current political situation is correct, it is important to begin our consideration of it not with a study of Fascism but rather with an attempt to estimate the forces in men's minds on which the diverse movements now labelled "Fascist" have based their influence. A study of these forces will be likely to tell us how much there is in common between these various movements and how far they represent a new political power emerging into activity on a world-wide scale, or rather merely a temporary wave of reaction against intolerable political and economic conditions. Let us ask, then, what is the state of mind which leads to the growth of movements which are at once anti-parliamentary and anti-Socialist, and to a willingness to employ violent methods in seeking an outlet from the present political and economic impasse.

In the first place there undoubtedly exists among a very large and growing section of the people in almost all the capitalist countries an uneasy feeling that both in political and in economic organisation the world is getting nowhere. This feeling existed to a substantial extent even before the coming of the world depression; and the magnitude of the depression has to some extent made us forget the strength of the forces which were, even before 1929, eroding the established political and economic systems of the advanced industrial countries. But of course the sense of futility has been greatly widened and deepened by the depression—perhaps unduly so, for it is by no means certain that the depression will not pass away and give place to a period of at least relative capitalist prosperity. If it does pass quickly enough there is likely to be a big backwash from the present condition of unrest, most of all in the United States, but to some extent in every country which has been seriously affected by the slump.

Secondly there is undoubtedly in the minds of a growing number of people a feeling that the existing forms both of political government and of economic and social organisation are definitely inappropriate to the tasks which they are supposed to fulfil. The parliamentary democratic system, whatever it may have been when it was newer, is now obviously a machine far more easily usable for keeping things pretty much as they are than for introducing drastic changes. It has lost, for the present at least, its capacity to do big things or to arouse big emotions, especially among the younger people who have grown up in the post-war world. This does not imply that there is yet, save in a few of the parliamentary countries, a really formidable conscious revolt against parliamentary institutions. But there is everywhere in these parliamentary countries a growing lack of respect for them and a marked unwillingness to rally enthusiastically to their defence.

Thirdly, there exists in all the advanced industrial countries a growing sense of vast potential wealth going foolishly to waste. This sense exists most strongly of all among the technically educated, who have a keener sense than others of the incongruity of destitution in the midst of rapidly advancing productivity. This sense of incongruity makes men ready to say that, whatever the right system of political and economic organisation may be—and many people do not profess to know at all clearly what it is—the one thing evident is that we have not got the right system now. This turns many men into cynics, or, when cynicism begins to pall, into potential revolutionaries of one sort or another.

Fourthly, there is a growing weariness of cynicism itself. Men are growing tired of shrugging their shoulders and saying that nothing is any good, or at least that no good can come out of political activity. They are coming more and more to demand new values in place of the old values that have decayed or ceased to appeal to their minds. This weariness of cynicism, like the conscious cynicism which preceded it, exists most obviously among the intelligentsia, but it spreads down among other classes of the populations of the developed countries to a much greater extent than many people are willing to believe. Taken by itself it is an entirely unconstructive force; for as the negation of a negation it simply exposes people to any political infection that may happen to be prevalent.

Fifthly, there is a very widespread fear of insecurity among all those who have hitherto possessed security in some measure. This applies primarily to the entire class of property-owners, both large and small, who form so large an element in advanced economic Societies; and it applies also to those whose superior education has hitherto counted for them as a form of property capable of yielding them an income well above the average, and in addition to a certain section of the better-paid working class. It is a powerful force impelling property-owners both large and small to support any movement that promises to smash Socialism and thus ensure the continuance of a Society based on the private ownership of the means of production and the retention of class differences. The skilled workers it impels rather towards Socialism, wherever Socialism appears to be a practicable and workmanlike policy; while the intermediate group of "intellectual proletarians" may be impelled either way according to the circumstances of each particular country. In one way or another, this fear of insecurity has been undoubtedly the main *economic* driving force behind the various movements which are lumped together under the name "Fascist."

Sixthly, there exists, as something distinct from the fear of a Socialist system of public ownership, a special and intense fear of Communism regarded as an alien creed seeking to impose world domination. This attitude has been steadily inculcated in men's minds by years of propaganda directed against the Soviet Union, and this propaganda has undoubtedly met with a good deal of success. Nor is it without a certain element of truth as matters stand. Communism as distinct from West European Socialism is felt not only as a political and economic but even more strongly as a cultural challenge, threatening to tear up by the roots all the social values to which men have been used in the capitalist countries of Western Europe and in the United States. Men feel that Communism seeks to impose upon them a radically different way of living, inspired not by the advanced civilisations of the West but rather by those of the semi-barbarous Eastern fringe. The Nazis, with their constant stress on their mission to defend Western Europe against the menace of barbarism from the East, are only exaggerating a sentiment which finds a wide response in minds which have been formed by a culture based on an age-long system of class inequality. Naturally this fear of the East is not so much felt, except by the upper classes, in the countries of Eastern and South-Eastern Europe; and in Asia the reaction to Communism takes quite different forms, dividing men between those who fear it as a Western doctrine seeking to impose itself upon Eastern culture and those who regard it as a more Eastern-like gospel than the gospels which they have hitherto been offered from the West. Of course, in Asia as well the response to Communism is different in different economic classes; but the sense that Communism is more assimilable in the Eastern peasant countries than European Parliamentarism also counts in determining India's and China's response.

Seventhly, there exists a very general sense, at any rate among the younger people, of the futility of all the old political parties, from Socialists at one end to various types of Conservatives at the other. This deters the new generation of electors from joining with any enthusiasm in the work and organisation of the older parties, and it makes especially against parliamentary Socialism because the parliamentary Socialists rely more than other parties on the support of a large rank and file of voluntary helpers. Moreover, the strength of the parliamentary Socialist appeal has been undoubtedly weakened in a number of countries by the fact that the tenure of office by Socialist Governments has failed to make any vital difference to the situation, though of course the Socialists are able to point to the fact that in these cases their Governments have had no clear majority behind them, and no real opportunity for applying a Socialist policy. In addition parliamentary Socialism has lost caste because of the ease with which it crumpled up in both Italy and Germany as soon as it was opposed by physical force. The apparent failure of Socialist Governments makes many of the younger people ready to say "You see these Socialists are no good after all"; while the collapse of German and Italian Socialism makes them say "Look what cowards these Socialists are when it comes to the point." The fact that the Socialists may have valid answers, or that they can reasonably point out the extreme difficulty of constructing Socialism by parliamentary methods, does not save them from these criticisms. The ordinary man, especially the young man, does not make excuses—he draws inferences. Nor is he wholly wrong. Socialist leadership has been weak and ineffective in most of the parliamentary countries.

Eighthly, the prolongation of political and economic disorder has led to a powerful outbreak of political "Gawdsaking." There are more and more people who, without knowing what they want to do, say, "For Gawd's sake let's do something." This means that the gospels which make the most compelling appeals are those which appear to offer their supporters the opportunity for acting as well as thinking. Men want to march about the streets, dress up in special shirts, make loud political noises on all possible occasions. For these activities give them a sense that they are doing something instead of merely sitting still. Communists as well as the various types of Fascist make every effort to enlist this desire for activity on their side, and actually give their members far more real work to do than the older parties. But it is far more dangerous to be an active Communist than an active Fascist. In a good many countries if you are a Fascist you can do a lot of brawling and kicking without getting very much kicked yourself, whereas active Communists in general get short shrift.

THE REVIVAL OF NATIONALISM

Ninthly, there is a strong revival of nationalist feeling. We have left this till the last deliberately because it differs from all the other feelings that we have been attempting to analyse in being at bottom a flight from the terrifying complications of modern world problems back to a notion deeply rooted in man's social tradition. This is not because the sentiment of nationality is itself particularly old. Indeed, over the greater part of Europe it is definitely modern, and there was very little strength in it till it was stirred up by the proselytising zeal of the French Revolution. There was nationalist sentiment before that; there is much of it, for example, in Shakespeare's historical plays, but Elizabethan England was exceptionally nationalist for any period earlier than the nineteenth century. Nationalism as a powerful political force in Europe came to birth in the period following the

French Revolution and was thereafter for a time associated in men's minds with Liberal movements for the establishment of responsible government on a national basis.

But though nationalism is relatively new, that which underlies the sense of nationalism in men to-day is exceedingly old. For the modern nation has succeeded in becoming the heir of the far older tradition of social solidarity, sometimes called the "herd instinct," which has been growing up from the earliest family groups down through tribal communities to the modern Nation-State. When men are afraid, they want something to huddle round, and the Nation-State has become in the modern world the social unit round which they gather. This sense of herd or tribal solidarity has been always also a sense of the foreignness of everything outside the herd; and nationalism correspondingly issues to-day in a sense of the externality and unintelligibility and potential dangerousness of everything outside the nation. Men are saying: "We don't understand all this internationalism. It carries us into commitments with people who are not our kin, and we don't know where we are being carried. In a world of insecurity the only sure thing to trust to is the familiar nation-group." So we get a great weakening of the drive towards internationalism in men's minds which accompanied the creation of the League of Nations and the return to peace after the last war. Nationalism becomes stronger everywhere; and where there has been foreign oppression, as in Germany, or a sense of national inferiority, as in Italy, the nationalist spirit breaks out in the most extravagant forms. Racialism is one extreme expression of it.

It is quite true that there is some growth of internationalist sentiment to set against this recrudescence of the anti-foreigner complex. Many men have come to see that if the world is to be rescued from disaster it must be organised on international or even in some respects on cosmopolitan lines. But this rational response to the existing situation exists mainly among a limited section of the populations of the various countries, and is largely confined to politically educated people. It is strongest perhaps at the moment in France, though France is often accused of being the most nationalist of countries. For the French, as a highly educated people in a political sense, are well aware that there is no escape for them from the world problems through any policy of national isolation. They want to build up international safeguards and guarantees, which they conceive in a far more realistic form than the majority of internationalists in other countries; but they are distrustful of the possibilities of success, and as the world stands to-day who shall blame them for their mistrust?

THE RIGHTS OF PROPERTY

These seem to be the fundamental factors which constitute the psychological situation on which the various movements called Fascist have everywhere been based. But it is necessary to take account also of certain secondary factors—by which we mean factors that are not so much of independent importance as derived from one or more of the primary factors which have already been set out. First among these secondary factors has been the vehement reassertion of the rights of private property by large and small property-owners alike. This arises out of the fear of insecurity of which we have spoken above. It creates at one and the same time a hatred of Socialism, which threatens to sweep away altogether private property in the means of production, and a milder dislike of large-scale capitalist organisation, which restricts the opportunities open to the small property-owner and sometimes threatens him with expropriation. But of these two reactions the hatred against Socialism goes infinitely the deeper, since Socialism, with its proposal to eliminate private property in all the essential means of production, unites all owners of such property against it—for the fact that the Socialists propose to confer property in personal possessions on a larger section of the population which has virtually no private property now does not appeal to those who fear the loss of the existing properties on which their superior economic position is based. Large-scale Capitalism, on the other hand, threatens only the small firm or the private *entrepreneur,* and offers to many property-holders ample compensation in the diffused ownership of stocks and shares. Therefore, if it comes to a struggle between Socialism and large-scale Capitalism, the mass of small property-owners is far more likely to take the capitalist than the Socialist side.

It is true that there exists among a large section of the middle class to-day a strong dislike of bankers and financiers as a special form of the sentiment against the large property-owner, and that this dislike has been greatly heightened by the appalling currency muddles and financial scandals of recent years. This "small capitalist anti-banker complex" meets and mingles with a second complex of the same sort which comes from a very different source. This second complex exists among the working class, which has come to regard the banker and the financier as the outstanding representatives of the capitalist system, whereas the anti-banker middle class regards them as the enemies of a sound capitalist system. The mingling of these two streams leads to constant confusion of policies, as when the *Daily Express* and the Labour Party are both found supporting the nationalisation of the Bank of England, but for very different reasons.

THE DEMAND FOR STATE INTERVENTION

Secondly, there is on all hands a growing demand for State intervention to help any section of the community which feels the pinch of economic adversity. The basis of this demand has in the main nothing to do with the doctrine of Socialism. It is simply a derivative of the "Gawdsaking" attitude. Those who appeal to the State for help in their troubles are for the most part simply saying "For Gawd's sake can't somebody do something," and turning to the politicians as the most obvious targets for their demands. The demand for State intervention is from the standpoint of most of those who make it simply a demand that somebody else shall get to work to clean up the mess. When the State does not intervene, or when State intervention only creates fresh muddles, the demand turns into advocacy of a change of political institutions. The demand for State intervention thus arises out of the first of our primary considerations, and is powerfully reinforced by the second.

Thirdly, there is a flight from representative institutions to personal leadership. This is a perfectly familiar happening in times of serious crisis, and like the recrudescence of nationalism it is largely a reversion to ancient ways of thought. It is still easier for men to put their faith in a person than in a gospel, or at least to embody their faith in a gospel in the person of an individual leader. But this demand for personal leadership is rather the consequence of the primary forces already analysed than itself an independent force. It is to be placed among the secondary rather than the primary factors in the situation.

Fourthly, there is an undoubted tendency to think of politics less in terms of discussion and more in terms of violence and coercion. This, too, is a secondary reaction. It is in the main the blind hitting out that comes of a sense of frustration. It is the action of the man who kicks the chair against which he has barked his shin. But this does not make it the less dangerous. It is, indeed, the most dangerous of all the factors that go to make up the political mind of to-day. For it puts men in a mood in which they will hit first and think afterwards, and it thus leads directly to national states of mind which will facilitate war and to a situation which weakens the inhibitions that a long tradition of tranquillity has set against civil war.

These forces, which are for the most part world-wide in their influence, are capable of taking very different forms according both to the differences of conditions between one country and another and to the quality of leadership that is forthcoming in each country and class. It is misleading simply to lump together all the movements which arise out of them under the one name of Fascism, for Fascism is only one possible response to a situation of this sort. For example, many of the forces which have just been described are certainly very powerful to-day in the United States. But it would be entirely a misnomer to call President Roosevelt's policy Fascist. It is not Fascism, but a different way of mobilising and directing the same sentiments in men's minds.

THE AMERICAN EXPERIMENT

The essence of Rooseveltism, as we understand it, is that it is an emergency programme of an experimental character. It is not, like some forms of Fascism, an attempt to curb large-scale Capitalism in the interests of the small business man, though it does direct itself largely against bankers and financiers, who have been obviously responsible for exaggerating in a high degree the troubles of the United States. It is anti-banker, but it is not anti-big-business; rather the other way, for the Codes under the Industrial Recovery Act on the whole help large-scale Capitalism more than small. The effect of the National Recovery Act has been to remove for the time at least many of the old prohibitions on combination among large-scale businesses and to abrogate a large part of the Sherman anti-trust law. The American Government is attempting to curb the banker and the stock market operator in the interest of the investing classes, including large and small capitalists alike, and to regulate financial and commercial conditions in the interests of the property-owning farmers. But in both these respects it aims rather at applying State regulation in order to restore American business prosperity on the old lines than at building a new system. It is an attempt to set American Capitalism on its feet again with the full intention of removing many, though not all, of the new "controls" as soon as this has been successfully done. It is not an attempt to establish a new form of State-controlled Capitalism. Nor is there anything essentially new in America in the attempt to apply forms of State control which are designed to protect individualism rather than to supersede it. America nationalised her Central Banking system when she set up the Federal Reserve Banks in 1913 after the financial crisis of 1907. The American Federal Government, within the limits set by the Constitution, has been active in interference with large-scale business for a long time past. It has prohibited trusts, and aimed at limiting monopolies of any and every sort; and that it has largely failed in these endeavours does not mean that the attempt has not been seriously made. President Roosevelt has had to go very much further than any of his predecessors with this policy, and has been able to go very much further because of the extraordinary severity of the American economic crisis. But it is quite a mistake to suppose that President Roosevelt is either a Socialist wishful to supersede American Capitalism or a Fascist thinking in terms of a fundamental change in American political institutions.

On these grounds it is reasonable to draw a sharp contrast between what President Roosevelt is doing in the United States and what is happening in Europe where Fascist or other anti-parliamentary movements have gained control. For European Fascism, as it exists in Italy and Germany, is definitely aiming at a permanent change both in the political structure of the State and in the State's relation to economic affairs. It seeks to rebuild the capitalist system on a new basis as a State-controlled Capitalism run in the interests of the middle classes and of the *rentiers,* including the small traders and small agricultural producers, and to do this not simply as a means of dealing with a temporary emergency but on a permanent basis as a bulwark against Socialism. European Fascism is in fact a definite alternative form of Capitalism to the mainly *laissez-faire* Capitalism of the nineteenth century, and its leaders have set out to establish a kind of State that will be permanently proof against the attacks of equalitarian Socialism by building up the Corporative State as an embodiment of authoritative and dictatorial power. They have thrown over both economic and political Liberalism lastingly, and not merely for the purpose of overcoming the economic crisis; and their fundamental objective is the destruction of Socialism far more than the re-establishment of economic prosperity.

SEMI-FASCIST MOVEMENTS

What has been said in the last paragraph applies to the Fascist systems that have been created in Germany and Italy, but it does not necessarily apply to the numerous other movements in European countries that are commonly called "Fascist." Fascism in Great Britain, for example, has not yet developed far enough for its nature to be plain. It is at the moment little more than a planless revolt by miscellaneous elements of discontent against the ineffectiveness of the parliamentary system and the growth of constitutional Socialism. If economic conditions in Great Britain became substantially worse, it might assume a menacing form and take on the characteristic qualities of Italian or German Fascism; and the same result might be produced by the advent of a strong Socialist Government to power. But so far British Fascism can hardly be said to possess a policy, for it is impossible to discover in the orations of Sir Oswald Mosley or the other leaders even the rudiments of a constructive political doctrine. Again, to speak of French Fascism is also at present largely a misnomer. The French Royalists and the adherents of the *Action Française* are not Fascists in the German or Italian sense; they are just violent reactionaries. M. Tardieu and some other French politicians of the Right may have "Fascist" tendencies; but there is no *popular* French Fascist movement as yet. Nor does there appear to be even the beginning of such a movement outside Paris. Austrian Fascism, again, is not easy to classify. It began under Herr Dollfuss's leadership as a sort of Christian Corporativism, a very old thing which goes back far beyond the creation of the Austrian Republic in 1918. A sort of Guild State was being advocated by the Austrian Christian Social Party well back in the past century. Herr Dollfuss owed his power to the support of a Fascist movement, but he himself could hardly be classified as a Fascist in either the Italian or the German sense. The *Heimwehr,* on the other hand, has based itself largely on the imitation of Italian Fascism, as the Austrian Nazis have on that of German Nazism. But the backing of the *Heimwehr* differs radically from that of Mussolini's Fascists, in that it is based in fact far more on a body of peasants still following the lead of the old landowning class, and far less upon the ex-soldier and middle-class elements on which Signor Mussolini mainly relied. The *Heimwehr* is in a social sense far more reactionary than either Italian Fascism or German Nazism. It is, in effect, much more reactionary landlordism, allied with reactionary clericalism and dressed up in Fascist clothes, than a popular demagogic movement. As for the "Fascisms" which at present exist in Rumania, Bulgaria, and other States of Eastern Europe, they too represent even more a resort to violence by the older forces of the extreme Right than the emergence of a new force aiming at a different kind of State. Nowadays the extreme Right seems to resort everywhere to "Fascist" methods and forms of organisation, but it does not follow that there is any real community of social or economic policy among the various groups which are alike in repudiating both Socialism and the parliamentary State.

FASCISM AND SOCIALISM

Between Fascism in the true sense as it exists in Italy and Germany, on the one hand, and all forms of Socialism and Communism on the other, there is, as often between extreme opposites, something in common, which helps to explain the frequency of transferences from the one extreme to the other. They do all set out from a conception of the need for the co-ordinated control of economic and social life. They do all want to create an authoritative central power in the community which will be able to assume the ultimate control of the economic as well as the political life of the people. But their differences are of course far more important than these points of resemblance. The fundamental difference between them is that, whereas both Socialists and Communists want to build up this authoritative control for the purpose of securing economic and social equality, the Fascists want it for the exactly opposite purpose of preventing this equality. Accordingly, whereas Socialists and Communists propose to take all the vital industries and services under public ownership with the object of securing command for society as a whole over the entire social income, Fascism proposes to leave industries and services under private ownership, subject to a regulation by the State which is designed to preserve the rights of property and therewith to safeguard the recipients of private incomes from property in the possession of those incomes. Fascism is State-controlled Capitalism operated in the interests of the broad mass of property-owners, its conception of property-owning being of course wide enough to include the possession of a superior type of education reserved for a few as in effect a form of property.

But it is also highly relevant that Fascism is nationalist. For there is an economic as well as a political reason for its nationalism. It must be nationalist because the national State is the only available instrument for guarding the rights of property against Socialist attack. This necessity explains the eagerness with which Fascist leaders play upon nationalist sentiment. But it does not, of course, explain the existence or the strength of the sentiment to which they are able to appeal. For the nationalist sentiment iself, though it is reinforced by economic considerations, does not depend mainly upon them, but arises rather in its present heightened state from the power of fear and the threat of insecurity to drive men back to primitive loyalties. Nationalism in its more exaggerated forms is the outcome of a fear complex expressing itself no longer in a group or tribal loyalty on a small scale but in a sense of the nation as the embodiment of collective power. International Socialism or anything that requires world-wide collaboration is apt to seem terrifying to the minds of men who can think or feel easily only in terms of things nearer home. This is the fatal weakness that besets the present propaganda of internationalism. The idea of international friendship and cosmopolitan collaboration possesses a strong humanitarian appeal. When men are tranquil it elicits a ready response in their minds. But they are unable to attach it to any institution which seems capable of defending it against attack. The League of Nations, weakly founded upon a collaboration between the Governments of sovereign States, has been quite unable to make a position for itself in men's minds as an international institution commanding collective loyalty. Consequently, when men are afraid, their internationalism is apt to slip off them, and they revert easily to nationalist sentiments which can find expression in loyalty to an objective institution of which they feel themselves a part. Only the force of a strong intellectual conviction, or a sense of intolerable oppression, is powerful enough in times of crisis to overcome this tendency; and strong as Socialism has become in many countries it is still in its internationalist appeal only skin-deep among the greater part of those who have been accustomed to give it political support in national affairs.

BOOK II

POLITICAL SYSTEMS OF TO-DAY

1. INTRODUCTION

THE HISTORY of political organisation in the world is a very long one and contains the record of a number of very diverse systems. Subsequent chapters of this book describe the political systems existing in some of the principal countries at the present time; but it is of the highest importance to realise that these systems do not by any means exhaust all the possibilities of political organisation. Even if we leave out primitive communities altogether and consider only those comparatively developed entities which mankind has agreed to call States, and if we further confine ourselves to States which actually exist or have existed in the world, omitting those, such as the *Republic* of Plato, whose only existence has been in men's minds, we find the most bewildering variety.

We find, for example, that "States" may be of almost any size, varying from the tiny City-State of ancient times to a great modern nation like the United States of America or a would-be world empire like that of Rome. We find, further, that they may be formed upon almost any basis, of which the basis of neighbourhood is only the easiest and most frequent. It is true that a State can hardly be formed except out of people who associate on a basis of neighbourhood—though the Catholic Church, in the days in which it possessed temporal power, came near to doing without even this; but if the neighbourhood basis be taken for granted, there are many other additional bonds of union. States may consist, as do many States in the modern world, predominantly of those who speak a common language; yet in the past groups speaking the same language have been bitterly hostile to one another, as in the case of the ancient Greek city-states or the medieval States of Italy and the Low Countries; and most modern States, whatever their present linguistic uniformity, have been formed out of communities which at the time of the State's formation spoke many different tongues. The United States of America is a modern example of a community in which the possession of a common language, enforced firmly upon immigrant stocks, is one of the chief political bonds; yet English-speaking Canada has not joined that federation, and the spread of English in British India is helping to create, not an English, but an Indian nation.

States may be bound together by the possession of common institutions, in particular of a common legal system, as in the Roman Empire. They may also be formed upon the basis of a common religious creed, like the Empire of the Moslem Arabs, or the city of Geneva under Calvin, or of a common political creed, as the U.S.S.R. is to-day, or of a common ethic and common social institutions, as was the Chinese Empire for many generations. But neither a common religion nor a common political creed necessarily unites those who hold it in a single State. The Catholic States of medieval Europe fought one another with undiminishing energy; and the modern States which have embraced parliamentary democracy have not shown any tendency to combine one with another. At the present time the sentiment called nationalism, from whatever source it springs, seems the most potent bond of union in the Western world; but this is not true, even to-day, of the peoples which compose the Union of Socialist Soviet Republics, and it was certainly not a fact over large periods of the world's history, and may in the future again cease to be a fact.

States may live to themselves alone, not interfering with their neighbour States, or they may set out to conquer their neighbours, either for the purely predatory purpose of taking their land or imposing tribute upon them, as was the case with the ancient Empires of Assyria, Babylon, Persia and Rome—though the Roman Empire, of course, came to be much more than a mere machine for the exaction of tribute—or for the spreading of a particular creed or political institution, as the Arabs spread the religion of Mahomet by the sword. Or, again, they may simply plant offshoots of themselves in distant parts, as the Phœnician and Greek cities planted colonies on the shores of the Mediterranean. Most States appear to possess some form of machinery for internal coercion and external defence and attack, though the researches of archæologists in the Near East and parts of India seem to indicate that States have existed which had no weapons of war at all.

In their internal working, also, States show an infinite amount of divergence. They may admit to the privileges of citizenship all those who live within their borders, or most of them, or hardly any of them; they may grant or deny citizenship to the poor, to the rich, to women, to those of alien birth or imperfect education or unpopular opinions, and they may have various grades and qualities of citizenship. They may select those who are to carry on the work of administration on grounds of birth, or wealth, or education or occupation, or religious or political probity, or even by the casting of lots. They may devise all manner of expedients to secure the consent or co-operation of those who are governed, or they may have no formal machinery at all for this purpose, and simply trust to luck and the good sense of the governors. They may be federal or highly centralised, or anything between these two extremes. There have even been States, like China over many centuries, which possessed nothing that we should call a political system, and yet were in no sense of the word uncivilised; and there have also been States, such as the Roman Republic, which existed successfully for generations under a political system which most observers would unhesitatingly pronounce to be unworkable. The Roman republican constitution, with its college of ten tribunes of whom any one was entitled to veto the operation of any law, is perhaps the outstanding example of a system of government which seems, on the face of it, certain to lead to a deadlock; yet the Roman constitution appears to have functioned quite adequately for a long time until social changes in Roman society caused it to collapse. The British House of Lords is not the only example of a logically indefensible institution which yet manages to survive; and it would not be far wrong to say that there is no form of constitution, however odd, which has not succeeded in working at some time in some place.

Political systems, therefore, have varied very greatly at different stages of the world's history and in different parts of the world. Present-day Western institutions, and still more Western political thinkers, have been enormously influenced, in particular, by the experiences of ancient Greece and Rome; and much of our modern political controversies is still stated in classical terms. Of the two words which are most bandied about in political argument to-day, democracy and dictatorship, the former is Athenian and the latter Roman. It is therefore of some importance, if we are to clarify our political thought, to see what these terms meant in origin and how far their meaning has in fact been modified by time and by changed economic and social conditions.

GREEK DEMOCRACY

Democracy, as a term and as an idea, was invented in the Athens of the fifth century before Christ, though no modern democrat would accept the Athenian State as a full democracy. Democracy means "government by the people"; and since the abolition of slavery in the West and the introduction of universal suffrage no Western democrats can really allow a State to be fully democratic which does not grant political rights to all, or nearly all, its adult inhabitants, though they may differ about the machinery through which those rights should be exercised. But in Athens the number of persons who possessed full citizen rights, compared with the total number of residents in Attica, was small. Not only were slaves, as all over the ancient world, excluded; citizen rights were also denied to women, and to the very large class who could not show Athenian parentage on both sides. Athenian "democracy" thus meant in reality the rule of a comparatively small privileged minority: nevertheless, within that class there was democracy, in the most extreme sense of the term, based— as alone democracy can be based—on an equal opportunity and equal social rights. Athens did not enjoy economic equality, even among her citizens; but the inequalities of wealth were not sufficient, in the days of Pericles at all events, to result in the creation of social classes or exploitation of persons nominally equal before the law, and the system of public taxation was really designed to make the rich contribute in due proportion to the needs of society. Perhaps the main indication of the real general feeling of equality among the citizens—*isonomia,* as a speaker in Herodotus calls it—was the use of the lot to determine the holders of all the public offices except the most important, whose holders were selected by ballot. Even in a State where government was as comparatively small and simple a thing as it was in Athens, such a system could not have worked at all unless the citizens had been able to rely reasonably upon one another's competence and education. Leadership was secured for the State, not by the creation of an office with plenary powers, but through the personal qualities of such a leader as Pericles, and by the "ostracism"—i.e. banishment without disgrace—of leaders with rival attitudes which threatened to turn the policy of the State into a perpetual see-saw.

There has never been a State so democratic as ancient Athens, even with the qualifications which we have observed. Quasi-democracies existed, indeed, in some of the city-states of medieval Europe, and in the city of Geneva when it was ruled by the "Saints" under Calvin; but in both these cases democracy was very much tempered, in the medieval cities by the existence of differences of class and status which were reflected in the government, and in Geneva by the religious elements, which in effect reserved positions of authority for those predestined for salvation. The Calvinist system, as the history of many Puritan churches has shown, is less anti-democratic than many, in that no person is barred by differences of birth or wealth from entering the ranks of the elect; but it is certainly not a free democracy of equals.

It must be emphasised, however, that not merely is the democracy of Athens unique, it is also likely to remain so. Even apart from the system of slavery, whose return to the modern world is at the least improbable, the Athenian system is essentially a system for a tiny society, a society in which all citizens who are interested in politics can really come together and talk things over, in which everyone knows his neighbours and his neighbours' qualifications, and in which the business of the State has not become so complicated as to demand special expertise and specialised knowledge which the mass of citizens, however well-educated, cannot possibly acquire. It is as impossible for a modern State to turn itself into an Athenian democracy as for a modern man to grow a tail. Whence, then, comes the undoubted appeal and influence of ancient Athens in the modern world—an appeal which cannot entirely be put down to the accident which has preserved classical Greek as part of the education of the unfortunate sons of the wealthier classes, for it is and has been felt, throughout two thousand years, by many who had no knowledge of Greek?

Partly the reason is that Athenian "democracy," while it is nowhere practised in politics, is in fact practised, no doubt with modifications, in a great many modern institutions, clubs, societies, Trade Unions, and so on, which, while not part of the political system in the strict sense, do form a large part of society and to many of their members count for much more than their political affiliations. Not one of us lives in a political democracy, but we nearly all have practical experience, in one way and another, of the working of small democratic societies of equals, and it is this practical experience which accounts for some of the discontent with the political shams which go under the name of democratic States to-day. More important, however, is the fact that Athens was the first State to be formed, not on a religious or other authoritarian basis, but on a basis of free secular culture. *Parrhesia*—free speech—was as essential a part of Athenian democracy as *isonomia,* and if free speech did not extend to the toleration of Socrates in time of war, this only indicates that there are always limits to toleration, even in the freest community. The trial of Socrates reads very differently from the trials of witches in New England.

Athenian conformity was a conformity not of creed, but of ideas and culture, and of culture, in particular, of such a high standard and vitality that it long outlasted the peculiar institutions of the Athenian and the other Greek city-states. When Alexander of Macedon proceeded from the conquest of the Greek cities to that of the whole of the Near East, it was the Greek language and the philosophy and literature of Greece that his armies and the cities which he planted spread from Cyrenaica to the borders of Afghanistan; and the Romans, following two hundred years later in his footsteps, found themselves the masters of a whole host of communities whose ruling classes spoke Greek and discussed the Stoic and Epicurean philosophies, and which had grafted, in some cases with curious effects, scraps of Greek political institutions on to their ancient traditional ways.

THE ROMAN IMPERIAL SYSTEM

The Hellenisation of the Near East in one way greatly simplified the problem of the Romans. The Roman Empire, like Athenian democracy, is a unique historical phenomenon, and one which also appears unlikely to recur, though its influence is still as visible in the political and legal institutions of Western Europe as the influence of Athens in its thought; and there are still ways in which modern Empires might learn lessons from Rome. With the details of the Roman system we are not here concerned, though we may observe that, although dictator is a Latin word, modern dictators do not really resemble the dictators of ancient Rome. The Roman dictator was a person invested with plenary powers for the express purposes of rescuing the State from a particular impasse—a sort of temporary High Commissioner—and his powers were to be laid down after a very short time. What the Fascist and Nazi advocates of dictatorship mean to advocate is not dictatorship, but Cæsarism. There is much in common between the constitutional position of Augustus and that of Mussolini.

The Roman Empire, like its predecessors in Persia, Babylon, Assyria, etc., came into being as a result of military conquest, the motives of each particular conquest varying from desire for tribute and the personal ambitions of individual commanders, to the establishment of order and safety for travel and commerce in various parts of the world. As in the case of the earlier empires, also, its political system was an autocracy based on the autocrat's command of the army. But there the likeness stops; for the earlier empires made no attempt to follow up their conquests by the establishment of a common civilisation, and even Alexander, whatever may have been his intentions, died before he had had time to do more than initiate the diffusion of Hellenic culture. The Roman Empire did much more than this. Fundamentally, it aimed at turning every conquered province into a replica of Italy and every conquered city into a replica of Rome, and, further, at the establishment, in all areas, of cities and city-life. It tried, as Virgil puts it, "to enforce the arts of peace," and by the arts of peace it meant city civilisation. Where the Greeks had gone before them, the Romans found cities already in existence, speaking Greek and imbued with Greek ideals, and the eastern half of the Roman Empire thus remained, throughout its history, Greek rather than Roman. But the Romans themselves had derived so much of their ideas from Greek sources that there was no serious clash, and most of the specifically Roman contributions to political science were able easily to fit in with the older traditions; while in the West, except for a few earlier settlements such as Marseilles, the Roman seed was sown in virgin soil.

The Roman Empire was thus the greatest single experiment in political assimilation and urbanisation that the world has known. It was the Roman belief that all men who counted (leaving out, as ever in the ancient world, the slaves and subject cultivators of the soil) ought to live in cities as much like Rome as possible; and accordingly every excavation of a Roman city discloses baths, monuments, public buildings and public inscriptions of all kinds which differ very little one from another. Nor was the assimilation confined to the external appearance of the cities; there were also the common language, the common legal institutions and even the endeavour to introduce wherever practicable social institutions and social classes similar to those which were to be found in Rome itself. This assimilation was remarkably successful. Much may be said in criticism of the Roman system itself and indeed of the Roman character; the Romans were not a merciful people, and it cannot even be asserted that they were always either just or honest in their dealings. But their political system as a whole did avowedly aim at the practical realisation of universal justice; and it cannot be denied that no other empire has succeeded, to anything like the same extent, in turning its subjects into loyal and even devoted citizens, while preserving for them their pride in their own locality. St. Paul proclaims with equal vigour his citizenship of Rome and his citizenship of Tarsus; and wide differences of birthplace seem to have affected hardly at all the relations between citizens of the empire. Nationalist movements and minorities were practically unknown, and the Roman legions were never required as permanent garrisons for towns except on the frontiers. The vast system collapsed in the end because city civilisation is expensive, and the sheer cost of administration, coupled with that of defence against barbarians without, proved too much for the productive system, at all events in the West, to sustain; but the heritage of common culture and common law, handed down through the medium of Latin and the Catholic Church, has been of immense influence in moulding the political forms of Europe up to the twentieth century. Even to-day, it has been the Roman Catholic Church which has stood up most strongly, both in Germany and Italy, in face of the inordinate modern growth of nationalism, resisting *Gleichschaltung* in the former country and forcing its own recognition as an independent power in the latter.

OTHER INSTITUTIONS

The political experiences of Rome and Athens have called for special comment, as being forces that have been of most account in the making of Europe and hence, to a great extent, of the American continent. It must be realised, however, that this applies only to the West, and may not continue to apply for ever even there. Not only has the greater part of Asia been almost entirely uninfluenced by these institutions, so that the historical explanation of the political life of Chinese and Indians is to be sought not in the classics but in the teachings of Confucius and the traditional life of China, or in the Indian village community and the doctrines of Buddhism and Hinduism which are so difficult for Western intellects to grasp; there are also indications that new types of institution, also alien, yet not so alien, may prove more fertile in the East than the remains of Plato's teaching or the Roman canon law. Communism, as a creed, still arouses the fiercest emotional reactions among the bulk of Europeans, yet many will be found to be getting inspiration from the political institutions which Communism has evolved in its growth on Russian soil. Of these, as of the definitely Eastern peoples, we speak in later chapters; for the moment it may suffice to remind the reader that political systems are of many types and of the most varied provenance.

2. THE POLITICAL SYSTEM OF GREAT BRITAIN

THE POLITICAL SYSTEM of Great Britain is very peculiar and quite unique. This is the first fact which any student of politics must grasp, particularly if he be an English student. For the fact that certain parts of the British system have commanded in the past considerable general admiration among the articulate thinkers of other countries and have been widely imitated elsewhere has caused to arise a belief, almost universally held by Englishmen before the war and not uncommon even in these latter days, that the nations at large were destined inevitably to embrace in the long run the entire system, and has obscured the plain truth that, except in the case of a few distant areas inhabited chiefly by British emigrants, the countries which have borrowed English political institutions have changed them so much in the borrowing as to leave little more likeness than the name. Even in the United States the representative bodies which arose in direct imitation of the Mother of Parliaments look and behave in a manner very different from their parent.[1]

[1] For example Great Britain is technically a monarchy; it is generally referred to

THE TRADITION OF BRITISH POLITICS

The uniqueness of Great Britain is a matter of historical growth, and can quite clearly be traced to such historical factors as the peculiar course of the Reformation in England, the poverty in the sixteenth and seventeenth centuries of the English Crown, and, by far the most important, the immense and sudden growth in the material resources of the country which began in the eighteenth century and which we call the Industrial Revolution. It was the Industrial Revolution which made nineteenth-century Britain into a strange and separate country, which took its population off the land and raised their standard of life, which steadily increased Liberalism and liberal institutions within its own borders, until two of the chief problems which confront every Continental politician, viz., the peasantry, and the possibility of monarchical and clerical tyranny, were literally unknown to the pre-war Englishman. Not merely in its institutions, but in its theories and ideas, and to a very large extent in its literature and art also, nineteenth-century England was a world apart—but a world living not of itself alone but on supplies and tribute which its enormous economic start enabled it to draw from less advanced countries. Nineteenth-century Britain was in comparison with other nations a *bourgeois* of comfort and leisure, and its political liberties were built, no less than the Parthenon of Periclean Athens, upon the tribute of subject peoples. Occasionally, and towards the latter part of the century, one finds a dim uncomfortable realisation of this fact penetrating the minds of the more liberal among British politicians: the contrast between the home practice and the imperial policy becomes, as in the case of the British occupation of Egypt, unpleasingly obvious and creates a psychological disturbance which has to resolve itself into comforting fantasies like the "white man's burden" or what his enemies were pleased to call Gladstone's "hypocrisy." Neither the policy nor the practice, however, was seriously affected.

It was the Industrial Revolution which made the present system. But that system would not be what it is nor have grown up as it did

---

as a democracy; but it is perfectly clear to the unprejudiced observer that Great Britain is an oligarchy—an oligarchy tempered by a large element of reverence for pure individualism and one which has worked out in long practice an elaborate machinery for securing the consent of the mass of the people, and even for ascertaining the desires of that mass when it has any which are felt to be of any importance had it not been for other and prior factors. Had not the Crown been so poor and its direct power to influence industry virtually removed long before the arrival of new inventions, we should not have found the new manufacturing middle class growing up with a view that life was divided firmly into two compartments—politics, and trade and industry—of which politics was the business of the State and trade and industry a sphere in which the State was generally speaking a nuisance and to be admitted only with very great caution.[1] This had the curious supplementary result that politics, being more or less divorced from the sordid business of money-making, was enabled to become a comparatively pure and noble occupation, and to receive some of the reverence normally given to the Church. "Entering politics," as a study of nineteenth-century novels will show, was a course for Young Men with Vocations—not for shady touts.

Nor, if the power of the Crown and the former feudal aristocracy had not been removed with such comparative ease and painlessness—the only serious armed clash, the Civil War, being a tea party compared with Continental Revolutions—would the tradition of continuity in government have gained anything like the strength it has. There has never been a lasting political revolution in Britain, in the sense of an introduction in a single act or series of acts of a new political system. Cromwell, in the *Instrument of Government,* did try to introduce such a system; and his reward was a clean sweep of all the Cromwellian institutions, and the Restoration. The other largish changes, such as the 1688 "Revolution" or the Reform Act of 1832, have altered only some parts of the system, leaving other parts, important and unimportant, to be altered gradually in conformity or not altered at all. Nor has there been any violent readjustment of class relationships, such as we find in the French or the Russian Revolutions. There have only been minor modifications, and the educational system of Great Britain, to take only the most obvious example, still displays the clearest possible example of abiding class distinctions.

Further, the later "revolutions" have tended to leave the actual administration of government to be carried on by the same individuals or groups as before, on the understanding that they govern in accordance with the broad instructions of the side that has won the

---

[1] It should be noted that this statement is not true of finance proper. Ever since the institution of the National Debt and the Bank of England, the financial interests of Britain have been able to use the State machinery in accordance with their own policies without any inconvenient friction.

day. Even of 1660 this is true. Charles II, a Stuart, returned on the perfectly plain understanding that he reversed the policy of previous Stuarts; when James II went back on this understanding he was dismissed exactly as a recalcitrant bailiff might be dismissed, and replaced by a king whose views were more congenial to the governing class. Only very slowly did the governing class actually push the King out of participation in government. Similarly, when in 1832 the manufacturing middle classes asserted and obtained their right to political power, they made little direct use of it at first. The personnel even of Parliaments and still more of Cabinets underwent surprisingly few immediate changes; and after 1867, when the town artisan received the franchise, it was thirty years and more before a working-class party appeared in Parliament. In 1832, in fact, the British governing oligarchy definitely decided against the policy of the "clean sweep" or spoils system, and it was only a matter of time before this decision was reflected in the reform of the Civil Service.

This tradition of government has certain manifest advantages; it provides the minimum of dislocation and distress if those who know the machine are allowed to guide it during a change of policy; it does not introduce complications with foreign Governments; and it renders difficult certain naïve stupidities of parties recently come to power. The British Cabinets of 1832 to 1846 justly earned high praise for public service, while the parallel Governments of Louis Philippe in France were showing to the world an example of greedy commercial intrigue.

THE BRITISH CONSTITUTION

The British Constitution, though of very great antiquity, does not exist. Great Britain, unlike the great majority of "civilised" States, including the United States of America, has no written Constitution which is unalterable save by a special procedure. The "Constitution" of Great Britain is what the courts of Great Britain, interpreting the Common Law and the Statutes passed by the High Court of Parliament, have declared it to be; and at any moment either a new interpretation by the courts or a new Act of Parliament may alter that "Constitution" in any way. Strictly speaking, therefore, it is not possible to act "unconstitutionally" in Great Britain; it is only possible to act illegally. The word "unconstitutional" in this country is a term of political abuse, and implies that the political opponents of the writer or speaker are acting or are about to act in a manner which he considers at variance with the traditional usages of British politics. These traditional usages, as we have seen, are deeply founded in British political practice, so much so in fact that some of the most important of British political institutions, such as the position of the Prime Minister, have no legal basis whatsoever. A proposal that the Prime Minister should be appointed by the Trades Union Congress, or the Federation of British Industries, or the National Temperance League, would not be in the least unconstitutional; it would merely be shocking.

This is sometimes held to produce great flexibility in English political life. It may; on the other hand it may have exactly the opposite effect. On the one hand, as there is in theory nothing which the British Parliament cannot do if it chooses, and no methods which it cannot adopt, it is possible to carry through very far-reaching changes to which there is either no serious opposition or no opposition that can be mobilised in sufficient force in time; on the other, the mass of tradition which clings about all British political procedure—the ludicrous ceremonial of Parliament and the Law Courts, for example—coupled with the continued existence of ancient statutes and regulations (such as laws of Edward III) which can at any time be revived and pressed into service, renders the carrying of legislation against serious opposition, particularly wealthy opposition, extremely difficult even if no account is taken of the further problem of enforcing the legislation when passed. The British public, as has been often observed, has, for the last hundred years at any rate, been remarkably law-abiding. It is said that the words "I'll come quietly" are the real basis of British political life. Nevertheless, there are not wanting indications of a pretty strong latent power of resistance to, or sabotage of, legislation which is generally or partially unpopular.[1]

THE HOUSE OF COMMONS

The legislative organ of Great Britain is the King in Parliament—that is to say, the Crown, the House of Commons and the House of Lords, each of which must be considered separately in its turn. Logically, perhaps, one should begin by considering the first of these, but

[1] E.g. the passive resisters' movement of the early twentieth century, the militant suffragettes, the 1913 revolt of the army officers in Ulster, the successful defiance by the South Wales miners of the Munitions of War Act, and in general the small attention paid to motoring or betting legislation.

the House of Commons bulks so much larger in the public eye, even to the extent of being what most people mean by "Parliament," that it is simpler to discuss it first.

Historically, the House of Commons originated, like most representative bodies in monarchical countries, in the need of the monarch for funds. The Parliaments of the Plantagenets were summoned in order that their members might pledge their constituents to pay taxes for the upkeep of the realm, to finance wars, or to make good the extravagances of the King. The business of Supply is the most ancient business of the House of Commons. Naturally, however, even from the first the granting of supplies tended to become conditional on the redressing of certain stated grievances; and it is from the petitions of redress which early Parliaments presented to the King that all the multifarious business of present-day Parliaments ultimately derives. It should be noted that the British Parliament, unlike the States-General of France before 1789, has only two Estates; the clergy do not form a separate Estate, and only wealthy clerics, in the persons of certain bishops, are in practice admitted to the legislature at all.

The struggles of the seventeenth century finally settled the subordination of the Crown to the financial power of Parliament, and with the dawn of the eighteenth century a seat in the House of Commons became an asset as well as a job. In earlier days membership of Parliament was both unpopular and intermittent; the representatives were gathered together—when they did not succeed in escaping—transacted their business and departed. Even in the seventeenth century members of Parliament, such as Andrew Marvell, were paid by their constituents to represent them. But after 1688, when parliamentary government was really established, membership of Parliament came to be a prize for which large sums were paid.[1] This state of things was not seriously altered by the 1832 or by any other Reform Act: after 1832, it is true, it was no longer possible to buy a seat in a straightforward manner, or directly to bribe the electors; but the expense of canvassing and propaganda among the ever-increasing electorate has gone far to make up the difference, and the actual expenses connected with sitting in Parliament are high. Even now, when the amount which may be spent on elections (though not on "nursing" a

[1] The working of this system was made more easy by the extraordinary state of representation in the eighteenth-century Parliament, which enabled the oligarchy to dispose of "rotten-borough seats" with a minimum of trouble.

constituency) is limited by statute, and when a salary is paid to M.P.s, membership is practically open only to those above a certain standard of income or to those whose expenses can be paid by some organisation, whether a political party or a propagandist body, which has thus to some extent taken the place of the boroughmongers of George III's day.

The House of Commons is elected either every five years or when the King agrees to a dissolution, on the basis of what, since the granting of the vote in 1928 to women between 21 and 30, is in effect adult suffrage. There is still a certain amount of plural voting, notably in the university constituencies, where the supposedly better educated part of the population is given an extra vote, this normally resulting in the election of a dozen or so M.P.s of extremely reactionary views. Certain classes of persons, notably clergymen and bankrupts, are debarred from standing for Parliament, and a much larger number, of course, are kept out, either expressly or in practice, by the conditions of their employment. The electors as such are consulted upon political issues only when an election takes place; no such device as the referendum has found favour in Britain. "Interests," however, particularly when organised, are regularly consulted before controversial legislation is introduced. Very rarely, as in the case of the 1929 De-rating Act, such consultation is accompanied by public newspaper discussion. As regards foreign policy, other than commercial policy, there is generally no consultation at all.

Comparatively little, however, of the time of Parliament is devoted to new legislation of any importance.[1] Many people do not realise to what an extent the original function of Parliament, to act through its control of finance as a check on the arbitrary power of the Crown, hobbles its present-day procedure. So much of the very structure of administration, such as the Army Act and the bulk of Government expenditure and taxation, has to be separately voted every year, and passed, moreover, through a complicated system of debates and divisions which seem framed to provide the maximum of facilities for obstruction and the least for real discussion, that no devices either for limiting talk or for the transferring of business to standing committees have so far availed to prevent impossible congestion. Therefore, since the range of matters regulated by Parliament grows wider every

[1] More, however, than of the time of the French *Chambre des Députés;* see section on France.

decade, and new legislation must in fact be passed by even the most *fainéant* administration, the habit has grown up of passing Acts which are in effect incomplete, leaving many important details to be filled in by the Minister (i.e. in practice by the Civil Service) through Orders or Regulations subject to a varying amount of parliamentary control in particular cases. This method, first widely adopted during the war in the case of the Defence of the Realm Act, protest against which could be easily shown to be unpatriotic, has been used since on less controversial subjects—and is certain to be used far more extensively in the future, despite allegations that it involves a dangerous increase in "bureaucracy."

THE HOUSE OF LORDS

No Act of the House of Commons, however passed, can become law until it has been passed also by the House of Lords and countersigned by the King. Under the Parliament Act of 1911, however, any Act which has been passed three times in three successive sessions by the House of Commons is deemed also to have passed the House of Lords; and any Bill which the Speaker of the Commons has certified as "financial" cannot be either amended in any respect or rejected by the House of Lords. Rules are laid down to guide the Speaker in defining what is or is not a "financial" measure; but in practice he has a considerable discretion.

The House of Lords, as everyone knows, is one of the most extraordinary institutions in the world. It includes all peers of the realm of England and Wales, with a sprinkling of peers from Scotland and Ireland and the major dignitaries of the Church of England. Its numbers can be increased at any time by the King creating more peers, either of himself or at the behest of a political party, but there is no known method of reducing them. At the present time its membership could not possibly find accommodation in the Chamber which is reserved for it, and the great majority of its members are never seen to enter the Parliament buildings. It is, of course, highly Conservative in character, and in spite of the Parliament Act, it will be seen that its power to obstruct legislation without acting in any way illegally is very great. If it happens that the House of Commons is in control of a party whose political views differ from those of the majority of the Lords, a deadlock seems inevitable. On the two occasions in British history in which such a deadlock has arisen, it was solved by the Crown intervening on the side of the House of Commons with a threat to create a large number of new peers. Proposals are often mooted to remove this way out, and these generally involve a reform of the House itself so as to make it a more logical barrier against revolution.

THE CROWN

The Crown is in a somewhat different position; and here it is necessary to draw a distinction between the legal position of the Crown and the personal position of the King and the royal family. The political power of the Crown has been limited during the last two centuries by the growth of a tradition of non-interference rather than by legal enactment. For example, the royal right of veto has never been limited by law, though it is a long time since it has been used; but nobody knows, as a matter of fact, what the King's Coronation Oath could or could not be held to cover. The legal position of the Crown as regards property, rates and taxes, the law of libel and many other matters has been to a certain extent defined in ways that do not concern us here; the personal power of the royal house is quite another matter.

First, the King is an individual; and the political loyalty of Englishmen generally tends to be given to individuals rather than ideas. This in itself is important. Add to it that the King is the "fountain of honour"; not only does the whole of that small wealthy section known as Society look up to the King as its apex; not only is every title received from the King's hands; the very smallest decoration which is granted to soldiers or Civil Servants comes from the King. Add again that the personal popularity and esteem in which the King is held have increased enormously in the last hundred, and even in the last twenty years. Little over a hundred years ago popular publications could openly insult George IV; twenty-five years ago they could poke fun at Edward VII; but to-day the national sense of humour is in abeyance when it approaches the steps of the Throne. It will be seen that the real political power of the Crown is a factor which no one can at the moment pretend to gauge.

It only remains to be added that the Crown is now the only formal link between Great Britain and the self-governing Dominions. The allegiance of Canada, Australia and the rest is not to the Mother of Parliaments, but to the King; and the Crown, acting through the Privy Council, alone can settle their disputes with the mother country.

THE PARTY SYSTEM

These are the three parts of the legislative machine, a machine, it would appear at first sight, designed less to facilitate than to obstruct legislation of any kind. In fact the machine, like the machine of the United States, would not, in the complicated modern world, work at all were it not driven by another machine, viz. the party system. The traditional practice of British politics, which was put into shape by the later nineteenth century building upon eighteenth-century foundations, assumes that the Government is formed by the members of a single party which has gained a majority of the parliamentary seats at a General Election. The leader of this party becomes Prime Minister, and himself selects his Cabinet from the members of either House, subject to the necessity of placating various interests and passions and of meeting the claims based on long service which the British system creates in such numbers. Occasionally and under exceptional circumstances a coalition Government may be formed, either when, as during the war, an extraordinary crisis obscures traditional differences, or when a section of one party is temporarily so indignant with its colleagues as to change sides. But these coalitions are usually of short duration. The present National Government is obviously a coalition in little more than name.

The foregoing paragraph assumes implicitly the existence of not more than two important parties in the State; and such, in the heyday of the parliamentary system, was the case. During the late nineteenth and early twentieth centuries the Conservative and Liberal Parties enjoyed alternating spells of government. Towards the end of the period, it is true, the situation was complicated by the existence of two blocs which, while voting normally on the side of the Liberals, yet had a separate political existence: these were the Irish Nationalists and the small Labour Party, based mainly on Trade Union support. Since the 1921 Treaty, the Nationalists have disappeared as a party, while, with the disintegration of the Liberals since the war, the Labour Party has politically to a large extent taken their place as an alternative to Conservative administration. Fundamentally, the British political system remains an alternation of two parties, with this difference, that the Labour Party is at present both numerically weaker and, on paper at any rate, more fundamentally divided in policy from its opponents than were the Liberals in the days of Queen Victoria.

For to the serious student of history it is not the difference but the fundamental agreement between Liberals and Conservatives that marks nineteenth-century history. No Government, once the 1832 Reform Bill was passed and accepted, ever seriously desired or tried to undo legislation passed by its rivals, and, as a matter of fact, the reform legislation of the century, including actual changes in the franchise, was brought forward indifferently by either party. More-over, after 1832, real political oppression and real reaction as under-stood on the Continent were unknown in Great Britain. All nineteenth-century Governments were in fact in home affairs liberal Governments, and the questions at issue between them were not even how much reform should be introduced but what particular type of reform most interested the particular grouping of voters who composed the two parties—as the Conservatives tended to support factory reform and the Liberals to curtail the power of landowners.[1] On fundamental questions there was no difference, and no doubt, therefore, that it was the duty of the opposition party to submit to its rivals' proposals when all recognised means of obstruction had been exhausted. The rise of the Labour Party, with political and social principles definitely opposed to those of the Conservatives, has raised potentially a quite different problem. So far, however, the two mi-nority Labour Governments which have held office have not at-tempted, even if in fact they desired, effectively to challenge the opposition of Capitalism; even the Conservative Act whose immedi-ate repeal was most loudly announced, the Trade Union Act of 1927, was allowed to remain on the statute book.

Both Liberal and Conservative Parties have been organised in much the same way. They have a considerable membership, grouped in constituency associations, which do not, however, control either the central organisation or the policy of the party, though they may, if determined, cause considerable trouble over the selection of a candi-date for any particular constituency. The Central Office of either

---

[1] There were also certain social differences, brought out perhaps most clearly in the fact that the Conservatives tended to be supporters of the Church of England and the Liberals to rely on the Nonconformist vote. It should, however, be remem-bered that Gladstone was a strong Churchman; even here the difference was not absolute.

party is controlled by the leaders of the party *plus* its chief financial supporters, including both those who support from conviction and those who are actuated by a sense of rewards to come. Within Parliament policy is determined by the leaders subject to the necessity of avoiding a serious revolt among their followers. Both parties hold an annual representative conference whose decisions are in no sense binding on the party, but which acts as a useful means of testing the general opinion of its supporters. In general it may be said that the Conservative Party Conference is more reactionary than the Conservative leaders and the Liberal Conference more reformist than the Liberals.

The Labour Party, owing largely to the circumstances of its origin, differs in many respects from the older pair. In essence it is a class party, founded upon the numerical and financial support of the great Trade Unions of manual workers.[1] The Trade Unions, therefore, to some extent take the place of the wealthy subscribers to the funds of the other parties, but with this difference, that the extent of Trade Union subscriptions and the amount of influence which the Trade Unions have in determination of party policy at annual conferences are both matters of public knowledge. To the Union membership must be added, however, a large number of Socialist and Radical individuals, organised up till 1918 in affiliated Socialist associations such as the Fabian Society and the Independent Labour Party, and since then to a much greater extent in the individual members' sections of the constituency Labour parties—to which also the local branches of the Unions are commonly affiliated. The individual members also, as is natural, include a large number of women. The number of individual members has been increasing rapidly of recent years, but is still very much less than the membership of the affiliated Unions, or, of course, than the number of convinced Labour voters; as, however, it is composed of the more determined and more articulate part of the movement, it pulls much more than its numerical weight in the putting forward and expressing of party policy, though the final decisions at Conference rest with the voting power of the great Unions. This state of things has led to much wild assertion about the determination of party policy, some maintaining that the "sensible" Labour supporter is driven by the Trade Unions to take up a violent anti-social (i.e. anti-capitalist) attitude, others that the

[1] Excluding, since 1927, the Unions of Post Office workers and Civil Servants.

dead weight of the uninstructed Trade Union vote acts as a drag upon the keen and intelligent Socialist. As a generalisation neither remark is true.

Party policy is determined by the Party Conference and interpreted between Conferences by the party executive, which is elected by the Conference upon the principle of representation of the main interests. As discussion within the party is organised upon principles of democracy, learned from nineteenth-century parliamentarism, this means that in the first place there is a very great deal of local and sectional debate upon issues that are to come before the Conference and secondly that many issues which small groups desire to press cannot, owing to exigencies of time, be discussed at all, and are shelved or steam-rollered. A good deal of the half articulate discontent which the keen Labour worker feels with his party is due to the fact that the Party Conference has developed into a kind of semi-parliament with a congestion of business closely resembling that of Parliament itself, without as yet evolving any effective technique for dealing with it.

It should be added that neither the Conference nor the executive controls the elected members of Parliament. As far as these are concerned, the Party when in office (though not when in opposition) has followed national tradition by placing its leader in supreme control and giving him the right to select his own Ministers. The leader, it is true, must actually be elected by the M.P.s; but beyond that their relations, either to him or to the Party Conference, are not defined. The most that can be said is that both in Parliament and in the country the ordinary individual has more say in the Labour Party than in either of the older parties. The extraordinary individual has probably rather less.

Of recent years, and as a reflection of changing political events in the outside world, two parties have arisen which deny the value of Parliament—the Communists and the Fascists. Neither of these, though they run parliamentary candidates, at present has any seats in the House of Commons. The Communist Party, with a policy taken verbatim from the very different conditions of Russia in 1917, and with a political ineptness bordering on insanity, has so far enrolled practically nobody except a few thousands of those victims of the slump for whom official Labour policy has been able to do nothing; the Fascists, helped financially by some rich men, and stimulated by recent events in Germany, have been gaining recruits among the *petite bourgeoisie*. They are still, however, nearly as unpopular with Conservative leaders as the Communists are with Labour.

There is no space here to discuss at all fully the methods employed by the several parties for recruitment and propaganda. It should be realised, however, that political propaganda is in rather a peculiar position in Great Britain owing to the twin institutions of the British Press and the British Broadcasting Corporation. The Press, largely centralised in London, controlled to an enormous extent by millionaire advertisers, renders the task of political propaganda on a wide scale one which practically depends on the control of large quantities of money. The B.B.C., on the other hand, is not controlled by advertisers, but is, owing to its monopoly, completely controlled by the governing class, and while there are obvious limits, as has been shown in America, to the power which can be exercised by moneybags considered in themselves, nobody yet knows from experience to what extent class control of wireless propaganda can be extended. The net effect is that in Great Britain minorities which have not the advantage of either rich or influential supporters find their task one of extraordinary difficulty.

LOCAL GOVERNMENT

The British system of local government is actually more ancient than Parliament itself. It was completely reformed during the nineteenth century, and as a matter of fact the bulk of the present local governing authorities go back no further than that century. Nevertheless, the tradition remains to a certain extent, and the enormous independence which the British boroughs secured during the seventeenth and eighteenth centuries is reflected in the present state of things. The central Government has no general right of interference in the actions of local Councils. Such powers of interference as it possesses, great though they are in some fields, are derived either from special statutes or indirectly through the system of central subsidies to local funds which is comprehensively described as "grants in aid." There is in British local government no officer, such as the French *Préfet,* who is appointed by the State with wide powers of universal control.

The constitution of local Councils follows broadly the pattern set by the House of Commons. That is to say, they are all elected upon a wide franchise, and at the present time they are all "omnibus" bodies, elected to deal with any and every function of local government. Owing to the fact that these Councils have not passed through the peculiar historical development of Parliament, they have also avoided some of its peculiar inefficiencies in working, and a really effective City Council, such as that of Manchester, could easily give the House of Commons a lesson in the efficient conduct of business. Partly for the same reason, they have in some cases not developed a party system such as that which obtains in the House of Commons. With the rise of Labour a party system shows signs of springing up, which in the majority of Councils is expressed in the form of the Labour Party *versus* the rest. But there are still many minor Councils in which there are either no parties or parties based on purely local or ephemeral issues. The fact that members of the local Councils, unlike M.P.s, are not paid, hinders the development of parties by keeping large numbers of the working classes off the Councils.

Local Councils have a great amount of self-government, but, unlike Parliament, they are not omnicompetent. They have to work within limits which have been either laid down or confirmed by the great nineteenth-century statutes, and where a local Council in the opinion of the courts exceeds the powers legally assigned to it it will quickly be pulled up for acting *ultra vires*. Nor is it at all easy in practice for any local Council to secure an extension of the powers thus granted to it. It needs fresh legislation of one kind and another, and fresh legislation is both difficult and very expensive to secure. In effect, therefore, Councils are severely restricted in the class of activity which is generally called municipal enterprise.

For the rest, the Councils are elected for comparatively small areas of very varying size and wealth. There is no means by which Councils can be combined over a single larger area. Where co-ordination for certain purposes, e.g. transport, becomes an urgent necessity, it has to be effected either by voluntary co-operation or by special legislation. To a large extent, the Councils are not self-supporting, because their direct income is for the most part drawn from an obsolete rating system which presumes that every locality should be able to provide for the local services which it requires, and that the value of the land or buildings occupied by a citizen of a locality is an adequate indication of the amount which he can afford to contribute to those services. Whatever may have been the case in the sixteenth century, when this system was instituted, the assumption is obviously quite untrue to-day, and the central Government has therefore been forced to contribute sums provided by the general body of income-tax payers to eke out local deficiencies. It will be seen that the opportunity for central control provided by this grant-in-aid system is very great, and that a recalcitrant Council can be disciplined to almost any extent by the threat of withdrawal or reduction of grant. Hence there is in fact a considerably greater control by the central Government of local services than would appear upon the surface. But it should be emphasized that this control has to be exercised within strictly defined limits. It has seldom happened that the central body has gone so far as to suspend locally elected councillors from administration, and this so far has only occurred in connection with some direct attempt in particularly poor areas to make the rich pay more towards the upkeep of their poorer brethren.

Besides the directly elected Councils there are also a number of public and semi-public bodies which are otherwise constituted. Examples of these are the various Harbour Boards, the Central Electricity Board and the British Broadcasting Corporation, of which mention has already been made. Space forbids more than a reference to these bodies, but it is probable that they are destined to be extended over a considerably wider sphere in the near future.

THE JUDICIARY

Such is the direct machinery of legislation, local and national. In the sphere of administration, the machinery of justice and the machinery of the Civil Service fall to be considered. The British judicial system is as ancient as Parliament, but was very extensively reformed during the 'seventies, and the system against which Dickens delivered his attacks has very largely ceased to exist. British justice may roughly be divided into two parts—High Justice and Low Justice. The function of High Justice, i.e. the High Court in its various Divisions, the Courts of Appeal and the House of Lords as a final appeal court, is not merely to enforce the law but to interpret it—that is to say, to explain in the light largely of past decisions what the law on a particular issue really is. The Courts cannot make law themselves, or, like the Supreme Court in the United States, annul a statute by declaring it unconstitutional. But the power of interpretation of Acts can sometimes produce very surprising results—results quite at variance with the intentions of the framers of the Acts in question.

When this has occurred, the law then *is* what the final court has declared it to be, however many established practices it upsets, or whatever the views of Parliament or of any individual. There is no remedy, however great the inconvenience, but that of passing a new Act, which may make matters better or may introduce fresh complications, or both.

This system is administered by the closely organised legal profession, which is divided in England and Wales into barristers and solicitors. Of these two branches the barristers, whose main business is to plead in the courts, though they also do a certain amount of advisory work, are held in higher social esteem; they undergo a long and expensive training, and they alone are eligible to become judges. British judges are appointed from the ranks of distinguished barristers, who for one reason or another are willing to resign the generally much higher fees that they can earn as advocates in favour of the comparatively ill-paid but less hard-working security of the judicial bench; once they have become judges they are practically irremovable. They are, therefore, in general men of mature years, belonging to the middle or upper middle classes, who have received a highly specialised training through their lives, which has been directed to make them as nearly possible immune from any but legal considerations; as in fact, however, judges, like other persons, are human beings with lives of their own, they are in practice moved, consciously or unconsciously, by the motives and ideas which are current among the class in which they have been brought up.

High Justice is very expensive, partly by tradition and partly because the chief litigants, who are wealthy corporations, are more concerned to purchase the best quality of law and to run the price up against their competitors than to get decisions either cheaply or expeditiously. This has the effect that High Court justice is practically closed to persons of small or moderate means unless they find themselves there in response to a criminal charge, and even then it is difficult for them to obtain adequate defence. Of recent years efforts have been made to reduce costs and to arrange cheap or free legal defence for those who are too poor to pay high fees; but it cannot be said that more than a fringe of the problem has yet been touched.

Low Justice, which includes the County Courts and the Courts of the Magistrates, paid and unpaid, is naturally cheaper; but in some cases, at any rate, it is also of poorer quality. County Courts are presided over by paid judges, and the stipendiary magistrates in London and the large towns are also paid. But to a large extent local justice is dispensed by benches of unpaid J.P.s, who may or may not know something of the law, and who tend, being unpaid, to be drawn largely from members of the leisured and semi-leisured classes. It is not contended that a magistrate is necessarily the worse for being rather ignorant of the law; in fact both history and present-day experience go to show that strict attention to law not infrequently involves the flouting of equity. But to decide cases on a basis of equity and justice implies certain preconceived ideas about the nature of justice, and particularly where class issues are concerned a man's idea of justice is commonly that which is prevalent in the class in which he was brought up. The very varying attitudes of Benches to motoring offences and offences under the Game Laws will provide plenty of examples. It should further be added that whatever any magistrate's idea of justice, he is *ex hypothesi* sitting on the Bench in order to administer the law; and the gaps in the legal knowledge of himself and his fellows are in practice more often than not filled in by the magistrate's clerk, who is generally a local solicitor.

CIVIL SERVICE AND POLICE

Finally we come to the strictly administrative class of Government officials. Considered as an instrument adapted to its purpose the British Civil Service is probably the best in the world. Up to 1832 the Civil Service was a source of patronage to the party in power and their friends, and was, as much as or more than Parliament, a home of jobbery and corruption. During the nineteenth century, however, the two great parties, as has been said, abandoned the spoils system, accepted the desirability of a permanent trained staff which could be relied upon to continue its job of administration no matter who was nominally giving the orders, and after a long struggle the system was reformed, mainly by the substitution of open competitive examination for other forms of selection. Corruption, as a result, has almost entirely ceased; for a highly placed Civil Servant to be convicted of bribery would certainly amount to a major political scandal. In the municipal service the process has gone much less far; there is no general qualifying examination—though this has been often enough urged—for municipal servants; and there is still a fair amount of minor bribery and jobbery, particularly in the smaller areas. This also, however, is on the decline.

To a certain extent the reforms in the Civil Service have brought about its "democratisation," even in its upper layers. Success in the examination for first division Civil Servants is in theory open to anyone who can achieve an education of the standard of Oxford and Cambridge; and for most Civil Service appointments no question is asked about the candidate's origin or how he acquired his education. It will be seen, however, that the mere existence of a standard set by Oxford and Cambridge is in itself an intangible class barrier to anyone coming from the lower classes who is not of very exceptional ability; and in one great department, at any rate, there is still very little pretence of democracy. In the Foreign Office strong preference is still given to candidates educated at one or another of the well-known "public" schools; and it would appear that a small dose of this principle is now being applied to the Metropolitan Police Force. Women, if they are unmarried, are admitted to the lower ranks of the Civil Service and to a few of the higher posts.

As Civil Service appointments are permanent in the sense of not being changed with a change of Government, and as Civil Servants, unless they resign, normally retain their posts until they reach the pensionable age, the higher ranks acquire very great competence and prestige—particularly since they are supposed to have no political affiliations; and their influence on legislation as well as administration is considerable. They have no power to interpret the law as the Courts have, and they are themselves open to the ordinary processes of law. There is no *droit administratif* in Britain, though in practice an officer of the Crown who incurs a penalty through over-zeal or reasonable error is generally protected or indemnified by his department. But the advice of the higher Civil Servants very much affects the content and the form of the legislation which is proposed or passed, and there has been a tendency of recent years more and more to place expressly upon "the Minister," i.e. in effect upon the Civil Service, the actual function of interpreting particular statutes or parts of statutes. Furthermore, the tradition of the Civil Service, which is now of quite respectable antiquity, dictates in large measure the method of day-to-day administration, so that the Cabinet Secretariat and the leading Treasury officials, to take the chief examples, are a very potent factor in any Government, and incline from their upbringing and from the nature of the case to help preserve that continuity of policy which we have already seen to be the basis of British parliamentary government. Of the municipal Civil Service this is less true; but the tendency is nevertheless the same.

Actual enforcement of the provisions of the law is in the hands of the unarmed police force, of which only the Metropolitan section is under direct Government control, though by means of financial pressure the Home Office can to a large extent interfere with provincial police forces, and proposals have been made from time to time to increase Home Office control still further. Behind the police force stand, of course, in the last resort the Army and Navy and the carefully selected Air Force. There has, however, been great reluctance to use the armed forces in case of civil dispute, though they have occasionally been employed to put down major strikes.

THE EMPIRE

This brief sketch of necessity has taken no account of the British Empire. Nor could the Empire be adequately described except in a section which would be at least as long again. It should not, however, be forgotten that the British political system does not live to itself alone; Britain is the centre of a vast and unique system which includes territories in every state of government, from the smallest Crown Colony to the Dominion of Canada. As regards those territories which are inhabited largely by white men (and with them the Union of South Africa, in spite of its coloured population, falls to be included) the sole link other than sentimental ties is the allegiance to the British Crown, and the fact that the great Dominions do not keep up armed forces of their own and rely upon the British Navy for defence. This fact is of particular importance in the case of Australia. The self-governing Dominions, ever since a Constitution was granted to the two Canadas in 1840, have settled their own methods of government, generally on lines which were believed to correspond with the British system; in the case of the rest, there is no general rule, and the separate arrangements provide for varying amounts of independence of the home Government, together with amounts, also varying, of representative institutions granted to the native population. In general it may be said that the British Empire, apart from the Dominions, knows very little of nineteenth-century democracy.

This, then, is the British political system—a system, as should have become clear, of extraordinary toughness and resilience, based upon a social system and supported by an educational system both of which, in spite of surface alterations, have changed very little in fundamentals during the past fifty years. Whether it will continue thus, and whether the social changes which changing economic conditions demand will succeed in translating themselves into political institutions without causing breaches in the system is a question which involves larger considerations than can be discussed at the end of a chapter.

3. THE POLITICAL SYSTEM OF FRANCE

THE ECONOMIC BLIZZARD of the last few years did not hit France till comparatively late in the day, and before the events of February 1934 it could be said that of all the major countries, with the possible exception of Great Britain, France, in spite of her unstable Governments, had the most stable political system. The instability of French Ministries, indeed, was supposed to be the main feature of the Third Republic; and was undoubtedly a fact, though the official records of French Ministries exaggerate it. For as the fall of a French Cabinet does not, as generally in Great Britain, imply the dissolution of the Chamber, but merely a "reconstruction" which often results in the formation of a new Cabinet bearing a remarkably close resemblance to the one which has just fallen, the list of "Cabinets" no more indicates real shifts in the policy of the French Government than the list of "scenes" in the ordinary text of a Shakespeare play indicates a real shifting of the scenery. Beneath this changing façade, however, there existed a real stability of political institutions, which had grown up, albeit slowly, with the passage of years.

This stability, patent as it was to the outside world, was perhaps less patent to the French themselves. For nearly a hundred years, indeed, France had been regarded as the home *par excellence* of political flightiness; and not all remember that when the Third Republic was formed nobody expected it to endure. "The Republic," said Thiers, "divides us least"; and accordingly the Republic was created. But its constitution was framed to facilitate the re-establishment of the monarchy, and a large part of those who agreed to its formation did so in the confident hope that the monarchy would be re-established as soon as the supporters of rival claimants could compose their differences. Unfortunately for their hopes, they were unable to agree in time; the Republic took root, and an amendment of 1884 added to the text of the constitution the words, "The Republican form of government cannot be the object of revision." The sixty years' life of the Republic, and the extreme unlikelihood of any return to monarchy, caused Europe as a whole to forget the stormy past; the French, however, who have in many ways the longest political memories of any people in Europe except the Poles, forgot it far less than their neighbours, and this recollection accounts in part for some of the features of French political life which occasionally puzzle the observer.

THE REPUBLIC AND FRENCH SOCIETY

The stability of the Republic derived from the comparative stability of French social and economic life. Not only did the Republic divide the French least; it also quite clearly suits them best, even during these past months of discontent, and is likely to continue to do so unless their economic and social institutions undergo a fundamental change. The basic shape of French economic life was settled by the Revolution, which at one and the same time created a free and independent peasantry and liberated from feudal, monarchical and clerical control its urban counterpart, the small *entrepreneurs* and manufacturers in the towns; and it has remained substantially unchanged ever since. It is of course true that France, like other countries, has felt the effects of the Industrial Revolution; large-scale production, great industrialists, and an urban proletariat have made their appearance, but to an extent far less than in either Great Britain, Germany or the United States. French industry, even since the acquisition of the comparatively highly-industrialised provinces of Alsace-Lorraine, is still on balance small-scale industry distributed over a very wide area; groups of *grande industrie,* like the *Comité*

des Forges, while they undoubtedly do exercise political influence,
particularly in the parties of the Right, are not really the sinister
Napoleons which inflamed imaginations have figured to themselves;
and the French wage-workers, concentrated only in a few large
manufacturing centres, and otherwise scattered all over the country
in small groups, remain, in ideas and policy, much more like the
Paris workmen who made the 1848 Revolution and the Commune
of 1871 than their English contemporaries, for example, resemble
their Chartist forbears. The chief change which both foreign and
native observers have noticed has been the decline, during the last
thirty years, in the importance of Paris as a leader of French thought.

The importance of the stable and permanent peasantry is the first
feature of modern France to which all must bear witness. No less
important is the huge class of *rentiers,* particularly of very small
rentiers, which overlaps, of course, to a certain extent the peasant
class. This class also makes for a high degree of stability. For the
rentier is of his nature conservative in the social sense, though that
does not necessarily mean that he is conservative in the strictly
political sense. Many French peasants and *rentiers* habitually vote
with the Left, just as the English Labour voters include some of the
most conservative-minded Englishmen. The last thing which the
French *rentier* wants is a social upheaval, though, with that sense
of reality which is peculiarly a French attribute, he is prepared, in
the last resort, stoically to cut his losses. At long last, the French
rentier has resigned himself more thoroughly to the final disappearance of the money invested in Russian Tsarist bonds than has
the British capitalist to the disappointment of his bright hopes of the
Lena Goldfields. This class of Frenchmen is conservative; and it
is also timid, and sees danger approaching a very long way off.
French politicians often seem to be emulating the White Queen,
and bewailing loudly a disaster which may overtake them next
week—a policy which has been known to hasten the approach of
the disaster in question.

One should also notice, as factors in French social life, the extraordinary persistence of the French family system, which accounts in
part for the absence in France not only of women's suffrage but of
any important women's rights movement, and the widespread class
of French professional workers of all kinds, including the *petits
fonctionnaires,* which, partly owing to the French educational sys-

tem, is far less socially divided from the rest of the community than is the professional class in Great Britain. Finally—quantitatively impossible to estimate but practically of very great importance—one must also realise the strength of French belief in the essential superiority of French culture and French life, literature and art, a belief which goes back far beyond the foundations of the Republic. The French do really believe that they are the most civilised people in the world, that they, and almost they alone, have upheld the standards of civilisation since the days of Charlemagne, if not, indeed, since the days of Augustus, and that the rest of humanity are barbarians by comparison. This is as apparent in the writings of a Radical like M. André Siegfried as in the most impassioned declamations of the *Action Française;* and though it cannot be evaluated in any known currency, it is undoubtedly one of the most important elements in the shape of French life.

FRANCE SINCE THE REVOLUTION

It has been said that the social shape of modern France was really settled by the Revolution. The same cannot be said of its political institutions. The revolutionaries of 1789 and onwards, inspired by the writings of Rousseau and of the extreme democrats of the eighteenth century, sought to set up a régime of perfect individual political equality combined with the unquestioned preservation of individual property rights. Even at the time there were not wanting those who, like Babeuf, desired social and economic equality to follow upon political equality; but they were quickly crushed by the great majority of small *bourgeois* who were the guiding force of the Revolution. However, the makers of the Revolution, partly because it was attacked by the Powers in concert before it had had time to get on its feet, and partly because the extreme individualism of their idea of democracy made difficult the creation of a strong and disciplined party in the country (such as the Russian Communist Party) which should carry through the programme of the Revolution by means of a steadily-applied policy of administration, failed to create a stable Government, and so fell before the First Empire. It was the breakdown of administration, particularly military and financial administration, and the chaotic experiments of unguided revolutionaries, rather than any doctrinal excesses of Robespierre or his associates, that accounted for the easy triumph of Napoleon;

and of Napoleon's régime it was the personal autocracy that fell, and the efficient and centralised administration that remained. The administrative system of France is Bonapartist to this day; though in the absence of a Bonaparte it does not function quite in the manner which Napoleon would have approved.

But with the fall of Napoleon fell also much that the classes which made the Revolution were determined to secure. Much of the *ancien régime*, censorship of the Press and suppression of public meetings, a franchise far more restricted than that of Napoleon, and clerical domination, returned with the Bourbons after Waterloo; and the battle for political democracy had to be fought all over again, first in 1830 with only a partial victory, and again, with more violence, in 1848. In 1848, once more, the working class of Paris, inspired by a new generation of definitely Socialist teachers, raised the standard of social equality, and again they were defeated. But the Republic was not yet firmly established. Only three years after 1848 Louis Napoleon succeeded in making another Empire, though an Empire with a basis distinctly more democratic than that of his predecessor; and if his foreign policy had not landed him in the disastrous Franco-Prussian War, the Second Empire might have enjoyed a very much longer life than it did. In the confusion caused by the collapse of the Empire, and while the Prussian troops were actually at her gates, Paris, following on this occasion Karl Marx rather than Louis Blanc, tried again to lead the country towards social revolution; and this time succeeded to the extent of maintaining for nearly two months the first Socialist administration in Europe. But the final verdict was no less decisive than that of 1848. The Paris Commune was suppressed in blood, and out of the ruins of the Commune and the Empire, by a series of unromantic compromises, the Third Republic was born.

FRENCH ATTITUDES TO POLITICS

The foregoing excursus into nineteenth-century history has been necessary in order to help make clear the attitude of the Frenchman to his own Government. Whatever foreign observers might think, the Frenchman has never felt at all certain that the Republic and the institutions of individualist democracy are by any means finally secured. He does not forget that many of those who agreed with the constitution of 1875 did so in the belief that it was only preparing the way for a royal restoration; he knows that General Boulanger in 1889 aimed at another *coup d'état,* and that ten years later the Dreyfus Case came near to causing a revolution in the State; and he observes that there are still to be seen (and, very definitely, to be heard) Legitimists, Orleanists, Bonapartists, and other persons who refuse to accept, even in theory, the Republican régime, and who, for the most part, are friends and allies of that clericalism which he still regards as the enemy of the Republic as it was in the 'seventies. Accordingly, the French people continue to suffer from periodic fears that the Republic may be destroyed; and these fears are reflected in their political institutions. They will preserve a strong executive and administrative machine, in order that the Republic may be able to defend itself with decision and rapidity against any would-be Napoleons; but they will keep the Government itself, in ordinary times, weak and in jeopardy, lest it be tempted to try any dangerous experiments of its own. In particular, they will regard with the utmost suspicion any attempt by an individual to rise above the ruck of his fellows and to act in a dictatorial or even a Prime Ministerial manner; and if momentary exigencies compel them to yield for a time to the leadership of some personality such as Clemenceau or Poincaré, once the emergency is past they will replace him as rapidly as possible in his proper position. Even at the time of writing, when governmental inefficiency combined with the high cost of living has given rise to an unusual amount of political disturbance, it is significant to see how little in the way of plenary power has really been granted to M. Doumergue.

Fear for the Republic, then, is one of the dominating forces in French political life. But it is not the only influential fear. Ever since 1870 France, with her nearly stationary population and her established economy, has been living in recurrent fear of her great expanding continental neighbour. Fear of German expansion, and a real and deep dislike and distrust of German culture and German modes of thought, have been quite as potent political forces as the fear for the Republic; and it would not be far off the mark to say that the major swings of French politics have been from Governments of the Left, based on fear of reaction, to Governments of the Right, based on fear of Germany.[1]

[1] At any rate, up till the beginning of 1933 this seemed to be the case; though since then the great change in German politics seems to be driving the French to

One more generalisation should be added to complete the picture. The ordinary Frenchman is both more interested in politics and more politically educated than the majority of his contemporaries in other lands. Of the latter fact no one can doubt who has compared the French popular Press and the news summaries of French wireless stations with, say, the British penny dailies and the news bulletins of the B.B.C. Only the Moscow *Izvestia* gives anything like the quantity of political, particularly foreign political information that is served up to the French public, and *Izvestia* is a Government-controlled newspaper, with a public which has to take what its rulers think good for it. As to the former, one may see in much French literature, and in the casual discussion and expression of Frenchmen, a lively interest both in the contemporary doings of politics and in their basic principles. It is not an interest in the unpleasing sense in which the word is sometimes used in America or in Great Britain, to denote an interest which is primarily secret and of the pocket—and to say this is not in the least to imply that French politics are of a fanatical purity or free from all thought of private advantage. It is a public interest which likes to discuss aloud and in full the machinery and aims of the Republic, and which is a little apt to decorate some quite minor dispute in a Cabinet, involving the dropping of two or three very minor politicians, with thunderous rhetoric that would be more appropriate to the downfall of Napoleon; and it is perfectly compatible with a firm intention of keeping the political machine in its proper place, and of seeing that it does not interfere more than is desirable with the legitimate occupation of the individual—such, for example, as keeping his money in his pocket, and not handing it over to the income tax authorities. Such as it is, this interest guides and dominates French political life. It may be true that all nations get the kind of Governments they deserve; in the case of the French it is not quite absurd to suggest that they get the kind of Government which they like, however much they may also like to abuse it.

THE REPUBLICAN CONSTITUTION

The governmental system of France at the present time is regulated by the constitution of 1875, which has been amended, though

---

hope rather in a general semi-pacific European alliance than in a bristling national policy to save them from Nazi aggression.

not substantially, in 1879, 1884, and 1926. At the time of its estab-lishment, the constitution of the Republic was supposed to be imitative of the political system of Great Britain, which was, at the time, the only established parliamentary system available for imitation. Owing, however, to the very different historical circum-stances, the French constitution has in practice borne only a very shadowy likeness to the British.[1] The constitution can be revised by both houses of the Assembly through a special procedure. The electors are not consulted about revision.

Like the British system, the French constitution makes provision for a single titular head, the President, and a legislative assembly consisting of two houses. But at once differences begin to appear. The French President has more power in theory than the British Crown, and his public interventions in politics have been more frequent. But of course no official elected for a term can ever attain to the amount of wide personal influence and authority which is enjoyed by a hereditary monarch; and as the French President is not elected by the French people—French politicians have too vivid a recollection of the experience of the *coup d'état* of Napoleon III to be anxious to try *plébescites*—he does not possess the popular sanction which is the basis of the power of the President of the United States.

And as there can be no king in France, so there can be no House of Lords in a country which has virtually abolished hereditary aris-tocracy. A House of Lords grows, and is not made; no constitution-mongers could invent one for a new country. The makers of the French constitution accordingly had to find a new basis for their Senate or Upper House.

THE PRESIDENT

The President of the French Republic is elected by the National Assembly, i.e. the two Houses of Parliament sitting together. He is elected for seven years, and according to the constitution can be re-elected to any extent; but in fact no President has held office for more than a single term except Grévy, who resigned two years after his re-election. He must be elected by a clear majority. On

[1] It should be emphasised that the constitution of 1875 was not a "clean sweep," or a root and branch reshaping of the political system. It was, in essence, a definite restatement of all that was undecided in the form of national government; but it left the administrative system, and also the system of local government, substantially unaltered.

paper it would appear that the President has fairly wide powers and discretion, for he is "irresponsible," that is to say, he can only be called to account for treason, and that only by the Chamber of Deputies, with the Senate acting as a high court to try him. Nominally, he appoints the Ministers, but in fact he only appoints the Prime Minister, and that subject to the approval of the representative machine, as the Ministers are responsible to that machine and not to him. He can, in practice, exercise a good deal of influence in the choice of Ministers, and can generally keep out one whom he dislikes. But any attempt to force through his own policy is quite another matter. Strong Presidents may try; but Millerand, one of the strongest in recent history, failed and had to resign the Presidency.

Nominally, again, the President, with the consent of the Senate, can order a dissolution of the lower house; but Marshal MacMahon, the only President to make use of this power, received such a rebuff that no subsequent President has attempted it. The President can, however, summon meetings of either house, and he can also adjourn them for short periods, send to them Presidential messages and refer their decisions back to them for reconsideration. He can veto Bills; but in practice he does not. He nominates to office under the Republic; but as every such act has to be countersigned by a Minister—ostensibly to "relieve the President from onerous responsibility"—this power, like our Royal Assent, is simply a rubber stamp. The most considerable power that remains to the President is the power to conclude treaties of alliance (not treaties of peace or commercial treaties, which require ratification by both houses) with the consent of a single Minister only. This power was used by Poincaré in 1917, for instance, with the connivance of Briand; but the circumstances were rather exceptional. It follows that the President is more or less of an ornamental cipher in public affairs. Millerand, who alone of recent Presidents seriously attempted to dictate policy, found it impossible. But, as an ornament, the President is very well-equipped; his official salary is extremely high and enables him to entertain foreign political leaders (which is now his main job) in a thoroughly satisfactory manner while retaining a reasonable income for his own purposes.

THE NATIONAL ASSEMBLY

The National Assembly consists of two houses, the Senate and the Chamber of Deputies. Of these, the Chamber of Deputies has at present 612 members, elected by manhood suffrage—though, as conscripts are ineligible to vote, the great majority of Frenchmen cannot exercise the suffrage until they are twenty-two or over. The voting takes place in single-member constituencies, though the French have twice experimented for a short time with voting for party lists over wider areas; and there is a second ballot in cases where no candidate has a clear majority. Under the constitution, any or all candidates may go forward to the second ballot, and even at that stage new candidates may be introduced; but generally candidates with little chance withdraw, and it is common for the second ballot to contain two names only. The Chamber, unless dissolved by the President, is elected every four years.

The Senate is constituted so as to be, as far as possible, that Assembly of "Elder Statesmen" of whom most advocates of a Second Chamber profess to desire that Chamber to consist. Accordingly, the first qualification for a Senator is that he should be at least forty; and when elected he sits for nine years, one-third of the Senators retiring every three years. Senators are not directly elected; the body which elects a Senator is a departmental assembly or electoral college consisting of all the deputies whose constituencies lie within the department, the members of the departmental council and of the *conseils d'arrondissement* (sub-divisions of the department), and delegates from the municipal councils. A clear majority is necessary for election on either the first or the second ballot; only at the third ballot can a candidate with a relative majority, or what the Americans call a "plurality," take his seat. Representation in the Senate is heavily weighted in favour of the rural areas; thus in the department of the Seine, Paris, with over one-half the population, chooses only one-ninth of the Senatorial electors, and in the composition of the electoral colleges generally, though there is since 1884 an element of proportionality, the large towns are badly underrepresented.[1] The distribution of seats, the method of election, and the age of Senators, all go towards securing that the Senate shall be a body generally conservative and intent to preserve the *status quo*. No Socialist was elected to the Senate until 1919, and in social legislation the Senate has a magnificent record of bills rejected or killed

[1] This is intentional in the constitution, and not, as was to a large extent the British rotten borough system, a result of shifts in the population. Paris, and most of the large towns, were just as populous, relatively to the rest of France, in 1875 as they are to-day.

by delay. It should not, however, be assumed that the Senate is monarchist in opinion or disposed to favour Fascist or semi-Fascist movements. In political matters the Senate is more Radical than the Chamber when the Chamber has a Right majority. Conservatism, in France, means the policy of those who desire to conserve the political and social institutions of 1875.

The Senate and the Chamber have practically equal powers, except that finance bills must originate in the Chamber (though they may be amended or rejected by the Senate), and that the Senate retains certain judicial powers, particularly in cases of high treason. There is no court, as in the United States, which can declare acts of the Senate or the Chamber unconstitutional. Constitutionally, the French legislative assembly, like the British, can make any laws it pleases and can alter the constitution, if it likes, by the prescribed procedure. All laws, however, must be passed by both houses, and there is no provision for what is to be done in case of a deadlock, except as regards amendment of the constitution. In practice, where deadlocks have arisen, they have been solved by one or other house giving way; but the habit of the Senate is rather to delay bills than to reject them outright. Bills do not drop at the end of a session as they do in England, and can be proceeded with in the next session from the point at which they were left. Nevertheless, the output of legislation in France is small. Both Senators and Deputies receive a salary.

"ASSIMILATION" AND THE COLONIES

One curious feature of the French constitution is that both Senate and Chamber contain representatives from some, but not all, of the French colonial possessions. This is due to the old doctrine of "assimilation" which used to govern French colonial policy, and which derives directly from the theories of the eighteenth-century revolutionaries and ultimately, in all probability, from the practice of the Roman Empire. In its simple form, it implies a belief that ability to co-operate in a particular set of political institutions is not a question of race, colour, or place of birth, but solely of education in and acceptance of the institutions, so that any French subject in any part of the world, once he has understood and accepted the French constitution, is as capable of being an active French citizen as any other. It is thus a highly rationalist theory, taking no account of historical or cultural differences; but those who pour scorn upon it, as a theory, forget that under the Roman Empire "assimilation" did actually take place over some hundreds of years, that the Russian Soviet constitution envisages a possible "assimilation" of other nationalities which may adopt Communist institutions, and that the strength of the classical French literary and educational tradition makes it far more possible to teach a subject "Frenchness," if one may coin a word, than it is to teach "Englishness" or "Germanity." The comparative freedom of the French from colour-prejudice (though not from the anti-Semitism so strongly fostered by the Catholic Church) helps in this.

However, "assimilation" has not occurred in practice. No one can believe for a moment that the inhabitants of the great French possessions in tropical Africa or south-western Asia have become or are in the least likely to become Frenchmen. Actually, the white population in the French colonies available for the practical work of "assimilation" is very small; the two chief areas to which Frenchmen have emigrated in any large numbers, French Canada and Louisiana, having been lost to France by the early nineteenth century. "Assimilation" as a theory has now been replaced by the policy of "association," which aims rather at turning the colonies into protectorates, with some development of native institutions. No French colony, however, has anything like the self-government of a British Dominion, and colonial policy is still firmly subordinated to that of the home government.

The relics of "assimilation," however, are to be found in the Senators and Deputies elected for the colonies as though they were departments of France, and in the tendency, slightly tempered of recent years, to govern the colonies bureaucratically by administrative officials, as though they were departments of France. The franchise, for the purpose of the election of deputies, varies fantastically: Senegalese may vote, but Arabs may not; the Indian towns have 50,000 Indian and 500 French voters, whereas in Cochin-China, out of 3 millions, 2,000 have votes, of whom three-quarters are French officials. This system, or rather absence of system, has few defenders; and proposals are commonly made, without much success, for its reform.

THE CABINET

As in England, so in France the Cabinet is selected by the Prime Minister, and consists of the principal heads of the Departments of

State, who may be drawn from members of either Chamber, but may not vote while in office. Cabinet meetings are of two kinds, the *Conseil des Ministres,* which the President attends and at which he can express an opinion, and the *Conseil de Cabinet,* at which he is not present. The relative importance of the two types of meeting depends in practice upon the personality of the President.

French Cabinets are, as everyone knows, much weaker and more unstable than English Cabinets. The constitutional reason for this is that no French Cabinet can hold over either Chamber the threat of dissolution; deputies, once elected, are in practice irremovable for four years, and so can destroy a Cabinet without risk to their own position. One of the periodic demands of would-be "strong" Governments is to be given the right of dissolution; but so far it has not been granted. Thus a French Cabinet, if it does not wish to resign, must be ready at all times to submit to defeat on minor points; and further, the power of "interpellation," i.e. the right of any deputy to tackle any Minister on any point of his policy, and to carry the matter to a general debate in which the entire policy of the Ministry may be pulled to pieces, places any Cabinet very much at the mercy of individual deputies. It is true that the Cabinet, by reason of its power to appoint and dismiss any public official, has on paper powers of control of administrative policy which the British Cabinet does not possess; but in practice this control is largely in the hands of individual Ministers and is used for the "sweetening" of individual deputies rather than as an instrument of general policy. The long reign of M. Chiappe as *Préfet* of the Paris police,[1] while Governments of the Left were in power, and the furious outcry which followed his removal, are a case in point. The French give their Governments large paper powers, but snap and worry continually at any efforts to use them.

FRENCH POLITICAL PARTIES

This system of infinitely collapsible Cabinets could hardly exist in a country where there were strong and clearly-defined parties; but in France there are no strong parties. In fact, it is even doubtful how many parties there are, and for what, if anything, each of them stands. Reference-books on the French party system quite often vary considerably in their classification of parties; and even the most permanent-looking parties, such as the Radical-Socialists and the

[1] A position of great importance, owing to the absence of a *maire* of Paris.

Socialists, are apt to suffer from splits and re-formations. French parties are thus not really parties, but groups, and splits and secessions take place so much oftener than elections that the phenomenon of a group which has no ascertainable vote in the country (because it is a split from a larger group) wandering irresponsibly about the Chamber and making and upsetting Cabinets, is not at all unusual. Nor is this because France is hopelessly torn, as some of the newer Continental nations are, between religious, economic, and racial factions which cannot by any known means be reconciled in a single party or parties. Aside from the Communists and the extreme Right, there is no really irreconcilable party in France; and even the troubles of the minority in Alsace appear to be calming down.

The French political parties—there are twenty of them, according to the latest reliable count, as well as a handful of persons so independent that no party can contain them—are generally grouped under the three headings, Right, Centre and Left. This grouping is, however, rather misleading to the English reader, because it obscures the fact that the views of the Centre Parties are in general what we should call Conservative, and that it is quite seldom that any of their members vote with the Left for any length of time. The Right, on the other hand, is both small in numbers and wild-cat in policy; it can never form a Government by itself, and French Governments of the Right, such as the *Bloc National,* are really formed by the Centre with the occasional acquiescence of the Right and some support from the more Centrist of the Left parties.

On the extreme right[1] is the anti-republican group, the monarchists and the Bonapartists and the *Action Française* with its very noisy henchmen the *Camelots du Roi;* and balancing them on the far left the Communists in two factions. Next on the right come several groups of Republicans, Republican Democrats, and so forth; and following, nominally in the centre, but really right-wing, the Republican Centre (M. Tardieu's party), the Republicans of the Left, and the Radical Left, the last two of which occasionally support Cabinets of the Left on some issues. Then comes the Left, whose main base consists of the two largest parties in French politics, the Radical-Socialists and the Socialists. (It must be remembered that

---

[1] Not officially represented in either house, though certain members have royalist leanings. The parties are here described as they appear in the Chamber. The Senate has a rather different party grouping, though the main lines are the same.

the Radical-Socialists are not in the least Socialist in the English sense; they are a party of small *bourgeois,* and the word Socialist in their name indicates no more than that they supported more liberal social legislation at the beginning of this century.) Around these two flutter four or five groups of dissident or dissatisfied Radicals and Socialists; but any French Government of the Left is formed by the Radical-Socialists in some form or another with the support, on varying terms, of the Socialist Party or as much of it as can be induced to support. The Socialist Party has never, except during the war, been tempted into a coalition; but as no Cabinet of the Left can remain in office without Socialist support, the Socialists can generally force concessions up to a point. It will be seen from the foregoing that the French elector has virtually no say in the appointment of Ministries; for nobody can possibly tell who the Ministers are likely to be. The British elector voting Labour knows more or less for whom as well as for what he is voting; but votes given for Radical-Socialist candidates carry no guarantee that, even if the Left wins, M. Herriot will be in the Cabinet.

French Governments, in spite of this multiplicity of parties, do tend to show a fairly simple series of swings between Left and Right, even apart from swings in the composition of the assembly. Governments of the Right tend to fall more from generic French distrust of a strong executive and a right-wing policy than from any other cause; even in 1926 M. Poincaré, called in to save the State, could only get his measures put into effect by investing himself with extra-parliamentary powers. Governments of the Left find their worst snags in finance. But obscuring these major swings are perpetual minor crises, arising out of Ministers who suddenly desert or become violently unpopular, or due to some unattractive or unwise action of the Cabinet, or to scandals affecting one or more of its members. French politics are full of "scandals," of which the *affaire Stavisky* is only the latest and noisiest. When any of these eventualities occurs, the Cabinet generally falls, to reappear, after several sea-changes, as a new Cabinet looking very much like the old one.

THE ADMINISTRATIVE SYSTEM

This musical chairs atmosphere could not, however, be maintained in government if there were not, actually, considerably more continuity in administration. As has been said, the French administrative system derives from Napoleon and is highly centralised. The same applies to the system of local government, which is also part of the *Code Napoléon*. French local government has far less democracy than British; the elective bodies which Napoleon threw in as sops to popular feeling are still as powerless as he left them. The largest unit in France is the *département,* governed by a *Préfet* appointed from Paris; the *département* is divided into *arrondissements,* each governed by a *sous-préfet* who is appointed from Paris but placed under the orders of the *Préfet*. Under the *Préfet* also are the smallest divisions, the *communes*[1] small and great. Each *commune* has a *maire* elected by the communal council, who may be dismissed by the President or suspended by the Ministry of the Interior. The *Préfet* wields practically despotic powers; it is true that his rule in each area is tempered by the existence of elected councils, which have at any rate the right of remonstrance, and certain other functions as well; but in practice these are advisory rather than governmental bodies. There also exist a great many institutions which are advisory in name as well as in fact, and which are commonly composed of delegates from bodies such as trade unions and corporations. French individualist democracy does not like associations, and has only grudgingly recognised their right to exist at all; but in practice they have come to play a fairly large part by their "advising" of administrators.

The system of *droit administratif* further illustrates the undemocratic character of the machine. Under that system servants of the State cannot be tried in the ordinary courts for acts committed in their official capacity, but appear before special tribunals constituted for that purpose. These tribunals are controlled by a special section of the *conseil d'état,* which is the highest administrative tribunal of France. According to most authorities, however, the administrative tribunals are not slower to convict for breach of official duty than are the ordinary courts of England.

It would thus appear that French local life is under the despotic control of a protected bureaucracy, itself acting under the direct orders of the central executive. In practice this rigidity is softened in working by several factors, of which the weakness of French government is one. The *Préfet* acts under orders from the Ministry of the

[1] The three largest cities, Paris, Lyons and Marseilles, have special constitutions of their own, e.g. there is no *maire* of Paris.

Interior, it is true; but it is difficult for the *Préfet* to be made to act in accordance with a strict policy when the personnel of his masters is continually changing, when he who is Minister of the Interior to-day may not be Minister to-morrow, and when to-morrow's Minister, whatever his general political views, may have quite different views on local affairs. He is not likely, except in extreme cases, to dismiss the *Préfet,* for there is no general "spoils system" in French politics, but he is quite likely to order the *Préfet* to change his course of action, or to refuse to back him up in a course of action which he has already embarked upon, or to ask for some changes in minor offices to be made in order to please the deputies for the area, or the brothers, cousins and aunts of the deputies. Furthermore, a *Préfet* may always be entangled among varying orders from various Ministers, or may, by adroit manœuvring, succeed in causing them to fall over one another. The local government of France is centralised in very minute detail, so that it is necessary to acquire permits and authorisations from a great number of departments of State before quite simple pieces of local work can be put in hand. The fencing-in of a field which borders on a main road, for example, requires the consent of nineteen different authorities, each necessitating a separate application to Paris. This state of things has now been recognised to have become an administrative nuisance, and thoroughgoing reforms are from time to time demanded. The position of reformers is, however, complicated because the reform of local government, in France, rapidly becomes involved with regionalist issues. And French regionalists are not, like English regionalists, essentially local government reformers who want to see the areas of administration widened; they are also apt to be politicians who want a very large degree of autonomy for vast provinces, hoping in this way to revive areas of ancient tradition, such as La Vendée, in which royalist and clerical feeling can grow unchecked by the heavy hand of the republican government. In many cases, "regionalist," to a Frenchman, connotes "reactionary"; and hence proposals for the reform of local government are apt to be regarded with suspicion. In the meantime, however, the system affords ample opportunity to a *Préfet* anxious to avoid carrying out obnoxious orders.

Finally, there is the influence of the deputy to be considered. The preceding pages should have made it clear that the individualism and factionalism of French politics make the individual deputy far more of a personality, far more someone whose favour must be personally courted by a would-be Minister than is the average British M.P. At any moment, by interpellation or by raising a scandal, the deputy can upset the Minister's fair prospects; and he therefore requires conciliation. The prime concern of the majority of deputies is with the areas which return them to the Chamber, and their interests therefore tend to be the interests of those areas, the local assistance which they need, and the State jobs which can be provided for their voters. Hence the deputy is continually exacting from the Minister, as the price of his support, local concessions of various sorts, and hence too the deputy is in a position to remark to local officials who show too much zeal or too much sense of their personal importance that the advocacy of the commune or department at headquarters will materially suffer if the deputy feels that he cannot in honesty continue to support the claims of its officials. French local officials, as every observer has noticed, are apt to be very fierce and dictatorial and to bristle with an air of *droit administratif;* but it is a fierceness which seems conscious that it may at any moment be put suddenly into its place and told to "lie down, good dog." There is little of the bored and serene unconsciousness of any possible consequences which characterises the unimaginative type of British administrator. French civil servants are, however, in a much stronger position *vis-à-vis* their employers than British civil servants, with their long tradition of patient obedience. In the case of the British, the possibility of the higher ranks of the service sabotaging the work of Ministers with whom they were in violent political disagreement has been canvassed, but open revolt is at least very unlikely, and salary reductions are commonly accepted with no more than a grumble. But the French civil service has more than once put a Cabinet in jeopardy.

PROBLEMS OF FRENCH POLITICS

This brings us to the question of the "corruption" of French political life, which can easily be exaggerated, and is often exaggerated, largely because the French newspapers make such a noise about any case of corruption, and treat it not with weary amusement, as the Americans do, nor, like the British, with a hasty veiling of the unpleasant sight, but as a full-dress public spectacle demanding the oratory of Danton to do justice to it. French politics are not pure; there is a good deal of jobbery, particularly in regard to minor public offices, and a good deal of palm-greasing on a smallish scale, and occasionally some dubious connections between politicians and financiers which explode into first-rate scandals like the Oustric and Stavisky affairs. The French Press, also, particularly a portion of the Paris dailies, if one can trust half of what is commonly believed, is remarkably venal and continually in receipt of subsidies from some interest or another—including, in some cases, foreign political interests.

But it all does not amount to very much; the transactions, with a few notable exceptions, are on a small scale. The Frenchman is as economical in his bribery as he is in everything else; and an American boss could probably buy up most of the Paris Press for less than it would cost him to acquire a street-car franchise in his own home town. (In the case of the Press, at any rate, the venality matters less because there are so many newspapers; if one bought paper proclaims one set of views, another has generally been bribed to say the exact opposite; and there are no millionaire advertisers, as in Great Britain, who are in a position to suppress *all* advocacy of certain points of view.) The whole thing is evidence of a slightly slatternly standard of public morality, no doubt; but it does not mean very much more than that. And, just as the admirable French food is often produced in kitchens whose appearance would scandalise an American used to getting his food out of nice clean cans, so the state of French politics indicates that there are worse things in the world than a little dirt.

The future of politics in France, as in all countries, depends upon the economic factor; and at the time of writing this factor is uncertain. The effects of the slump, and of French financial policy, are coming home to roost in the form of unemployment, high prices, and the loss of foreign tourist traffic; and the international outlook, with the Nazis vociferating across the frontier, is also dark. It was high prices and mismanagement, rather than the Stavisky case, which produced the troubles in the spring; and French newspapers are now full of the demands that something should be done, somebody be made to suffer, and a plan be produced, with which other countries have for some time been familiar. Nevertheless, it does not at the moment look as though any major social upheaval of the kind which produces a constitutional cataclysm were coming. Socialism is weaker in France than in most countries which are not under a dictatorship, and a good deal of the French Socialist vote has no specifically Socialist views, but votes Socialist through a general desire to be on the Left. The voter who complained to his deputy, who having been elected six months before as a Radical-Socialist still belonged to that party, "Mais, alors vous n'avancez pas!" is not untypical of the Socialist vote in the South; and while there may be local strikes and *émeutes* of vigour, a Socialist Government in France appears very unlikely to arrive, or to last longer than a couple of days.

Nor has Fascism any great hold outside Paris, though the tendency of all French parties to call their opponents "Fascists" rather conceals this. The rioting of the spring was mainly provoked by reactionary elements whose community with Fascism proper lies only in their tendency to idealise violence. The class which made the strength of the Nazi movement in Germany, the ruined and angry *petite bourgeoisie* of intellectuals and small shopkeepers, is not yet ruined in France, or even particularly angry, though rising prices have caused a good deal of discontent and heart-searching. This class does, as a matter of fact, largely control the Government, and has no need of a revolution to enable it to seize power.

It is not, of course, suggested that this state of things is necessarily permanent, or that a serious worsening in the economic situation might not yet produce startling results. There is no reason to suppose that the French have actually lost their capacity for revolution. But at the present time there is more cry than wool; and even the Paris rioters, with all the support which economic discomfort has rallied to their side, belong largely to the upper *bourgeoisie,* and are, besides, deeply committed to royalist and clerical policies which are anathema to the majority of French citizens. Some administrative changes will probably result from the present discontents; but it is doubtful whether, as things stand at present, they will be anything more than superficial.

4. THE POLITICAL SYSTEM OF
THE UNITED STATES

IT IS A MATTER of great difficulty to write upon the political system of the United States at the present time; and this not only for the obvious reasons. Clearly, it is difficult to write with any certainty of the great experiment, not only in methods of government but in political control of economic life, which President Roosevelt is at the moment making, while neither the results of that experiment nor the course of economic conditions is or can be known; so that whatever comments the writer makes may be nullified, by the time his words are in print, by some unexpected turn of events. But even if there were no slump and no Roosevelt, the present would still be a turning-point, and the future of American politics and political institutions one of great uncertainty.

For the United States has, of recent years, quite clearly reached the end of a long period which has covered, in effect, the whole of her history from the War of Independence to the European War. The time during which she was growing into a State is over, and she now has to face the largely different problems of how a formed and settled State is to be governed and what institutions it is to preserve out of those which were found suitable for a State in the process of evolution.

SPECIAL CHARACTERISTICS OF AMERICAN SOCIETY

The main characteristics of growing America were the infinite availability of land at practically no cost, the continual stream of immigrants, and, to a rather less degree, the practically continuous existence of a large economic surplus, and the isolation, both by economic barriers and by political choice, of the United States from Europe. All these, to a greater or less degree, have disappeared during the last fifteen years. The "squatter" is no more to be seen; all the land has been taken up, and there is nowhere for him to squat, even if, under present economic circumstances, the prospects of squatting were rather more rosy than they are. (It is the slump which has put an end to a development which at one time looked possible, the penetration by American squatters of Western Canada.) The effect of this, in cutting off from the city worker the prospect of setting up as an independent farmer, has hardly yet begun to be felt; its most obvious symptom is the terrific bread-lines which have been seen in every American city during the past three winters; but its final effects are obviously going to be very much greater, in the practical denial of the possibility, axiomatic in American thought for over a hundred years, for every man, if he possesses courage and ability, to rise to wealth and influence, and in the gradual growth of something more like the British class-system. In a sense, of course, there is a class-system in present-day America, in the sense that there is an upper layer of rich, and a very much larger substructure of persons of low incomes who have in reality only an infinitesimal chance of rising into the upper layer. A recent study of the social origins of American business leaders shows that, in spite of popular myths, the percentage who come from anything but comfortable homes is very small. Nevertheless, this layering of the population yet lacks many of the elements of a class-classification, in particular, that conscious acceptance of "station in life" which is such a feature of the British class-system. The American proletariat, partly owing to racial difficulties, is as yet non-homogeneous, the craftsmen, organised in Unions affiliated to the American Federation of Labor, feeling little sympathy with and sometimes definite hostility to the mass of unskilled, who include so many foreign-born or negro workers. It should also be remembered that the United States contains a large number of small farmers, who, when allowance is made for the much higher general standard of life, may be said to correspond to the peasant populations of the Old World. Many people still think of farming in America as essentially large-scale. This, except for the cattle-ranching States, is not true. The typical American wheat-grower farms 150 acres or thereabouts, and the same is true, since the abolition of slavery, of the great majority of the cotton-growers of the South. The "small man" is as much a feature of America as he is of France, in agriculture though not in industry.

With the free land has disappeared the immigrant; at least, he is now only admitted in small and grudging degree and after a careful process of handpicking. This means that the American nation is now complete, as it were, in personnel; and that the problem of "Americanisation," except as regards the negroes, will grow progressively less and less. The difficulties of this problem have, it is true, been exaggerated in some quarters. It is undeniable that the existence of large blocks of German, Scandinavian or Irish immigrants in certain States has given rise to particular problems in those States; and it is also true that the streaming-in, particularly during the later years of heavy immigration from South-Eastern Europe, of masses of illiterate voters of alien traditions has made the government of some large cities peculiarly difficult and accounts in part for the power of such institutions as Tammany Hall. Nevertheless, the observer must feel that the agents of Americanisation, particularly the immense force of Evangelical and Methodist Christianity and the universal system of education, have on the whole met with remarkable success. Wide differences may still exist, and New York may not be America; but a Serb in the United States rapidly becomes something very different from a Serb in the mountains of Serbia. Even the Roman Catholic Church, that most international of forces, wears a strange aspect on the other side of the Atlantic. No minority of voluntary immigrants has given the United States half so much trouble as those unfortunate involuntary immigrants who go under the name of the Negro Problem; though in the case of civilisations so difficult to assimilate as those of China and Japan she has perhaps been wise in deciding, as far as possible, to keep their representatives out.

The economic surplus may not have disappeared for ever; but it certainly has for the time, as the most recent budget figures show; and whether or not it returns, its vanishing at the moment marks a great break in the system of "share-out" which has been a continuing feature of American government at least since 1836, and of which such incidents as the rapid paying-off of a large part of the War Loans and the remarkable ramp of the Civil War pensions list were only minor manifestations. We shall return to this point on a later page, for it is impossible to understand American history or American politics unless the perpetual existence of this surplus is borne in mind.

At the moment, however, the surplus has gone, gone almost within a night. And it has gone partly owing to forces and events without the American Continent. It used to be commonplace that "isolationism" and the Monroe Doctrine made up an all-sufficient policy for the United States; that with her enormous natural resources and her great home market she needed only to sit tight and enter into European politics merely, as in the case of the "Open Door" policy in China and even of the European War, for the purpose of teaching European nations better manners. This has proved untrue. Apart from her special anxieties with regard to Japan, the United States has discovered that economic changes and their effects can cross oceans. Whatever the political propagandists might say, President Wilson neither kept the United States out of the European War nor brought them in. Individual American financiers and traders had effectively brought them in long before the President declared war, and the effect of the war debt and reparations problems on internal American economics showed quite clearly that they had not yet come out. The present efforts of President Roosevelt at the moment of writing are directed largely to rebuilding American economic prosperity on lines as autonomous as possible; whether or not they will be successful remains to be seen.

AMERICAN DEMOCRACY

One more general comment must be made by way of introduction. That is, that the American system is, in theory at least, both popular and democratic in a sense that even the French system is not. The idea of popular control lies deep in the heart of American political institutions, and this not merely because they carry the principle of direct election, as some would think, to extremes. It is true that the Constitution itself, under the guidance of Alexander Hamilton, was framed so as to secure that popular control should, if possible, trip over its own feet; but again and again the right of popular control has asserted itself. The ease with which President Roosevelt, elected upon a great popular wave by a frightened people, was able to manipulate the most cumbrous Constitution in the world, is an instance, as is, in another way, the mass of absurd laws which manage to get passed by State legislatures. The American believes that law and the Constitution should do what the people desire them to do—even though the law which the people desire to have passed is incapable of enforcement, and would have the most surprising effects if it could be enforced.

Further, the American system is democratic, with a rough, frontier, equalitarian democracy. The States have in many ways equal rights, in the election of Senators, for example, and to a less extent in the distribution of public money and offices; and one American, particularly one hundred-per-cent American, is theoretically as good as another. It is true that American democracy is somewhat Darwinian in its practical working; it believes in the survival of the fittest,[1] and not even American democracy can get round the fact that the fittest in the modern world are commonly those who possess the largest incomes. But since the southern aristocracy of planters, to which Washington and the first Presidents belonged, shaken by the victory of

[1] One may notice a *reductio ad absurdum* of this in the wild exaggeration of competition in the U.S.A. Competitions in "tree-sitting," in swallowing ices, in reading the Bible as fast as possible, etc., all seem to give the winners some mysterious stamp of worth.

Andrew Jackson in 1828, was destroyed as the result of the Civil War, there has never been a dominant class in the United States, though there have been dominant interests. Whatever the hopes of Henry James and other expatriates, America has never succeeded in developing an oligarchy—in which it most notably differs from Great Britain. "Privilege" is a word which is bitterly hated; hence the terror of capitalist monopoly, expressed in Theodore Roosevelt's "trust-busting" campaign. That view is really a seventeenth-century anti-Stuart view, and modern experience is rapidly altering it. The only group that has been systematically kept under has been that of the negroes in the south; and snobbery about birth, though it is to be found in the States as well as anywhere else, has never made a caste system. As has been suggested, it may be that a class alignment will develop with changing conditions; but so far it is individualism that holds the field—individualism that is compatible with an enormous gregariousness and ability to join together in associations and machines of every kind.

THE FEDERAL CONSTITUTION

The United States is a very large country, and its political system large and difficult, the more so because many of its institutions, in the course of generations, have come to work in a way far other than that intended by their founders. In the first place, the United States is a federation, and the student therefore has to consider, not merely the Constitution of the United States itself, but those of forty-eight member States, as well as the position of territories, such as Alaska or Hawaii, which have not risen to the dignity of Statehood, before he can turn his attention to the local governments of the cities and rural areas. As it is a federation, and as the Federal Government only possesses the powers which the States in the Constitution have agreed to hand to it, it might be more logical to begin with a description of the State Governments. But in practice, whatever the intention of the founding fathers, modern economic conditions and modern transport have so worked towards integration of the whole nation, that the Federal institutions are now of much more positive importance than those of the individual States. We shall therefore begin with the Federal Constitution, which was drafted in 1787, eleven years after the Declaration of Independence, and came into effect in 1789.

The Constitution of the United States recognises three separate and independent bodies; the legislative, consisting of the Senate and the House of Representatives, both of which are now elected by popular vote; the executive, consisting of the elected President and the officers appointed by him; and the judicial, consisting of the Supreme Court, whose members are appointed by the President but are practically irremovable, and such lesser courts as the legislative body may from time to time determine. This principle of "the separation of powers" was in accordance with the most up-to-date political thinking in the eighteenth century; it was considered to be the best way of ensuring that democracy would not run away with itself and act in an ultra-democratic manner, and as such it commanded the support of the respectable founders of the American Republic, who disliked the "rabble" and the prospects of anything like the French Revolution in its later stages quite as much as they disliked King George III. Thus, on paper, Congress (that is, the two elected Houses) cannot pass laws without the President's signature; the President cannot initiate legislation; and, even if these two powers are united, the Supreme Court can at any time thwart them by declaring that a particular law violates the Constitution. (The Constitutions of the separate States have, with slight variations, embodied the same general principle.) In practice, the "separation of powers" has not worked with the rigidity that was anticipated. The use of the President's veto on Congressional Bills has bridged one gap; so has the practice known as "senatorial courtesy," under which the Senators from each State have generally had a veto on appointments made within that State. Even the Supreme Court has not been completely deaf to political considerations; Mr. Dooley once announced that "the Supreme Court follows th' iliction returns," and in the early days of the present Roosevelt administration the possibility of "packing" the Supreme Court in order to avoid the danger of a legal decision upsetting the Roosevelt programme was freely canvassed. In matters that are not of immediate urgency, however, the possibility of a deadlock between a President and a hostile Congress, or of a hold-up by the Supreme Court, remains as a considerable nuisance, more especially as the Constitution is very hard to alter.

The procedure for amending the Constitution is slow and cumbrous. In fact, during the hundred and forty-six years of its life, only twenty-one amendments have been passed, of which ten were passed immediately after it took effect and really as a result of bargaining in the discussions. Of the rest, four are of quite minor importance, and were only directed at removing certain inconveniences; one enabled the Federal authorities to levy a Federal income tax, one gave votes to women throughout the Union, and one abolished negro slavery. One, the Eighteenth Amendment enacting prohibition, proved unworkable and has been repealed by the Twenty-first Amendment; and the remaining two, which forbade the vote and other privileges of citizenship to be refused to any citizen on the ground of "race, colour, or previous condition of servitude," are not in effective operation in the States to which they were particularly intended to apply.[1] It is perhaps significant that the Twentieth Amendment, which abolished the ridiculous "lame-duck" session of Congress by providing that the President should assume office two months and not five after election, and which raised no question of high principle, took ten years of agitation to pass. The American Constitution is not easily altered—on paper.

THE PRESIDENT

The President is a constitutional monarch, elected every four years. He is not, however, elected directly by the voters, but by an electoral college, consisting of representatives of every State to a number equal to the whole number of Senators and Representatives to which that State is entitled in Congress. If no candidate for the Presidency has a clear majority of the electoral college, the House of Representatives has to decide between the leading candidates. The original idea, no doubt, was that the electoral college should solemnly and in due order consider the merits of rival candidates; but in all recent elections the results have been so clear that the electoral college has been merely a recording body, and the House of Representatives has not been called upon. If, however, at any time serious splits or re-alignments of the great parties should take place, curious results might occur, as after the end of the "Virginian dynasty" in 1828.

The President has no constitutional control over Congress; he cannot dissolve it, or introduce legislation, though in practice he can always get members of his party to introduce any legislation which he desires. He can, however, veto within ten days any Congressional

[1] The Fourteenth Amendment, however, has also had a considerable effect on labour legislation in the Union.

legislation, and his veto can only be overridden by a two-thirds vote of both Houses; the Presidential veto has been in fact considerably used to stop minor and sectional as well as major legislation. He can also appoint his Cabinet with much greater freedom than can an English Prime Minister. In point of fact, the Cabinet of the United States is not a Cabinet, but a meeting of the President's servants, who may be anybody he chooses. A President who had "forgotten Goschen" would have no reason to be distressed at the omission; he could replace Goschen by a Civil Servant, or a University Professor, and nobody would turn a hair. See, for example, the extraordinary proportion of entirely unknown men (in politics) whom Roosevelt II put into his Cabinet.

The President is *ex officio* commander-in-chief of the forces, and has treaty-making powers, subject to the consent of the Senate by a two-thirds vote; and he appoints to and dismisses from all Federal offices, including the diplomatic and consular services. He can be impeached, while in office, by the Senate; but only one President, Andrew Johnson, was actually impeached, and in his case the impeachment failed. Otherwise there is no means of controlling or interfering with the President in office; and he is therefore a monarch within the limits of the Constitution. But he is a monarch without a dynasty: since Washington set the precedent by refusing a third nomination, no President has served for more than two terms, and Presidents have found considerable difficulty in nominating their successors as the Roman Emperors did theirs, though Roosevelt I succeeded in getting Taft elected in 1908. The "reign" of a President is therefore limited to eight years at most, unless the present President breaks the tradition.

If the President dies while in office, the Vice-President, who is elected at the same time, but, since 1804, by a separate vote, becomes President. As, however, the Vice-President, apart from being President of the Senate, has practically no political functions, the office is generally filled by a nonentity, or "sound party man." The sole exception was Theodore Roosevelt, who actually became President through the assassination of McKinley.

THE CONGRESS

The American Congress consists of two Houses, both of whose consent is necessary to the passing of legislation, though bills for raising revenue can only be introduced into the House of Representatives. Both Houses are (since 1913) elected by direct vote, nominally of all citizens; but in most of the former slave States persons of negro blood are by one means or another prevented from voting.

The House of Representatives is elected every two years on a State basis, the number of representatives allotted to each State being roughly proportioned to population. The Territories are represented in Congress by representatives who may speak but may not vote. The allotment of representatives is supposed to be revised after each census; but in the twentieth century there has been a tendency to delay revision. Within the States, the distribution of Congressional seats is decided by the State legislature; and it is alleged that there is a good deal of gerrymandering and discrimination in the process, mostly in favour of the rural as against the city areas. This point, to which we shall have to return in discussing the government of States, illustrates the battle between country and city, which is one of the main issues in American politics which the American party system does not disclose. Congressmen, like Senators, may not hold any executive office; but more important than this is the provision which requires that a Congressman must be resident in the State which he represents.[1] This at once makes the House much more of a delegate body than the British House of Commons; it also makes it impossible for a party leader, unseated in his own State, to find, as British Cabinet Ministers have again and again found, a seat in another part of the country; and (as the same constitutional rule also applies to the Senate) it practically debars a Republican who lives in Georgia or a Democrat living in Vermont from a seat in either House. Herein, it will be seen, the Federal system is a bar to free popular choice of any public politician but the President. It also leads, in some States, to a sort of rotation of the office of Congressman, which generally encourages mediocrity. The House of Representatives, like the Senate, has regular committees; it has also an elected Speaker of its own who has considerable powers over debate. There is not nearly so much unrestricted freedom of debate in Congress as there is in the Senate.

The Senate is composed of ninety-six elected persons, two from each State. Senators serve for six years, one-third being elected every

[1] In practice, a Congressman must actually reside in his own Congressional district —as though Mr. Ramsay MacDonald were forced to live in Seaham.

two years. The Senate is thus not at all representative of the United
States in a numerical sense, Delaware, which elects one Congressman, sending up the same number of Senators as New York, which
has forty-five. Nevertheless—or possibly for that reason—seats in the
Senate are much more sought after than seats in the Lower House,
and tend to be filled by men of some political weight. Most of the
American politicians of whom the outside world has heard, excluding Presidents, millionaires, leading gangsters, and mayors of Chicago and New York, are Senators; and there is even a tendency in
some States, such as Wisconsin since the rise of the La Follettes, towards the emergence of a hereditary principle. The complete freedom of debate in the Senate, under which any single Senator may
keep the floor as long as his breath holds out and may discourse upon
any subject under the sun,[1] together with the necessity of securing a
two-thirds majority of the Senate for the endorsement of treaties,[2]
has given more external interest to the debates in the Upper House;
and the provision of the Constitution under which Presidential appointments, including those of judges of the Supreme Court, must be
made "with the advice and consent of the Senate," provides that
body with a direct interest in administration.

THE SUPREME COURT

The Supreme Court of the United States consists of nine judges.
It has, according to the Constitution, original jurisdiction "in all
cases affecting ambassadors, other public ministers and consuls, and
those in which a State shall be a party"; and appellate jurisdiction
in other cases. There are also lower Federal courts, as may be decided by Congress, for the enforcement of Federal law; their activities were greatly increased by the passing of the Eighteenth
Amendment. The powers of the Supreme Court as set out in the
Constitution, however, give little hint of the real importance of that
body, which is, that it is the final court of review of constitutional
law. If, on a case brought before it, the Supreme Court decides that

[1] Senators have been known in the past to read aloud their entire literary output,
thus securing for it the immortality of print in the Congressional Record. Since 1917
a very mild form of control has been introduced, by which two-thirds of the Senate
can impose the closure.

[2] Roosevelt I found the attitude of the Senate on foreign policy so exasperating
that he took to concluding "agreements" instead of formal treaties; but that policy
cannot be applied in all cases, and the fate of the Versailles Treaty in the Senate
should be fresh in most people's memories.

a Federal law, or a State law, "violates the Constitution," that law is nullified. As the Constitution is drawn upon exceedingly broad lines, it follows that there is a very wide field for political interpretations of it by the Supreme Court, and decisions have from time to time been given by it which have seemed to outside observers to have little or nothing to do with legal considerations. The most famous decision of the Supreme Court was given in the Dred Scott case, which was one of the proximate causes of the Civil War; but its other activities, particularly in the domain of social legislation, have given rise to more than a little comment.

THE STATE CONSTITUTIONS

It is not possible, within the space at our disposal, to give more than a very brief review of the constitutions of all the forty-eight States of the Union. They vary a good deal in comparatively minor matters, with varying local economic and social conditions; but their likenesses, both to one another and to the Federal Constitution, are more important than their differences. Like the Federal Constitution, they are all written; and, like it, they all provide for the "separation of powers." They all have, under one name or another, a Supreme Appeal Court which performs for the laws of the State the functions which the U. S. Supreme Court performs for the Union. They all have an elected Governor, with wide powers, including a veto on legislation, and, up to a point, the power to appoint and dismiss State officials; and they all have an elected legislature of two houses. The method and term of election of those houses varies from State to State; on the whole, however, there is the same tendency towards over-representation of the rural areas as we have already noticed in the Federal Congress. In Georgia, for example, every one of the counties is given the same weight in Senatorial elections; the average county population is 18,000, but Fulton County, which contains Atlanta, has 300,000, with the same representation. The farmers, however, owing to the operation of the general property tax, contribute heavily to the upkeep of the States. The social enmity between city and rural areas has been, for some time, one of the realities of American political life; it gains force from the fact that the immigrant, particularly the poor immigrant, generally settles first in the cities, and the hatred shown by the country voter for the "wicked city" is one aspect of Americanisation. It was, probably, one of the forces in the enactment of prohibition. The steady growth of the cities, however, is a fact which no exercise of votes can stop, and with the closing-down of immigration it may be that this particular issue is destined to become of gradually decreasing importance. This does not imply that the small farmer is on the decline. As indicated earlier, he is one of the major factors in American economics; all that is meant is that the cultural divergence between him and the city-dweller seems likely to diminish.

The main differences between the State and Federal constitutions are three. The State constitutions, though not all of them are on paper easier of amendment, are in practice more often amended; in a good number of States, the constitution contains some provision, such as the initiative or the referendum, for direct popular control of legislation; and in many cases a number of the higher State officials are popularly elected, instead of being appointed by the Governor. Otherwise, what has been said of the Federal Government applies in general to the State machinery, save that as the issues are State issues, except when it is a question of constitutional amendment or the giving of an opinion on some Federal question, the debates in State legislatures are of less consequence and attract less political talent than those in Congress.

LOCAL GOVERNMENT

Below the State machinery is the machinery of local government, of which little can be said here, except that it also is elective, and consists, generally speaking, of the cities and the county districts. The government of the cities is of three main types, that of a mayor and council, that of an elected board of commissioners, and that of a city manager, who is himself generally chosen by a small elected body. The counties are governed by elected county boards, and in the older States there are generally township meetings or councils under them for the small urban areas; but this system has not been widely extended in the south and west. In addition to these, however, there is also in many States a whole host of particular authorities, sanitary boards, parks and drainage boards and the like, recalling the confusion of local government in nineteenth-century England. It is said that there are no less than 415 local governing bodies in Chicago and Cook County, each with its own tax-levying and borrowing powers. With all these authorities to be chosen, and with the State legislatures and Governors and State judges as well, and Congress and the President into the bargain, it is not surprising that it sometimes seems as though the American citizen could spend all his days voting—a fact which is not without its bearing on the working of the system.

AMERICAN IMPERIALISM

There is no room here for a discussion of American imperialism—"dollar diplomacy," as it is sometimes called. But it should be realised that, apart from the comparatively unimportant territorial conquests of the United States in such areas as Hawaii, the operation of the Monroe Doctrine meant that the United States, having forbidden European Powers to interfere to protect their capital invested in the South American States, in effect had guaranteed that "normal" capitalist conditions would prevail in those States. Hence some very dubious financial and other transactions, in Nicaragua, Mexico, and elsewhere, regarding which, to do it justice, American public opinion has always been uncomfortable.

THE PARTY SYSTEM

The working of American political institutions, to European observers, is almost more difficult and bewildering than the institutions themselves. Parties, there, do not appear to mean what they mean in the Old World; a Republican or Democratic Party Convention is not in the least like, nor does it behave like, an English Party Conference; and there are institutions such as "direct primaries," "party bosses," and the "spoils system," to say nothing of bodies such as Tammany Hall, which appear to have no parallel in the other countries with democratic representative governments. Nevertheless, these institutions owe their continuing power, if not their existence, to the nature of the American party system; and unless that system is understood it is impossible to make sense of the rest.

America has no party system, in the sense in which those words were understood in nineteenth-century Britain. There are two great parties, the Republicans and the Democrats; but it is merely misleading to say that the Republicans are "like the Conservatives." Since the disappearance of the Federalists, there has never been a Conservative Party in America; and whatever the Democrats are they are certainly not Liberal. Even the most cynical observer of British politics is forced to admit that the Conservative and Liberal Parties, for all their likenesses, had a quite considerable difference of programme and policy; between the programmes of the Republicans and the Democrats there is, as nearly as possible, no difference at all. It is true that the Republicans have tended, on the whole, to put up the tariff, and the Democrats to favour the farmers and currency policies that would please the farmers; but the Democrats have always advocated a tariff for revenue purposes,[1] and in the great currency controversy of the 'nineties a large number of "Gold Democrats" would have nothing to do with Bryan. There is more force in the contention that the Republicans have tended to be the party of "Big Business"—though it was Republicans who passed the Sherman Anti-Trust Laws; but this is due far less to any principles of the Republicans than to the fact that from 1860 until 1932 the Republicans were, with hardly any intervals, the party in power, and Big Business naturally tends to attach itself to the Ins rather than to the Outs. There is practically no difference between the "platforms" of the two parties; the issues which excite public interest, such as Prohibition, cut right across party affiliations; and the various groups which are formed from time to time on what British observers would call "party lines," like the Granger movement of the 'seventies, often tell their adherents to vote Republican or Democrat as seems best in the several States. This does not apply to the Socialists, who have always kept themselves separate. But the Socialist vote over the country is very small. The two great parties are machines for securing control of the administration; and that is all.

The reason for this state of things is mainly historical. Before the Civil War, there were in the United States parties whose political programmes could be distinguished. But the Democrats, who alone can trace their existence back to the foundations of the American Republic,[2] came to base their party upon two main issues, the right of the constituent States to reject Federal legislation that was not to their liking (which drove them in the end to uphold the right of secession), and the maintenance of slavery. Both these claims were

---

[1] The voting of Democratic Senators on the 1930 tariff should disprove the suggestion that Democrats have anything Free Trade about them.

[2] Jefferson's party called themselves Republicans at the beginning, and only gradually adopted the present name. The first President to be generally called a Democrat was Andrew Jackson (elected 1828).

finally defeated in the Civil War, and the *raison d'être* of the Democratic Party thus cut away. Had the Civil War ended, as Lincoln intended it to end, in reconciliation and a co-operative reconstruction, the way might have been clear for the building up of new parties on a basis of differing policies. But whether or not Lincoln's idea could have been translated into practice, his assassination ensured that this was not even attempted; and the new "Republican" Party, formed in the main out of a combination of Unionists and anti-slavery men, treated the beaten South in a spirit which suggests the Treaty of Versailles. Andrew Johnson, Lincoln's successor, and a former Democrat, gained no support for a more lenient policy and himself suffered impeachment.

There is no need to recall here in detail the mistakes and follies of the Republicans in the "reconstruction" period. The effect, which is what concerns us, was that the Democratic Party was preserved as a sullen beaten minority, drawing its main support from States which had to readjust themselves to a new system of economy based on wage-labour, and which were also half ruined by the extravagance of the "carpet-bag" régimes,[1] facing a party equally sectional, but based mainly upon the New England and other Northern manufacturing States, whose wealth had been growing by leaps and bounds even during the war. Under these circumstances the Democrats became a party of *revanche,* a party which saw its enemies in power—and dividing, during the immediate post-war years, the spoils of victory in a peculiarly shameless way. Their only policy was to hold on solidly and to hope that, by collecting support in the Western States which had had little interest in the war, and in those border States and immigrant States (such as New York) which had been less under the influence of the Abolitionists, they would be strong enough to get in time the reversion of the power and profits, when a sufficient number of persons had become tired of the Republicans. Eventually this came to pass; a Democratic President was elected in 1884, and 1892 saw a reasonable Democratic majority, which, however, the slump of 1893 destroyed. Not until 1932—for Wilson in 1912 came in through a split in the Republican Party—was there anything resembling a Democratic landslide; and no one can pretend

[1] The "carpet-baggers" were Northern Republicans sent down to organise the negro and "poor white" vote in the conquered States so as to make sure that the former leaders were effectively crushed. The Ku Klux Klan was the reply to this naked policy of repression.

that the triumph of Roosevelt II was due to anything but the economic weather. Up till the present, then, the Democrats have been,
with only slight intervals, the party of the Outs, hoping some time
to get in, and the voting strength and distribution of the two parties
has remained basically what it was in 1876 or thereabouts.

The two parties thus are in essence sectional—sectional by States,
and in doubtful States even sectional by area. They are not divided
in policy; the battles of policy, as has been said, have been conducted
by individuals and groups largely, though not entirely, within the
Party framework. For what, then, have the parties fought? For the
right to govern and to acquire the power to dispose, not merely of
public offices, but also of that economic surplus which, as we said at
the beginning of this chapter, has been one of the most essential features of the American political system.

To say this is not wholly to condemn the system. It is true that it
has produced a great deal of plain corruption of the type which is
castigated by every American radical or reformer; it is true that the
"spoils system," the distribution of public contracts, the graft in
public offices, and the sheer handing-out of dollops of public money,
as, for instance, in Civil War pensions,[1] always amount to a scandal
of sorts and sometimes to a scandal of very large dimensions; but,
after all, the surplus was there, and it had to be divided somehow.
The explanation lies not in the particular depravity of any individuals, but in the general attitude of American business to politics, which
differs greatly from the attitude of English business in the nineteenth
century. American business does not regard the State as something
which should interfere as little as possible with industrial life, or
politics as a career too lofty for the rough-and-tumble of reality; it
takes the simple view that the State was made for the service of the
people, and as the most important part of the people is the business
community, the State must serve the business community. The
spectacular ease with which the Roosevelt National Recovery Programme was able to overleap all constitutional difficulties was largely
due to the fact that American business, alarmed by the sudden disappearance of the surplus, came stampeding to the State machine
with demands that it should bring the surplus back again, and indicated that no scruples or prejudices of legislators should be allowed

---

[1] The fear of creating a new and vast opportunity for graft is undoubtedly one
reason, though a minor reason, which has operated to prevent the introduction of
unemployment insurance into the United States.

to stand in the way of their plain duty. The bulk of politicians in America are, directly or indirectly, consciously or unconsciously, the servants of business, and the ethics of American politics merely reflect the ethics of American business, which are much the same as the business ethics of any nationality. (This is not to say that American politics cannot be highly moral at times; business men are often delighted to procure a law which forbids the other fellow to steal, or swear, or behave himself in an unseemly manner. It is the general ethic, however, which determines the political code.)

THE SPOILS SYSTEM

The "spoils system" is one of the features of American politics to which critics most often point. Put simply, the spoils system is the practice under which an incoming President or State Governor turns out those appointed officials who do not belong to his own party, and replaces them from the ranks of the faithful. Its germ is to be found in the cancellation by Jefferson in 1801 of appointments made by his predecessor as he was about to quit office; but as a system it dates from the "clean sweep" made by Jackson in 1829. It has, obviously, been the chief reason which prevented, until quite recently, the development of an American Civil Service; and, while its results have not been as uniformly bad as its critics make out, it has undoubtedly resulted in some very peculiar appointments. The policy of a clean sweep is not, of course, a peculiarity of the United States. Where a single party, with revolutionary aims, comes into power, a clean sweep is inevitable, as both Communist and Fascist Governments have declared. It is hardly less certain when two parties within the State hold views that are irreconcilable; it would have been impossible to leave Democrats in high official positions during the Civil War. But where there is no irreconcilable difference of party policy, and particularly where, as in America, there is really no difference at all, then the "clean sweep" becomes the "spoils system," and a standing invitation to political corruption. It further forces an altogether undesirable amount of the President's time and attention to be spent on "securing his fences," seeing that plums are tidily distributed and that no important interest is left out in the cold.[1] Almost the only countervailing advantage is that a strong President can bring

[1] It is generally believed that one President at least perished in six weeks from the burden, and another (Garfield) was undoubtedly shot by a disappointed office-seeker.

a tiresome group to heel by threatening to withhold patronage from their friends. The great days of the spoils system, however, are over. The magnificent corruption of General Grant's administrations startled even business ethic; and from 1877 onwards more and more offices were removed from the sphere of appointment and filled by competitive examination. Nowadays, the great field of "appointments" is the Federal Post Office with its hundreds of thousands of jobs; but the sphere of examination is very wide, and is slowly building up an American Civil Service which approximates more to the British, though it has, as yet, nothing like its power and prestige.

THE PARTY MACHINES

In a political system which is directed so largely by the simple counting of votes, the right to these and other plums of office can only be secured by the steady and thorough organisation of votes and voters. This is the more necessary since, as already mentioned, there are so many elections in American life, so many areas, cities, counties, States, and Federal Government, in which a victory at the polls means a cut at the surplus; and, more important, because voting for the larger elections is conducted so much on a territorial basis that carelessness or miscalculation in one small area may quite easily have disastrous consequences. On one occasion, at any rate, it was a matter of a thousand votes that swung the great State of New York over to the Democratic side and brought a Democrat in as President. It is therefore necessary to see that the voter, particularly the foreign or illiterate voter, is brought safely into the proper fold; and accordingly both parties have evolved strong party machines which in all the different centres collect and poll the voters, and in return for this service, receive a fair share of the pickings that are the result of victory. Largely, of course, the party machines, like party organisations in any country, are paid for by wealthy supporters of the party; but to a certain extent they draw—and did much more fifty and sixty years ago—on percentages paid up by the fortunate who obtain political office. In the United States, however, this system of party organisation has gone much further than in any European country. In Great Britain, for example, every candidate, and every election agent, knows that it is desirable, if the seat is likely to be contested, that the local party headquarters should make itself into a kind of unofficial enquiry bureau and welfare centre, and in some constituencies this practice has been carried much further than in others. But all British efforts pale before the social and political organisation of such a body as Tammany Hall,[1] with its "chiefs," its "ward" and "precinct" captains, its paid lawyers and friends at court, and its intense and practical means of assisting the poor voter in his difficulties with the law and the complexities of city life—and, of course, the rich voter who desires more substantial advantages. The political machines of the United States do not solicit votes for nothing; they exist to help the voter in the ways in which he needs help, and to impress upon him the value of supporting the Republican or Democratic Party as the case may be; and the result is that they are able to dispose of blocks of votes, not with absolute certainty, for this is an uncertain world, but at any rate approximately according to calculation. There is room, of course, in the elections themselves for a certain amount of manipulation. There is not much plain slugging still left, even in Chicago—less than in many European elections—and, except in the case of the negroes in the South, there is little wholesale disfranchisement; but in a good many American elections, particularly in State and local elections, there are enough charges of personation, etc. flung about to make it clear that the ballot is not entirely free from extraneous influences. As to direct "corruption," that obviously varies from State to State and from time to time. Tammany Hall had a magnificent orgy during the 'seventies, and recently Chicago, Pennsylvania and Illinois have been a good deal before the public eye; but the very real services rendered by the machines to the voters whose support they solicit should not be forgotten. The poor immigrant is only following the example of his betters in giving his suffrage to those who help him most effectively.

THE PARTY CONVENTIONS

It only remains to deal with the party conventions, and with the primaries. The national Party Convention is the machine for selecting the Party Presidential candidate, and for drawing up the platform upon which the Presidential election has to be fought. As there is no difference between the policies of the two parties, the platform does

[1] Tammany Hall is, of course, much older than the party machinery as a whole. But it is, in effect, the Democratic machine in New York, and the organisation of other machines, though they receive less publicity, does not differ materially from that of Tammany.

not matter very much, though it is generally desirable to find an issue or two on which public feeling can be aroused and for which the other party can be blamed, as the Democrats in 1920 went down to defeat on Wilson's foreign policy, and the Republicans in 1932, with less real justification, on Hoover's failure to prevent or cure the slump. The interest lies in the choice of candidate, which is achieved by means of bargaining between the bosses who control big State blocks of delegates, coupled with an attempt by the delegates generally to "spot a winner," i.e. to choose a man whose personality enables him to be easily advertised to the innocent voter as a desirable Cæsar. Sometimes this procedure leads to the adoption of a candidate of real popularity on his popular merits, as Bryan in 1896 ran away with the Democratic nomination, though not with the Presidency; sometimes to the sliding-in of a harmless-looking creature to whom nobody objects, as happened in the nomination of Warren Gamaliel Harding. Occasionally it is found impossible to reach an agreement, and there is a split, involving a rival convention and a rival candidate at the elections, as Roosevelt I split with Taft in 1912; but these occasions are rare, and it is rare, also, for a separate party, except the Socialists, to run a convention and candidate of their own. The elder La Follette did so in 1924; but after his defeat his machine went back to its Republican home. The essential of the nominating convention is the bargaining with votes, and the arrival, by outward process of singing, shouting, and processions which seem odd to anyone used to the solemnities of English party procedure, at the choice of a candidate whom all factions can be induced to support. The above description relates to conventions for Presidential nominations; *mutatis mutandis,* what has been said applies also to conventions held for less august purposes.

THE PRIMARY

The primary, that peculiarly American institution, is more interesting. In essence, it is a means of introducing some element of public control into the choice of delegates to party conventions or party candidates for office, and derives its existence from the sectional character of the great parties. As, normally, in about half the States of the Union, one party is in permanent control, the candidates nominated by that party's machine are bound to carry the elections, and therefore, if a single boss, or a few bosses, are not to control all the offices, some means must be found of democratically influencing the choice of party candidates. This means is the party primary. Instead of the delegates to the national party convention and the party candidates for office being nominated, as they used to be, by local conventions, in all but a very few States it is now compulsory for the parties to hold preliminary elections, under State-made rules, at which the delegates or candidates are voted upon. The rules vary from State to State. There is generally some qualification, either the presentation of a large number of nominating papers, or the production of a party membership roll of some size, or the deposit or payment of a substantial sum, which is necessary before a candidate's name can appear on the primary list. Some States allow a candidate's name to go forward if he has a bare majority; others provide for a second ballot. Generally speaking, candidates defeated in the primaries may run at the election as independents if they choose.

The main difference arises between the forms of primary prescribed by States. In the open primaries of Wisconsin, Montana and Colorado, the primaries of all parties are held together, and the voter is given the ballot papers of all parties, and marks the one for which he intends (presumably) to vote. In the closed primaries, the voter can only take part in the primary of a single party; but the devices for securing that he is confined to his own primary vary from one of enrolment on the party register to a mere promise to vote for the party in the election—which obviously may or may not be fulfilled. One result of this is that in some States it is easy for the voter to assist in the choice of candidates for the opposite party, so that where a State is doubtfully Republican, for example, the Democratic voter may seek to serve his party by voting in the Republican primary for the most unpopular Republican candidate for governor, and *vice versa*. The extent to which primaries are used varies from State to State, some States using them even in the Presidential elections. They are on the whole a curious device, an attempt to bring back popular voting into a system which had almost managed to destroy it.

THE FUTURE OF AMERICAN POLITICS

The future of American politics, as has been said, is almost impossible to prophesy, for so much depends upon the development of economic forces which cannot be foreseen with any accuracy. At the time of writing, the curious two-party system which is practically a no-party system, but which effectively bars the creation of a party system, appears to be as firmly established as ever; and the fate of new parties and even of independent groups has not been happy. Even the combination which seems to have most economic *raison d'être,* that of the Western farmers with the city proletariat, both of whom suffer from financial manipulations and the depredations of big business, has not yet got very far. The Socialist Party continues to plough its lonely furrow; but, opposed by the boss-ridden machinery of Trade Unions belonging to the American Federation of Labor and composed largely of theoreticians and the foreign-born, it has hardly yet reached the position of British Socialism before the birth of the Labour Party; and at the present rate of progress, unless class-distinctions grow up with amazing rapidity, it will be years before it can hope to do more than capture a city here and there. Meantime the sheer expense and elaborateness of the party machines and their hold upon the electorate of all classes make the organisation of a new party far harder than it would be in any other country.

What the last year has shown, however, is that the apparent clumsiness, the checks and balances, of the American Constitution do not stand in the way of considerable changes nearly so much as had been thought. The American people can still, in the last resort, bend its political system to its will, or, at least, to the will of such members of it as can make themselves heard; but the instrument of that bending, it is important to observe, has been the President, not a party. It is not the Democratic Party, but Franklin Roosevelt, who has brought about the present changes; and his rule is therefore a popular dictatorship, which must, however, unless there is a break in a tradition which is as old as the Republic itself, come automatically to an end in six years' time at longest. The remarkable flexibility which the Roosevelt organisation has shown does not essentially affect the main issue, whatever its interest for students of political machinery. Whether there will be a break, whether the Roosevelt policies will result in a real re-alignment of political forces on a basis of real political differences, and, further, whether any progress will be made meanwhile towards the solving of such basic and permanent problems of American life as the negro question and the economic position of the farmers and the wage-labour which is now beginning to recognise that it can never hope to rise to wealth and position, can only be a matter of conjecture.

5. THE POLITICAL SYSTEM OF ITALY

IT IS NOT PART of the purpose of this chapter to discuss the rights and wrongs of the methods employed by the Fascists in seizing power in Italy. These, ever since 1923, have been the theme of innumerable books and pamphlets in which the details can be studied. It is of course clear that the Fascists both gained and consolidated their power by means which violently shocked liberal opinion and which included both torture and mass terrorism, though on a smaller scale and with much less hideous accompaniment than in the case of the Nazi revolution in Germany. Mussolini came to power as the leader of a minority and for some time had to be careful not to rouse against himself the mass of the country. At one point, even, a single crime, the murder of Matteotti, was sufficient severely to shake his position. These facts, however, are not and never have been denied by Fascists; and their defence, when they see the necessity of making one, is not that they have not killed, imprisoned and banished their opponents, but that such action is both necessary and desirable and further that at least as many Fascists were killed in the early days by Communist and Socialist rioters. Under the circumstances, Fascism being now a comparatively established system, it is more profitable to discuss what circumstances facilitated its establishment and what are its intentions and performances than to enter into controversies about the exact degree of violence which its inception involved.

PRE-WAR ITALY

The Fascist Party arrived at power in Italy by the use of violent means to destroy a parliamentary Government of very great weakness. But Italian Parliaments had long been very weak, and sporadic recourse to violence, in the south particularly, had long been a feature of Italian political life. Except for its strength and cohesion there was nothing very new about *Fascismo* until it began to develop its new political creed. Italy, during the late nineteenth century in particular, was in the unhappy position of a country which had had forced upon it a *bourgeois* parliamentary system before it had developed in anything like sufficiency the *bourgeois* social and economic institutions which were necessary to sustain it. Italy in 1860 was a country of deep poverty and a very high percentage of illiteracy. It had little industry, and, in the absence of coal, no means of developing it. Furthermore, its agriculture was at a very low state of productivity, and large areas which ought to have contributed highly to production were unable to do so without the aid of great and expensive improvements. The agricultural system—or rather systems, for there were many—were not at all satisfactory, including on the one hand minute holdings too small to support a family and with no reserve for improvement, and on the other the vast estates of the south, and Sicily in particular, deriving from the *latifundia* of Roman times, owned by absentee landlords and farmed by bailiffs who administered some of the most degraded and poverty-stricken labour in Europe. To this should be added that Italy was then, and for long remained, in effect two countries with different climates and habits—the north, containing the bulk of industry, the most prosperous farmers, and the most highly educated individuals, and the south, agricultural, poor and illiterate, and retaining much of the manners and customs of medieval times.

The coming of the Kingdom of Italy did nothing to alter any of these factors. The change was a political and not a social one. There was, for example, no attempt made to redistribute the land and create a numerous independent peasantry as in France after 1789. Actually the cost of the wars of liberation and of the absolutely necessary elements of unification such as railroad building added greatly to the economic burdens of a struggling country. Little was done to alleviate the tension between north and south, and to this tension had to be added, particularly after the capture of Rome in 1870, the steady sullen hostility of the Catholic Church and the personnel of the Vatican to the new State. For more than forty years after the establishment of the Kingdom, Italian Catholics were either forbidden to vote or discouraged from voting, and in a country whose population is so overwhelmingly Catholic these instructions, even if not obeyed, were a perpetual source of friction.

It might have been economically more fortunate for Italy if the new Kingdom had been able to become a "benevolent despotism" and to put financial and industrial development under a strong hand for a time. However, the movement for Italian liberation had been carried on under the direction of Mazzini and the nineteenth-century Liberals, and the Constitution which was now extended to the whole of Italy was that granted in 1848 by Charles Albert of Savoy to his subjects, i.e. a constitutional monarchy with a Senate and an elected Chamber, the franchise for the Chamber being fairly restricted at first, though a series of extensions had turned it into manhood suffrage by the time that the parliamentary régime fell.

But with a *bourgeoisie* few in numbers and an illiterate peasantry, the materials wherewith to work a parliamentary system were lacking. For the time a Conservative oligarchy succeeded in holding together and in governing with moderate success. But after its fall in 1876 there was nothing to take its place but a confusion of corrupt and unprincipled groups of the "Left," which ran the country into debt, plundered the public funds, changed sides in whole or in part with perfect readiness, and generally encouraged in the country a system of corruption and rigging of elections which would have done credit to the worst governed American city. They even developed, in such institutions as the Camorra in Naples, a type of gangster which could provide an example for any racketeer. The real evil, however, lay not in the iniquities of particular politicians, but in the absence of any solid basis, economic or political, for the parliamentary system.

Before the war, indeed, there had grown up a fairly strong Socialist Party in Italy, which had earned for itself the reputation of being the most disinterested and least corrupt of the parties of the Left. It was, however, violently opposed by the Catholic Church, and it further suffered from disagreements within its own ranks. Italian Labour had always had large Syndicalist elements; strikes were frequent, and a part of the Italian Trade Union movement was strongly Syndicalist. There was always, in the Italian Socialist Party, a latent disagreement between the revolutionary and reformist elements, and this broke out in a split over the seizure of Tripoli in 1912, and again, more violently, over Italy's entry into the European war, which was supported by some of those, including Mussolini, who had been most hotly opposed to the Tripoli adventure. The bulk of the Socialists remained against the war, and as time went on grew more and more revolutionary. But as Socialist strength grew, so the

Church organised in opposition to it. Even before the war the ban on voting by Catholics had to all intents and purposes been removed; and after it was over, the Socialists found themselves confronted with a Catholic political party of strength almost equal to their own—the *Popolari,* based mainly on the southern peasantry, and led by Don Sturzo.

The existence of the *Popolari* made it impossible for the Italian Socialists to make a revolution on the Russian or French model with peasant support, and no real collaboration was possible between two parties whose principles were so widely apart. It was this stalemate between the only two parties of any strength or respectability and the consequent breakdown of all administration, coupled with an "inferiority complex" of very long growth among the Italian people, that made possible Mussolini's *coup d'état.*

For the young Italian Kingdom, in addition to all its other troubles, aspired to be a member of the Concert of Europe on equal terms with such long-established and wealthy States as Great Britain, France, and Austria-Hungary. It was conscious of a past at least as brilliant as that of any of its neighbours. It had been assured by romantic friends of the *Risorgimento* of its high destiny and innate abilities, which were only awaiting the moment of liberation from Hapsburg and Bourbon tyranny to blossom;[1] it believed these assurances and set out, on the morrow of its emancipation, to "commence Great Power" on a totally inadequate income—only to find, as the Irish have found at a later date, that while a country in chains may be admired and romanticised, the same country liberated is apt to be regarded merely as a nuisance. The story of Italian diplomacy before the war is largely the story of a succession of fruitless attempts to obtain a real recognition of equality from the Great Powers, and a different series of attempts, equally fruitless, but more disastrous because more expensive, to found an Italian colonial empire which could be matched with the British or the French. Italy is the only Power to have met with a really serious and lasting defeat in African imperial enterprise,[2] and even Tripoli, snatched in haste from a Turkish Empire already collapsing and involved in struggles with its own subjects, has been to date more of a liability than an asset.

[1] See, for example, Swinburne's *Songs before Sunrise,* Meredith's *Vittoria,* and much literature of a similar kind.

[2] In 1896, at the battle of Adowa in Abyssinia.

THE WAR AND THE FASCISTI

Such was the mood in which Italy entered the European war, largely as a result of balancing the offers made to her by either side, and hoping to find that in the end, if the wild promises of the Allies were fulfilled, she would at last be a really great Power. But the experiences of the war were disappointing. Not only did the Italian army undergo the great Caporetto defeat, which caused the Allies to lecture Italy very severely, and for which the final driving off of the Austrian army did little to compensate; not only did Italy suffer very heavily from war privations accentuated by maladministration; the Peace Treaties also signally failed to fulfil the promises made earlier. Italy got none of the German colonies, nor any part of Asia Minor, and on her north-eastern frontier she obtained far less than she desired, and had also to watch the new State of Yugoslavia extending itself along the Dalmatian coast. At one point, in fury, the Italian delegates actually withdrew from the proceedings at Versailles, and President Wilson's attempt to appeal to the Italian people over the heads of their representatives aroused bitter resentment. D'Annunzio's seizure of Fiume in 1919 was only a spectacular example of the feeling of anger and frustration which was one of the results of the Peace Conference. These circumstances, coupled with the breakdown of home government, gave the Fascists their opportunity. The first *Fascio di Combattimento* was founded in March 1919 by Mussolini and other Socialists who had supported the war. To begin with, its programme was Socialist, though not Communist; but it was, even at that date, both nationalist and anti-pacifist, and its main first source of membership was the discontented ex-soldiers, though it also came to include an increasing number of peasants and members of the *petite bourgeoisie*. It supported certain of the strikes and peasant risings of the years 1919–1920; but it was at variance with the official Socialists because of their leanings towards Russian Communism.

The first two years of the existence of the Fascists were full of strikes and disturbances, culminating in the seizure of the factories by the metal-workers in the autumn of 1920. When this last movement collapsed, as it was bound to do unless the Socialists were prepared to embark on positive revolutionary action, the way was open for the Fascists. It was clear that the Socialists and the *Popolari* could govern neither separately nor in combination; and the nominal Governments grew more and more powerless. Under these circumstances, the Fascists, reinforced in 1921 by D'Annunzio, took up a definitely anti-Socialist attitude,[1] and there were several preliminary skirmishes between the two parties in cities such as Bologna—skirmishes in which the better-organised and more ruthless party generally won. In the elections of 1921, the Fascists returned 35 deputies; and in the autumn of 1922 this party, small in the Chamber, but strong in the country, decided on a *coup d'état*. Their policy had been already modified so as to secure the support of the large employers and the army chiefs, and the support of the army forced the King's hand. With the King not daring, even if he wished, to proclaim martial law, the March on Rome became a safe venture, and Mussolini was in power, though with a nominal opposition still so large that he had to walk cautiously at first, and it was not until 1928, for example, that he ventured to make actual changes in the composition of the Parliament from which he had already taken away all real power. The Fascists did not, as some of their propaganda suggests, "deliver Italy from a Socialist revolution," for the likelihood of that had passed long before the *coup d'état;* what they did was to rescue the country from having no government at all.

When we have described the present political system, we shall deal with the general policy of *Fascismo*. It should, however, be emphasised at this point that, whatever the present policy, it has no continuity at all with that of the past. The first programme of the original *Fasci di Combattimento* was almost indistinguishable from that of any left-wing Socialist body in any country. It was republican, feminist, anti-clerical, and in favour of socialisation and a liberal international policy. All these elements have long since disappeared from *Fascismo,* and the special contribution which it is now endeavouring to make to political theory, i.e. the idea of the Corporative State, derives not from earlier Fascist programmes, but in part from the teachings of Hegel, and in part from the pre-war ideas of the Christian Socials (of whom Dr. Dollfuss may be taken as an example) and possibly to some extent from Mussolini's own past leanings towards Syndicalism. The only item of its policy to which Fascism has held consistently true is its nationalism. Even in its early days the internationalism which it advocated was not an interna-

---

[1] The Socialists themselves split in the summer of 1921 and again in October 1922.

tionalism of the Communist type, but a federal internationalism based on sovereign States. For the rest, the body of theory which now goes by the name of *Fascismo* has been built up largely by Mussolini himself in the course of the development of his party in action. It may be said very definitely of *Fascismo,* in sharp contrast to Communism, that it did not know what it thought until it saw what it had done.

THE PRESENT CONSTITUTION

Although Fascism is one of the most definite political systems in Europe, and although it has been in power in Italy for twelve years, the actual constitution of the country of its origin is still to some extent in a transitional state. As has been already said, Mussolini came to power not, like Hitler, as the result of a large popular vote, but as the leader of a small minority. He has therefore been unable to proceed more than a step at a time, and while those steps have certainly been drastic they have not up to the present resulted in the complete transformation of the Italian State into a Corporative Society. Accordingly the formal framework of the State is still the Constitution of 1848, though the changes in working made under the Fascist régime have in practice altered it almost out of recognition.

Italy is still, then, in form a constitutional monarchy. The King is the final power in the State, and it is the King who appoints and dismisses the Head of the State, who is also Prime Minister and Secretary of State, and, upon his suggestion, the other Ministers. The law of December 1925, however, contains certain provisions relating to the Head of the State which serve to differentiate his position sharply from that of the Prime Minister in the parliamentary countries. It is there provided, for example, that no proposal can be submitted to either Chamber without the concurrence of the Head of the State, and that he can re-submit to the Chambers proposals which have been rejected, and special penalties are laid down for anyone who makes an attempt on the life, integrity or liberty of the Head of the State. The Head of the State may also hold, in addition to his own office, the portfolios of any number of Ministries, and in practice much of Mussolini's power is actually derived from such concentration.

There is a Senate, which is now of practically no importance; it consists of princes of the royal blood who have attained their majority plus a number of life members nominated by the King from persons of over forty years of age who have attained celebrity by one means or another. As there is no legal limit to the number of Senators, it would be possible for the Government at any moment to pack it to any extent. In practice, however, it has never been found necessary to do so.

The Chamber of Deputies also remains, but the electoral law of 1928 has turned that Chamber into a body quite different from any other parliamentary Chamber in the world. Under that law the whole country forms a single constituency, choosing 400 deputies, but the choice is not free. The Fascist Grand Council compiles the list of names from nominations sent into it by the thirteen National Confederations of employers and workers (see below) and by certain other associations. It has the right to add other nominations of its own, and has used this right, according to the most recent study of the system, to increase the proportion of Fascists and members of the upper classes who appear on the list. The list of 400 so compiled is presented as a whole to the electors, who have the right to vote for or against but not for any alternative list. In the extremely improbable event of the Grand Council's list being rejected, a procedure which also requires nominations to be submitted in the first instance through associations is laid down for fresh elections. In the two elections, however (1929 and 1934), which have been held under the new law, in the first ninety and the second ninety-six per cent of the entire electorate voted the Fascist list, and it may be regarded as certain that while the Fascist régime endures and as long as the Chamber of Deputies is permitted to exist, the Fascist Grand Council will in fact nominate its members. The right to vote is possessed by all Italian citizens over twenty-one (or over eighteen if married with children) who either contribute to, or are in the service of, a syndicate or association recognised under the law of 1926, or pay at least 100 lire a year in direct taxation, or are priests, or employees of the State, or of a Commune. The actual vote, however, matters little, and will matter progressively less as the Fascist State proceeds further in the direction of "Corporativeness." The present position of the Chamber is a curious half-way house, and Mussolini has announced his intention of superseding it altogether when his projected corporate institutions are in full being. In the meantime it is actually a body of slight importance, for the real direction of policy rests with the Fascist Grand Council, working through the present corporate institutions and the Fascist Party. Both the Grand Council and the Party are now regulated by a law of December 1929.

The Grand Council consists (a) of four life members, the quadrumvirs of the March on Rome (i.e. Mussolini and three others), (b) of certain persons holding important offices, such as the principal Ministers of State, the Secretary of the Fascist Party, the Head of the Fascist Militia and the Presidents of the National Confederations, (c) of persons nominated by the Head of the State, as a reward for good service, for a period of three years with possibility of renewal. There is no limit to the numbers of this third category. It will be seen, therefore, that the Grand Council is mainly nominated by the Head of the State himself. The Fascist Party has a General Secretary, a Directory or governing body, and local secretaries, all of whom are nominated directly by the Head of the State.

The system of provincial administration has been reorganised by the Fascists and is now highly centralised. The general plan is much the same as that of France, but the central control is naturally very much stronger. Each province is under a *Podestà* corresponding to the French *Préfet,* who is appointed by the Government and directly responsible to it, with very wide powers for the preservation of order. There are also provincial "Rectorates" taking the place of the former provincial Councils. Their functions are purely advisory. They are appointed by royal decree, i.e. in effect by the Head of the State, and their deliberations are private. This does not mean that they have no effect on the proceedings of the *Podestà,* particularly where their membership is composed of tried Fascists, but that, outside the Fascist Party, there is no popular control or criticism in local affairs.

THE CORPORATIVE SYSTEM

We must now turn to the special contribution of *Fascismo* to political practice, which is the Corporative System. This system is based essentially upon the idea that the representation of functions provides a better basis for government than the general representation of individuals which was established by the nineteenth-century parliamentary system. It is an idea which Fascism shares with Guild Socialism, and with Syndicalism. But its application of the idea is made radically different because of its deliberate preservation of social classes. The intention is that the whole of the economic life of Italy and much of what we should call its political life shall be directed by a system of Corporations representing workers, employers and independent professionals in all industries and services. Until the summer of this year only one Corporation, the Corporation of the Stage, had been formed, and the National Council of Corporations, though it had come into existence, contained no representatives of Corporations but only a number of members from other bodies which were considered of sufficient importance to be represented on it.[1] At its head was placed a Minister of Corporations, who was Mussolini himself, and whose functions included general direction of industry, commerce, labour and social insurance. But the Council itself acted only as an advisory body and an organ of discussion. It was given power to issue regulations, but in most cases only at the request of the Minister of Corporations; and though some Fascist writers desired this power to be rapidly extended, Mussolini was very cautious in extending it. The really operative bodies, therefore, were the Syndical Associations of Workers and Employers, united in thir-teen[2] National Confederations of which six represented workers, six employers, and one professions. We have already met these Confederations as bodies which nominate candidates for parliamentary elections. Within the Confederations there are National Associations, Provincial Associations, and Local Associations, and it is worthy of note that legal recognition is not given to the local association of the workers but only to the Provincial Association. Local workers' associations are not bodies recognised at law.

The Syndical Associations are those which are recognised by the State, which has the right to lay down certain provisions with regard to their rules and objects. The objects of most associations, for example, must contain definite professions of Fascist faith. The officials of the associations must also be Fascists. Even when these conditions are fulfilled recognition does not necessarily follow automatically. The State still retains its right not to recognise any particular association. When an association is formed and recognised it becomes the association for the whole of the category of workers or employers covered by it, and all engaged in this occupation must pay a contribu-

---

[1] For recent developments relating to the Corporations, see the end of this chapter.
[2] To be reduced to nine when the latest decree comes into force.

tion to it whether they are members or not.[1] Membership of the association involves the payment of a further fee, though not necessarily a regular contribution, and carries with it certain privileges of which the right to participate in the assembly for the election of officials is one. Democratic voting is thus preserved by the Fascist State in the Corporative institutions, though even here there is considerable control by appointed officials and the State has the right to refuse to accept the election of a particular official. Membership is not freely open to all. Only persons of suitable moral and political character are admitted, and it is laid down that the associations are to concern themselves with the conduct of their members in matters not strictly relating to their occupations—as in England the British Medical Association's canons of "professional conduct" seem to relate mainly to actions which most people would not suppose were particularly connected with professional ability.

The main function of the Syndical Associations is to draw up the collective contracts under which Italian economic life is now regulated. There has to be a collective contract for each industry or service; and this collective contract, once made, is binding upon all who take part in the service, whether members of the associations or not. The scope of the collective contracts goes well beyond the mere question of wages. They do regulate wages and hours and holidays; they also regulate the conditions of employment, circumstances under which dismissal is allowed, and arrangements for unemployment insurance and for pay during sickness. They are made for four years at a time and renewed or revised at the end of the period. As is well known, strikes and lockouts are absolutely forbidden. Disputes which arise in industry are dealt with either by the ordinary courts or by the special labour courts. The associations also discuss matters connected with the industry and pay contributions to the expenses of such social institutions as the *Opera Nazionale Dopolavoro,* the maternity and child welfare institutes, and technical schools. There are provincial corporate Economic Councils which consist of representatives from the Employers' and Workers' Syndicates in the province and are discussive bodies, taking for the present the place of the provincial Corporations which are intended to be set up when the

---

[1] In practice, a much higher proportion of workers than of employers are members of their Syndical Associations.

National Corporations come into being. Up to the present time, at any rate, the whole system is avowedly and deliberately built upon class associations.

FASCIST POLICY IN PRACTICE

The institutions of *Fascismo* have been set out above in the barest possible terms. Certain other features of the régime, such as the suppression of opposition parties and the stern Press censorship, extending so far as to bring pressure upon communities of Italians living outside Italy, e.g. in the United States, will occur to everyone. But these, like the extensive programme of public works upon which the régime has embarked, are not so much features of the Constitution as of the working policy of *Fascismo,* to which we must now turn.

As has been said, the political theory of *Fascismo* is largely empirical, having been worked out *ambulando,* and it will therefore be convenient if for the moment we leave the more formulated doctrine as expressed in Mussolini's speeches and articles on one side and set out the main points of Fascist policy as exemplified in its actions to date.

Fascist policy, then, is monarchical, in that it recognizes and perpetuates the monarchy and professes to derive the authority of all Ministers, including that of the Head of the State himself, immediately from the royal source. Beyond this, it is also highly autocratic. The chief officers of State are expressly to be appointed by the Head of the State, and neither in the Fascist Grand Council nor in the Fascist Party is there any pretence of democratic election. There is, as we have seen, a certain amount of democracy in the Syndical Associations; whether this will be extended to the Corporations and whether it will be a free or a sternly controlled democracy must be a matter for conjecture. At present the control of Italian life rests with the Fascist Party, and the control of the Fascist Party with Mussolini, whose dictatorship has much more of a legal basis than, for example, that of Kemal in Turkey.

Fascismo is also clerical, in the sense that since the Concordat of 1929 it has definitely come to terms with the Catholic Church. In this respect Mussolini has succeeded in doing what all previous rulers of Italy have failed to do—enlisting the active support of the Church on his side though there is still some bickering between them. Exactly what this will involve in the future is not yet quite clear, but it seems obvious that the State will have to pay for the Concordat by at any rate upholding the social views of the Catholic Church upon such questions as private property and the position of women. At the moment of writing Church and State appear to be happily in accord on both these points. Fascism is anti-feminist in the sense in which the word is commonly understood in Western Europe. That is to say, it endeavours to confine women to the occupations connected with replenishing and preserving the population, to prevent them from entering into competition with men, and generally to preserve and even to accentuate the differences between the sexes.[1] Furthermore, it is now avowedly committed to maintaining both the institution of private property and the existing alignment of classes. Mussolini does not recognise the absolute right of private property owners in the sense in which it was put forward by the extreme individualists of the nineteenth century—in which he is at one with the medieval tradition of the Church. He will not, in so far as he has the power, allow private property owners to act in a manner contrary to the interests of the State. But, subject to that proviso, *Fascismo* upholds private property and has even been at pains to declare that the setting up of certain State institutions, such as the *Istituto Mobiliare,* which might seem to impinge on the rights of property owners, is not intended to be in the remotest degree a step towards socialisation.

Even more definite is the preservation of social classes. The very idea of the Corporative system rests upon the fundamental principle that the classes of employers and workers are fixed and differentiated for ever and can only be harmonised but not destroyed by the State. And the special provision, such as the system of *Dopolavoro,* which the Fascist State makes for the employed class is again based on this idea of differentiation. In this respect, therefore, the Fascist ideal is fundamentally opposed to that of Socialism, which is based upon the equality of men. Equality, to a Fascist, is a dangerous and nonsensical chimera. To him functionalism and functional representation presuppose the continued existence of inequality.

That the Fascist ideal is nationalist is almost too much of a truism to state. What exactly this means and how far it implies imperialism as well as nationalism in the strict sense is examined elsewhere. Suffice it to say for the moment that *Fascismo* knows and recognises no authority higher than that of the national State and that it demands on the one hand that the national State shall act in the best interests

[1] See, for example, Mussolini's regulation of immodest attire for Italian women.

of the people as a whole, and expects on the other that the people will individually and collectively live in and for the State.

THE THEORY OF FASCISMO

For the last main characteristic of *Fascismo* is that it is *étatiste* in the most extreme sense, or, in its own jargon, totalitarian. And this point leads us from our objective observation of *Fascismo* in action to a consideration of its present ideals as expounded by its Head. To the Mussolini of to-day the State is not, as to the nineteenth-century individualist, a nuisance inevitably attendant upon collective life, or even, as to the Russian Communist, a necessary instrument of transition to a new social order. It is a mystical conception which at once completes and transcends the individual. "The State," he says, "becomes the conscience and will of the people"; and again, "it is the State which shapes individuals to civic virtue, which makes them conscious of their social purposes, and which leads them to unity. The State harmonises their interests in a system of justice. The State spreads the triumphs of intellect throughout the domain of science, of art, of law, and of humanity; it raises mankind from the simple life of the tribe to the highest human expression of power, which is empire. It hands down through the ages the names of those who perished in preserving it or obeying its commands, and it presents as examples to the generations to come the captains who widened its boundaries and the men of genius who crowned it with glory. Where the love of the State grows faint, and dissolvent and centrifugal tendencies of individuals and groups grow strong, there nations are advancing to death."[1]

This conception of the State, it will be seen, is highly mystical as well as idealist. In part it is derived from Hegel, whose conception of the Nation-State provided the basis for most of the reactionary political philosophies of nineteenth-century Europe. But in borrowing from Hegel, Fascism has taken the reactionary part of his doctrine—that which relates to the nature of the State—and left out his dynamic treatment of human history. The Hegelian Dialectic, which to many is Hegel's real and fruitful contribution to philosophy, is nowhere to be found in Mussolini. The "Totalitarianism" of *Fascismo* is really a simpler idea than Hegel's complex conception. Its derivation can be seen partly in the passionate popular nationalism that was taught to Europe by the soldiers of the French Revolution, and partly,

[1] Mussolini, *Il Fascismo*.

to go even further back, in the City-State patriotism of Ancient Greece. There are phrases in the funeral speech of Pericles that have something in common with the words of Mussolini quoted above. But besides these semi-conscious derivations, there is also in Fascist nationalism an element which is wholly irrational—an element akin to family or tribal loyalty, which is simply the instinct to try and find the strongest group for mutual defence against the storm. The world to-day is full of storms, economic and political. The Fascist, and still more the Nazi, is to a certain extent proclaiming and exalting what appears to be the safest unit of shelter against them—which is to-day the Nation-State. The *sacre egoismo* about which Mussolini used at one time to talk so much is at bottom little more than tribal solidarity grown aggressive.

Be this as it may, the full Fascist creed demands of every citizen complete and active loyalty to the State. "Nothing without the State; nothing against the State; nothing beyond the State." The citizen can feel no loyalty which is superior or which conflicts: if he does, he is *ipso facto* a bad citizen. It is this belief which has enabled Mussolini to launch without fear his Corporative programme. The Corporative institutions are only the machinery of administration. It is believed by the Fascists that they are actually better instruments than any parliamentary or similar institutions based upon representation of individuals. But the whole possibility of their working as they are intended to do and not developing particularist policies of their own, depends upon the belief that the State will always transcend and control them. In Mussolini's view, his is the one Government in the world which could safely encourage the formation of large capitalist trusts[1] and of all-embracing Trade Unions because his is the one Government which can effectively lay down the functions of these bodies and see that they do not overstep them. The comparative weakness of capitalist combination in Italy and the fact that the pre-existing Trade Unions were all destroyed and replaced by Unions under direct Fascist control has given a certain amount of colour to his contention.

ORGANISATION OF FASCISMO

This idea of the State has an obvious appeal to youth, and especially to vigorous youth, which wants to be up and doing, as well as to the many who find balanced loyalties and conflicting obligations

[1] Though in practice Fascism has supported the small employer to a certain extent.

very hard to endure and are always yearning after a single authority or creed which shall satisfy all their demands and answer all their questions. The internal propaganda and discipline of *Fascismo,* also, are in many ways admirably fitted to drive home its ideal. The complete control of the Press ensures that none but Fascist doctrines are spread among the people, and it is reinforced by the Fascist control of popular education. Further the Fascist Party itself is exceedingly carefully picked and trained. There are ancillary organisations of youth and children (as in the parallel case of Russia) which are busy training up young Fascists, and there are special Fascist institutions such as the educational bodies and the Fascist militia which provide ample means of using the particular talents of the Fascist party member to the best advantage. It must be admitted by any impartial observer that Mussolini, at the price of crushing out liberal and dissentient opinion and of practically forbidding spontaneous combination, has succeeded in enlisting the active and eager co-operation of a great many Italians, with results which are clearly visible in such matters as public health and general efficiency. To this general appreciation of what Fascism has achieved, however, three qualifications, all of great importance, must be made. The first relates to the position of Mussolini himself, which is one of complete and absolute dictatorship. Mussolini has made the very existence of the Italian State depend upon himself in practice by keeping in his own hands the principal Ministries, himself making the principal appointments and allowing no rival near the throne;[1] in theory by associating his own personality in everybody's minds directly with the State itself. "A dictatorship," said one of his strongest supporters, "is a very different matter when you all love the dictator." Possibly; but if the dictator is mortal it is not so certain that everyone will love his successor. It may be that the system now being built up is strong enough to find a successor to Mussolini, and to function even if that successor be a much weaker man. But in any event this system, like any other system of individual autocracy, puts the policy and welfare of the country at the mercy of a single brain.

The second point is the affection shown by Fascism for violence. This is not merely a question of violence committed in the course of accession to power, or even as a means of consolidation of power. It is inherent in the Fascist creed. "Fascism," says Mussolini, "believes

[1] See, for example, the supersession of General Balbo last year.

neither in the possibility nor in the desirability of perpetual peace";
it envisages life in terms of continued struggle and it appeals throughout to a combination of faith and force rather than to reason. Mussolini asks his supporters to "think with their blood and not with their
brains"—i.e. in effect, not to think at all. For this reason Fascism is
a world-wide factor making for violence and "hundred-per-centism"
and against rationality, argument, tolerance and willingness to come
to terms with opponents, and it is significant that wherever Fascist
parties have appeared in other countries their immediate and loudest
appeal has always been to force of the most direct and simple kind.

Finally there is the difficulty inherent in all mystical conceptions
of the Nation-State, that the perfect Nation-State can only exist in a
world all by itself. If there is to be nothing beyond or outside the
State that State must exist to and for itself alone. It cannot recognise
the rights of any other State. In fact to be logical it cannot even
recognise the existence of any other State. To this extent the idea of
Fascism in power in a single State out of many is unrealistic—a contradiction in terms. And this lack of realism produces very dangerous
results in the world of to-day. Nobody can possibly predict what a
Fascist State will do in the international field. For the international
field, as it presents itself to a supporter of the League of Nations, for
example, is something of which, from its own premises, the Totalitarian State is unable to take cognisance. It can only really regard
other nations either as inventions of the devil, like Communist Russia, or as tribes which have not yet attained to the dignity of statehood. Furthermore, what is to happen when the perfect Totalitarian
State is confronted, not with a Communist State or a liberal parliamentary democracy, but with another perfect Totalitarian State
claiming a similar uniqueness of authority? What happens, in fact,
when Mussolini's Italy meets Hitler's Germany?[1] *Sacre egoismo* then
shares the fate of the principle advocated by some educationalists
that the child must on no account be thwarted, and discovers the
difficulty of applying that policy in a family which contains more
than one child.

It is true that up to the time of writing these words, the extreme
has not yet happened. Fascism has not set out to conquer the world
in arms, and Mussolini has for some years in fact behaved with great

[1] The Nazis may in fact be influenced more by Spengler than by Hegel, but the
essence of their claims is the same.

circumspection, at any rate as regards the greater Powers. He has not, except in the single case of Corfu, invaded the territory of other States and has even remained in connection with the League of Nations. But his real view of the function of the Fascist State in the world may perhaps be gathered from the following brief passage: "One can conceive an Empire, that is to say a nation, which shall directly or indirectly guide other nations without this necessitating the conquest of a square kilometre of territory." This is an almost exact description of Mussolini's recent policy with regard to Austria, and the result of this combined with the beginnings of a clash of one *sacre egoismo* against another can be read over the bodies of the workers of Vienna.

THE FUTURE OF FASCISMO

What is to be the future of the Fascist system? In the last resort, of course, the length of time for which Fascism will endure depends upon how far the system of Fascist education and propaganda can sustain the theory of the Fascists that the idea of nationality transcends class distinctions. Undoubtedly at the moment the Fascist system is popular in the country of its origin. Even the most bitterly hostile *émigrés* admit that if a free vote of the people were taken in Italy to-day, Mussolini would be triumphantly put back in power. This support has, of course, been secured in part by crushing all minorities and by deliberate indoctrination of the people, particularly the young. But it must be said that it is also based on certain tangible advantages which Fascism has given to the people. It is true that when Mussolini seized power the country was in such a state of political and economic chaos that it would have been hardly possible for any settled government not to introduce some improvement, and some of the improvements of Fascism, the cleansing and tidying up of administration and the stimulation of production and of productive efficiency, are improvements which in this sense can be called obvious. Fascism, however, has done more than that. It has made a very great and in some respects successful effort to improve public health and the housing condition of the workers, and has given also to some of them unemployment benefit, and to more comparative security in their jobs, and various provisions for education and amusement which are considerably in advance of what has been done in the parliamentary countries. The effects of collective contracts have been to steady and to a certain extent to level up the rates of the worst-paid workers. All this has meant a good deal to the Italian worker, even if the unemployment pay is very tiny, and Mussolini's public works programme and the existence of bodies like the Fascist militia have meant that in practice some of the unemployment consequent upon the slump has been mitigated. All these have so far tended to keep the worker from active discontent at the fact that wage levels have really fallen under the new administration. But no State that is not wholly self-contained can save its workers from the effects of general economic conditions. Italy has felt the slump badly, and the great efforts to balance trade returns have naturally tended to reduce the standard of life. Much of Mussolini's original support was derived from the smaller employers and small proprietors, and though he has up to the present been able to help the large industrialists in addition, there is no certainty that his small supporters will for ever feel that community of interest with the large employers or with the workers on which he relies. Quite apart, then, from what might happen in the event of war, it is not at all certain that fundamental contradictions will not develop within the framework of the Totalitarian State—that, in effect, the class struggle which Mussolini claims to have liquidated will not again appear in another form if economic conditions worsen, which is particularly possible in view of the high birth rate, the decline in emigration, and the effect of the reduced death rates which any attempts at sanitation are bound to produce. On one occasion already (in 1928) a National Syndicate of workers in all industries was dissolved because it developed "revolutionary Syndicalist," i.e. class-conscious, tendencies; and what has happened once may happen again.

NOTE. The most recent law relating to the Corporations was published in the *Gazzetta Uffiziale* in February 1934, and according to speeches made by Mussolini while this book was passing through the press, is to come into force immediately. At the same time, there is to be a considerable regrouping of occupations, so that the economic system of Italy will henceforward be ideologically perfect, or, as Mussolini likes to say, will form a "great tree of production." This involves the regrouping of the Syndicates into nine instead of thirteen Confederations.

The constitution of each several Corporation is to be laid down by decree of the Head of the State, on the proposition of the Minister of Corporations and the Central Committee of the National Council of Corporations. The President of the Corporation must be a Minister or the secretary of the Fascist Party, and the number, nature, and representation of its constituent bodies must be approved by decree of the Head of the State; it is thus hoped to secure that the Corporations will conform in all respects to the wishes of the State. Exactly how the Corporations are to be constituted is not yet perfectly clear; they are to be based upon associations of employers and workers, which appears at the time of writing to mean the Fascist Syndicates. But the National Confederations have no part in them, and, while the new law expressly allows the Confederations to remain in being, it does not seem to view them with favour, presumably because they may have a tendency to become organisations of class. The Corporations are to have general powers over productive discipline, certain price-fixing powers, and functions of conciliation in case of disputes over the collective contracts; and it is clear, from Mussolini's speeches, that the intention is to develop as rapidly as possible their legislative functions. The National Council of Corporations remains in being for the present; but the Head of the State has power to alter its constitution.

6. THE POLITICAL SYSTEM OF GERMANY

NAZI GERMANY presents a baffling problem for anyone who attempts to give a simple explanation of its political system; for it is still quite impossible to predict either what the final structure of the new German Reich will be or on what principles its policy will ultimately be based. The Nazi political system is still in process of rapid evolution, and there exist within the party which has made itself the exclusive master of the new Germany currents of policy so divergent as to defy confident prophecy. Nevertheless, where much is utterly uncertain, some things do stand out plainly, and it seems best to devote the greater part of this necessarily brief chapter to those features of the Nazi system and policy which appear to be relatively fixed and permanent.

Among these things the most obvious is that the new Germany is intensely and aggressively nationalist. Nationalism was strong in the pre-war German Empire, for Bismarck's creation stood above all else for the notion of German unity. But Hitler's Empire goes far beyond Bismarck's in its emphasis on national solidarity, and the Nazis have already accomplished a measure of German political unification of which Bismarck and the Hohenzollerns were only able to dream. Pre-war Germany was a federation of largely autonomous States, each with its own dynasty or individual form of government; and all the smaller States, from Bavaria downwards, were jealous of the Prussian leadership, even while they accepted it as the necessary condition of German union. But the Nazis, within a few weeks of assuming office, had accomplished what Bismarck had never dared even to attempt, by destroying entirely the independence of the Governments of the separate German States and establishing over all Germany the single authority of the Reich. The separate States still exist, but they have become under the Nazis mere administrative units within which the policy laid down by the dominant party is applied without question under the authority of governors appointed by the central Government. Nor can it be taken for certain that even this shadow of the separate States will long survive, for the Nazis are clearly determined to break up the territorial divisions within Germany so thoroughly as to make their restoration by any subsequent change of government as difficult as they possibly can.

The ill-fated Weimar Republic established after the war prepared the way for this decisive unification of the German Reich; for when the reigning families of the separate States shared the fate of the Hohenzollerns, the chief obstacle to national unification was at once removed. The provincial republican Governments could put no such barriers in the way of centralisation as existed when rulers claiming hereditary rights sat on the thrones of the numerous German States. Moreover, the Weimar Constitution itself greatly expanded the functions and powers of the Central Government and—most important of all—largely centralised the control of finance. Under the Republic the constituent States, or *Lände,* received their revenues mainly by way of grants out of the proceeds of national taxation, and this system went a long way towards undermining their effective autonomy. In destroying the Weimar Republic the Nazis were able to inherit and to push much further its centralising tendency, so as to make of Germany for the first time a single and thoroughly unified State as far as its machinery of administration was concerned. It does not, of course, follow, that the Nazis have been equally successful in stamping out separatist feeling, which undoubtedly retains a strong hold over a large part of South Germany, despite the ease with which the Governments of Bavaria and the other southern States crumpled up in the face of the Nazi attack.

THE NAZI MOVEMENT

This process of political unification was inherent in the Nazi movement, which was essentially a reassertion of German nationhood against the humiliations imposed on Germany under the Versailles Treaty. The Weimar Republic, born out of Germany's defeat in the war, and fatally compromised by its attempts at "fulfilment" of the obligations imposed by the Treaty, became in the eyes of patriotic Germans the symbol of national impotence and humiliation. The Nazis were finally raised to power under the intense pressure of economic distress arising out of the world crisis; but it is unlikely that they would ever have conquered Germany if they had depended on economic forces alone. They were victorious because they were able to rally behind them the support not only of a large middle-class threatened with proletarianisation and a peasantry ground down by economic attrition, but also of that great mass of nationalist sentiment which saw in the Republic the embodiment of national humiliation and blamed its economic adversities upon the politicians who had attempted to meet the demands for reparations and had trusted to conciliation rather than defiance as a means of restoring Germany to her place among the great Powers.

The Nazis stood from the very beginning of their movement for the policy of defiance instead of accommodation. They played without ceasing on the resentments which had been aroused by the enforced acceptance of German "war guilt" by the politicians who had set their hands to the Treaty of Peace. They claimed, not without truth, that Germany's place among the nations would be re-established far more effectively by defiant resistance than by a policy of compliance. This was not true in the years immediately after the war, when Germany was far too weak successfully to defy the Allies, and the Allies were still in far too militant a mood to endure defiance. The Ruhr occupation, which led up to the Dawes Plan and the policy of "fulfilment," plainly showed that Germany was at that stage not in a situation to resist. But the Nazi view became more and more true as the war receded into the background and the Governments of the Allied countries became less likely to take aggressive military action against a German reassertion of equality. Even in 1923 Great Britain opposed the French policy of occupying the Ruhr; and by the time the Nazis had grown strong enough to count seriously in German affairs France, too, had passed over to a political mood which made a renewal of Poincaré's aggressive methods highly unlikely. Germany had only to screw herself up to the point of defying her conquerors to be able to defy them with impunity; and in face of the vacillations and internal dissensions of the parties which dominated the Weimar Republic this situation combined with the distress due to the economic crisis to give the Nazis their chance.

Nazism in its economic aspect was above all a movement of property-owners and middle-class people directed against the threat of proletarianisation. It enlisted behind it the property-owning peasants, the shopkeepers and small employers, the "intellectual proletariat," which could find no outlet for its abilities, and, as it grew more powerful, an increasing section of the great capitalists as well. Under the Weimar Republic, Germany was drifting steadily towards a bastard kind of semi-Socialism which lacked all the driving force of a real Socialist system, and yet sapped by high taxation the vitals of private enterprise. The Socialists were strong enough to press for concessions which cost money in the interests of the unemployed and the wage-earners, but not, in face of the divisions in their own ranks and of their own mental hesitations, to set about the building up of a Socialist State. The State was continually extending its control over the economic life of Germany, not in pursuance of a policy of Socialist construction, but because it was being compelled to step in to assist and to control wherever the capitalist system decisively broke down. But these extensions of State control were usually made in ways which merely inhibited private Capitalism without setting any constructive forces in its place. Germany had no revolutionary Socialist Government such as existed in Russia, able to enlist new impulses of social service and emulation on its side, but a régime of perpetual compromise, taking control of economic affairs not because it wanted to but because it had to, and consequently making the worst of both worlds.

Against this policy were arrayed at one extreme the Communists, threatening revolution, and growing in strength as they attracted to their party the younger workers whom the unconstructive opportunism of the Social Democrats repelled. But Communism, unable to detach the older workers from their allegiance to Social Democracy, could only divide the working class, while raising up against it the united resistance of the entire body of property-owners, large and small; and even among the workers who became Communists a growing number drifted away afterwards to the Nazis when they realised that the division of the working-class forces between Communism and Social Democracy was a fatal obstacle to the victory of Socialism.

German Nazism has often been represented as simply a reactionary economic movement of the middle classes and the peasants, supported by the large capitalists and, more hesitantly, by the older aristocracy, against the menace of Socialism. That it was a movement of this sort is beyond doubt. But if it had been no more than this, it would certainly not have conquered power with the thoroughness of its present victory. The essential thing about Nazism is that it managed to fuse nationalist sentiment and the fear and dislike of Socialism into a combined force too strong to be resisted. The Communists, preaching an internationalist doctrine of revolution, and proclaiming that the workers have no country, outraged the feelings of national resentment at the subjection of Germany.

The Social Democrats, standing for compromise and "fulfilment," lost ground fast among the younger workers as economic distress became more severe. They succeeded to the end in holding the allegiance of the majority of the older workers; but between 1928 and November 1932 their representation in the *Reichstag* fell from 153 to 121, despite a rise of 85 in the total number of seats. The Social Democratic vote fell by nearly two millions, whereas the total vote rose by nearly four millions. Meanwhile, the Communists had increased their vote by over two and a half millions and their seats from 54 to 100, while the Nazis, who polled less than a million votes and got only 12 seats in 1928, got 230 seats in July 1932, and 196 after their setback in November, and polled 13,700,000 and 11,700,000 votes on these two occasions.

In the period immediately succeeding the war, the Social Democrats were the leading party, and had the government in their hands.

They had, however, no clear majority in the new *Reichstag,* and up to 1922 they governed in coalition with the moderate *bourgeois* parties, steadily losing ground and being forced to the adoption of a *bourgeois* programme. From 1922 to 1928, save for a brief interlude in 1923, after the Ruhr occupation, the Socialists were in opposition; but their gains at the election of 1928 brought them back to office as the leading element in a coalition, which lasted until it was broken in 1930, as a result of the economic crisis. Thereafter Brüning governed Germany, as the representative of the *bourgeois* parties, until he too fell in face of the further advance of the crisis, and gave place to von Papen.

Throughout the period since 1918, the *bourgeois* parties, compelled to act, if not always in alliance with the Social Democrats, at all events on the basis of some sort of accommodation with them—for there were no other conditions on which the Weimar Constitution could be made to work at all—were never able to put forward any clear policy of their own. Nor had they such a policy; for they represented a number of different and conflicting *bourgeois* tendencies, from the People's Party, backed by the big industrialists, through the Catholic Centre Party to the largely Jewish and intellectual Democrats.

In consequence of the hesitations and failures of the middle parties, including both the Social Democrats and the *bourgeois* groups, the youth of Germany, suffering and resentful under both economic and political repressions, was ready to listen with enthusiasm to the Nazi orators, who, free from responsibility, and suffering in themselves the neuroses of defeat and internal instability, were ready to make the wildest and most inconsistent promises to anyone who would aid them in reasserting the manhood of the German people.

The Nazi movement, in fact, could never have existed at all in anything like the form which it has actually assumed except among a nation of neurotics. The neurotic atmosphere which did actually exist in post-war Germany is explained partly by something inherent in the German and especially the Prussian character, but also by the experiences through which the German people has passed in recent years. The Germans were starved not only during the war but for some time afterwards, and this starvation reacted both on the national physique and upon the national mind. In addition to being starved they were humiliated not merely by defeat, or even by the harshness of the terms imposed upon them, but by being compelled to "eat dirt" and treated, long after the war was over, as outcasts to be received back only on probation and after long delay into the comity of civilised nations. Every day something happened to remind them of the accursed Treaty and to bring the national humiliation back into their minds. All this might have been overcome if Germany had been able to settle down within her new frontiers to build up a new national State; and for a time after the institution of the Dawes Plan and the stabilisation of the mark it did seem as if the forces of unrest and mental disturbance were about to recede. Between 1924 and 1929 it did look as if the policy of "fulfilment" might have some real chance of success; and if at this stage the Allies had possessed the wisdom to give up their claims to reparations and to take Germany back fully and frankly as an equal into the comity of nations what has happened since might have been averted.

But there was no such foresight among the Allied statesmen. Germany, in order to meet the claim for reparations, was compelled to borrow fantastically large sums from abroad, and to rebuild her economic system on a basis consistent only with a rapidly advancing volume of international commerce. She gambled on world prosperity, but she was compelled to gamble in this way because there was no alternative method of building up a sufficient export surplus to meet the charge both for reparations and for the new capital which she had borrowed for use in economic development. Consequently the coming of the world slump hit Germany desperately hard because her industrial system had been so reconstructed as to be most sensitive to the falling off in world trade, and because her financial system had been far too precariously reconstructed to stand the strain of a serious crisis. Between 1929 and 1932 the Germans carried on somehow; but they were compelled to tighten their belts more and more until the Brüning Government, which appeared to them as the instrument of their distress, had lost all basis of popular support and was simply waiting to be pushed over by the first powerful group that ventured to lift a hand against it.

NAZIS AND NATIONALISTS

Yet the Nazis did not succeed at once to the lost inheritance of the Weimar Republic, for there were other claimants also in the field. The working class had indeed surrendered, on account of its divi-

sions, its claim to the succession of authority. But the old governing classes of pre-war Germany had been watching the situation
with increasing hope that, between the Socialists on the one hand
and the Nazis on the other, they might yet contrive to slip in and
reassert their lost power. They possessed the great advantage that
Field-Marshal Hindenburg, elected as President against Hitler as
the defender of the Republic, was on their side; and when they
thought their chance had come at last, the President, dismissing
Brüning, called to the office of Chancellor in his place not Hitler
but von Papen, as a representative of the old aristocratic and landowning classes. These classes hoped, by installing their own nominee
in power, to use the Nazis as means to their own reactionary ends.
They were willing to be as nationalist as the Nazis could possibly
desire, and they trusted, by taking an aggressively nationalist line,
to win over a sufficient part of the Nazi following to render impotent
the more democratic elements in the Nazi movement. They were
willing to have Hitler and other Nazis in the Government; for
they thought that if they could get a coalition Government under
their own auspices they would have little difficulty in determining
its policy. Hitler they regarded as a magnificent agitator, but as a
person who was likely to fizzle out rapidly when he was once admitted to office as the partner of men with a hereditary capacity for
government. Hitler, however, was well aware that entry into a Government dominated by the Nationalists would at this stage be likely
to wreck the prospects of his movement, and to send a great mass
of his discontented following over to the Socialist side. He was quite
ready to make an alliance with the Nationalists when it suited him,
but he meant that alliance to be made at his own time and on his
own terms. In face of his refusal to collaborate, the von Papen
Ministry soon showed itself impotent to rally sufficient support to
carry on the government of the country. Von Papen lasted some
months because he had President Hindenburg behind him; but in
due course the reactionaries realised that he was bound to fail and
determined to try an alternative method of keeping control in their
own hands. Where von Papen had failed to enlist support, perhaps
General von Schleicher, drawn no less than von Papen from the old
governing classes, might succeed, by a more conciliatory policy towards the Left, in enlisting, if not the Socialist Party, at any rate the
Trade Unions behind a Government of the Right.

But von Schleicher was even less successful than his predecessor in holding the eruptive forces in check. Von Papen, angry at being displaced, began immediately to intrigue with the Nazis; and von Papen rather than von Schleicher had the President's ear. Consequently the von Schleicher Ministry lasted only a few weeks before the President and the reactionaries made up their minds to ally themselves with the Nazis, even on Hitler's terms, in the hope that, even if they had to accept Hitler as Chancellor, they could so ring him round with reactionary Nationalist Cabinet colleagues as to compel him to follow their own rather than the Nazi policy.

By this time Hitler and his advisers deemed that their chance had come. Hitler was perfectly willing to accept von Papen as Vice-Chancellor and to admit von Papen's friends to the Cabinet, because he felt abundantly strong enough, provided that he held the Chancellorship, to take complete power for his own party over the Nationalists' heads. That he was right and that the Nationalists were in the short run wrong, subsequent events have demonstrated with the utmost possible clarity. For the Nazis both knew quite clearly what they meant to do and how they meant to do it, and had behind them a huge popular following which was able by brutally forcible methods to carry their policy immediately into effect through the length and breadth of Germany. The old Nationalists were little more than a clique of aristocrats, bureaucrats and soldiers with no widespread popular following. The Nazis were a mass movement; and their leaders were past-masters at using their organised and disciplined rank and file as instruments for the seizure of every post of vantage throughout the country.

It is important at this point to realise that Hitler, in coming to the Chancellorship at the constitutional summons of President Hindenburg, was carrying out exactly the programme which he had laid down for himself years before, and insisted on throughout the entire period of the Nazi agitation after the failure of his ill-conceived Munich *putsch* of 1923. After that first failure Hitler evidently made up his mind that the revolution in Germany would have to be made, up to a certain point, not by the direct use of armed force but within the forms of constitutionalism. He set out to create a movement so powerful and highly organised that it would be impossible for any-one to continue to govern the country without its support, in the confidence that, if he could once raise his movement to this point of indispensability, there would be no alternative to summoning him constitutionally to office. Again and again, in the course of the Nazi advance, Hitler stressed the constitutional character of the movement, and this is precisely what he meant. He was "constitutional," not in the sense that he had the smallest intention of respecting constitutional methods when he had once attained to power, but in the sense that he meant to get power in the first instance as the head of a constitutionally summoned Government, which would then be free to tear up the Constitution under which it had been brought to power. Hitler's "constitutionalism" did not mean that he eschewed the use of force; for he built up, side by side with the political organisation of the National Socialist Party, his storm troops to act as the spearhead of the movement. The constant clashes between the Nazi storm-troopers on the one hand and the Communists, and to a less extent the Republican *Reichsbanner,* on the other, served a double purpose. They trained his storm-troopers in the arts of political violence, and they also raised the temper of the movement to a point which served to make it ruthless when its opportunity came for the exercise of unrestrained authority. In addition the uniforms and the marches and the adoption of military slogans and methods of organisation exerted a strong influence over the minds of a people smarting under defeat and prohibited from armed equality with their late antagonists. Hitler and those who worked with him were sound psychologists; and they created precisely the form of organisation which was required for the sort of "constitutional" revolution which they had in mind.

NAZI POLICY

As we have seen, the Nazi movement was built up on a mingling of nationalist and economic appeals. In both respects the policy of its leaders seems to have been that of assembling together every slogan that they thought capable of attracting followers, with very little regard for either consistency or commonsense. But perhaps this impression, which one gets very strongly from a reading of Nazi propaganda, speeches and writings, exaggerates the element of conscious hypocrisy in the movement. To a great extent the Nazi leaders as well as those who followed them were in a state of mind which enabled them to believe idiotic and self-contradictory things. The absurd exaggerations of their Nordic propaganda and of their continual fulminations against the Jews were not for the most part conscious hypocrisy, but irrationalism rendered proof against argument by the high emotional content with which it was charged. There was probably more conscious hypocrisy in the perpetual ambiguities and contradictions of their economic programme, but even here they had probably worked themselves up into a state of feeling in which it was perfectly possible for two and two to make simultaneously five and three in their minds.

Anyone who reads the earlier economic pronouncements of the National Socialist Party is bound to be struck by the extraordinary inconsistency between what the Nazis were aiming at on paper and what they have actually done. The tone of their early pronouncements was throughout strongly anti-capitalist, and even to a great extent socialistic. There was any amount of denunciation of financiers and capitalists and of insistence not merely on the establishment of State authority over industry in the national interest, but even on positive socialisation of large-scale enterprise. This anti-capitalist element in Nazi propaganda was undoubtedly an important factor in attracting to it large sections of the German youth, who either came to National Socialism after a period of Communism or Social Democracy, or reached it direct because they were repelled by the internationalist attitude of Communists and Social Democrats alike. Even to-day this socialistic element in the Nazi movement is undoubtedly very large among the rank and file, and extends to some of the leaders, including Herr Goebbels, whereas General Goering represents the out-and-out reactionary and militarist wing of the party. But at no stage has National Socialism, though it has used Socialist slogans in order to wean followers away from the Socialist parties, been really Socialist in its outlook. There is in it a real element of hostility to large-scale Capitalism, and especially to large-scale finance. But this hostility is conceived far more from the point of view of the tradesman, the small employer, the peasant and the intellectual worker than from that of the manual working class. Hitler himself is a highly class-conscious person, but the class of which he is conscious is precisely that which stands between the large-scale capitalist and the workman.

Nazi economic policy, stripped of its propagandist contradictions, has been from the outset essentially a policy of preserving the superior social status and income of the middle classes in Society against both large-scale Capitalism and Socialism. It is against the bankers and financiers who threaten to overwhelm the small men with a vast burden of debt. It is against the trusts, which threaten to crush out the competition of the small business, against the multiple stores and the chain stores and the large merchants who stand between the small-scale producer and his market. All these it sets out to curb and to control so as to preserve the position of the small capitalist. But it is conscious that it cannot destroy these forces without destroying the very basis on which the property of the intermediate classes rests. It therefore seeks to build up a State powerful enough not to destroy, but to dominate the financiers and the large-scale capitalists in the interests of the general mass of property owners. But its hostility to Socialism goes infinitely deeper than this; for its quarrel with the large property owner is only secondary, and the small property owner is at most only threatened with a quite gradual attrition at his hands, whereas the Socialists are aiming at a rapid and complete supersession of all forms of private property in the essential means of production, and at a levelling of incomes which would destroy the cherished social superiority of the middle class. Accordingly, when it comes to the point, the Nazi movement has shown itself fully prepared to enter into an alliance with large-scale Capitalism in order to fight the Socialists, trusting that if it can successfully liquidate its major antagonists it will then be able to control to a sufficient extent the activities of its ally.

The large-scale capitalists, for their part, for a long time looked askance at the Nazis because of their denunciations of big business. But it was not long before a few of them, notably Herr Thyssen, saw that the Nazi movement was the one force in Germany capable of standing out against the gradual advance of some form of Socialism, and therefore came over to its side. Herr Thyssen and other great industrialists helped to finance the Nazi movement even in the days when Nazi orators spent a large part of their time in denouncing people of this sort; and by and by the number of large-scale capitalists who backed the Nazis very greatly increased, though most of the great bankers and industrialists remained within the fold of the reactionary Nationalist and People's Parties, and only came over to support the Nazis when Nazis and Nationalists finally made a formal alliance.

It follows from what has been said that the Nazi movement, when it came to power, was prepared to take as its first task the complete liquidation of Socialism. But it had also to throw some sops to its own anti-capitalist following. This it attempted to do by declaring war upon one section of the German capitalist world and thus throwing up a smoke-screen for the protection of the rest. All its anti-capitalist venom was concentrated upon the Jewish shopkeepers and industrialists and bankers, in the hope that the purgation of German industry from non-Nordic influences would suffice to keep its anti-capitalist followers busy until the process of liquidating the Socialists had been successfully carried through to the bitter end. Even so it was necessary to make exceptions. Jewish banking, especially, is so strongly entrenched in the German financial world that little has been done to interfere with it. But there has been plenty of baiting of Jewish shopkeepers and even of Jewish industrialists; and to a large extent the need of the Nazis to provide an outlet for anti-capitalist feeling seems to have been satisfied in this way.

THE NAZIS AND THE WORKERS

The vital question, however, remains whether, having liquidated Socialism, the Nazis are destined to become the tools or the masters of large-scale German Capitalism. Undoubtedly there is on this point an internal struggle proceeding within the party. So far everything that the Nazis have done has favoured the great industrialists, for the power of the Trade Unions has been broken, and this has led to a sharp fall in wages and a widespread worsening of the conditions of labour. The industrialist has certainly up to the present got his money's worth. But the working-class following of the Nazis will hardly be content for long with the situation which has been created by the break-up of the old Trade Union movement. Before the revolution the Nazis had organised a widespread system of factory cells of their own, and these cells had shown some tendencies to collaborate in strike action with the Social Democratic Trade Unions. Unless something is done to satisfy industrial claims, there is likely before long to be trouble within the ranks of the Nazi movement itself, and a rallying point for working-class discontent which is denied an outlet in Trade Union or political organisation. Accordingly the Nazis have already begun to build up a mass organisation of their own in the industrial field. All the workers of Germany are being enrolled in the new Nazi "Labour Front" under the authoritative leadership of Dr. Ley. But in order to prevent this body from acquiring the characteristics of a Trade Union movement of the familiar type, employers and technicians and managers as well as rank and file workers are being enrolled in a common organisation, and the Labour Front as a whole is being organised under a system of control from above through picked Nazi leaders. Like Mussolini in Italy, the Nazis are aiming at finding an outlet for working-class energies through cultural and recreative activities rather than in the workshops themselves. They are building up, in imitation of the Fascist *Dopolavoro* institutions, a system of well-equipped clubs and centres under the auspices of the Labour Front, at which there are to be cheap meals and free entertainments on a lavish scale, coupled with educational opportunities for indoctrination in the Nazi faith.

But clearly the conditions of labour cannot be left unregulated. Under the Weimar Republic there had been built up in Germany an elaborate system for the settlement of trade disputes by arbitration before public officials, and this system the Nazis have taken over practically unchanged, altering only the personnel of the courts before which Labour disputes are to be decided. They have, however, added to the machinery which existed under the Republic a new and highly significant form of tribunal, the "Court of Honour." There are to be, in industrial establishments of any size, Courts of Honour before which workmen can be brought for any invasion of the factory discipline, and before which, with formal equality, workmen are to be entitled to bring complaints against the conduct of the management. These bodies, which are to be presided over by Nazi officials, are certain to be made use of for the prevention of any potentially dangerous forms of industrial agitation, for it is expressly laid down in the new code formulated for the Labour Front that workmen accused of stirring up unrest in the factories can be brought before the Court of Honour for trial and sentence. With the fate of incarceration in a concentration camp hanging over the offender, this is likely to be a highly effective method for the present of damping down Labour unrest. Moreover, the Works Councils which existed under the Republic have been drastically reorganised, and shorn of most of their powers. Obviously, for the present the Nazis are determined to enforce a strong discipline in the factories, and rely on their ability to keep the working-class elements in their own ranks for some time sufficiently hostile to the Socialist workers to prevent any development of a common solidarity. Unless, however, the Nazi State is able to bring about an improvement in working-class conditions, which it has so far very greatly worsened, these measures can hardly be effective in the long run in preventing a revival of Labour unrest.

Whatever may be the state of feeling among the manual workers —and there is no doubt that it is at present sharply divided, or that the Nazis have since their victory acquired a considerable measure of working-class support—there can be no question that the Nazi régime at present commands the adherence of the great mass of the younger people in Germany outside the ranks of the working class. It is applauded not only as the movement which has saved Germany from Socialism, or perhaps even Communism, but also and still more vociferously as the instrument whereby Germany has been restored to national self-respect and to real equality among the great nations.

GLEICHSCHALTUNG

The policy which the Nazis have followed in organising the Labour Front is an application of the more general principle which underlies their policy as a whole. The essence of it can be summed up in one untranslatable word—*Gleichschaltung*—which they themselves proclaim as the guiding principle for the construction of the Nazi State. *Gleichschaltung* means in effect that all forms of social organisation, both governmental and non-governmental, that are important in the working of German society, are to be assimilated to a common type and brought under leaders animated by a common policy. There are to be tolerated within the new State no organisations that stand apart from the State or claim independent rights of criticism and opposition; and no one is to be allowed to hold any important position either in a public office or in any voluntary association that counts in the moulding of action and opinion, unless he is either a devout Nazi or at the very least sufficiently in sympathy with the Nazis to be counted upon as an agent for the execution of their policy. *Gleichschaltung* is thus partly a question of the forms of organisation, which have all to be brought under a common model of authoritarian leadership as against the democratic principle of power proceeding from below; but it is also a question of the actual choice of leaders, who are to get their authority from the controlling group in the Nazi State and are thus to regard themselves rather as agents of a central Nazi power, entrusted with the guidance of some particular organisation in accordance with State needs, than as the representatives of any particular section of the German people. The complete destruction of the Trade Unions, as well as of all the political parties with the exception of the National Socialist Party, proceeds directly from this conception of *Gleichschaltung;* and so does the bringing within the State's authority of all manner of voluntary organisations, including not only the Co-operative Societies but all the various Youth Movements, Sports Associations, and cultural and recreational bodies of any and every kind. The *Reichswehr,* however, Germany's professional army, remains unassimilated.

NAZISM AND THE CHURCHES

Nor have the Nazis stopped short even at this point, for they have also aimed at making the German Churches fall in with the requirements of the "totalitarian" State. The German Protestant Churches, hitherto organised in several different denominations, mainly on a local basis within the borders of each separate State, have been firmly consolidated into a single body, over which has been set as leader a Nazi Bishop appointed by the Government, with a mission to reorganise the entire unified Church so as to make its attitude and doctrine conform to Nazi ideas. It is common knowledge that this attempt to assimilate the Church to the Nazi régime has led to a fierce internal struggle, involving the one organised movement of resistance—apart from the Catholic Church, which has not been directly attacked, except in its political aspect—that the Nazis have yet encountered since their coming to power. It is probable that this movement of opposition would not have become articulate if the Nazis had confined themselves to an attempt to institutionalise the German Churches under the auspices of the State; for German Protestantism, ever since the days of Luther, has been insistent on the recognition of the claims of the temporal power. But the Nazi attempt to capture the Churches went in fact far beyond this. There had arisen within the National Socialist Party an extraordinary new version of Christianity re-interpreted in accordance with Nordic racialist ideas, which threw over a large part of Christian doctrine and acclaimed the necessity for a purified Nordic Church from which all non-Nordic elements would be ruthlessly expelled. This "German Christian" movement in its more extreme manifestations shocked the consciences of many who were perfectly prepared to accept the reorganisation of the Church as an institution under State control, provided only that the State left untouched the essential Christian doctrines. Consequently there arose within the reorganised Church a struggle between the apostles of "Nordic Christianity" and those who, while affirming their loyalty to the Nazi State, sought to preserve the gospel undefiled. The Pastors' Emergency League in Prussia and similar organisations in the other States demanded the removal from positions of authority of "Nordic" Bishops and other Church leaders whom they were unable to recognise as fellow-Christians. The Nazi Reichsbishop retorted by fulminations against the Pastors' Emergency League, and threats to dispossess the recusants of their benefices and to invoke against them the full power of the State. The bishops, most of whom were at first on the side of the Pastors' Emergency League, thereupon abandoned their resistance, and it seemed as if the League's power had been successfully broken. Nevertheless it appears that the struggle is not yet over. There remains acute resentment within the body of the unified German Protestant Church; and the Nazis, while they have succeeded in beating down the organised opposition of the Pastors, seem for a time to have moderated their policy and to be holding back the more extreme elements among their German Christian followers. In this they are partly guided, no doubt, by the protests which "German Christianity" has aroused in foreign Churches, as well as by the strength of the opposition at home. For Hitler has far too much elementary common sense to wish to rouse against himself the united conscience of an outraged Christendom.

In the case of the Catholic Church the Nazis have been compelled to proceed with far more caution than in dealing with other denominations; for Catholicism, being in its essence an international doctrine embodied in the Catholic Church as an international institution, cannot possibly accept, as national State Churches can and have accepted, the domination of the State. The Nazis, after their accession to power, proceeded promptly to the liquidation of the Catholic Centre Party in the Reich and of its allied parties in Bavaria and elsewhere; but in proclaiming their hostility to political Catholicism they were careful at the outset to refrain from any attack on the spiritual institutions of the Catholics, and to seek the toleration, if not the approval, of the Pope by means of a Concordat. German Catholics have therefore enjoyed substantially more spiritual liberty

than German Protestants. But there have been many incidents arising out of clashes between Catholic priests and zealous Nazi propagandists, and of late relations between the Pope and the Nazis have
grown more and more strained. Catholicism in effect remains within
Nazi Germany as the one organised civilian element that has been
able so far openly and successfully to stand out against the policy of
Gleichschaltung.

Elsewhere *Gleichschaltung* has been applied with ruthless thoroughness. There survive, indeed, numerous persons in important
positions in the business and educational worlds who are not actual
members of the Nazi Party. The attempt to push *Gleichschaltung*
to the point of staffing all important positions with actual Nazis
would have involved far too great a dislocation to be politically
practicable. It would have rendered German business organisation
utterly inefficient, and would have aroused so much feeling as seriously to menace the Nazi power. But where men who are not Nazis
remain in positions of importance and authority, they are subject to
constant surveillance, at any rate unless they belong to the small
group of very great capitalists whom the Nazis dare not at present
interfere with on any account. Lesser non-Nazis who retain their
posts live in a condition of constant insecurity, never knowing when
they may be superseded or accused of conduct disloyal to the policy
of the new State. This makes them timid in action, anxious to curry
favour in order to hold their posts, and quite incapable of any combined effort to assert their independence. Apart from the Catholic
Church, and the still unsettled issue of German Protestantism, the
only organised civilian force which the Nazis have not succeeded in
subordinating to their authority is that of Big Business and high
finance.

THE NAZIS AND THE CONSTITUTION

It is natural to ask at this point under what constitutional forms
this extraordinarily extensive dictatorship of the Nazi Party has been
built up. Hitler, as the authoritative head of the Nazis, is to all
intents and purposes the dictator of Germany. Under what constitutional forms does he hold his power? This question is not at all
easy to answer; for in effect the Constitution of Germany is still in
the melting-pot, and no one yet knows precisely what the institutions
of the new Reich are intended to be.

Hindenburg remained President of the Reich up to the time of his death, and to that extent the Republican structure of Germany remained in being. Hitler was Chancellor, summoned to that post by the President in the exercise of his constitutional power. Hitler governed with the aid of a Cabinet which, in accordance with the German precedent, consisted rather of subordinates than of equal colleagues. But the position became far more complicated after Hindenburg's death; for Hitler thereupon assumed by decree the office of President while retaining that of Chancellor, despite the fact that the powers and status of the President had been specifically excepted from the emergency powers of legislation by decree conferred upon the Nazi Government. This assumption of dual office was indeed promptly ratified by one of those plebiscites to which the Nazis resort when they desire to give their actions a cover of democratic authority; but the concentration of all power in the hands of the Führer nevertheless startled German opinion. It was especially important in that it gave Hitler, as President, supreme command of the regular army, the *Reichswehr,* which was at once, even before the plebiscite, made to take an oath of allegiance to its new commander.

Hitler has thus gathered up in his own person the entire supreme power of the Reich—executive and legislative, and extending to the army and the law courts as well as the Civil Service. There still exists, indeed, a *Reichstag* chosen by universal suffrage; but, although the *Reichstag* exists as an organ of the supreme party, it has been shorn of all real power. Under a Bill passed in March 1933, immediately after the Nazi revolution, the Government was given power to enact laws without any reference to the *Reichstag,* and even without the requirement of the President's signature. The *Reichstag* has thus become not a legislative body but merely an assembly of Nazi leaders which can be called together from time to time in order to listen to important Government pronouncements. It has no control over what is to be done, and under a law of July 1933 it appears that the Government, when it does consult the people, intends to do this not by appealing to the *Reichstag,* but by the use of the popular referendum. This was in fact the method employed when Germany decided to leave the League of Nations and the Disarmament Conference.

Under the Weimar Constitution the Parliament consisted of two Chambers, the *Reichstag,* elected by universal suffrage, and the *Reichsrat,* representing the constituent States of the Reich. But in

April 1933 the Nazis enacted a measure which completely destroyed the system of parliamentary government in the various States, and handed over practically complete power in each State to a *Statthalter*, appointed by the Reich Government. This made the *Reichsrat*, though it continued in existence for a time, obviously functionless in relation to the new unified Constitution, and it has now completely disappeared in accordance with the decision to abolish the constituent States as units of government, and to centralise completely the control of political policy.

Hitler as head of the Nazi Party thus owes his authority in the Reich to his dual position as both President and Chancellor, and to the powers conferred upon the Government by a *Reichstag* in which the voice of the opposition has been completely silenced. The Government can, under the new Constitution, pass precisely what laws it likes, without reference to any other authority and without any limitation upon what it chooses to do. This means that complete authority in the shaping of the new State is conferred upon the leaders of the National Socialist Party; and as the theory of the Party is that of authoritative leadership from above, this means in effect that Hitler possesses absolute power, subject only to the necessity of carrying with him a sufficient amount of consent among the influential leaders of his Party. Yet this completely dictatorial power has been assumed without the necessity for acting at any point outside the letter of the Constitution, though its spirit has been constantly invaded. For Hitler got his power first by being summoned to the office of Chancellor by the President; secondly by getting conferred upon him by a subservient Parliament powers so extreme as to amount to a complete abdication by it of all control over the legislative process; and thirdly, on Hindenburg's death, by assuming the Presidency while still retaining his office as Chancellor. The old Civil Service, however, remains in administrative control.

The way was prepared for this constitutional *coup d'état* by the events of the years preceding the accession of the Nazis to power. For Germany's embarrassments and the difficulty of securing a working majority in the *Reichstag* had compelled successive Chancellors to assume greater and greater powers for themselves, and also to make steadily increasing use of the somewhat ambiguous but extensive powers conferred upon the President under the Weimar

Constitution. These presidential powers remain nominally in being, and may yet possibly be invoked. But Hitler has taken advantage of a situation which had already produced an exceedingly authoritative form of governmental control to concentrate in himself not only the enlarged powers which had accrued to previous Chancellors but also those which, under the Weimar Constitution, had been placed in the hands of the President. He has thus succeeded for the time being in accumulating in his own person all the sources of political authority within the Reich.

No such constitutional revolution would have been possible in a country really habituated to the forms of parliamentary government. The fact is that not only was pre-war Germany never a parliamentary State in any real sense of the term, but even the Weimar Republic, despite its adoption on paper of a thoroughly parliamentary constitution, never worked in practice as a parliamentary State in anything like the same sense as Great Britain or France. The idea of personal leadership remained latent in the powers accorded to the Chancellor as against the members of his Cabinet, and also in the wide authority conferred upon the President for action in cases of emergency. And the failure to build up party government into an effective instrument constantly required the use of powers which were intended by those who framed the Constitution only to be invoked very rarely in order to deal with a quite exceptional condition of crisis. Germany under the Weimar Republic was in a continual state of crisis, and recurrent crises prevented parliamentarism from ever finding its feet.

NAZI FOREIGN POLICY

Armed with this completely authoritative power, the Nazis set out both to establish the policy of *Gleichschaltung* in every sphere of German life and to reaffirm Germany's place among the great nations. As we have seen, it is not easy to give any clear account of the constitutional structure which they are building up internally as the embodiment of this policy; and it is not much easier to define their attitude in international affairs. Undoubtedly Germany is set on rearming, at least up to the level of the other Great Powers; and undoubtedly there is under the Third Reich a constant exaltation of the virtues of the warrior and a constant insistence on war as a training ground for national valour. With this attitude goes a determination to assert Germany's influence as a world Power, and to undo in one way or another the consequences of the German defeat of 1918. There is not the smallest doubt that Germany in her present mood is an aggressive State constituting a continuous and serious danger to world peace. What is not easy is to say how far this German assertiveness involves a demand for the extension of the actual territory of the Reich.

From the first the Nazis have put up a claim to apply their Nordic policy of *Gleichschaltung* to all German peoples no matter where they live; and accordingly powerful Nazi movements have arisen not only in Danzig and in the Saar, which have been claimed as territories to which Germany possesses an indefeasible right, but also in Austria and in the German-speaking parts of Czechoslovakia, Switzerland, and several other States. The Nazis claim the right to imbue Nordic peoples, wherever they live, with the Nazi spirit, so as to make them responsive to the new leadership which has arisen within the Reich. But it is not clear even to themselves how far this claim to "Nazify" all Germans carries with it a claim to political control over all the territories in which Germans live. Undoubtedly Germany means to regain the Saar, and is setting great hopes on victory in the plebiscite which has to be held in 1935 under the auspices of the League of Nations. On this point the Germans are not prepared to compromise. They mean to reabsorb the Saar within the territory of the Reich, if not as a result of victory in the plebiscite, then in some other way. In the early months after the Nazi revolution it seemed as if their policy was the same in Danzig and the Polish Corridor; but the conclusion of a ten years' Pact between Nazi Germany and a Poland now also governed on what are broadly Fascist lines has modified the situation, as it seems to imply a willingness of the Germans at least to postpone their aspirations on the Polish frontier to the success of their claims in the west and south. In Danzig they have, indeed, hit on an alternative method of establishing their supremacy; for by capturing the government of Danzig through the local Nazis they have established a complete control over the Free City and its territory without any actual annexation, and the Nazi régime in Danzig seems now to be working without any great friction with the Poles, who have, under the system set up by the Peace Treaty, rights in the commerce of the Free City.

This system of political control without annexation is obviously capable of being applied elsewhere, and it seems to be the policy which the Germans have hoped to pursue in their dealings with Austria. Up to the present at any rate the German Nazis probably have shrunk back from provoking the tremendous international crisis which would be bound to follow their success in absorbing Austria into the Reich. What they have hoped for is rather that the Austrian Nazis, with their barely concealed help, would succeed in overthrowing the Dollfuss Government and in establishing a Nazi Austria, which, remaining nominally independent, would be in all matters subservient to, and unified with, Germany. Annexation would of course be likely to follow in the long run; but for the time being the Nazis could get all they want if they could establish a Nazi Austria with which they could then proceed to enter into close political arrangements—giving the Austrians economic advantages as a *quid pro quo.* The economic boycott of Austria by Germany, and especially the interdiction of the tourist traffic, has done Austria very serious economic harm, and this power to offer economic advantages to an Austria assimilated to the Reich was one of the powerful weapons of the Nazis in their campaign against the Dollfuss Government and its Italian backers. For though Italy has now entered into an economic pact with Austria and Hungary, and is doing her best to offer economic advantages that will keep these countries out of the German sphere of influence, the Italian market is, from the standpoint of both countries, a very inferior alternative to that of Germany.

This policy, however, suffered a serious setback as a consequence of the abortive Nazi *Putsch* in Austria in August 1934. The assassination of Dollfuss by the Nazis threatened to provoke a first-class international crisis. Italy moved troops to the Austrian frontier, and threatened to intervene. Hitler, for his part, did not dare, for fear of international reactions, to allow the Austrian Nazi Legion, which had been trained in Germany for precisely this event, to cross the frontier and take part in the *Putsch*. The German Ambassador in Vienna was recalled for allowing himself to get mixed up with negotiating for a safe conduct for the rebels; and Herr Habicht, the German Nazi who had been in charge of propaganda on the "Austrian front," received his *congé*. Hitler announced his intention of sending von Papen to Vienna as a special envoy to "re-establish amity," and made haste to disclaim all aggressive intentions against the new Catholic-Fascist Government which replaced that of Dollfuss in Austria.

Meanwhile, the Austrian Nazi *Putsch* was successfully put down by the *Heimwehr* and the regular army, though there is no certainty that it may not be renewed at a later stage. For the present, however, German ambitions to include Austria within the Nazi sphere of influence have been foiled, and the Austrian State continues to look to Italy rather than Germany as its suzerain protector.

In Czechoslovakia and in Switzerland the situation is largely different. German-speaking people do indeed predominate in Switzerland; but the long tradition of Swiss neutrality and independence will take a great deal of breaking down, and although there are active Nazi elements in the territory of the Swiss Confederation it seems most unlikely that Germany will succeed in applying there her policy of *Gleichschaltung* in face of the existence both of the large French and Italian minorities and of a powerful and well-organised Socialist movement which has been recently gaining strength. Germany can disturb Swiss politics, but she can hardly hope to do more than that. In Czechoslovakia the Nazi menace is more immediately dangerous. The Germans in Czechoslovakia constitute only a small minority of the total population. But they are closely concentrated in certain parts of the country near the German border, and they have been, ever since the constitution of the Czechoslovak State, strongly organised as a national minority in parties of their own, which refused for a long time to take any part in the working of the State machine. The Nazi Party in Czechoslovakia has been proscribed and officially dissolved, but it continues to exist and to exercise a dangerous subversive influence; and its existence within a State lying between Germany and Austria and intimately involved in all the vexed political issues of the Danubian region constitutes one of the major dangers to the preservation of European peace.

In addition to proclaiming their mission to express the cultural and political unity of the "Nordic" peoples, the Nazis in Germany often proclaim a second gospel, that of the defence of the West against the menace of Russian Communism. In their appeals to the public opinion of the Western countries they seek constantly to represent themselves as the saviours of Western Europe from the barbarism of the East, embodied in the threat of Communist revolution; and this mission to save Europe from the East sometimes expresses itself in far-reaching projects for the invasion and dismemberment of Soviet Russia. At the World Economic Conference of 1933 Herr

Hugenberg indiscreetly put forward a colossal plan for the invasion of Russia, with the object of detaching the Ukraine and constituting it as a separate State which would provide a field for German expansion by means of colonisation by German settlers; and though this plan was promptly repudiated by the Nazi Government, projects of this order have undoubtedly been very widely canvassed in Germany during the past year. In seeking to ally herself closely with Poland, Germany is not above offering to compensate the Poles for her claims to an extension of territory by offering them a share in the spoils of Russia; and though the Poles are at present co-signatories with the Soviet Government of a pact of non-aggression, there is of course no guarantee that this will be permanently observed. Grandiose projects of this order float constantly about in the Nazi consciousness together with aspirations for the recovery of the lost Colonies, or for the building up of a new Colonial Empire; but the Nazi leaders, however fantastically they may dream, are sufficiently hard-headed realists to postpone ideas of this type to the achievement of their more immediate objects. What Germany wants for the present is a rearmament sufficient to establish her as the equal of any other European Power, and a reassertion of her claims in the West and the South of Europe so formidably backed by military power that none of her rivals will dare to stand out against her. For that reason her attention has been concentrated largely on securing control of Austria; for Austria is evidently the key to the re-establishment of German influence in South-Eastern Europe. A Nazi Austria would replace Germany astride of the Danube and enable her to begin once again her ambitious planning of penetration through South-Eastern Europe into Asia. That is why she is at present cultivating the friendship of Bulgaria, which remains outside the new Balkan Pact drafted early in 1934 between Yugoslavia, Rumania, Greece and Turkey.

NAZISM AND WAR

Nazi Germany is undoubtedly a most serious menace to world peace; but it would be a mistake to conclude from this that her policy constitutes an immediate threat of European war. On the contrary, it is plainly to Germany's advantage to preserve the peace, if she can do this without sacrifice of her policy of rearmament and penetration, until she has become again powerful enough to stand a chance of

success in war. It would be madness on the part of the Nazis to provoke a renewed European war until they have had time, by replenishing their armaments and training up a new generation in the arts
of war, to overcome the inferiority forced upon them under the Versailles Treaty. Although rearmament is undoubtedly proceeding fast,
and military training faster still, and these facts are plainly reflected
in the 1934 German Budget, the Nazis are hampered in building up
their military strength by the necessity which they still feel of not
violating too openly the letter of the Treaty of Versailles. Their
policy is one of gradual encroachment upon the terms of the Treaty
without any overt act that can easily be treated by the League of
Nations or by the victors at Versailles as a decisive breach of international obligations. They are breaking down the Treaty a step at a
time by the improvement of their facilities for the manufacture of the
prohibited arms, by extending constantly the military character of
the training provided for the Nazi following and for the general
body of the German youth, by stretching to the utmost the facilities
which civil aviation gives for military preparedness, and by pressing
continually upon the Powers the need for fresh concessions in the
sphere of rearmament. But though Germany is rearming fast under
these limiting conditions, it is bound to be some time before she can
regard herself as ready to stand up to her possible enemies in war.
Nor is it certain that the Germans do mean war, even in the long
run; for they would undoubtedly prefer to secure their objects without the great risks to their supremacy which war would be bound
to involve. An aggressive war would inevitably bring about a large-
scale revival of Socialist opposition inside the country. It would
menace the power of the Nazis from within as well as from without.
Therefore Herr Hitler, when he proclaims in his speeches addressed
to the world at large the German will to peace, is not wholly insincere; he does want peace—provided he can get without war everything that he regards as essential for the re-establishment of German
greatness, and he is even prepared to go to considerable lengths of
concession in order to avoid a war for which he is by no means as
yet prepared. That he does not need to make many concessions in
practice is because his possible antagonists are fully as reluctant to
go to war as he is himself. But a peace maintained on these terms is
obviously of the most precarious. For nations do not as a rule make
war out of deliberate intention, but rather because they pursue even

at the risk of war policies of which the inevitable outcome is a clash of national and imperial ambitions which only war can resolve. When such policies are pursued by a Government which bases its hold on the people largely on its exaltation of the warlike virtues the danger that the ultimate outcome will be war is bound to be very greatly increased. It is impossible to avoid the conclusion that in international matters the policy of Nazi Germany, whatever its deliberate intentions, makes for a situation calculated to stir up such antagonisms in Europe as to make war, if not imminent, at any rate probable in the long run.

NAZI ECONOMIC POLICY

In the sphere of economic policy, it is much harder to say what will be the outcome of Nazi control. During the period of reconstruction and rationalisation which followed the stabilisation of the mark in 1924, the Germans rebuilt their economic system on a basis which demanded for its successful working a very large export trade in manufactured products. The reorganised German industries were capable of working at very low cost, provided that they could find markets for a great and expanding output. But as they were very highly mechanised, their costs of production were bound to rise very sharply if output had to be reduced below the level necessary to carry the high capital costs of rationalisation. The collapse of the world market necessarily involved a great contraction of German exports, and thereby destroyed Germany's ability either to meet the claims for reparations, added to the burdens of the new capital debts which she had incurred for the purposes of rationalisation, or to afford a good standard of living for her own population. There arose from the industrialists a demand for sharp reductions in wages in order to lower costs for the purpose of maintaining German exports; and at the same time imports had to be curtailed heavily on account of the shortage of the means of payment, and this curtailment of imports carried with it the necessity of a fall in the German standard of living. Germany was driven towards a greater reliance on the domestic market, and towards an attempt to expand her own agricultural production in order to reduce imports of foodstuffs.

Under these circumstances the Nazis, basing their power on the support of the peasants and of the smaller industrialists who were producing largely for the home market began to proclaim a doctrine of economic self-sufficiency, *autarkie,* as the national economic policy corresponding to the nationalist aspirations of the party in the political sphere. This *autarkie* was to a great extent the economic policy of the Nazis before their assumption of power, but since they came to office they have realised to an increasing extent the enormous dislocation of the German economy which any attempt to rebuild it on a basis of self-sufficiency would involve. For in order to become self-sufficient Germany would have to scrap a large part of the new industrial plant which she has acquired since 1924 and to establish a totally new balance both between industry and agriculture and between the different types of industry. To attempt this would bring the Nazis into sharp conflict with the great industrialists, whose power is concentrated largely in the industries producing for export.

Consequently the economic policy of Nazi Germany is based on a compromise between *autarkie* and the re-establishment of the export trades. Germany is setting out to increase permanently the production of home-grown foodstuffs, in order to decrease her dependence on imports, but even more in order to consolidate her position among the peasants and to keep the landowners in a good temper with the new régime. But it is necessary at the same time to find an outlet for German exports and especially for the products of the reorganised heavy industries. In face of the general development of Economic Nationalism in recent years and the consequent contraction of the former German markets, this involves looking for markets in which the German exporter can hope to command a political advantage. The policy of rebuilding export trade thus works in with the Nazi movement for *Gleichschaltung* and political penetration in Eastern and Southern Europe. Even more than before the war Germany, now deprived of her colonial empire, looks for an outlet for her manufactures and for the future export of capital to the less developed countries of Eastern and Southern Europe. The desire to rebuild her trade with Poland is one of the motives underlying the recent German-Polish *entente,* and already steps are being taken to bring to an end the customs war with Poland which has been in existence since the disputes over the Silesian frontier after the war. The Nazification of Austria would be of immense help in pushing this policy of economic penetration into Southern Europe, for the assimilation of Austria would prepare the way for economic arrangements between Germany and the Danubian and Balkan States. It is true that this policy of economic penetration of Eastern and Southern Europe is bound to come to some extent into conflict with the policy of internal self-sufficiency in the supplies of foodstuffs. For the countries to which Germany wishes to export her manufactures have themselves large surpluses of agricultural products for which they are seeking markets, and the Germans will be compelled to admit an increasing quantity of their products if they are to have any hope of expanding their trade in these areas. Consequently the antinomy between the purely nationalist policy of *autarkie* and the imperialist policy of economic penetration remains unresolved, and the outcome is bound to be a compromise between the two. For the Germans can afford neither to relax their attempts to provide a satisfactory market for the products of German agriculture, nor to do without the large volume of foreign trade in manufactures which the structure of German Capitalism imperatively requires. This antinomy, however, is nothing new. It existed under the pre-war German Empire, and was the basis of the foreign policy of Bismarck and his successors, with its compromise between concessions to the junker landowners and advantages offered to the German industrialists.

Internally the Nazis are still contending with very great economic difficulties. There has been undoubtedly a substantial reduction in unemployment since Hitler assumed power, but a considerable part of this decrease seems to have been secured not as the result of a real improvement in the position of industry but rather by forcible manipulations of the economic machine. Employers have been compelled by Government and Nazi pressure to take on more workers, especially Nazis. They have been encouraged to dismiss women, to whose participation in industry as well as in public life the Nazis profess a rooted objection. There has been also an extensive dismissal of Jews, Socialists, and other political and racial "undesirables," who have been largely deprived of their claims to unemployment benefit, and have thus disappeared out of the unemployment statistics. Moreover, additional labour has been taken on not at full wage-cost to the employer, but with the aid of large subsidies from the State; and there has been a considerable introduction of part-time employment with the object of spreading the available volume of work over a larger number of workers. Thus the employer has gained the advantage of cheap labour and has been the more ready on this account to accept Nazi orders with regard to the engagement and dismissal of particular classes of workers.

Apart from this the Nazis have hardly yet shown their hand in matters of internal economic policy. They inherited from the Brüning Government a system which involved a very high degree of State control; for in the course of the depression the Government had been compelled to come to the assistance of the heavy industries and the banks up to a point at which the State had become virtually the owner of the greater part of the banking system and had acquired a large participation in the share capital of a number of the leading industries. This gave the State great power over the direction of industry, even before the Nazi revolution; and the power thus acquired fell into the hands of the Nazis together with the governmental authority. There is, however, no clear sign yet of the way in which the Nazis mean in the long run to use this power. They have made no attempt to browbeat the employers in the same way as they have browbeaten the working class. They have been tender in their dealings with the great industrialists, despite the denunciation of Big Business which was one of the propaganda instruments by which they climbed to power. They have been anxious to disarm capitalist opposition to the new régime, and they have found no difficulty in securing capitalist support as long as they are prepared to play the capitalist game by attacking wage-rates and destroying working-class organisations.

THE FUTURE OF NAZISM

But will the Nazi system survive? In Nazism, as it came to power, there were many conflicting currents. A numerically strong left wing, centred in the Storm Troops, looked for economic benefits and combined with extreme nationalism a hankering to pull down the rich and mighty. Goebbels and Roehm were regarded as leaders of this faction, while Goering led the more purely nationalist and anti-socialist wing, with Hitler, the Führer who can do no wrong, poised ambiguously between. The Storm Troops were indispensable to Hitler's rise to power; and they could not have been recruited or relied on unless they had been fed on anti-capitalist and anti-aristocratic, as well as nationalist, slogans. But when Hitler had won power, and liquidated the Socialist and Liberal oppositions, the Storm Troops, calling for radical promises to be redeemed, became a nuisance. In the summer of 1934 the Führer turned suddenly on the old associates who had helped him to power. A plot, real or imaginary, was discovered. Hitler and Goering swooped down on the Storm Troop leaders: Roehm and Heines and numerous others were shot, and many more imprisoned. Opportunity was taken to kill two birds with one stone. The ex-Chancellor, von Schleicher, was alleged to have been implicated with Roehm: he and his wife were murdered. Numerous arrests and killings of alleged right- as well as left-wing plotters were carried out with dramatic swiftness. Goebbels, who would have been more naturally among the victims, was found with his habitual suppleness at Hitler's side.

But what is the outcome? By destroying the Storm Troops—for it almost amounts to that—Hitler has weakened his own left. He has still General Goering's picked "S.S." force to uphold the Nazi terror; and Goering also controls the police. But, with the Storm Troops subdued, the ultimate power in Germany veers towards the *Reichswehr,* the professional army which the Treaty allowed her to keep. The *Reichswehr,* officered largely by aristocrats, is not Nazi, but far more Nationalist in the old sense; and the same is true of a very large number of the civil servants in every department of German public life. Has Hitler, in suppressing his own extremists, prepared the way for a reaction to a purely militarist régime of the old aristocratic type, by which he himself will in due course be cast down? Or is he getting ready to discard from National Socialism the last of its socialistic trappings and appear himself as the incongruous leader of such a reaction? We do not venture to prophesy; but assuredly the *coup* of midsummer 1934 has put the Nazi régime back into the melting-pot, and the future of Germany will be settled, not only by Hitler and Goering, but also by the strongly entrenched permanent officials and, last but not least, by the military power of the *Reichswehr.*

The situation has, of course, been greatly altered by the death of President Hindenburg and the assumption by Hitler of the Presidency in addition to his office as Chancellor. Hindenburg's prestige afforded a powerful support to the Nazi régime among the German upper and middle classes; and, though by assuming the double office Hitler has made himself head of the Army as well as of the executive, and has thus widened greatly the apparent basis of his power, there are many who think that the Nazi régime will be weakened by having to stand exclusively on its own legs, without the support of Hindenburg's tremendous national prestige.

7. THE POLITICAL SYSTEM OF SOVIET RUSSIA

SOVIET RUSSIA has passed through a violent revolutionary upheaval which is still in process of working out its results. The Communist Revolution in Russia was far more and far more fundamentally a revolution than either the immediately post-war revolutions in the defeated States, or the more recent Fascist revolutions in Italy and Germany, because it changed not merely the political machine and political institutions, but also the entire economic and social system. Such comparisons as are made between the Russian and, say, the Italian and German systems, though based on certain undeniable similarities, only convey at most half the truth. The similarities exist because there exist also similarities between men, whatever the system under which they live, and societies faced with certain objective factors, such as the need to repel invasion or rapidly to increase production, will commonly tend to adopt in some measure like expedients to enlist the active co-operation of their populations. There are some things in common between the Fascist and Communist theories, notably their insistence on the power of the State, but the main resemblances are on matters of political technique; and the fact that present-day Russian political technique bears a likeness, in some respects, to Fascist political technique is far less important than their fundamental differences.

For Russia, to the Western observer, is essentially a country of perpetual shock and surprise—a country which appears to be standing on its head. The visitor from the West, whether he is horrified or exhilarated, cannot fail to be continually struck by one paradox after another, one after another reversal of institutions which he had taken for granted all his life. He finds a country with social relationships entirely new, where the complicated class-structure of the West has disappeared, and in its place, apart from the diminishing and suppressed class of persons held to be of *bourgeois* origin or counter-revolutionary practice, there is only a single vast class, divided, but not at all rigidly divided, into occupational groupings. He finds, also, that the social value and importance attached to the various occupations is quite different from the values given by his own society. If the order of priority in which rations and privileges are assigned to the different groups be taken as a rough indication of the esteem in which they are held—it is, owing to the economics of the Soviet price-policy, a better indication than the wages or salaries paid—he will find soldiers, Government officials of the higher rank, and manual workers in important branches of heavy industry ranked together, whereas persons who do not work are ranked lowest of all. Again, he will find a great alteration in the professed motives of men and the purposes of social life; and he may observe that a considerable change in sex-relationships and the position of women has come about, almost as a minor event, in the course of the Revolution.

Further, he will see that the sharp distinction which (particularly if he is English) he has learned to draw between things political and things economic does not exist in the Russian State. In a sense, every question in Russia is a political question and every worker a State employee. He will see a country which contains only one political party, but that so different from the parties which he knows in Great Britain and the United States as to be almost deserving of a different name; where no change of Government would appear to be possible without another revolution, but where changes *in* government, in the policy of government, and in the personnel of the governors are taking place from day to day; and, finally, where a stiff theoretic dogmatism and a tight State control in matters felt to be essential co-exist, not merely with a high degree of flexibility in policy and administration, which is possibly not surprising, but with a degree of public criticism and discussion and of conscious collaboration on the part of large numbers of the population, which is unparalleled since the days of the City-State. This he will find affecting the very appearance of the towns, the clothes and conversation of the people, the articles in the newspapers, and the subject-matter of the plays and films; and he will be hard put to it, particularly if he has a mind that readily receives impressions, to distinguish between the specifically Communist features of the new régime and those which are due to the position of the Soviet State in a capitalist world, and further between what is likely to be permanent and what transient in its social life.

THE BASIS OF THE STATE

The political institutions, in the narrow sense, of the Soviet State, i.e. those which are embodied in its Constitution, are comparatively simple, and we describe them briefly below. Far more important, however, for an understanding of Russia than the institutions themselves, which may at any moment be modified, is the theory upon which the Soviet State is based and the practical instruments adopted for translating that theory into social action. The importance of this is very difficult for the English reader—though less so for the American—to realise. For the British political system is wholly empirical and traditional and has never been based on any formulated theory whatever, though various thinkers, like John Locke, have upon occasion attempted to evolve a theory to fit the facts, even as Fascist Italy seems now to be developing an explanatory political theory of its own. The Russian State has been built according to the sociological theory of Karl Marx, as laid down first in the *Communist Manifesto* of 1848, and interpreted in practice by Nicolai Lenin; and the policy of the revolutionary leaders has followed with singular fidelity the lines prescribed for it more than eighty years ago, as can be seen from a comparison of the programme of revolution laid down by Marx with the measures actually taken by the revolutionary Government.

The Marxist theory lays down that the transition from a capitalist to a Communist society must be carried through by a dictatorship of the proletariat (i.e. the wage-earning classes) acting upon social institutions evolved by the proletariat itself. This is the method by which the Revolution was in fact achieved; and the theory forms the basis of the Constitution of 1923, though only part of it is actually expressed in that Constitution. It was the revolt of the Russian proletariat, aided by the disaffected army, that made the Revolution; the institutions which it evolved were the Soviets, or Councils of Workmen, Soldiers and Peasants; and the instrument of proletarian dictatorship was, and is, the Communist Party.

Two points should here be noticed, both of which are peculiar to the Russian situation. The first is that the Russian proletariat in 1917, though numerically insignificant as compared with the vast mass of the Russian people, was very highly "proletarianised" in the Marxist sense. It was both oppressed and remarkably concentrated in large towns and great factories; it was not scattered all over the country in small groups, like the French wage-workers; it had, under the Tsarist régime, no "stake in the country," as has the British Trade Unionist, nor hope of individual advancement such as gleamed before the American worker. It was, as nearly as possible, pure proletariat, pure wage-slave, organised by its masters in gangs which were as nearly as possible chain-gangs; and it was thus admirably fitted to make a proletarian revolution. But—and this leads to the second point—the Russian proletariat was, as has been said, comparatively small in numbers, and could not carry through a revolution without enlisting the support of the peasantry by giving them the land. But to create a vast class of peasant proprietors would have been to destroy the Revolution; accordingly, the most strenuous efforts of the revolutionary leaders, over the past sixteen years, have been directed to "proletarianising" the peasant, not, indeed, in the capitalist sense because, Capitalism having been destroyed in Russia, there cannot be any proletariat as we know it in the West, but by collectivising, by force or propaganda as seems expedient, the mind and institutions of the peasant, so as to bring them into harmony with those of the industrial worker. Hence the preponderance assigned in the Constitution to the urban Soviets, and hence, too, the merciless war against recalcitrant peasants (*kulaki*) and even against whole districts which resisted the policy of collectivisation, as well as the continual drive of propaganda into the rural areas. It is too soon to say whether this policy, which, though essential to the Revolution, undoubtedly produced great economic difficulties as well as political repression, has succeeded; what can be said at the time of writing is that the worst dangers appear to have been surmounted, and that without seriously endangering the political State.

CONSTITUTION OF THE U.S.S.R.

The Constitution itself is comparatively simple. The Union of Socialist Soviet Republics is in form a close federation of seven Soviet Republics, of which the Russian Socialist Federal Soviet Republic, stretching from Leningrad to Vladivostok and right down the Volga to the Caspian Sea, is much the largest member. Of the others the most important is the Ukrainian Socialist Soviet Republic, whose capital is Kiev, which has an older civilisation than Moscow. The Ukraine did not join the Union until 1920; its adhesion even then was due largely to fear of the Poles and of such White generals as Petliura; and it is the only part of the Union in which separatist feeling has remained strong enough to give recurrent cause of anxiety. Some of the member Republics themselves include autonomous republics and autonomous regions, of which the Tartar Republic, the German Republic of the Volga, and the Republics of Georgia, Armenia and Azerbaijan perhaps call for special mention.

The Union is a close federation; that is to say, the powers which are given to the federal authority are very large indeed. They include, for example, foreign trade and foreign relations, defence (including defence against "counter-revolution," which was long the province of the State Political Department or G.P.U.), the direction of national economic policy and internal trade, taxation, and the organisation of labour and labour legislation. The chief features of both economic and political life are thus concentrated in the federal machinery, and the subjects on which there is large republican autonomy are mainly those, such as education and public health, in which most countries allow a good deal of local freedom. The Republics have, however—and this is very important—full cultural autonomy of speech, writing and printing. As this was rigorously denied to the nationalities under the Tsars, it represents an immense reversal of policy from a régime of extreme oppression to one that is more liberal than those pursued by the bulk of European nations; and it is further a means by which other neighbouring States which might adopt a Communist system—Afghanistan, for example, or Chinese Turkestan, or one of the Succession States of the old Russian Empire— might enter the Soviet federation. The Soviet Union, though its leaders are Russian and Russian its main language, is not in theory a national unit, but a federation based on the possession of common Socialist institutions and a common social theory—Marxian Communism: this is one of the many ways in which it differs from any other political entity in the modern world, as it differs from the Empires of Rome and Islam in not extending its boundaries by force of arms. On paper, at any rate, any of the constituent Republics has also the right to secede from the Union: whether secession would be permitted in practice may be open to doubt, but the right at least is there.

Within the Union, the franchise is uniform, and open to all of either sex, excepting persons employing hired labour for profit (this includes *kulaki*) or living on unearned income, monks and priests, imbeciles, and former agents of the Tsarist régime. The vote itself, owing to the working of the Soviet system, is of comparatively minor importance; but the vote is only a part of "civil rights," which include such essentials as Trade Union membership, ration card, right to share in the many social services which the State provides, and so on. The loss of civil rights, in fact, amounts to a kind of semi-outlawry, and commonly follows conviction for any serious offence. It should be noted that the position of women is one of absolute social and political equality; the Soviet marriage laws, the institution of equal pay, and the provision on a large scale of public clinics and nurseries, have gone far to ensure that this nominal equality is a real one, and not, as in the case of our own Sex Disqualification Removal Act, a mere declaratory statement with very little practical effect.

The political system, as set out in the Constitution, is in form a pyramid, based on the Soviets and built up by delegation from below. At the bottom there are the small town and rural Soviets, including Soviets for large factories which send delegates to form district Soviets, and so on, up to the central Congress of Soviets, which meets as a rule annually, and is, according to the Constitution, the supreme authority for the whole of the Union. Throughout, urban areas are more heavily represented than rural areas in Soviet congresses; thus, Article 9 of the Constitution reads:

"The Congress of Soviets of the Union of Socialist Soviet Republics is composed of representatives of town and township Soviets on the basis of one deputy for each 25,000 electors and of representatives of provincial Congresses of Soviets on the basis of one deputy for each 125,000 of the population."

The Congress of Soviets elects the Council of the Union, a large body which with the Council of Nationalities (representative of the allied and autonomous Republics) forms the Central Executive Committee of the Union. This body, however, is too large to meet often; and between its meetings the government is in the hands of its Presidium, which consists of twenty-one members appointed from the two bodies which make up the Central Executive. Directly below the Presidium, and subject to its orders, is the Council of People's

Commissaries, which consists of the heads of the chief State Departments and hence corresponds in composition to the British Cabinet. Below again are a tremendous and changing variety of Councils, Commissions, and Committees, created to deal with the vast complexity of Government business in a socialised State; but, interesting as they and their functions are, there is no space to describe them here. The Supreme Court of the Union, the Commissariat of Workmen's and Peasants' Inspection (R.K.I.) and the G.P.U., were also set up directly under the Constitution. The two last-named institutions have been abolished this year; it is announced that the work of inspection is henceforward to be performed by a committee of the Communist Party, and that of defence against counter-revolution by the machinery of the ordinary courts, with only such reference of special cases to military tribunals as is provided for in the constitutions of a number of other countries.

There is no President of the Soviet Union, though the Central Executive Committee has several presidents, and there is a President of the Council of Commissars. The latter was the post held by Lenin, but since his time it has become of considerably less importance.

The above is a very brief summary of the Soviet Constitution, which is, in itself, not at all a complicated or difficult document. But no summary of the Constitution can give any idea of the real political life of Russia, for the simple reason that so much of the vital part of that life finds no mention at all in the Constitution.

In the first place, the Constitution envisages only one type of Marx's "working-class organisations," viz. the Soviets. This is no doubt natural, since the Soviets were the bodies which sprang up spontaneously before and during the revolutionary period, and they were also the bodies which conferred political authority on the revolutionary government. The government of Russia is, as the Constitution states, a government derived from and based on the Soviets. But the Soviets are not by any means the only spontaneously arising working-class bodies; and in the field of administration, as distinct from that of legislation, there is a whole host of bodies, some of them showing considerably more vitality than the Soviets, which must be taken into account. For it must be continually remembered that in a socialised community "administration" covers a very much wider field than we are accustomed to assign to it in a capitalist country. When the whole of industry, trade, and transport, to go no further, is the direct concern of the State, "administration" comes to cover the entire sphere of what we now call private enterprise, as well as of public works, and the organs of administration become of an importance greatly exceeding that of the British civil and municipal services or of the more purely political machinery.

THE COLLECTIVES

To a certain extent, Soviet administration is run from above, under the orders of the various commissariats and departments, as in most other countries, and it also makes use, as many other countries have done at times, of working-class bodies which existed before the Revolution, such as the Trade Unions and Co-operative Societies.[1] But to a very much greater extent than in any other country it is run from below, by spontaneously-uprising groups and committees which form themselves around any and every job or institution and which take to themselves social functions over a very wide field. Every factory, for example, has its factory committee which concerns itself fully with the social life of the factory workers, with the factory kitchens, the factory club, the factory housing estate if there is one, as there frequently is, the factory crêche, and to a certain extent with the education of the factory children. As collectivisation proceeds in the villages, the same sort of organisation is springing up in connection with the *kolkhozi* or collective farms. The same thing can be found in connection with non-productive institutions, such as schools, prisons, and reformatories—even in a house for the reclamation of prostitutes!—though since the main preoccupation of the Revolution is with the manual workers from whom its support came, less stress is laid upon these than upon the factory units.

It is a little difficult to convey to anyone brought up upon Western ideas of formal democracy exactly the scope and function of these bodies—for which a compendious general name is "the collectives." In the first place, it is sometimes quite difficult to find out how they are chosen; in most cases they seem to be elected after a fashion, but not necessarily in any strict or formal sense. And when, by whatever means, they are chosen, though they are undoubtedly responsible to those in whose name they speak, it is very difficult to arrive at a definition of that responsibility or to find out how it works. Often

---

[1] The Trade Unions are now, since taking over the functions of the Commissariat of Labour, actually an important part of the Government machine.

there seems no provision for challenging any decision or any member of the factory committee; it seems to be assumed that the committee will in some way succeed in carrying out the general will of those it represents, which is a curious reminiscence of Rousseau in a Marxist country.

Nor is the function of the factory committee anywhere defined. One thing is certain; it is not "control of production" in the sense of which early Socialists of the producers' co-operation type envisaged it. Ever since the brief and disastrous experiment of 1918–1919, the direct control of production has been firmly in the hands of the factory management, itself controlled by the State productive organs. (This cannot be quite the case with *kolkhozi,* but of them it is too soon to speak.) Nor is it a control over wages and labour conditions, which are also settled from above. To a large extent it is a function of criticism and complaint; the means open to any Russian worker of voicing his discontent with the conditions and methods of his factory appear to be legion. But the collective is not wholly or even mainly an organ of criticism. It is also definitely co-operating in production and in the planning of production; in the tremendous Union-wide surge of discussion that preceded the launching of the Five Year Plan the workers' collectives played a very large part, and no less a part in its carrying-out and its modification, as circumstances seemed to require it. Further, there are all the social and cultural activities referred to above as well as the functions of acting as a sort of court of first instance to try offences against the discipline of the institution in question. (Prisoners, in Russia, try prisoners who break prison rules.) In fact, the "collective" sometimes appears to be more of a kind of combination of parish council, local bench, and rotary club than an organ of production—which is perhaps to say no more than that it has no parallel in the West.

Be that as it may, and be it formed as it may, the "collective" is undoubtedly one of the most vital and most interesting phenomena of present-day Russia. It is the institution which vivifies the whole, which brings into active co-operation and citizenship the vigour of any citizen of the Republic who has vigour to be used; and it is the only body which makes tolerable and workable by human creatures the tight discipline which a socialised society struggling for existence in a capitalist world must needs enforce. It may not be possible of transplantation to other countries which have not the same strong communal traditions as have the Russians; but, as it is, it has at the very least the merit of being a very valuable contribution to the perennial problem of democratic social life.

THE COMMUNIST PARTY

The collectives appear nowhere in the Soviet Constitution. Nor does the Communist Party, which is at least as important in the system, and more so for the revolutionary period. The Communist Party, it has been epigrammatically said, differs from all other known political parties in that it is very hard to join and comparatively easy to leave; but the difference is wider than that. Historically, the Communist Party is simply the majority faction (Bolsheviks) of the old Russian Social Democratic Party, which divided in 1903 on questions mainly of doctrinal difference; but since in the summer of 1917, between the first and second Revolutions, it decided to put itself at the head of the forces opposed to the Provisional Government, and raised the cry "All Power to the Soviets" (i.e. the working-class organisations) it has been in fact the instrument of proletarian dictatorship. Whether it so considered itself at the moment of revolution is immaterial; it was abundantly clear within a very short while that unless there was a strong, disciplined and clear-headed party to take command, the Revolution would collapse into chaos and civil war; and the Bolsheviks, under Lenin's guidance, became that party.

The institutions of Russian political and social life, legislative and administrative, are as described above. But the policy, in both legislation and administration, is decided by the Communist Party. It follows that the really important policy debates are conducted, not at the Congress of Soviets, but in the periodic Congresses of the Communist Party, and that the real authority, whatever the Constitution may say, is the Communist Party Congress, and, between Congresses, its Executive or *Politburo,* whose secretary is Stalin. This dominance is secured by the comparatively simple method of seeing that key positions are occupied by Communist Party members, and that Communist Party members or at any rate persons of proved Communist faith are present on local Soviets and important "collectives" in sufficient numbers to make sure that these bodies toe the party line. It is not, of course, suggested that *all* executive positions are occupied by Party members; the Party membership[1] is not nearly inclusive

---

[1] Something over two million at the time of writing. But the numbers are subject to very great variation, partly owing to deliberate policy of the heads.

enough for that to be so, and there are millions of convinced Communists who for one reason and another are not in the Party. Opinions differ about the proportions, and practice differs also; but undoubtedly of high executive positions practically all are held by Party members, and among the Soviets the more important the Soviet the larger proportion of Party members it contains.

The method of dominance has been called simple, and it can be simply stated. But, of course, this does not mean that it is at all easy in practice. It involves a Party membership with a very high quotient of discipline, conscious devotion, and—particularly as Russia advances to be an economically developed country—of practical and intellectual ability. As this advance takes place, it is found more and more that ideological orthodoxy cannot make up for practical incompetence, and the Communist desiring to reach high position must be prepared to undergo other tests than those of faith, though faith is, and will probably remain, the greatest single desideratum.

Accordingly, the Communist Party must be both a dedicated and a carefully hand-picked body, and the strongest measures are taken to ensure that this end is achieved. In the days before the Revolution the discipline was in effect imposed by external circumstances—the fear of exile or death. An outlawed or proscribed party does not commonly attract to itself weaklings or place-seekers, and if a few such do arrive in it, the conditions of work soon harden or drive them out. Since the Revolution, however, a new discipline has had to be achieved.

In the first place, the general character of the membership is kept strictly overhauled, with a view to seeing that the proportion of industrial workers remains high, so that the Party does not lose its proletarian character. Entry to the party is always easier, other things being equal, for an industrial worker than for anyone else; but in addition, in the course of the great drives and purges which periodically change, in greater or less degree, the composition of the Party, one frequently finds *en bloc* enlistments of industrial workers of various classes. Secondly, no one can, generally speaking, be admitted to the Party unless he or she has passed through, first, a searching test which in many cases almost amounts to a stiff examination, and secondly a period of probation during which the merits of the candidate are weighed. By these means it is hoped to secure that, both in character and ability and in understanding of the Communist cause, the new members are well-fitted to undertake their task. Lastly, there is a very high code of personal service and personal conduct among Party members. They are expected, as a matter of course, to undertake voluntary work of many kinds, either on their own initiative or at the behest of their Party cell; they are also expected not to indulge private whims or amusements to an extent which interferes with their public efficiency; and in general they are expected to set a standard of Communist conduct (or, in work, "Bolshevik tempo") which shall be an example to the rest of the community. Until quite recently, there was a fairly low upward limit to the amount of salary which a Party member might receive. This proved impossible or unwise to retain; but the principle remains.[1]

The same procedure is followed, though it is rather less rigidly applied, in the case of the junior Communist associations, the Komsomols, whose membership of nearly five million runs from 16 to 24 years, and the Pioneers for the school-children. Both organisations have a probation period for would-be members and tests before entrance; and both demand special service as a condition of membership. In the case of the Pioneers, the effect somewhat resembles that of a glorified Boy Scout movement, with this important difference, that the Pioneers are part of the social structure of the State and are called upon to undertake, not one "good deed per day" in a haphazard manner, but definitely prescribed portions of social service. The Komsomols, owing to the comparative youth of the executive in a revolutionary country, play a much larger part in actual administration than a similar organisation could hope to do in the West; many persons holding responsible posts are Komsomols.

The orthodoxy of the Party is maintained by its leaders, following out and interpreting the decisions of the Party Congress. In effect, Party policy has really been determined by one man, by Lenin until 1923, and since, after a struggle among personalities, by Stalin. But neither Lenin nor Stalin has gained or held his position by virtue of any particular office. Lenin was chairman of the Council of People's Commissars, Stalin is secretary of the Party; but neither of these posts carries with it leadership, which is only given by triumph at

[1] The standard of conduct concerns itself much less narrowly with the department of life which in the West is the sole content of the word "moral" than in, say, the United States. Conduct unbefitting a Communist is much more often slackness or pilfering than sexual irregularity, though spectacular aberrations are not condoned save in exceptional cases. But Communist Puritanism is not Evangelical Puritanism.

the Party Congress. It was not until after some years of struggle that Stalin established his right to the succession over the Trotskyites; but since that episode closed with the expulsion of Trotsky in 1927, there has been no such spectacular conflict, and individual dissidents from Party policy have been removed without much publicity.

There is no room for dissident groups within the Party. "Factionalism" is one of the most heinous Party sins. The observer therefore naturally enquires to what extent the Party is itself democratic in the sense of representing in its policy the views of its membership. Obviously, this question cannot really be satisfactorily answered except by a long-service Party member; it may be noticed, however, that the Trotsky controversy was fiercely debated, up and down the country and through the Press, long before a decision was finally reached, and that, while conformity with Party decisions is rigorously demanded, and "minorities," that love of Western liberalism, are regarded with horror, the Communist Party, like other Russian institutions, seems in practice to allow a good deal of local and individual discretion on matters not felt to be essential to the safety of the Union. Nor have the recusants, even in exile, generally attacked the Party itself, whatever they may have said about Stalin and his friends.

The Communist Party has been likened to the Fascist and Nazi Parties on the one hand, and to the Jesuit Order on the other. Neither comparison gives anything like a true picture. The Communists share with the first-named parties the demand of personal service from their members, and the determination to run all the organs of society in accordance with a theory and policy of their own. The Fascists resemble the Communists rather more than do the Nazis, at any rate at the present time, both because their membership is more selective than that of the Nazis, and because their propaganda contains more intellectual appeal than do the wild emotional speeches of the Nazi leaders. In the actual technique of propaganda, of course, there is considerable similarity. But, quite apart from the vast differences between a Socialist and a non-Socialist theory of society, the Communists stand well apart from the Fascists, as regards both their highly selective membership and the stern intellectual orthodoxy required of it. As to the Jesuits, it should suffice to say that the Communist Party is not an Order; its members have received no separatist training but undergo the education given to the youth of Russia at large; they are not cut off from the world, either by celibacy or any other distinguishing condition; and the Party is not a hierarchy. Its authoritarianism comes from its dogma, and not from positions reserved for the interpreters of that dogma.

THE TWO SIDES OF THE SOVIET RÉGIME

Students of Russian politics are often puzzled and perplexed by apparent contradictions between what appears to be the height of enlightenment and what equally appears to be the height of obscurantism. When all allowance is made for propaganda on both sides, it remains difficult to reconcile the Soviet child labour code with the persecution of the *kulaki,* or the treatment of ordinary criminals, as exemplified in reformatory camps like *Bolshevo,* with the behaviour of the G.P.U. to persons suspected of counter-revolutionary activities. It is in this latter instance that the explanation of the contradiction lies.

Soviet Russia is a country which has two sides. The obverse is a socialised community living, and struggling for its existence, in a capitalist world, guided, in part though not wholly, by Marxist doctrine, and prepared to employ every possible expedient in order to save the Revolution; the reverse is a country of continual Socialist experiments, some successful, some unsuccessful, but all based on assumptions which have little or nothing to do with Marx, whose writings, indeed, afford no guidance whatever as regards the details of life in a socialised State. To the first aspect belong the Constitution itself, and its basing upon the foundation of Soviets; to it, also, belongs the strong and merciless drive towards the collectivisation of the countryside, in order that no class of peasant proprietors should arise to turn revolutionary Russia into a counterpart of modern France; and with these goes also the apparatus of defence against enemies abroad and traitors at home, the Red Army and the G.P.U. To it, again, belongs the foreign policy of the Soviet Government, though this is far less Marxist than the other features mentioned, for the simple reason that the Marxian philosophy does not include prescriptions for the conduct of a Socialist State in a capitalist world.

The Marxian analysis has been generally taken to assume a world-wide breakdown of imperialist Capitalism, with the consequent arrival of Socialism on all sides, if not with absolute simultaneity, at least more or less at the same time; and for a brief while after the October Revolution it seemed as if this prophecy was likely to be fulfilled. There was a political revolution in Germany which looked like the prelude to a much more far-reaching social revolution; in Bavaria and Hungary Soviet Governments were actually set up; even in Great Britain the industrial workers and the returning soldiers created a situation that momentarily alarmed the governing classes. The Russians, at all events, believed that world revolution was only just round the corner; they had little hope, at that time, of preserving their own revolution without the assistance of other Socialist communities; and they set up immediately the Third International of Communist political parties (Comintern) and the Red International of Labour Unions (Profintern) to help foment revolution in the capitalist countries. But as time passed it soon became clear that not only was world revolution far away, but no other country was going immediately to follow the Russian example; and after they had disposed of their civil war and their foreign invaders, the Russians had to decide whether to pursue the policy of stirring up revolutions outside, or to try and come to terms with the capitalist world. The struggle between these two policies formed part of the great battle between Trotsky and Stalin, and in it the adherents of world revolution were decisively beaten. The Red Internationals were not disbanded, for the Russians are still Communist and Communism is still an international creed, and the Red Flag must be kept flying all over the world; but they received less and less attention. Russia's foreign policy has become definitely empirical, aimed at keeping on the best terms possible, without sacrifice of her own Socialism, with countries which she knows would welcome its destruction, even taking part in the activities of the once-abominated capitalist League of Nations, and showing her Communism principally by special encouragement and friendliness towards such Eastern and Near-Eastern countries as might possibly follow her course of economic development, i.e. leap straight to advanced industrialism without the preliminary stages through which the West has passed.

Turning now to the reverse side, we have no space to detail all the social experiments of the Soviet régime; but there is general agreement among all observers that, in intention if not always in achievement, the Russian laws and institutions which deal with women and children, education, culture, and similar departments of life are admirable, and that there has been a real attempt both to industrialise Russia without bringing in the inhumanities and horrors of the Western Industrial Revolution and to achieve something approaching a Socialist distribution of the available goods and services. These are matters of internal experimentation, and here all who are not root-and-branch opponents of any form of socialisation, including many who bitterly dislike the repressive side of modern Russia, agree that the Western world has very much to learn, if not slavishly to imitate, from the Russians. Perhaps the clearest example of the contrast is shown by the Russian legal and penal systems. On the one hand, the normal legal system of Russia is extraordinarily simple and informal; the procedure of the courts is easy to follow, and there is no complicated tangle of case-law. The legal profession is not, as in England, a caste apart; lay judges, who work at their trades between cases and who have only the minimum of legal instruction, sit with the permanent judges in all trial courts; pleaders are remunerated by salary and not by fees, and there is a universal endeavour to see that all that can be said in favour of the accused is said, and that his penalty, if he is found guilty, reasonably fits his crime. Furthermore, penalties are light, and there is a really amazing effort to secure that terms of imprisonment, for example, shall result in the curing of the prisoner.

In this, as in other matters, the Russian conception of a law or decree as "normative" causes much confusion in the Western mind. The Western idea of a "law" is something to which no exception should be allowed; a law which is not enforced is a bad law or a law badly administered. But a Russian law is as it were declaratory of what ought to be the general practice, and will be in force roughly in proportion to the importance which is attached to it, the practical possibility of its enforcement, and, in individual cases, the degree of hardship which its enforcement would entail. "Hard cases make bad law," says the English jurist, and can only temper the law in cases of patent injustice by complicated machinery of equity and pardon; but the Russian in practice entrusts the actual decision on the extent to which the law shall be enforced to the man on the spot, i.e. the collective, and relies upon inspective and cleansing bodies, such as the R.K.I., to see that this privilege is not abused. Hence the great discrepancy which observers notice with perplexity between the wide intentions of some of the Russian laws and the degree to which they are enforced. The *intention* is that they shall be the standard, as and when it is practicable.

On the other hand, there is the machinery of internal coercion, of which the G.P.U. with its army of plain-clothes spies, and practically unrestricted power of striking secretly at persons suspected of counter-revolutionary activities, was for long the outstanding example. It is true that in the summer of 1934 the G.P.U. was officially disbanded; and it is also probable that, as has been stated by an English non-Communist writer, it was never, in action, as terrible as it liked people to believe. But its liquidation does not by any means imply that political speech and action in Russia have yet secured even the limited freedom which they have in liberal-capitalist countries like France and Great Britain.

What is to be the future of these two elements in Russian political life? No one can answer this question: for the answer depends upon the success of the Russian socialised economy, and, even if that be assumed, upon the attitude taken up towards Russia by the outside world. The orthodox Marxist answer is that with the completion of Socialism "the State," i.e. the machinery of coercion, will "wither away." But the completion of Socialism certainly involves, if not a completely Socialist world, at any rate a world in which Socialist States do not have to go in continual fear of attack by their capitalist neighbours. Russian internal institutions have progressed at least far enough to show what can be done even under present circumstances; but no one who looks realistically at the way in which foreign nations, even those which are not at all likely to take actual part in an invasion, still regard the Russian system, can expect the machinery of coercion to do much "withering away" at present. A Russian who should propose immediate disarmament against the enemies of the Soviet either at home or abroad would be a political idiot. The real question, apart from success in the economic field, is whether the security which alone can make a relaxation possible can be achieved before the coercive institutions have acquired that secondary life of their own which has often in past history caused institutions to survive after they have ceased to have any practical utility and have even become noxious. There is always the danger that this may happen; and those who desire coercive institutions to wither, and the Socialist institutions to go on experimenting and developing should realise that the practical answer to their question lies not in Russia itself, but outside—in effect, in their own States.

8. THE POLITICAL SYSTEM OF TURKEY

OF ALL the dictatorships that have been created since 1918, that of Turkey is in practice the most complete and has been the most ruthless in its handling of opposition. It has been in effect the dictatorship of one man, gathering complete authority into his own hands and using his immense personal prestige and popularity both to stamp out all organised opposition and to enforce a clearly conceived national policy which has gone as far as that of Russia in altering the way of living of an entire people. This dictatorship of a single man has now behind it the support of a large and highly organised political party, which has been the only party allowed to exist, though more tolerance is at length being allowed to forms of opposition which do not challenge the fundamental institutions of the new régime. But the dictatorship is in form thoroughly democratic, based on a wide franchise to which women were admitted in 1931 (they got the municipal vote in 1930). On this franchise there is elected a Single-Chamber Assembly, which possesses both undivided legislative power and the right to appoint the President. Mustapha Kemal, who holds this office, is thus the choice of an assembly elected on a democratic basis; but in fact the members of the Assembly have all belonged to one party—Mustapha Kemal's own creation—and they have been in effect chosen by that party in the absence of any organised opposition. Equally with Italy or Germany, and more completely than Russia, Turkey has been in recent years a one-party State.

Mustapha Kemal owes this remarkable ascendancy, and his power to use it for the radical re-fashioning of the entire national life, to the overwhelming prestige which he enjoys as the saviour of his country. Turkey came out of the War not merely defeated and weak, but threatened with complete extinction as an independent State. Her old capital, Constantinople, was in Allied occupation, and her Sultan a mere tool in the hands of the Allies. Her territory was being dismembered and parcelled out among the Allies; and what was to be left nominally under Turkish rule was being divided up into spheres of influence by the Allied Powers. Luckily for the Turks, the Allies did not agree among themselves about the distribution of the spoils. There were constant dissensions between the British, the French, and the Italians; and these worked out to Turkey's profit. Great Britain must take most of the blame for the handling of the situation; for the British were chiefly behind that Greek invasion of Asia Minor which finally aroused among the Turks an irresistible wave of national feeling, and enabled Mustapha Kemal, as General of the Turkish National Army, to drive the Greeks in rout out of Asia Minor, and establish the new national Turkish State. The Allies were compelled to recognise the Turkish victory. The Sèvres Treaty of 1920, which had imposed onerous and humiliating terms upon the Turks, was torn up; and the Lausanne Treaty of 1923 gave Turkey back her independence within restricted frontiers that enabled her to begin building up her new State on a basis of national unity.

THE NEW TURKEY

The first thing to understand about the new Turkey is that it is utterly different from the old. The new Turkey is a national State, with a mainly homogeneous population, including since the mass exchanges of population with Greece and Bulgaria the vast majority of Turkish people, and not very many of other nationalities, though there still remain some "minority" problems, such as that of the Kurds in Asia Minor, as well as a large mixed population in Constantinople. Despite these minorities, present-day Turkey is essentially a national State; but that is precisely what the old heterogeneous Turkish Empire never was at any stage of its existence. The unity of the old Turkey was purely enforced and dynastic; it had no sense of internal community. What unity it had united it not as an empire, but as the centre of a religious movement extending far beyond its territorial boundaries; for the Sultan was Caliph as well as Sultan, and was thus the spiritual head of the entire Mohammedan world. The new Turkey, under Kemal, has swept this religious basis clean away. The Caliphate, retained for a brief while after the abolition of the Sultanate in 1922, was finally abolished in 1924; and Kemal built up the new Turkey on a completely secular basis, with secular education under the State and a new purely secular legal code, based on that of Switzerland, to take the place of the old religious code. Where the "Young Turks" failed to Westernise Turkey after the Revolution of 1908, Kemal has succeeded, because he has been able to build on nationalist foundations within a national territory that has lost its unwieldy and embarrassing empire.

For some time after the War there were two Governments in Turkey—the Sultan's Government in Constantinople, under Allied military control and with virtually no authority over the rest of the country, and the Government of the National Assembly at Angora, dominated by Kemal. The first assembly controlled by Kemal met at Erzerum in 1919; but the effective foundation of the new Turkey began with the Angora National Assembly of 1920, under whose auspices Kemal waged his victorious war against the Greeks. The Sultan's Government remained in being until 1922 when, Allied protection having been withdrawn, the Sultan fled and the Angora Government occupied Constantinople. The Angora Assembly had already proclaimed itself in 1920 to be the sole fount of authority, and had declared that the sovereignty of the Turkish nation belonged to the people; but only in 1922 was the Sultanate definitely abolished, and the Caliphate made a separate office, to be held by a member of the house of Osman, without temporal power, till it too was abolished in 1924. Before this latter step was taken, Turkey had been formally proclaimed a Republic in 1923, and Mustapha Kemal had been elected as its first President.

Up to this point, the real form which the Government of the new State was to assume had not been settled. Under the Fundamental Law voted by the Angora National Assembly in 1921, the Assembly was declared to be the sole representative of the people, and provision was made for its re-election every two years. Voting for the Assembly was to be indirect, through a system of electoral "colleges" chosen on a wide male suffrage. In the revised Constitution of 1924 indirect voting was retained, but the term of the single-chamber Assembly was extended to four years. Later, direct has replaced indirect voting, but the old system was still in use at the election of 1931, at which Kemal's Popular Party returned every candidate. In effect, the institution of the "one-party" State and the spread of literacy under the new educational system—the percentage of illiterates had been very high—are making the system of indirect election obsolete. Women received the municipal vote in 1930 and the national vote in 1931. Local Government has remained under strong central control. The territory of Turkey is divided into 63 *vilayets,* each under a *Vali* appointed by the Government. The smallest local units of government are the *nahiyes,* which are grouped into *Karas.* Each *Kara* is also under an official appointed by the State. Each *vilayet* and each *nahiye* has also an elected Council; but in the case of the *vilayet* this is more an advisory than a governing body.

Up to 1924, the new Turkish State was still dominated by the task of clearing up the disorder left over from the War. Mustapha Kemal was in effective command of the country by virtue of his position as leader of the victorious National Army which he himself had created; and on its loyalty he could thoroughly rely. He was President of the National Assembly, and under the new Constitution of 1924 therewith President of the Turkish Republic; and he had begun from 1923 to build up his Popular Party, with its governing statute opening with the words—"The goal of the Party is government by the people and for the people, together with the elevation of Turkey to the status of a modern State." The Party Statute goes on to declare for the complete separation of politics from religion, the abolition of all forms of class-privilege, and the complete equality of rights among all citizens, including both men and women. It urges the re-organisation of the Republic on modern lines, on a scientific and technical basis derived from the most advanced countries. The Party thus declared unequivocally as far back as 1923 for the entire programme of Westernisation which has since been carried into effect.

But, while Mustapha Kemal was in 1924 at the height of his prestige as a national leader, and already pressing forward actively with his policy of secularisation and development, he was still far short of being a dictator in the political sphere. Before he could establish his position of unquestioned predominance he had to do battle with what remained of the old "progressive" forces which, under the name of the "Committee of Union and Progress," had made the Turkish Revolution of 1908. Kemal had himself taken part in this movement, as a young officer at Salonika; but the political leaders who had governed Turkey after the Revolution had been discredited in the eyes of the people by the successive disasters of the Balkan Wars and of the World War, and thereafter by their subservience to the Allies in yielding to the terms of the Sèvres Treaty and acting as a puppet Government at Constantinople during the Allied occupation. These defects had lost the Young Turks their popular following; and, while not all the leaders opposed to Kemal shared in these handicaps, most did, and the few who did not were quite unable to stand out against him. These rivals, opposing Kemal's ascendancy, wanted to make Turkey into a Parliamentary State, with rival parties and the rest of the technique of Western parliamentarism. For a time Kemal's friend and follower, Ismet, was driven from office as Prime Minister, and the opposition of "Progressives," under Fehti Bey, assumed office, with a programme hostile to Kemal's demand for a centralised and disciplined State. Kemal thereupon asserted his authority over the Assembly, and, on the plea that the "liberal" policy of the Progressives had caused the Kurdish revolt, which he ruthlessly suppressed, drove Fehti from office, re-instated Ismet, and secured the passing of a "Law for the Preservation of Order," under which the entire opposition was speedily suppressed by a system of "Tribunals of Independence." A number of Kemal's leading opponents were executed, and others driven into exile; and he and his Popular Party, which he had founded in 1923, became undisputed masters of the situation.

KEMAL'S AUTHORITY

But even after his victory, Kemal carefully refrained from giving his ascendancy the form of an open dictatorship; nor has it that form to-day. Kemal is President of the Turkish Republic, elected to that office by vote of the National Assembly for the four-year period of the Assembly's own life, and eligible for re-election. As President he has no wide constitutional powers. He can send back to the Assembly a law of which he disapproves; but the Assembly can then re-vote it over his veto. He can appoint the Prime Minister, who then chooses his colleagues; but the Cabinet has to secure the approval of the Assembly. The President has no law-making power; nor are his acts valid without the counter-signature of the Prime Minister and the departmental Minister directly concerned.

But Kemal is not only President, but also Commander-in-Chief of the Army, and President of the Popular Party; and it is on this combination of offices that his authority is based. At bottom, however, it depends even more on his personal force and prestige than on any office, and it by no means follows that his successor will be able to inherit his power.

Since his victory of 1925, Mustapha Kemal has pressed on vigorously with his policy of transforming Turkey into an advanced national State, based on completely secular institutions, mainly modelled on Western Europe. The religious orders have been abolished and the schools completely secularised; compulsory elementary education has been introduced, and the elaborate Turkish alphabet replaced by that used in Europe; the language has been simplified; women have been granted complete educational and social, as well as political, equality with men; the marriage laws have been secularised and Westernised; European costumes have been made compulsory; the law courts have been completely re-modelled on Western lines. These reforms, which were expected by many observers to break Kemal's power against the strength of the old cultural and religious traditions, have in fact been carried through with astonishing success with the aid of strong government and the widespread energy of the Popular Party. There has been resentment, no doubt, but no open opposition since the ruthless stamping out of the Kurdish rebels and the Progressive Party.

TURKISH FOREIGN POLICY

This success has been greatly aided by the enlightened vigour of Turkish economic and international policy. Internationally, Turkey under Kemal has consolidated her position by making plain that she has neither the ambition nor the desire to regain her lost territories; and the sincerity of this attitude has been confirmed by the mass exchange of populations, above all by the mass removal of the Greeks from Asia Minor in return for Turks received from the enlarged Greek territory. This policy has been followed up by the conclusion of non-aggression pacts with all her neighbours, culminating in the entry into the League of Nations in 1932, and, most recently, by her partnership with Greece, Yugoslavia and Rumania in the Balkan Pact of 1934, which has not prevented her from remaining on good terms with Bulgaria. The first of all States to recognise the new Turkish Republic was Russia, with which she signed a Treaty embodying a complete settlement of boundaries in 1921; and ever since the Turks have remained on excellent terms with the U.S.S.R. Mustapha Kemal has been evidently influenced in his economic policy by the development of Economic Planning in Russia. Indeed, at the beginning of 1934 the Turks adopted a Five Year Plan of their own.

TURKEY'S ECONOMIC PROBLEMS

Turkey has been hard-hit economically by the conditions of post-war production and trade. Her handicraft industries used to produce a wide range of products for the world market; but these have been gradually ousted by mass-produced goods from the industrial countries, leaving her mainly dependent on agricultural exports, including tobacco. The sharp fall in the world prices of these exports created a very difficult economic situation. The Turkish Government, in order to save the peasants from ruin, adopted a system of very high protective tariffs, using the tariff revenue as a means of subsidising exports; and steps were also taken to develop home industries for the working up of agricultural products, especially sugar and cotton. In sugar Turkey is now equipped to be practically self-supporting; and great efforts are being made to improve the quality of native cotton, and to establish a cotton industry, largely with British machinery. The peasants are also being trained under State supervision in the use of agricultural machinery and advanced methods of cultivation.

One great problem for the Turks has been that of improving means of communication in Asia Minor, where the bulk of the population is now centred. Old Turkey had good European railways; but little effort had been made to open up the interior of Asia Minor. Now that fourteen millions of the Turkish people live in Asia and only one million in Europe, and the capital is at Angora instead of Constantinople, Turkey has become mainly an Asiatic State; and Kemal's plans of economic development depend absolutely on securing access to markets for the peasants of the Asiatic hinterland, as well as communications which will make easier the spread of the new methods and ideas. Accordingly, the Turkish Government has been very active in railway-building; and, although the work has had to be carried through largely by foreign firms and engineers, it has been done without incurring fresh foreign debts, at the cost of a capital burden which has fallen heavily on the current standard of life.

Already this policy has produced very big results. Between 1928 and 1932 the value of industrial production rose from £ (Turkish) 40,000,000 to £100,000,000; and railway mileage has been increased from 1,440 in 1923 to over 4,000. Moreover, Turkish economy has been, by a series of nationalist measures, freed from its previous domination by foreign capitalists. Foreign corporations operating in Turkey are now compelled to include Turkish directors, to employ Turks, and to use the Turkish language. Turkish shipping has been fostered by navigation laws reserving the coasting trade for native vessels; and an elaborate system of State control and State financing has been built up for the development of industry in native hands. Economically as well as politically, Turkish policy has been based on a thorough-going nationalism; but this Turkish nationalism is of a defensive and not of an imperialist type.

THE TURKISH POLITICAL SITUATION

If we compare the Turkish form of the "one-party" State, as it has developed under Kemal, with the proletarian dictatorship of Russia, or with the Fascist dictatorships of Italy and Germany, we observe, first, that in Turkey alone has the new system been founded mainly on nationalist considerations. The Soviet Union has recognised nationality, but is itself founded on internationalist and class ideas. Fascism in Italy and Germany has large elements of nationalism, but came to power even more as the antagonist of Socialism than as the standard-bearer of nationalism. But in Turkey there was no Socialist movement to combat. What brought Mustapha Kemal to power was a nationalist revolt against the attempts of the Allies to dismember and subject the Turkish territory. The Sultan lost his throne because he became a mere puppet in the hands of the Allies; and Kemal became arbiter of Turkey's fortunes because he beat the Greeks and compelled the Allies to abandon the Sèvres Treaty. The foundation of Kemal's authority was therefore military power, reinforced by national prestige; and his command of the Army's absolute loyalty enabled him to stamp pitilessly upon the political opposition that sought to prevent his dictatorship. Ultimately, his power still rests on the Army, and the stringent military control on the frontiers impresses this upon every visitor to Turkey; but he has now supplemented that source of authority by gathering round him a powerful political party, well organised and numerous throughout the country, and established through the dictatorship as the sole avenue to political influence or to playing a part in the great work of national reconstruction. Kemal has thus got behind him, since the complete destruction of the Opposition leaders, all the elements in the country—including a very large number of women—who are keen to work for the establishment of Turkey as an economically and culturally advanced country, adapting what is valuable in European institutions and European knowledge to serve its own special ends. All observers agree that the advances made during the eleven years' life of the new system have been astonishing, and that Turkey enjoys incomparably better government than ever before. Mustapha Kemal has not secured his ends without a brutality that is deeply shocking to the Western mind—at least as shocking as anything that has happened in Hitler's Germany. But there is no manner of doubt that he and his party have used their dictatorial power in the interest of the mass of the people, or that as a result of it the Turkish peasant is in process of becoming both more civilised and economically better off. Turkey under Kemal's dictatorship is no longer "the Sick Man of Europe," but the healthy and rapidly growing adolescent Republic of the Near East, on good terms alike with Russia and with her Balkan neighbours, intensely nationalist and yet in her nationalism no menace to any other State. These are undoubtedly great achievements for a country that seemed in 1918 to be at the point of final and complete dissolution.

9. THE POLITICAL SYSTEM OF JAPAN

IF YOU LOOK up the constitution of Japan in a standard work of reference, you will find that it bears a close resemblance to that of one of the parliamentary States of Western Europe. There is an Emperor, who appears to be a constitutional monarch, governing through a Cabinet of Ministers. There is a Parliament of two Chambers, one largely hereditary and the other elected, since 1925, by Manhood Suffrage and secret ballot. This Parliament passes laws, which require the Emperor's signature; and the popular Chamber passes the annual Budget, just like the British House of Commons. There is a Civil Service, under the control of the Cabinet Ministers, and a central control over local government which looks very like the system existing in France. There are two large political parties which appear alternately to provide the Government, and some smaller parties, which figure in it occasionally. At present, there is in office a "National" Government, consisting largely of officials, but including leading naval officers, obviously put in office with a view to the impending negotiations about naval armaments under the Washington Treaty.

In short, there appears to be all the regular paraphernalia of parliamentary democracy. But in fact the Japanese political system is not in the least like that of a parliamentary country. It is not very much more parliamentary than Nazi Germany or Fascist Italy; and it is in reality even more remote from Western "liberalism" than either of these, because its institutions rest on radically different social traditions and ways of thought. The true nature of a political system cannot be understood by merely mastering the formal structure of its institutions, but only by discovering how they really work.

Yet the Japanese system has been imitated largely from Western originals. Japan imitated Western political institutions after the great "Restoration" of 1867, just as she imitated Western industrial technique, Western banking, Western science, and Western armaments. But whereas in these other respects the adoption of Western methods involved a real conversion to Western practices, Japanese parliamentarism has never been more than skin-deep, and responsible parliamentary government has never existed, and certainly does not exist to-day.

PARLIAMENT AND THE ARMED FORCES

This weakness of Japanese parliamentarism is not mainly the result of a failure on the part of the parliamentary leaders to use the powers conferred upon them by the Constitution, but of a deliberate withholding of the powers required for the real effectiveness of parliamentary government. Thus, while Japan possesses a Cabinet and a Parliament which votes the annual Budget, in effect the Cabinet is responsible not to Parliament but to the "Emperor"— which means the influences surrounding the Emperor. The Cabinet is usually composed mainly of ministers drawn from the leading parliamentary party; but this does not apply to the ministers who preside over the fighting departments, since the fighting services are not under parliamentary control, but are within the exclusive domain of the Emperor. These services, responsible only to the Emperor, can put forward their own demands for expenditure, which the Cabinet has to accept; and a Party Cabinet can have forced upon it, as Ministers of War and Marine, colleagues whom it heartily dislikes and of whose policy it disapproves. This alone would reduce to a farce the "power of the purse," which is generally regarded as the keystone of the arch of parliamentary control. But Parliament does not even possess this power in relation to the Civil Services. It can indeed refuse to vote the Budget put before it; but if it does refuse the effect is not, as in a parliamentary country, to stop supply, for the Budget last voted thereafter remains in force until a new Budget is voted in its place. In other words, the old taxes remain, even if Parliament refuses to vote them; and as there is nothing to prevent the Emperor from borrowing to meet a deficit, the fighting services have always the whip hand of both Parliament and the civilian members of the Cabinet. The Army chiefs claim independent powers of executive action; and they have often pursued their own policy regardless of the views of their Cabinet colleagues. The offensive which resulted in the establishment of the puppet Emperor of Manchukuo was launched by the Army without the prior consent of the Cabinet.

This independent position of the fighting services is the key to the Japanese political situation. Of late the real controller of Japan's international policy has been far more the militarist War Minister, General Araki, than the Prime Minister or the Minister of Foreign Affairs; and now that Araki has resigned owing to illness, his power seems to have passed to his successor, who is also his nominee. The most effective check upon the War Minister's authority is, indeed, not the Cabinet, but rather a dignitary unknown to the formal Constitution of Japan, the so-called "Elder Statesman," Prince Saionji. Formerly there were a number of "Elder Statesmen," with a recognised right by custom to be consulted by the Emperor when vital questions of policy were being discussed; but now Prince Saionji is the only survivor regarded as possessing this claim—and he is very old. But for his moderating influence it is probable that Japanese policy would have been even more intransigeant than it has actually been. He is said to have tried to keep Japan within the League of Nations, and to have succeeded for a time; and he is said recently to have resisted the demands of the Army leaders for the replacement of the parliamentary Cabinet by a non-party Cabinet of officials that could be relied on to support the militarists' demands. Japanese parliamentarism is a puny thing; but the Army leaders are eager to do away with even the shadow of democracy which it represents, and to establish openly a dictatorial government of the type called "Fascist" in European countries.

THE RESTORATION AND AFTER

Japanese political conditions can hardly be understood without some reference to the so-called "Restoration" of 1867, which was the beginning of Japan's emergence as a Great Power. It is well known that up to the middle of the last century Japan was a feudal State, shut off from the rest of the world by stringent laws which denied all access to foreigners, and sought to keep the entire country immune from foreign influences. This isolation came sharply to an end when the American Naval Commander, Perry, demonstrated by bombardment the superior claims of Western civilisation, and compelled the Japanese to open their ports. Then followed further incidents— isolated onslaughts on foreign sailors by Japanese, and retaliatory educational bombardments by British naval vessels. These occurrences convinced the Japanese that in order to stand up to the West they must imitate its technique, and with extraordinary rapidity and thoroughness they set about the complete refashioning of their way of life. The first step was a political Revolution, made in form as a movement for the restoration of the Emperor's political power. For centuries before 1867 the Emperor, regarded with immense reverence as the religious and spiritual head of the State, had been wholly stripped of political authority, which was exercised by a hereditary officer, the Shogun, who held a Court of his own, and received the acknowledgment of the other feudal lords. The Shogun was himself a great feudal lord, ruling a large tract of territory under his direct control. The rest of the country was governed by other great feudal lords, much after the manner of a medieval feudal State in Europe. But in 1867 the last of the Shoguns was compelled to resign his power by a movement which, under the form of restoring all power to the Emperor, aimed at the complete modernisation of Japan by the introduction of European industries, arms and knowledge.

It is unnecessary here to detail the stages by which this remarkable movement accomplished its purpose. The Shogun's own estates were taken directly under the Imperial Government; and before long the other feudal lords were induced to resign their powers to the Emperor, and a feudal rebellion in part of the country was successfully crushed. A powerful group of bureaucrats, drawn mainly from the class of Samurai (fighting retainers of the feudal lords), made Japan into a highly centralised State under strong governmental control. The old nobles and the Samurai were persuaded to resign their privileges, and compensated by pensions which put an immense strain on the finances of the new State, and could be paid only with the help of money borrowed from abroad. The Constitution was at first mainly aristocratic, the Imperial Ministers governing with the aid of nominated Councils, whose form was often changed, without any representative basis. But in 1889 a Constitution embodying a form of parliamentarism was adopted, largely by way of imitation of Bismarckian Germany; and this Constitution, modified by the introduction of Manhood Suffrage in 1925, is still in force.

We have described the Samurai as fighting retainers of the feudal lords; but if they had been no more than this, modern Japan would be a very different country. For the Samurai, when they renounced their privileges and went over to the cause of Westernisation, carried with them their coherence as a group and the code of conduct—*Bushido*—in which they had been trained. It is hardly possible to describe *Bushido* in a few words. It is a moral code created by and for a class of warriors, exalting the military virtues above all others and involving some contempt for those who engage in commerce, extolling an ideal of devotion to the interests of the State as represented, since the "Restoration," by the person of the Emperor, and above all holding the Samurai together as a class even in face of the complete transformation of social conditions which they have helped to bring about. Inevitably, the Samurai dominate the fighting forces of the State; and no less inevitably, being closely connected with the land and not with industry or commerce, they are more inclined to take side with the impoverished peasants than with the great capitalists. This explains why the leaders of the Japanese Army and Navy, while intensely militaristic, are not social reactionaries when it comes to agrarian questions. It explains, too, why Samurai officers and peasant leaders have been found side by side in "Fascist" movements, and why Army officers have assassinated bankers and business men as readily as they have suppressed movements among the industrial workers.

THE JAPANESE CONSTITUTION

Japan has a Parliament of two Houses. The Upper House consists of four elements—an upper class of nobles who sit by right and for life, a second class of hereditary nobles elected by and from the various grades of nobility, persons nominated by the Emperor for eminent service to the State, and a person chosen by and from the fifteen richest taxpayers in each electoral area—this last a direct borrowing from the pre-war electoral system of Prussia. The Lower House was until 1925 elected on a restricted property franchise, but is now chosen by Manhood Suffrage by means of the ballot, which is workable in Japan because compulsory State education has practically wiped out illiteracy. The Ministry is usually so chosen as to command a majority in the Lower House; but it can be at any time dismissed, and the Lower House dissolved, by the Emperor—and in practice the Party summoned to power by the Emperor can usually secure a majority over its rivals. The Upper House, which cannot be dissolved, is re-elected every seven years, except the nobles who sit by right and the members appointed by the Emperor, who also serve for life. Bills must pass both Houses and require the Emperor's consent; but the Budget is initiated in the Lower House, which sits for four years, unless it is previously dissolved.

All this parliamentary apparatus means, as we saw, much less than it appears to mean, because the military departments are entirely outside the control of Parliament, and there is no effective "power of the purse." Nor do the rival parties in Japan stand for vitally different policies. The two leading parties at present are the Seiyukai and the Minseito; but they are more remarkable for their internal corruption, and for their close association with financial interests, than for their rivalry in political doctrine. Broadly, the Seiyukai Party is usually regarded as the political representative of the agrarian interests and as the associate of the great Mitsui Combine, a vast banking and industrial concern which ramifies into almost every leading branch of industry and trade, but is connected above all with internal trade and with armament-making. The Minseito Party, for its part, is more closely connected with the interests concerned in the export trade and is therefore commonly disposed to favour a more conciliatory foreign policy. But it too has close associations with the armaments industry; for whereas the Seiyukai leans upon the Mitsui Combine, the Minseito has depended on the rival Mitsubishi concern, which also bases its power largely on the armaments industry, and is also closely connected with every branch of engineering and shipbuilding, with coal and steel and electrical production, and of course with naval construction. The rival parties have thus been largely concerned with the securing of contracts for the financial groups which uphold their political fortunes; and there have been numerous financial scandals in recent years arising out of these connections.

Closely as both the leading parties are associated with the armaments industry, the military leaders stand for the most part outside them both, and constitute in effect a third, and strongest, party in the State. It is a point of substantial importance that there is in Japanese militarism a strong anti-capitalist tinge. The old Japanese social code put the soldier in the position of pre-eminence, and looked down upon the merchant as lower than the peasant or the artisan; and this feeling still survives strongly in the military classes, despite the intense industrial development through which the country has passed. The Japanese have more than any other people a "sense of the State," which expresses itself above all in an unbounded military loyalty. As we have seen, the members of the old warrior class of Samurai, who still dominate the country, preserve the traditional contempt for the merchants and financiers, and extend it to the politicians, whom they regard as the tools of these groups. Consequently, and also because many of the Samurai are poor, the extreme militarists are usually more sympathetic to the peasants, if not to the industrial workers influenced by Socialist ideas, than to the capitalists and the politicians. Even a section of those who were Socialists is now found working in alliance with the militarists in a sort of Fascist Party against the orthodox parliamentary parties; for in 1932 the Social Democratic Party split, and nearly half its members went over to a new "National Socialist" Party with a Fascist programme.

Indeed, the multiplication and constant readjustment of parties has been a highly significant feature of recent political developments in Japan. Quite recently, the Minseito Party in the Diet split, and Adachi, one of its leaders, carried over about thirty of its 146 members to a new "Fascist" Party, the *Kokumin Domei,* which advocates a one-party "totalitarian" State on the Fascist model. Further to the right is the aristocratic *Kokuhonska,* led by Hiranuma, which represents the old aristocratic elements; while far to the left is another party often described as "Fascist"—the *Seisanto,* or "Producers' " Party. This is a curious body, largely recruited from ex-Communists. It is strongly militarist, and believes in Japan's mission to liberate all the Far East from exploitation by the Western Powers. It works in closely with the military leaders, and with the powerful *Zaigo Gunjinkai,* or Reservists' Association, from which it draws much of its support. Its economic policy, however, is aggressively left-wing. It demands the socialisation of industry by the Emperor, to whom it professes absolute loyalty; and it acclaims this policy of socialisation as the logical sequel to the "Restoration" by which the Emperor resumed possession of the feudal fiefs in 1868. The *Seisanto* also works in closely with the Black Dragon Society, which has been the protagonist of the Pan-Asiatic Movement in Japan.

Socialism in Japan has passed through many vicissitudes in recent years. There was after the War a wave of Socialist feeling, especially among the intellectuals, followed by the growth of a considerable Communist movement after 1922. From 1928 onwards the Communist Party was suppressed, and nearly thirty thousand of its members suffered arrest. It still exists, underground; but much of its following has passed over to the *Seisanto.* The orthodox Socialist Party, *Shakai Jaishuto,* has not been suppressed, and has a few seats in the Diet. There has been also a left-wing Peasants' Party, the *Ronoto;* but this has shared the fate of the Communist Party, and is now working illegally, if it still exists.

THE JAPANESE PEASANTS AND WORKERS

The peasant problem is of vital importance. Japan is a crowded, mountainous country, of which a very large part is unsuitable for cultivation. There are great differences of climate, so that migration from the more to the less crowded parts is made difficult because of the unsuitability of the colder areas for settlers from the warmer districts. The same difference of climate has been one factor preventing any large-scale emigration of Japanese to Manchuria or the other areas under Japan's political control. But in these cases there is also the difficulty that the Japanese settler is unable to establish himself on the land in countries where the peasant standard of living is even lower than his own. Consequently, the central areas of Japan suffer from great over-population, which causes peasant holdings to be so small as to be barely capable in many cases of supporting the cultivators. Rice is, of course, the principal crop, though wheat and other cereals are grown in certain parts.

As a means of eking out the peasant standard of life, great attention has been given in the past to encouraging the production of raw silk, which has been largely exported to the United States. But the great fall in the American demand for silk and silk goods during the depression has hit the Japanese peasantry very hard indeed; and this has led to widespread peasant unrest, which has received some backing from the military leaders. On the other hand the two leading political parties, closely associated with industrial Capitalism, find in the necessities of the peasants a plentiful source of cheap factory labour, which enables them to undercut with cheap textiles and other exports the relatively high-wage products of the older countries. The deliberate depreciation of the Japanese currency has further stimulated exports, and caused a rise in internal prices, though this has not been nearly equal to the degree of the depreciation. It has, however, been big enough to aggravate the peasants' difficulties, and to increase peasant unrest, with the compensation, from the industrialists' standpoint, of swelling the supply of cheap factory labour, consisting largely of girls who are virtually sold by their impoverished parents into a period of years of factory slavery.

Among the industrial workers also there has been a great deal of unrest; and in certain sections Communist and Socialist ideas have received a ready hearing. But extremist movements have been severely repressed, particularly where they have been tinged with internationalism; and Japanese Trade Unionism, though it has not been crushed out, is weak and sharply divided among rival factions with widely different outlooks. It should, however, be remembered, first, that wage-standards in Japan are substantially higher than in India or China, and secondly that Trade Unionism has a far better foundation in Japan than elsewhere in the Far East because almost the entire population is literate.

JAPANESE "FASCISM"

In this situation, with the two leading political parties largely identified with rival groups of industrialists and financiers, and a sharp opposition between them and the military caste, which is constantly threatening to upset the Budget or compel the raising of higher taxes in order to meet the rapidly rising military expenditure, a continual state of tension exists. The allegation is constantly made that the politicians favour the enrichment of the interests which they represent at the expense of the claims of national honour and glory. Among the younger officers and adherents of the Military Party patriotic feeling runs exceedingly high, and finds expression in secret leagues whose members pledge themselves to the most extreme actions in what they hold to be the supreme interest of the State. These leagues have of late years resorted again and again to the assassination of high personages of whose attitude and policy they have disapproved. Hara, the first commoner to become Prime Minister of Japan, and the leader of the Seiyukai, was assassinated in 1921, as well as the President of the Yasuda Bank, the outstanding figure in the Japanese banking world. A second Prime Minister, Hamaguchi, was mortally wounded by an extreme Nationalist in 1930; and a third minister, Inukai, was killed by militarists in 1932. Assassination has thus become a regular weapon in the hands of the militarists; and offences of this sort, held to be actuated by patriotic motives, are treated with the most remarkable leniency. Thus, the Naval officers who murdered Inukai, after being sentenced to a term of imprisonment, were pardoned by the Emperor at the request of the militarists, and received a public ovation on their release.

To a great extent, Japan possesses already most of the characteristics that are associated in Europe with the "totalitarian" State. Local government is under a highly centralised control by officials appointed by the Central Authority, so that the locally elected Councils have very little power. The central administrative system is highly authoritarian and bureaucratic, and penetrates into every part of the national life, actively suppressing criticism and removing inconvenient persons from positions of influence. Industry and commerce have been fostered under strong State encouragement and control, with State participation and financial help in many types of enterprise; and the Japanese business man, in his dealings with the outside world, confidently expects the backing of the State authority to which he submits practically without question. The monetary system and commercial relations are managed under the control of the State to serve the national interest; and in the organisation of every branch of economic activity, including agriculture, Japan comes far nearer to possessing a "planned economy" than any other great State except Russia.

But whereas European Fascism, despite all the exaltation of the military virtues, has been a movement of citizens, in Japan extreme Nationalism bases its power directly upon the armed forces, with their assured immunity from parliamentary control. A civilian Fascism, with somewhat radical demands for the redress of peasants' grievances, has developed during the past few years; but it can hope to exert influence only to the extent to which it can gain the support of the military and naval leaders. Japan is, in fact, a State in which the supremacy of the military caste, after giving way for a time before the advance of parliamentary institutions modelled on those of Western Europe, has been sharply reasserted as parliamentarism has ceased to rank as the sole civilised model worthy of imitation. The Japanese, when they first decided to adopt Western institutions, selected Germany rather than France or Great Britain or the United States as a model for imitation, because the German system was more authoritarian and gave more power and prestige to the military caste. The defeat of Germany in 1918 and the apparent triumph of parliamentary democracy in Europe caused a forced and artificial development of parliamentarism in Japan. But the successful consolidation of Communism in Russia soon led to a revulsion of feeling, accentuated by the failure of the Japanese attempt to penetrate Siberia during the period of European anti-Communist crusading. For a time the rise of Russia produced a fashion for Socialist ideas; and the Japanese intelligentsia seemed to be heading for left-wing Socialism. But when it became clear that the Bolshevik world revolution was not going to happen, at any rate for some time, there was a further shift of opinion, accompanied by a suppression of the growing Communist and left-wing groups; and as soon as Fascism began to offer an alternative model in Europe, Japanese opinion veered strongly that way.

The movement did not become decisive until Germany, always

the most congenial of all States to the Japanese mind because it came nearest to the Japanese subordination of the individual to the aims of the nation, passed under Fascist rule. By this act the Germans seemed to their Eastern imitators to have wiped out the stigma of their defeat; and the German system regained all its lost prestige. Instinctively, Japan and Germany joined forces in repudiating the democratic tendencies embodied in the League of Nations. Both declared a *Kulturkampf* against Russian Communism; both proclaimed a sacred mission of national expansion and civilising self-assertion. The Germans set out to uphold the West against the advance of Russian "barbarism": Japan set out to establish her hegemony of the East against Russian Marxists and Western Capitalists alike. Japanese expansionism is largely the expression of militant nationalism armed with a mission to liberate the Eastern peoples from the Western exploiters.

JAPANESE EXPANSIONISM

Be it admitted that Japanese expansionism is also partly the outcome of serious internal economic difficulties. Both agriculturally and industrially the Japanese territory is sadly deficient in relation to the ambitions of the leaders of Japanese nationalism. The country is mountainous, and a very large part of it unfit for cultivation; and within the cultivated area the growing population presses more and more heavily on the means of subsistence. Difference of climatic conditions checks migration from the more to the less densely populated cultivable areas; and there is in the more populous districts an extreme sub-division of agricultural holdings which keeps the peasants down to a very low standard of life. Industrially, Japan is badly lacking in the raw materials needed for the development of her manufactures. Water-power she has been able to develop on a substantial scale. She has coal, but it is of poor quality; and she lacks iron as well as cotton and other textile materials, except silk. Consequently, she presses outward in the hope of finding both suitable areas for the settlement of surplus agricultural population, and sources of raw material supply which can be brought under her political control. Manchukuo attracts her expansionists because of its great undeveloped resources in raw materials; and Manchukuo is also a stepping-stone to the potential wealth of Inner Mongolia and Northern China. But agricultural settlement in these regions is difficult, because the Japanese settler will have to compete with peoples used to an even lower standard of life; and Japan, in her search for areas of mass colonisation, looks rather—since her settlers are shut out from Canada and the United States—to Borneo and New Guinea, the Northern Territory of Australia, and the Dutch East Indies.

Japanese advance in these directions is, however, barred by the established imperialisms of the West. Great Britain is bound to uphold the "White Australia" policy which is common to all sections of Australian political opinion; and the British and the Dutch would certainly stand together against any Japanese political aggression in the Indies. The Singapore Naval base is the outward and visible sign of Great Britain's determination to defend the Indian Ocean and the East Indian Islands against Japanese political penetration. The Philippines, now within the American Empire, may indeed soon present an easier target for attack; for the determination of the United States to restore their independence is more a sign of American unwillingness to defend an evidently indefensible position than of an ethical zeal for national self-determination. But the Philippines, even if the withdrawal of the Americans is likely to mean, sooner or later, their subordination to Japan, are far too insignificant a morsel to satisfy Japanese aspirations. Japan's leaders believe in their mission to dominate the Far East; they have annexed Korea and Formosa; they want China, whole or dismembered, to pass within their sphere of political control; they want to add Inner Mongolia as well as Manchukuo to their effective spheres of influence, and to establish their right, as against Russia's, to penetrate Eastern Asia with sword and doctrine. *Vis à vis* the Russians, they pursue their policy with a display of armed force, counting on Russia's fear of the repercussions of war in the East on her position in Europe. Meanwhile in China, in the East Indian Islands, and in India they pursue their aims at present mainly by commercial penetration, underselling with the aid of low-paid labour and the depreciated *yen* the products of Lancashire, and trying to make economic advance the basis for a policy of political aggression. For they hope, as fast as they drive out European manufactures, to drive out European political influence as well, and, established as the masters of Far Eastern trade, to be recognised as the natural leaders of the Asiatic peoples in a counter-crusade against European Imperialism.

Authoritative and militant institutions at home fit in best with this policy of external expansion and imperialist aggression. But there are forces in Japan that seek to stand out against the more extreme manifestations of this aggressive policy. For Japan, despite the long strides which she has made in industry and commerce, remains a poor country, with a predominantly peasant population living at a very low standard of life and a serious deficiency of capital for the financing of her ambitious expansionist programme. The strain of maintaining the very heavy armed forces is extreme; and with this is combined the necessity of subsidising the depressed agriculturists and providing from internal resources a large mass of capital for the development of industry. Civilian Finance Ministers, compelled to find the money for huge military expenditure over which they have no sort of control, struggle desperately with the problem of making both ends meet, and pay the penalty of death by assassination if they venture to stand out against militarist demands. If an unbalanced budget really ruined a country, as the financial pundits are always explaining that it must, assuredly Japan would have been conclusively ruined long ago.

Japan is not ruined, but on the contrary has been able actually to expand her production and trade at a time when other countries, more obedient to the dictates of financial orthodoxy, have suffered from declining trade and production and a very high level of unemployment. But these commercial advances have been purchased at a high price, especially at the expense of the unfortunate peasants. For this reason Japanese militarism, though it is well able at need to bend the politicians to its will, has to set bounds to its aggressiveness and to conduct its expansionist operations as far as possible "on the cheap." The Shanghai adventure was unduly expensive, and brought in no such economic returns as are to be found in Manchukuo; and the experience of Shanghai, where the Japanese forces encountered far tougher resistance than they had ever expected to meet, caused the militarists to proceed more cautiously towards the establishment of their supremacy in China. In 1915 it was mainly the United States that prevented Japan from pressing the more extreme of the "Twenty-one Demands" presented to China while the European Powers were too busily engaged in fighting one another to be able to intervene. After 1918, the United States again played a large part in compelling the liquidation of Japan's Siberian adventure. But to-day what checks the force of Japanese aggression is less the fear of the United States—much less that of Europe or the League—than the limitation of Japan's own financial resources. The Japanese leaders do not renounce their desire for Asiatic hegemony; indeed, in April 1934, they re-asserted it in an official pronouncement which was a direct challenge to the Western Powers. In this pronouncement, Japan virtually proclaimed a "Monroe Doctrine" for the Far East, bidding the Western Powers keep their hands off China, and refrain from giving her any sort of help that might strengthen her resistance to Japanese aggression. Europe's internal quarrels and America's conomic preoccupations furnished a convenient occasion for this staking out of the claim to exclusive domination in China. But, though Japan's militarists claim everything, for the present they realise the need for advancing by stages, and consolidating each conquest before moving on to the next. At the moment, Japan is assimilating Manchukuo: as soon as her military leaders feel ready for another bite, they will resume their activities, either against Russia or in Northern China, as immediate considerations of expediency may dictate.

There is to the Western mind—and especially to the minds of British and French individualists—something terrible about the certainty with which the Japanese leaders can count on the individual citizen to subordinate himself absolutely to the claims of the State. There seems to be nothing that a Japanese will not do if he holds that the State requires it of him. Something of this spirit exists also in Nazi Germany; and Mussolini has assiduously preached to the Italians the same "totalitarian" gospel. But in Europe this attitude, powerful as it can be made for a time, appears to most people as something artificial and imposed on men's minds by the temporary influence of a highly emotionalised creed, whereas in Japan it seems to arise naturally as the outcome of a strong national tradition which was only momentarily modified by the imitation of Western parliamentarism and is now resurrecting itself as strongly as ever before, and far more menacingly because it now appears armed with the economic and military weapons of the West. European Fascism, in its more militaristic and aggressive forms, seems to arise only as the response to a condition of acute crisis and distress, and to be likely to simmer down if only the crisis can be made less severe. Japanese Fascism scarcely seems to need a special stimulus of this sort; it seems rather to confront European civilisation for the first time with a barbaric and tribal fearlessness armed with its own scientific weapons.

There is, however, something by way of comfort. Japan's nearest neighbours are China and Russia; and both China and Russia are tough morsels to assimilate. Chinese armies may melt away before a Japanese attack; but China is too vast to be overrun or organised by all Japan's militarist zeal. Russia, by having to contend with an adversary near its base along an immense line of railway, may have difficulty in defending her Far Eastern territories—indeed, Vladivostok and the Amur Railway are probably incapable of being defended in a military sense, except by counter-attack from the air, now that Manchukuo has passed under Japanese control. But if the Japanese try to penetrate into Siberia, will they fare even as well as they fared in 1915 or in 1919, when Soviet Russia was far more defenceless than she is to-day? It is some comfort for the countries of the West—cold comfort, may be, but comfort none the less—that Japan, with her limited resources, is likely to have her hands full for a long time ahead with the problems of the territories nearest to Manchukuo, without embarking on decisive adventures against the territories and spheres of influence of the Western Powers. The comfort is colder for the Russians, who may have to share with China the brunt of Japan's militarist expansionism, but are deeply anxious to preserve peace in order to press on with their internal policy of economic development and political consolidation. The Japanese advance threatens, by absorbing Mongolia, to cut the Russians off from the hope of union with Soviet China, and to establish a powerful counterpoise to their influence all over Asia. But there is always for Russia the hope that Japan, in attempting more than her resources will allow her to accomplish, will provoke a powerful reaction throughout the East against her policy, and thus play into Russia's hands. For the Western Powers there is no such compensation; for, whether Japan or Russia ultimately dominates Asia, the loss of power and prestige is equally theirs. The half-heartedness of the League Powers in standing up to Japanese Imperialism in Manchuria is not unconnected with the fact that, of the two rival claimants for the allegiance of the East, they ultimately prefer Japan; for the Japanese only carry to its logical extreme the imperialist policy which they have constantly practised themselves, whereas the Russian "menace" stands not for the subjection but for the liberation of the Eastern peoples.

10. THE POLITICAL SYSTEM OF CHINA

To SPEAK of the political system of China is in one sense a misnomer; for the outstanding fact about China is that there is no political system in the Western sense. There is a Government at Nanking, under the effective control of Chiang Kai-shek: there is a Constitution, or Organic Law, of the Chinese Republic: the Republic possesses a President of the Government, and a Cabinet of Ministers, a system of Legislative, Executive and other Councils, a revenue gathered in from taxation, a Civil Service, and last but not least an Army. But this Government holds real jurisdiction only over a small part of the vast area of China; and much of its political and legal system exists on paper, and nowhere else.

There are other Governments in China besides the National Government at Nanking. Indeed, no one can possibly say how many Governments there are, or what precisely are the relations between them. First, there are provincial Governments, sometimes controlled by a single Governor or military leader, and sometimes under a governing Council of politicians, as at Canton. Some of these provincial authorities are under Nanking; indeed, in a very vague sense that is presumably true of all. But there is every variation from an effective acceptance of the control of Chiang Kai-shek's Government to a repudiation of all allegiance to it, usually coupled with a recognition of allegiance to China as a national unity which may some day come again to have an inclusive governing authority. But even this recognition of national unity is not universal. Manchukuo is technically Chinese territory; but the Manchurian Empire created and upheld by Japan repudiates all allegiance to China. Both Inner and Outer Mongolia are technically under Chinese sovereignty; but the Soviet Republic in Outer Mongolia is in fact closely allied to the U.S.S.R., and takes no orders from Nanking. Jehol has been added to Manchukuo; and Inner Mongolia is a disputed area between China, Manchukuo (or rather Japan), and the Mongolian Soviet Republic. Tibet is technically part of China; but it is politically far more within the British than the Chinese sphere of influence, and assuredly the Tibetan Government is quite unmoved by doings far away on the lower Yangtze. Sinkiang, or Chinese Turkestan, is also Chinese territory in a formal sense; but it is in fact the battleground of Central Asia, where local Moslem rulers contend for mastery with Chinese Governors, Communist insurgents and bandit armies, and no settled authority at present exists.

In addition to this, certain parts of Chinese territory are at present in occupation by foreign Powers as a result either of annexation or concessions under some sort of lease. Hongkong is a British possession, definitely annexed in 1841. The French, apart from their possessions in Indo-China, occupy the bay of Kwang-Chau-Wan in the south-west under a ninety-nine years' lease dating from 1898. Shanghai, with more than one million inhabitants, of whom all but about 30,000 are Chinese, is an International Settlement controlled by an international administration wholly independent of China. There are throughout the country numerous Treaty Ports, including some inland ports on the rivers, in which foreigners have special rights. The number of "concessions" has, indeed, been reduced by the return of Wei-hai-wei to China by the British Government in 1930, and of the Belgian Concession at Tientsin in 1931, and the British Concession at Hankow was never reoccupied after its seizure by the Chinese in 1926. But the existing foreign settlements on Chinese soil constitute a material diminution of the effective sovereignty of the Chinese Government, in that Shanghai and Hongkong especially command between them a larger part of Chinese external commerce, while Shanghai is by far the most important centre of Chinese industrial development.

Moreover, apart from these foreign possessions and the outlying areas which owe but a shadowy loyalty to the Chinese Government, there exist in China proper large but constantly shifting areas under Communist, or at any rate Soviet, control. The most important of these Soviet areas is in Kiangsi, lying between the area controlled by the Nanking Government and the southern area centred upon Canton. In Kiangsi a Soviet Government, aided by mountainous country, has maintained its independent existence for some years now, defying all Chiang Kai-shek's efforts to dislodge it. There are other Soviet areas, more constantly changing and less firmly controlled, in Honan and Hupeh, round the middle reaches of the Yangtze and further North; and there are yet others far in the interior round the upper Yangtze in Szechwan and further south in Yunnan. In Fukien, lying on the coast between the areas controlled by Nanking and Canton, an attempt to establish an independent left-wing Government in hostility to Chiang Kai-shek has recently been crushed, having failed to secure the support of the Canton leaders. The Canton Government alternately co-operates with and repudiates Nanking; but it has been to all intents and purposes under independent control. North China, centred upon Pekin, has no assured political orientation. It is ruled under provincial Governors and military leaders who at present owe a vague allegiance to Nanking, but are liable to change sides and come and go with bewildering rapidity. A number of them have been recently intriguing with Japan.

Thus over an area of more than two million square miles, or more than four million if Manchuria, Mongolia and Tibet are added, there is no settled political sovereignty, and for the most part no assured system of government. No one knows how many people live within this troubled area; but the lowest estimates put their number at about 450,000,000 and the highest at not much below 500,000,000. The Chinese are not far short of being a quarter of the entire human race.

Brought up in the notion that a strong State is a necessary condition of any sort of civilised living, we in the West are apt to be amazed that the Chinese, who are beyond doubt a highly civilised people, can manage to exist under these political conditions. When we hear of one civil war after another devastating vast and densely populated areas, of flood, pestilence and famine adding their toll to that of war, of millions evicted from their homes, of bandits marching about the country, living on the land and laying it waste, we are disposed to be astonished that the Chinese do not either sink into sheer barbarism, or by a determined effort make an end of the intolerable confusion and establish a strong Government capable of holding the country together. Western politicians and Western merchants are constantly crying out about the need for strong centralised Government, and giving their support to one leader after another who promises to unify the country. But again and again, even when unification seems for a moment to be almost achieved, China breaks up; and the lamentations begin afresh at the ruin of trade by the renewal of civil war, at the spending on armaments of money that ought to go to the payment of old debts to foreign bond-

holders—whose money has partly gone to pay for earlier armaments
—and at the Chinese habit of taking a dislike to the foreigner who
only wants China to have a government that will enable him to make
money out of her, and of boycotting his goods in the name of a
national consciousness he cannot fathom, because it fails to express
itself in an organised national State.

THE CHINESE VILLAGE

Yet, despite the lamentations of Western critics and of many
educated Chinese, the life of China does go on, not unaffected by
the disorders, but to a considerable extent regardless of them. Nor is
China nearly so ungoverned as a study of her political condition is
bound to suggest to the Western mind. The real unit of social government in China is something far smaller than the nation or the
twenty or so great Provinces into which the country is divided by long
administrative tradition. Whatever may happen nationally or provin-
cially, the village carries on much as before, unless it is actually in
the middle of the fighting; and, even if it is, no sooner do the soldiers
move on than the village sets about tending its wounds and resum-
ing its normal way of life. No threat or experience of devastation
stops the Chinaman from cultivating his land. From the worst areas,
such as parts of Shantung, where the same villages have been rav-
aged year after year, there has been a great exodus in search of
land in the less thickly inhabited regions. From such areas have
come the bulk of Chinese migrants to Manchuria and to Inner
Mongolia, where the cultivated area is pushed forward by fresh
settlers at the rate of several miles a year.

The village carries on; and it is able to carry on because of the
immense strength in China of the family as an institution. The
practice of ancestor-worship which prevails in China aptly sym-
bolises this strength. Whatever happens in the wider field of politics,
the family holds together as an economic and social unit, and the
grouping of families holds the village together. The family land,
often but a tiny area in a tract so densely populated that no more
than the barest subsistence can be got from it, is cultivated to yield
the last dose of product that an unlimited supply of manual labour
can secure without the aid of Western science. By no means all of
China is so densely populated as this suggests. There is more room
in the North than over most of the South, and there are still vast

empty spaces left far in the interior of Asia—largely desert now, but in part capable of being brought under use by irrigation, accomplished with the aid of intensive human labour. But the quintessential China of the Yangtze valley and the Southern Provinces is crowded to the utmost limit; and here the patient cultivator raises his rice, his green vegetables, and his silkworms, and ekes out his diet with soya beans and bamboo, and with fish. Further North, wheat and millet take the place of rice, and the ox of the buffalo. Population is less dense over much of the North; but the same essential type of village community exists, holding on tenaciously in face of floods and droughts, war lords and bandits, and a perpetual uncertainty in which the one thing certain is more trouble to come.

The family and the village hold together, and contrive to carry on through all the troubles. But they are by no means like the almost isolated and self-centred villages that exist among more primitive peoples. For China is a civilised country, with a very strong cultural unity and a truly remarkable freedom from rigid class distinctions. This is not to say that the typical peasant is an educated person, according to either Chinese or Western standards. But the educated class in China is drawn freely, generation after generation, from every stratum of the people except the lowest. By way of the age-long examination system, which persists through all the civil wars and changes of government, the son of the small cultivator can become the scholar; and in China the scholar is held in vast respect, and can usually be sure of the means of life. China's war lords and governors, moreover, do not form a class apart from the rest of the people in a hereditary sense. They are drawn from many groups and classes. China has no such system of hereditary distinctions and privileges as Japan, and no caste system like that of India to stand in the way of unity. Nor do religious differences obstruct unity. Most Chinese are Buddhists; but Buddhism, Taoism, and Confucianism—with its almost universally observed cult of ancestor-worship—exist side by side; and the same person may often practise all three. For Chinese religion differs profoundly from the religions of the Western world. Confucianism is broadly an ethical doctrine practically without ceremony or theology. It embodies an attitude to life rather than what we think of as religion, and above all it has no such emotional content as we associate with the religions of the West. Buddhism and Taoism, on the other hand, are largely ceremonial observances with very little of ethical content, as well as very little emotion. There is nothing inconsistent in a Confucian being also a Buddhist because the two hardly overlap; but even if a Chinaman is both, that does not make him a religious person in the Western sense of the word. Above all, Chinese religion has practically no influence on Chinese politics. Chinese ethics are personal and not political, and the Chinese are in no danger of finding their political aspirations side-tracked by religious differences. There are Mohammedans also—at least 20,000,000 and perhaps far more—and Chinese Christians—perhaps three or four millions. But the widespread system of Christian missions in China has not had much success in converting the people to Christianity. Its importance—which is very great—lies in the field of education and health far more than of religion. The Americans, who have been easily foremost in this field, have recognised this, and done far more to provide hospitals, schools, and colleges than unwanted churches.

Chinese Nationalists often complain that the rapid growth of mission schools and colleges has combined with the penetration of China by foreign capital to break down the old culture, and that the American action in applying the money from the Boxer Indemnity to education, especially the training of Chinese students in American universities and technical colleges, has greatly aggravated this tendency. Undoubtedly this policy has been an excellent stroke of business for the Americans; for it means that the bulk of the Chinese who have received technical education are familiar with American goods, standards, specifications, and methods of work, and therefore inclined to make purchases in the United States whenever they can. It is doubtless true that this Westernisation is breaking down the traditional forms of the old Chinese culture, which is being further undermined by the changed living conditions of the rapidly growing urban populations in the areas in which Western industrialism has taken root. Chinese Nationalist movements of all sorts have been led by men who have got their training largely outside China—in the United States, or in Western Europe, or in Japan, or latterly in the U.S.S.R. Sun Yat Sen, who made modern Chinese Nationalism, gathered his followers from among Chinese emigrants and exiles all over the world. Eugene Chen comes from Trinidad. Chiang Kai-shek got his military knowledge from Moscow. T. V. Soong, his chief ally and China's leading financial expert, is a graduate of Harvard, and Chiang Kai-shek's wife, who is Soong's sister, was at Wellesley College. A second sister, who married Sun Yat Sen, was at the Wesleyan College in Macon, Georgia. But this foreign—above all, American—influence, while it is greatly modifying the old cultural traditions, is not destroying Chinese culture, or making it merely imitative. The old cultural tradition is too strong for that; and already a new literature is arising that blends the old learning with the new lessons from the West. The diffusion of culture is made immensely the easier because China, with many spoken dialects, has long had but one written literary language. This is too complicated and laborious for wide diffusion; but its general acceptance paves the way for a common recognition of the Northern Mandarin dialect as the approved vernacular for the new literature that is springing up.

THE CHINESE REPUBLIC

The Chinese Republic, founded after the successful Revolution of 1911, dates from 1912. Under the leadership of the revolutionary organisation created from abroad by Sun Yat Sen, the South went over to the Revolution, and the Southerners were able to march north and dethrone the last of the Manchu dynasty—who has now been given a new throne in Manchukuo as the puppet of Japan. The Kuomintang, the Chinese Nationalist Party, was founded in the course of the Revolution to take the place of Sun Yat Sen's earlier organisation. Sun Yat Sen became the first President of the Chinese Republic, and China appeared to be on the point of establishing a democratic Republic on the model of the Western parliamentary democracy. But although the Southern armies were able to march north and conquer the country, driving before them the war lords of the Yangtze valley, the democratic movement had little strength in the Northern Provinces, where Yuan Shi-kai, at the head of a formidable force, would have been in a position to put up a strong resistance to its further advance. Yuan Shi-kai was willing enough to come to terms with the Republic, but not to accept the Presidency of Sun Yat Sen; and Yuan had behind him powerful elements which stood for a moderate revolution that would create as little disturbance as possible in the economic structure of Chinese society. In order to avert a further struggle and secure unity on the basis of the Republic, Sun Yat Sen resigned the Presidency after holding it only a few months, and Yuan Shi-kai became President in his place. Thus the new Chinese Republic began its career not under the radical auspices of Sun Yat Sen, who, since his death in 1925, has been canonised as the leader and inspirer of the new China, but under Yuan, who had certainly no intention of carrying out Sun's radical policy. That policy was embodied later in Sun Yat Sen's famous "Testament," which has since become the Bible of the Kuomintang. In his Testament, which sums up the ideas for which he had been working all his life, he proclaimed as the basis of the Republic the three master principles of Nationalism, Democracy and "Socialism." He wanted a Republic that would unify the Chinese nation into a strong power capable of flinging off external interference and aggression. He wanted the new national State to be organised on democratic principles derived largely from the West, and he preached a sort of "Socialism" which he interpreted, in terms of the economic structure of Chinese society, as "the right of the people to the means of life."

Yuan, however, was by no means minded to reorganise China on the basis of these ideas. Instead, he set to work promptly to consolidate his own personal ascendancy, and before long serious dissensions broke out in the ranks of the revolutionaries. In 1913 the South, under Sun's leadership, rose in revolt, which Yuan successfully repressed. Sun Yat Sen was driven out of Canton and found refuge in the far interior of China, where he set to work to rebuild the Nationalist movement. The next year came the European War, which gave Japan her opportunity. The Japanese, as one of the Allied Powers, promptly seized the German concessions in North China, overrunning Shantung; and in 1915 they presented to Yuan the famous "Twenty-one Demands," which would have destroyed Chinese independence, and established a virtual Japanese protectorate over the entire country. The European Powers, occupied by the war, could do nothing; and Yuan's policy was one of accommodation with Japan. But his attempts to compromise raised up acute discontent; and when, in December 1915, he proclaimed himself Emperor of China, a new revolution at once broke out. In the midst of the ensuing civil war Yuan died; and China thereupon fell definitely to pieces. For the next eight years the history of the country is that of the internecine struggles of rival war lords, each holding a province or two and seeking perpetually to oust his nearest neighbours, while a weak Government in Pekin, always the nominee of the local war-lord for the time in command of the area round the capital, professed to govern, but in fact exercised no authority within the country. In 1917, chiefly in the hope of enlisting European support against Japanese aggression, China, by the declaration of the Pekin Government, entered the war; and when the war was over an attempt was made at the Peace Conference to dislodge Japan from Shantung. This failing, China refused to sign the Versailles Treaty; but she entered the League of Nations, still under the auspices of a Government devoid of all real power.

But, even in this period, the Chinese showed that, lacking a national State, they could still act together. The anti-Japanese boycott of 1919 was a national movement, largely effective throughout the country, and of real influence on Japanese policy, which was sharply modified under American pressure at the Washington Conference of 1921. Under the Washington Nine-Power Treaty all the leading Powers, including Great Britain, the United States and Japan, agreed to respect the sovereign independence and territorial and administrative integrity of China. They agreed to the policy of equal treatment for the commerce of all nations in the Chinese market, and promised to refrain from taking advantage of Chinese political confusions to seek special privileges for themselves. Though this Treaty is now, since Japan's action in Manchuria, and her proclamation, in April 1934, of an exclusive claim to intervene in Chinese affairs, little more than a scrap of paper, it did for a time secure China some real immunity from foreign pressure.

The anti-Japanese movement of 1919 and the struggle over Shantung and other foreign spheres of influence caused a great revival of the Chinese Nationalist movement, represented by the Kuomintang. The leadership of this new movement was taken by the students, who enrolled themselves in very large numbers under the Nationalist banner and were largely responsible for organising the boycott of Japanese goods. The Chinese students, greatly increased in numbers by the spread of missionary colleges and schools, especially under the auspices of the Americans, constitute a highly important and influential section of the Chinese population, able by virtue of their superior education to take the lead in organising the masses of Chinese workers, especially those who are employed by businesses under the control of foreign capital. Chinese respect for

education and the absence of any rigid class structure make strongly
on the side of the student movement and of its political influence,
and in recent years the demand for an effective national Government and a strong national policy directed against the foreigner
has come most forcibly of all from the student groups. The students
were in 1919 enthusiastic followers of Sun Yat Sen, and thereafter
many of them came under the influence of Communist propaganda,
so that they have been throughout the most turbulent element in
the Kuomintang, and to-day compose the group of whose ability
in organisation and agitation the Nanking Government is most
afraid.

In the years immediately after the war Sun Yat Sen's influence,
weak in Northern China except among the students, remained powerful throughout the South, and from 1916 onwards the Kuomintang
was improving its organisation all over the country. Up to 1919 Sun
Yat Sen's ideas met with no effective challenge from the Left; but
from that point, with the establishment of the Russian Soviet Republic in Asiatic Russia, and especially after the enforced retreat of
the Japanese army from Siberia in 1919, Russian influence began
to count. Young Chinese students flocked into Russia, and soon
Russian agents began to preach the Communist gospel in China.
The Communist Party of China was founded in 1920.

THE KUOMINTANG AND THE COMMUNISTS

For some time the Communists and the Kuomintang worked in
opposition. But in 1923 Joffe, the Russian representative in China,
and Sun Yat Sen worked out terms of alliance, under which the
Communists were to enter the Kuomintang, while retaining their
own party organisation. Sun declared against the immediate introduction of Communism into China, and Joffe accepted this, guaran-
teeing Russian help for the firm establishment of Chinese national
independence under a unified Government. Thereafter Borodin was
sent to Canton to help the Chinese to organise a new revolutionary
Republic; and with him came General Blücher, to train the new
Chinese revolutionary army. Chiang Kai-shek, who had been in
Russia as Sun's emissary, was put at the head of the new Whampoa
Military Academy, from which were to emerge the leaders of the
new force. Politically, the Kuomintang was reorganised, at Borodin's
instance, largely on Communist lines, but necessarily without the

same solid proletarian basis, though steps were at once taken to set up unions of workers and peasants, on the model of the Soviets, all over the South. An attempt by the "right wing" at Canton to rise against the Russification of the national movement was put down in 1924.

The power of the Kuomintang and the Communists was at this stage limited to the South. The North and most of the Yangtze valley were still held by contending military leaders. Sun Yat Sen went North to Pekin in the hope of arranging a compromise with General Feng and the other Northern leaders, and there died in March 1925, leaving the revolutionary movement without a generally accepted leader. There ensued a struggle for power, from which Chiang Kai-shek emerged as leader, with Borodin's support, after Sun's favourite lieutenant, Liao Chung-kai, the original nominee of the Communists and the man most responsible for the alliance between them and the Kuomintang, had been assassinated.

Meanwhile, left-wing agitation was spreading fast in the Yangtze valley as well as in the South. Labour unions were being actively organised, and there were many strikes, directed especially against foreign capital, and anti-foreign demonstrations. On May 30th, 1925, British-led police in Shanghai fired on strike demonstrators; and an immense wave of anti-British feeling spread over the country, accompanied by an anti-British boycott from which British trade in China has never at all completely recovered. In 1926, heralded by this movement, Chiang led his new trained army north, driving out the local war-lords, and proclaiming everywhere the new revolution of the Kuomintang. An anti-Christian agitation swept over the country, and from place after place the missionaries were driven out. On the middle Yangtze the revolutionaries seized, with the Chinese towns, the foreign Concessions at Hankow, including the important British Concession. The International Settlement at Shanghai was garrisoned against the revolutionaries by a large international force, of which Great Britain supplied the biggest contingent. In March 1927, the national forces occupied Nanking, previously held by the Northerners; and the foreign quarters were looted, and a number of foreigners killed. American destroyers in the Yangtze fired on the city, to cover the evacuation of foreign residents.

The Nanking affair was the turning-point in the development of the new Chinese revolution. It caused a sharp revolt among the right wing of the Kuomintang against the Russians, whose anti-foreign propaganda was held to have caused the trouble. Chiang Kai-shek turned round, and, strongly financed by Chinese bankers and merchants and encouraged by foreign interests, formed a strongly anti-Communist Government of his own, and proceeded to drive the Russians and their adherents out of the movement. There were big massacres of Communists in Shanghai and other towns; and within a few weeks the Kuomintang had been reconstructed at the centre, under Chiang's leadership, on a strongly anti-Russian basis. This eclipse of the Russians was greatly helped by the discovery of the secret instructions which Borodin had received from Moscow, ordering him to get Communist Party members into all the key positions in the Kuomintang, to eliminate Sun's left-wing successors, to organise a purely workers' and peasants' army under Communist control in the Yangtze valley, to foster direct confiscation of land by the peasants without reference to the Government, and, finally, to prepare the way for the complete supersession of the Kuomintang by the Communist Party. These instructions Borodin had kept secret, presumably realising that it would be fatal to attempt to carry them out: their revelation alienated the left-wing elements in the Kuomintang, and enabled Chiang to establish his ascendancy without much opposition.

After 1927 Chiang Kai-shek, now backed by the right wing in China and by the foreign Governments, which regarded him as their saviour from Chinese Communism, ruled in Nanking. Great Britain accommodatingly gave up the Hankow Concession; the United States conceded full tariff autonomy and a revision of the unequal treaties, envisaging the complete abolition of extra-territoriality in the not distant future. Russia and certain other countries renounced their extra-territorial rights; and these concessions helped to force the other Powers to adopt a more accommodating attitude. But the question of extra-territoriality is not settled even to-day. The Nanking Government announced its abolition in 1930, but was compelled to postpone the operation of the new system by pressure from the Great Powers. However, from the time when the Nanking Government thrust out the Russians, foreign money was lent to China to enable Chiang to establish a strong Government; and great promises of reform were made. Between 1927 and 1930 the Nanking Government elaborated new codes of law, largely on

Western models, in an attempt to unify the administration of justice, and justify the abolition of the rights of extra-territoriality claimed for the nationals of foreign Powers. Foreign capital began again to be invested, especially in Shanghai; and tariff autonomy gave the Nanking Government a new source of revenue—for customs duties had previously been limited by treaty with the Powers to a maximum of five per cent. But most of the money that passed into the Government's hands continued to be spent on the army; for Chiang's writ did not, and still does not, run effectively over a large part of the country, and the Nanking Government itself could not last a day except on the basis of its military strength. Moreover, Chiang needs all his forces to keep himself in power and to make war upon the Soviets in Kiangsi and the Yangtze provinces. He has no soldiers to spare for fighting Japan. He sent practically no help to the Northern Generals for the Manchurian campaign; and the heroic resistance which the Chinese put up to Japan at Shanghai in 1932 was that of troops from the South—no friends of Chiang or his Government. For though it was from Canton, and on the basis of Cantonese strength, that Chiang set out to conquer China for the Kuomintang, his complete shift to the right soon alienated Southern support, and Canton, though it owes a vague allegiance to Nanking, has been in recent years practically independent.

THE CONSTITUTION OF CHINA

Accordingly, a description of the Constitution in force at Nanking is very far from being a complete description of the system under which China is governed—and would be so even if the Nanking Constitution were in practice what it is on paper, which it is not. The Nanking Government is, however, in form and intention a government for the entire country, resting directly upon the authority of the Kuomintang, as the party responsible for the national revolution; for after 1927 the right wing got control of the Kuomintang—for the time being. Moreover, the Constitution of 1928, adopted by the national conference of the party, is professedly based upon the principles laid down by Sun Yat Sen in the "Testament" which he left behind him; for this "Testament" has become the inspired scripture of Chinese Nationalism, ceremonially read aloud at party gatherings, a sacred writing to be interpreted, but never disputed. Under this Constitution, the governing authority is to be exercised by five

Yuan, or Councils—Executive, Legislative, Judicial, Examining and Controlling. These Councils are distinct from the Cabinet of Ministers, whose members serve as Presidents and Vice-Presidents of the various Councils, as well as heads of various departments of State. The Executive Council is the supreme executive authority, with power to set up ministries and define their duties, and to exercise general control over their work. The Executive Council submits to the Legislative Council, which is the supreme law-making body, drafts of Bills and treaties, and also the annual budget; and the Legislative Council can approve, amend or reject these measures. It is thus the nearest approach to a Parliament in the Constitution; but it is, like all the other Councils, a nominated body, drawn from the Kuomintang, and not chosen by any form of public election. The Judicial Council has final control of the courts of law, and has been responsible for the large measures of legal codification that have been carried out during the last few years, at any rate on paper. The Examining Council is in charge of the elaborate system of examinations for public office, which has from time immemorial played so large a part in the Chinese administrative machine and is likely to survive in any new system, however much it may be reformed on Western lines. No public officer is allowed to be appointed except after examination under the auspices of this Council. Finally, the Controlling Council supervises the administration of the entire public service, and is responsible for audit of all public accounts. Such is the "Fivefold System" on which the Constitution of China theoretically rests.

It must, however, be borne in mind that all these Councils are nominated bodies, whose members depend for their tenure of office on the Kuomintang. In theory, at any rate, the China that is governed from Nanking is as much a one-party State as Italy, or Germany, or the U.S.S.R. But in practice the system works out very differently; for though the entire Kuomintang professes devotion to the principles of Sun Yat Sen, there is in fact no such agreement on fundamental policy among its members as exists among Fascists or Nazis or Communists. The Kuomintang, even after the expulsion of the Communists, is a battleground for sharply conflicting tendencies. In its ranks are bankers and merchants acutely hostile to Socialism, Westernised intellectuals advocating every variety of liberal and Socialist doctrine, peasants and workers seeking remedies for immediate economic hardships and grievances, even military leaders who find it easier to keep control of their provinces by keeping in with Nanking—in effect, every element in the population of China, except the Communists, that has rallied to the Nationalist cause. At the Kuomintang's Conferences there is always a strong representation of groups to the left of Chiang Kai-shek, who can keep control only by playing off one section or interest against another, and because he has command of the largest military force. The "left" finds its support against Chiang chiefly in the South; and there have been again and again threats not merely of a split, but of positive civil war between rival groups, each protesting its entire loyalty to the doctrines of Sun Yat Sen. At any time, the Kuomintang may break asunder. Late in 1933, when the Fukien leaders, headed by Eugene Chen, broke away with the support of the Nineteenth Army—the defenders of Shanghai—it was touch and go whether the Canton leaders joined in or not against Chiang. In the event, they stood aloof, and allowed the Fukien revolt to be crushed. But there is no assurance that they too will not before long come to blows with the Nanking Government.

CHINA'S FUTURE

It is not surprising that in face of this perpetual condition of internal dissension in the Kuomintang, with its effective authority limited to a few provinces, constant warfare with the Communists in Central China, most of its funds drained away for military expenses, and practically independent provincial Governors holding tightly to as much as possible of the provincial revenues, the Nanking Government has not been able to advance far towards the social and economic reconstruction of China. It has, moreover, had constantly hanging over it the half-war with Japan over Manchukuo. The Japanese army has crossed the Great Wall, and been at the gates of Pekin ; and no one knows when it will decide on a further sweep forward into Inner Mongolia or Northern China. Chiang and his colleagues would probably come to terms with Japan if they dared, even on fairly humiliating conditions ; for Chiang is under no delusions about his power to stand up to the Japanese army. But open yielding to Japan would rouse a storm of protest from outraged Nationalists, especially in the South. It would certainly at present split the Kuomintang irreparably; and it might easily provoke that civil war which is constantly threatening between Nanking and Canton. So Chiang temporises, protesting against Japanese aggression, accepting financial help from the Western financiers who look to him to make the country safe for trade, appealing fruitlessly to the League of Nations for help, and still refusing to recognise formally the accomplished fact in Manchukuo, but carefully refraining from any serious encounter between his soldiers and the Japanese army. For him, the situation has its compensations; for as long as Japan keeps the Northern Chinese leaders busy, he has little to fear in that quarter from a revolt against his authority, and his soldiers are left free to wage war upon the Communist *enclaves* in Kiangsi and the middle Yangtze provinces.

Chiang has a very large army, of several hundred thousand men, apart from auxiliary forces and the virtually independent armies in provinces which yield little allegiance to Nanking. He is a trained soldier; and he has German advisers, who have taken the place of the expelled Russians, to help him improve discipline and introduce modern methods. But Chinese armies are almost invariably, by European or Japanese standards, of very low fighting quality. They run away easily, and often a whole army changes sides under its general in the middle of a campaign. Men join the army in China to get food, where food is terribly scarce, far more than to fight; and armies degenerate easily into bodies of bandits when their pay is allowed to fall into arrears. There is doubtless some good fighting material; but many of the units are inefficient as well as unreliable, and the provincial armies are often acutely short of munitions and even of rifles and equipment. This is even more the case with the Communist armies Chiang is fighting; for they depend for their supplies of munitions chiefly on what they can capture from their opponents. Away in the interior, they cannot easily smuggle in arms from abroad: nor could they pay for them even if the routes were open. Yet Chiang, despite the large forces and the superior supplies of munitions at his command, has so far failed to suppress the Communists. He is afraid to risk his best troops; and those he does send often desert or run away.

The idea that Chinese armies have practically no fighting value against foreign troops was so firmly established in most people's minds that the resistance offered by the Chinese Southern forces when the Japanese attacked Shanghai caused universal surprise.

It surprised Europe: it surprised the Japanese, who would probably never have launched the attack if they had expected to meet with any serious resistance; and, most of all, it surprised the Chinese themselves. But these Southern troops were exceptional. The Northern Chinese armies were able to offer only a feeble resistance when the Japanese army swept across Manchukuo and Jehol. Nevertheless, the Shanghai fighting showed that Chinese troops are fully capable of being trained to serious war-making; and it is quite unsafe to reckon on the continuance of China's military weakness. It is true that the Chinese, despite the size of their armies, are a most unmilitary people. They rank soldiers very low in the scale of prestige, and have had hitherto very little respect for martial virtues. But that they can fight when they are screwed up to the point of fighting for a cause in which they believe, both the Shanghai struggle and the Communist resistance to Chiang Kai-shek have plainly shown.

Out of the political chaos in China, what is to come? For a century past, she has been the prey of rival imperialisms which have sought to dismember her or to part out her territory into separate spheres of influence. Pieces of her territory have been annexed: foreign concessions and settlements have been established on her soil: the foreigner in China has claimed rights of extra-territoriality as from an uncivilised country. Tsarist Russia dominated Manchuria, thrust into Mongolia, and threatened Northern China before Japan drove her out. The British annexed Hongkong, and claimed the Yangtze valley as a sphere of influence. The French pushed into China proper from Indo-China in the South-West. The Japanese took Formosa and Korea, and later supplanted Germany in Shantung, and seized Manchuria and Jehol as well as Korea. Of the Great Powers active in the Pacific, only the Americans pursued steadily a policy of commercial penetration without annexation or political control over any part of the country; for the Americans wanted the "Open Door" throughout China, and not a particular and exclusive sphere of influence. The World War altered the situation, by removing for a time the pressure of the European Powers. But European Imperialism was promptly replaced by Japanese, as the "Twenty-one Demands" of 1915 plainly showed. After the war, Japan was restrained for a time by fear of a rupture with the combined forces of the European Powers and the United States; and Great Britain struggled hard to regain her lost hold on the Chinese market. But with the coming of the world crisis, and still more with the recrudescence of the war-danger which was the aftermath of the crisis, the European Powers and the United States had their hands too full at home to be formidable in the Far East; and Japan was able to resume her aggression, and to seize Manchuria despite the impotent protests of China and of the League of Nations, even though these protests received the endorsement of the United States.

Thus, on the surface of things, Japan far more than any other Power has seemed of late to be China's enemy. But there are cross-currents; for a growing body of opinion in Japan lays claim to a Pan-Asiatic mission, and proclaims a crusade for the liberation of all the Far East from Western domination. This appeal is not without echoes even in China, especially among those who feel that the choice for China lies between accommodation with Japan and with Soviet Russia, and prefer Japan because they fear Communism. That indeed is likely to be the choice; for the United States cannot dominate the Far East across the Pacific Ocean except in conjunction with the European Powers, and Europe has too many troubles of its own to be able to risk a struggle with Japan over China. In the long run, China seems destined either to go over to Communism or to become the subordinate ally of Japan. The struggle between Japan and the U.S.S.R. in the Far East is, ultimately, a struggle for the control of China. It is a fateful contest for all the world; for upon its outcome may well depend the future shape of world political systems. A Soviet China, linked with Soviet Russia, would assure in the long run the victory of Communism over a large part of Europe as well as in India. A China dominated by Japan would immensely increase the chances of a conquest of all the Far East, including India, not for Socialism, but for a militaristic Imperialism that would postpone for a further period all hope of world collaboration and world peace.

11. POLITICS AND POLICIES IN BRITISH INDIA

ALL THE COUNTRIES which we have selected for special discussion in this book are "self-governing" States, in the sense that they are governed by their own nationals—except India. We felt, however, that something must be said about the problem of Indian government, both because India is, next to China, the most populous country in the world, and because India can stand, far better than any other area, as the example of the control of one people by rulers appointed by and responsible to the Government of an Imperialist Power. Not that we are putting forward India as a "typical" case of Colonial government; for in the nature of things no case can be typical. Subject peoples in the Colonial Empires of the Great Powers are far too diverse in culture and civilisation, and live under conditions far too different, for any one country to stand as an example of all. Nevertheless, it seems better to devote a chapter to a single country than to attempt upon a number a collection of comments which would be necessarily too inadequate to be of any value.

Even in confining ourselves to British India,—for this chapter does not propose to deal with the Indian Native States, with their combined population of more than seventy millions—we are conscious that we can hope only to scratch the surface of an immensely varied and complex problem. For India, far more than China, is a congeries of peoples rather than a single homogeneous Society. There is far less a "typical" Indian than a "typical" Chinaman, far less of racial or religious or cultural or economic uniformity in Indian than in Chinese civilisation, though in China too the internal differences in some of these respects are very wide. It is often said that India is not a "nation" at all, but a "sub-continent"; and there is in this an element of truth. But this half-truth is often pushed much too far. What makes a nation is the possession of a national tradition and a national consciousness, much more than the existence of common racial characteristics, a common language, or even common customs and economic conditions. Whether or no All-India was a nation before the British conquest, common subjection to British rule has gone far towards creating a national movement, and making inevitable the treatment of the political future of All-India (except perhaps Burma) as a single problem.

That the British conquest has counted in creating Nationalism is seen not least in the fact that Indian Nationalist organisations are compelled to conduct most of their activities in the English language, for want of a common language of their own. There are twenty-two separate languages registered as spoken by more than a million people, and an immense number of less widely used languages and dialects. The most widely spoken language is Western Hindi, which is spoken by nearly a hundred million people; and the Nationalists are making efforts to diffuse the knowledge of Hindi throughout the country.

It has often been remarked that Great Britain, through the East India Company, conquered India in a fit of absence of mind. It is true that the conquest was never deliberately or consciously planned in advance, and that the extent of British India, as contrasted with the surviving Native States, is largely the result of a series of accidents. But the British undoubtedly went to India for economic advantage—trade and sheer loot—and extended their conquests first for the direct purpose of consolidating and expanding their economic opportunities, and later for that of maintaining law and order in the vast Empire which had fallen into their hands. British and not Indian interests were responsible for the establishment of British rule, and still dictate its maintenance. Indian trade is of vital importance to British industry; British investors have huge masses of capital invested in Indian bonds and enterprises; the loss of India would be a severe blow to the British economy as well as to British Imperial prestige. Economic and political considerations combine to make the rulers of Great Britain regard the continuance of the British dominion over India as an essential Imperial interest.

It is true that British people often argue that, whatever may be said of the past, British rule in India is now in India's own interest. It is argued that the British administrators are slowly civilising the country and improving its economic position; that they have reduced the frequency and amplitude of famines, and done at least something to advance public health and education; that, if India is in process of becoming a nation capable of self-government, that is the product of the British occupation, and will best be carried to completion under British influence; and finally that if the British forces and the British administrators were withdrawn to-day, India would fall to pieces and become speedily a prey to anarchy and civil war, perhaps only to fall before long again under alien rule. Some say that the Russians would come from the North, to lay the land waste with Bolshevism; others lay stress on the Japanese menace, and flaunt the spectre of a Pan-Asiatic movement under Japanese exploitation, as the coming terror of Europe.

These contentions, of course, are not wholly groundless. British occupation has engendered Indian Nationalism in a political sense, by way of opposition; but India has common cultural traditions that go back so far as to make the period of British rule seem but a moment beside an age. British administration has developed Indian foreign trade, equipped the country with a railway system, done something for irrigation and the prevention of sheer starvation, and something too for education based upon Western models. Moreover it is highly doubtful what would happen if the British forces and the British Civil Service were suddenly and completely withdrawn; and it is not impossible than an India set free from British control would break up into a number of separate units, or go over to Communism, or even become in time part of a Pan-Asiatic movement under the leadership of Japan.

INDIAN SOCIAL CONDITIONS

But there are very powerful considerations on the other side. Great Britain has been in effective occupation of a large part of India ever since the eighteenth century. Yet the rate of economic progress among the great mass of the Indian population has been, and still remains, appallingly slow. Railways have been built, and there has been latterly some growth of industrialisation upon Western models; but the great majority of the population of India still lives in villages at a terribly low standard of existence, carrying on agriculture by exceedingly primitive methods and with correspondingly low productivity. These villages are barely equipped at all with even the most rudimentary sanitary services; and very little has been done, or is being done, to combat even the most preventible diseases. Schools are few, and illiteracy is still far more frequent than literacy—only 14 per cent of males over five years old and 2 per cent of females being recorded as literate, whereas Japan, with a much shorter period of contact with Western civilisation, has already to all intents and purposes stamped illiteracy out. The competition of Western machine-made goods has destroyed the primitive village industries of the people, and thus both taken away their auxiliary earnings, as happened in the English countryside during the Industrial Revolution, and left them without occupation during the winter months. Gandhi's campaign for the development of the home-made cloth industry—*khaddar*—is no mere fad of a romantic eager to revive the past, but a practical attempt to relieve the poverty and uplift the standard of the Indian villager.

Moreover, when it is urged that India is beset by a host of social evils, from child-marriage to the monstrous evil of "untouchability," which would be left to flourish unchecked if the reforming hand of Britain were removed, it must not be overlooked that the alien rulers of India, precisely because they are aliens, are in a terribly weak position for assailing these evils. The British rulers, in order to maintain their hold on the country, must be constantly on their guard against arousing deep-seated native prejudices. The more advanced and educated sections of Indian opinion are already too hostile to alien domination to be placated except by the grant of a large measure of self-government. What the British in India fear is that these sections of opinion may be reinforced by the adherence of the less enlightened elements in the population. Accordingly, they are the more disposed to respect the prejudices and traditions of these elements for fear that any discontent roused among them may be exploited by the Nationalist movement. This explains the sheer failure of the Indian Government to give the more enlightened sections of Indian opinion any help at all in dealing with such problems as untouchability and child-marriage. This unhelpful attitude is often defended as praiseworthy respect for native customs; but the motive behind it is too mixed for this justification to be accepted. Doubtless, an alien ruling group should respect native customs; but it is a poor defence of alien rule that it positively stands between evil customs and the section of native opinion that is eager for their reform. Yet this is what the Government of India undoubtedly does to-day.

The slowness of economic and social improvement in the Indian villages is usually explained on the ground that the resources of the country are quite unable to stand the strain of a more rapid advance. It is very true that the Indian peasant is at present weighed down by very heavy rents and taxes—often combined into a single payment under the system of indirect collection of taxes through tax-farming land-owners or agents. But, in the first place, a very large part of what the peasant pays goes at present into the pockets of the land-owners, and does not reach the Government. Secondly, India is compelled to meet the cost of a large army of occupation, including native troops under British control, and of a very expensive Civil Service and Police establishment; and she has also to bear debt charges by no means all of which represent expenditure incurred for socially useful services. India has paid, and is still paying, a vast tribute to British owners of capital, as well as to native capitalists who are under British protection, and are therefore in many cases staunch supporters of the British rule.

It may be argued that India could advance no faster towards improved social and educational standards, or towards an improved standard of living for the mass of the people, if she were left to her own devices. This may be true; but it is far from self-evident. A people under alien rule neither feels nor has responsibility for its own improvement. It is hard, under such circumstances, to generate the enthusiastic will to progress which is needed to lift a nation out of poverty and stagnation. Would Denmark ever have built up her great Co-operative Movement if she had been governed by foreign rulers? Would Japan ever have accomplished her astonishing economic transformation if she had been conquered, as well as bombarded, by the forces of the Western Powers? Would Russia have made the strides forward that she has made, from almost desperate beginnings, under the Five-Year Plan if the active spirits among her people had not felt that theirs were the power and the responsibility of building up a new social order? There is force in the contention that it will need a social revolution to rouse the people of India to the task of destroying poverty and filth and illiteracy and superstition, and that there is no hope of these evils being destroyed by any prolongation of the British supremacy. At the least, self-government must go far enough to make Indians feel that the responsibility is theirs, and not that of an alien Government, and to give them the opportunity freely to tackle the task of national redemption in their own way.

THE INDIAN NATIONALIST MOVEMENT

That is the rational case for Indian revolution; and to that, in one way or another, India is destined to come unless the rulers of Great Britain can make up their minds to a concession of real self-government. Half-measures will certainly fail; for they will weaken British rule without creating real Indian responsibility in its place. But Great Britain cannot grant real self-government and at the same time continue to regard India as a factor in British military strength, or as a market to be preserved for British goods even against the will of the Indian people, or as an Imperial possession that must be retained within the Empire on grounds of world-prestige, or as a protection against the future advance of Russia or of Japan. The only condition on which effective self-government can be granted is that police and military, as well as civil, services shall be transferred to Indian control, and the question of India remaining within the Empire or not be left to be settled freely and without British pressure by the Indians themselves. Failing concessions as large as this, Great Britain may be able for some time yet to hold a disarmed and imperfectly united India by military and police force, with the aid of "Ordinances" repressing freedom of speech and writing and the constant gaoling of "agitators" regarded as dangerous; but it will be a sheer impossibility, under these conditions, to make any half-hearted concessions of partial self-government work even tolerably well. For most of the men who should be helping to build up a self-governing India will be in gaol, or at least adopting an attitude of "non-co-operation" and spending their energies in agitation against the Government.

This is the fatal weakness both in past Indian "Reforms," and in such solutions as were put forward in the Report of the Simon Commission, or at the Round Table Conferences, or are now being argued about in Great Britain. These reforms have been rejected as quite inadequate by the representative leaders of most sections of Indian opinion; and the Indian representatives with whom they have been discussed in the later stages are for the most part individuals who represent little except themselves. The Congress Movement, which is undoubtedly the most representative single Indian organisation, has been in recent years almost continually suppressed, and is constantly under threat of renewed suppression; and most of its leaders, and also those of Nationalist opinion among the Moslem minority, are or have been in gaol. India is under a repressive system of government by "Ordinance" which stifles all free discussion, except by illegal propaganda; and the prospects of a real concession of self-government have grown less since the National Government has both shown signs of whittling down earlier proposals for the future and intensified strong methods of government in the present.

It is true that, at the moment of writing, a section of the Indian Congress leaders, apparently with Gandhi's support, has decided to abandon for the time the policy of non-co-operation, and to reconstitute the Swaraj Party for the purpose of fighting the Provincial elections, and that the Government has responded by relaxing for the moment its persecution of the Congress, and allowing its leaders to meet openly in order to decide their policy. This may mean a real change in the situation; but it may be no more than a half-truce leading up to a renewal of the struggle. There is no sign that the Government has really changed its attitude, or is prepared to modify its repressive policy; and even if the Swaraj leaders do return to the Assemblies, there is no knowledge whether they will do this in order to "co-operate" or to obstruct.

It is often argued that the policy of repression is justified because Indian Nationalist organization does not represent Indian opinion, but only a half-educated minority eager to replace the British as the ruling power, and without backing from or understanding of the mass of the people. Doubtless, Indian Nationalism is the movement of an active minority; what Nationalist movement—what movement of any sort—ever did enlist the active support of more than a small minority, at any rate until it had actually attained to power? Doubtless the majority of the Indian village population takes no part in the Nationalist movement, or in politics of any kind; for peasant politics are apt to be of a very practical sort, and to become visible only when a revolution does actually happen. Doubtless, there is an element of half-baked Westernisation among a section of the Indian students. But are they more half-baked than the Nazis, or than the makers of modern Japan were when they began upon their task? Does a people ever look as if it would be able to govern itself until it is given the opportunity? Let us not forget how confidently most of the authorities predicted after 1917 the speedy dissolution of Soviet Russia.

Indian Nationalism is no more half-baked, and no more dominated by a limited class of intellectuals, than is inevitable under the conditions of its growth. Let us glance briefly at the character of this movement, which clearly provides the only possible basis for any real system of Indian self-government. The outstanding Nationalist organisation is the All-India National Congress; and in the Congress the outstanding figure has been Mahatma Gandhi. The Congress was founded in 1885, and was at first a "moderate" body, claiming no more than limited administrative reforms. Not till

1906, when it had already become an organisation of nation-wide influence, did it first formulate the demand for *Swaraj,* or "Home Rule" for India, by which it meant self-government within the British Empire. *Swaraj* is, however, a notion obviously admitting of different interpretations; and there was room within the Congress for persons who held wider and narrower views of its meaning. The tendency to widen it developed chiefly during and after the War. During the War, Annie Besant conducted a widespread campaign on behalf of "Dominion Home Rule" for India; and the rejection of this demand caused the Indian Congress, especially after the Russian Revolution and during the period when the new States of Europe were being set up on the declared basis of "national self-determination," to re-define its objectives in a more ambitious way. The "Amritsar Massacre" of 1919, and the repressive Rowlatt Act which accompanied it, exacerbated Indian opinion, and largely wrecked the chances of the new Constitution then about to be introduced under the Montagu-Chelmsford Reforms; and the Congress, under Gandhi's leadership, retaliated with the first campaign of non-violent "Civil Disobedience," which was withdrawn, at Gandhi's order, because it led to violence. Further measures of repression followed; and ever since 1920 the Indian Congress has been engaged in a constant struggle with the Government, periods of active conflict alternating with truces and temporary relaxations of the tension, as at the time when Gandhi came to London as the Congress representative at the Second Round Table Conference. But not until 1929 did the Congress explicitly define its policy as *Purna Swaraj,* or complete Home Rule, involving the right to entire independence; and even this demand is not interpreted as excluding India's continuance within the British Empire, provided she can continue voluntarily, with the recognised right of secession, and on terms of equal partnership.

The Indian National Congress is the leading Nationalist organisation, but it cannot claim to represent the whole of articulate Nationalist opinion. For, although its ranks are open to all, it consists in fact mainly of Hindus, who form the great majority of the population of India. The Moslems, as we shall see, have their separate organisations, sometimes acting with the Congress and sometimes in dispute with it; and the Congress, now committed to a far-reaching programme and in violent hostility to the Indian Government, does not carry with it the whole body of Hindu opinion. There are outside its ranks the Indian "Liberals," organised in a Liberal Federation which includes a good many well-known politicians and also some of the best known Labour leaders, such as Mr. Joshi; and there are also a number of other moderate groups, more prepared than the National Congress to collaborate in the working of reforms which fall short of complete self-government. But, whereas these other groups consist for the most part of leaders, personally important and influential in some cases, but without much organised following, the Congress has a great popular membership in most parts of the country, both directly and through the auxiliary movements and societies that work in association with it. The Indian Congress, while it is led mainly by intellectuals, has reached the villages as no other organisation has been able to do; and the six thousand delegates and even more numerous visitors who attend its annual Sessions, when it is not prevented from meeting by the Government, come from many thousands of towns and villages scattered all over the country. If Congress chose to "co-operate" in working either the present Indian Constitution or any other that is likely to be put in its place, there is little doubt of its ability to capture most of the seats not specially reserved for particular sections of the population.

The Congress, when it is able to act, elects annually a Congress Committee of 350 members; and this body chooses a Working Committee, or executive, of fifteen members. The Congress also chooses, by vote of its provincial organisations, a President for the year; and there is provision whereby a President names his substitute if he is put in prison or otherwise prevented from acting during his term of office. As Congress has been in recent years a persecuted body, it has been necessary to invoke this provision again and again; and the Working Committee has only been able to carry on its work underground. The entire organisation, however, is too strong and pervasive to be successfully suppressed; and its work has gone on in spite of the ban.

Among the auxiliary organisations of the Indian Congress the most important are the All-India Spinners' Association and the movement for the creation of *Ashrams* (Settlements) and National schools and other educational institutions, to which must now be added the special body created to carry on the campaign against untouchability. These auxiliary bodies endeavour to escape the ban imposed on Congress activities by confining themselves to non-political work; but actually they have been greatly interfered with by the police under the Ordinances. Many of the *Ashrams* have been raided and closed down; and in many villages the organisation for the provision of materials for spinning and weaving has been prevented from pursuing its work, on the ground that it has been engaging in political activities. The *Ashrams* are essentially Settlements where young Nationalists, chiefly under Gandhi's inspiration, live together and cultivate the ascetic life. As such, they have no political activity; but their members include many of the most ardent young Nationalists, and it is therefore natural that the *Ashrams* should be in fact the centres of much political as well as cultural and educational work. This does not mean that they are disguised political bodies; but under Gandhi's leadership there is no line to be drawn between political, cultural and religious activities, which are all, for him and his followers, parts of the same gospel.

UNTOUCHABILITY

For some time past Gandhi himself has been outside definitely political activity, having decided to devote himself entirely to the campaign on behalf of the untouchables. This is, of course, indirectly a political question; for the position of the untouchables was one of the most intractable problems that came up at the Round Table Conferences. The question was whether the untouchables were to be regarded as a quite separate element in the Indian electorate, and given seats of their own to which they would elect their own nominees, or whether they were to be treated as part of the Hindu majority. At the Conferences no agreement could be reached on this point; and Mr. Ramsay MacDonald, to whom the matter was referred, thereupon decided in favour of separate electorates. This decision outraged Hindu sentiment; for though the caste Hindus at present put monstrous disabilities and humiliations upon the untouchables in many parts of the country, excluding them from the temples and from all social intercourse with their co-religionists, they are nevertheless determined to have them regarded as Hindus, and not as a separate group with independent rights. Moreover, the large element of progressive Hindu opinion, headed by Gandhi, which is determined to make an end of the entire idea of untouchability, is equally determined not to allow the untouchables to be parted off from the general body of Hindus, on the ground that this would stand fatally in the way of success in the campaign for opening the temples and removing the indignities under which these unfortunates at present suffer.

Gandhi therefore met the decision to grant separate electorates with a threat to fast to death unless it was revoked; and this threat, which he began at once to put into force, compelled the disputing groups to come to a compromise, because no section was prepared, by standing out, to incur the tremendous odium of responsibility for Gandhi's death. On the basis agreed upon, and subsequently accepted by Great Britain, there is to be no separate electorate for the untouchables, but in the united Hindu electorate there is to be provision for a certain number of reserved seats for untouchable candidates.

This, however, does not mean that there is any agreement to remove the stigma of untouchability. There are said to be nearly forty-five million untouchables in India, of whom over twenty-eight millions are in Bengal, the United Provinces, and Bihar, where their condition is not so bad as in other parts of the country, especially Madras. Upon the removal of this stigma, and especially on opening the temples to the untouchables, Gandhi and his followers are now concentrating their attention, leaving the political leadership of the National Congress to men less active in the religious sphere. This involves a leftward movement of the Congress, which includes a powerful left wing led by men who have thrown off their religious beliefs, and approach political questions more in a secular spirit. Jawaharlal Nehru is now the outstanding among these younger Congress leaders; and, as we have seen in an earlier chapter of this book, he has come to some extent under Communist influence, though he is certainly not a Communist and his devotion to Gandhi remains firm and undoubted. For the moment, however, the immediate future of Congress policy is uncertain, owing to the calling off by Gandhi of the "civil disobedience" campaign, and the decisions of most of the Congress leaders to fight the forthcoming elections. This may mean, for a time, a return to a policy of "co-operation"; but co-operation cannot possibly be lasting unless very large concessions of self-government are speedily made.

COMMUNISM AND TRADE UNIONISM IN INDIA

Communism in India is firmly proscribed as an organised movement; and Indian Communist leaders are compelled to live in exile in Russia, whither a good many young Indians have been in recent years for training and education. There is a good deal of underground Communist activity in India, where the young Communists are always trying to penetrate the growing Trade Union organisation and to take the lead in strike movements. The very heavy sentences passed upon Trade Union leaders in the Meerut Conspiracy trial—since largely reduced on appeal—were based on the view that the Trade Unions involved in the case were under Communist influence. This was to some extent true, but it could not possibly justify the savage sentences passed on men against whom no crime was proved save that of stirring up strikes among the underpaid Indian workers.

Trade Unionism in India is still weak and inchoate. The Census of 1921 did indeed show over 33,000,000 workers dependent on industry, 18,000,000 on trade, and nearly 4,500,000 on transport, as against 229,000,000 dependent on agriculture, these figures including members of the family as well as the actual workers. But a large number of the industrial workers are engaged in small-scale occupations, and the statistics of factory employment for 1929 covered only 1,500,000 workers, of whom over a quarter of a million were women. Transport workers numbered 1,500,000, and industrial workers of all sorts just under 12,000,000 according to the Census of 1921. Even of the workers in large-scale industry, a large number are still in spirit villagers, and many go back to village life after a spell in the factories. The 28,000,000 employed agricultural workers, as distinct from peasant owners and tenant farmers, greatly outnumber the industrial proletariat.

Among the workers by far the best organised are the railwaymen, who have a National Federation claiming 160,000 members, and the section of the textile workers organised in the Ahmedabad Labour Union, under Gandhi's leadership. The rest of the organised workers, apart from a small Communist fraction, are split into two rival groups—the All-India Trade Union Congress and the National Federation of Trade Unions. The Trade Union Congress, which used to be the leading body, is mainly under the leadership of Nationalists belonging to the National Congress Party; but it has suffered more than one split of late, and has lost a good deal of its influence. The Federation, on the other hand, has been a moderate body led by Indian Liberals, who have tried to keep it apart from current politics, while professing an evolutionary Socialist object. It is affiliated to the International Federation of Trade Unions, and has been the body from which the Indian delegates at the International Labour Organisation have been chiefly drawn. The railwaymen's Federation has recently been making an active effort to persuade these two bodies to unite, in order to build up a single effective organisation. At present a good many Unions stand aloof from both; but the general temper of Indian Trade Unionism is strongly Nationalist as well as Socialist, and a good deal of its attention has been given to the task of pressing the claims of the working class upon the Indian National Congress and the other Nationalist groups.

POLITICAL GROUPINGS

According to the Census of 1921, there were in India nearly 217,000,000 Hindus, over 11,500,000 Buddhists, mostly in Burma, 3,250,000 Sikhs, nearly 10,000,000 adherents of tribal religions, over 1,000,000 Jains, 4,750,000 Christians, and 68,750,000 Moslems, besides small numbers professing other creeds. The Indian National Congress is primarily a Hindu organisation, though it claims to represent the Sikhs, the Jains, and the tribal religious groups as well. It does not effectively represent the Moslems, who possess separate All-Indian organisations of their own for both religious and political purposes. Politically, the All-India Moslem League has been hitherto the outstanding body, working sometimes in close alliance with the Congress and sometimes in dispute with it. The Moslems, as the most important racial and religious "minority," scattered to some extent all over the country but chiefly concentrated in Bengal, the Punjab and Kashmir, in all of which places they outnumber the Hindus, are determined to secure adequate representation in any Indian representative system that may be established, and sometimes inclined to side with the British against the Hindus with the object of getting recognition of their claims. There are, however, among Moslems as well as Hindus all shades of opinion, from groups willing to co-operate in working an Indian Constitution still under British control, by way of "Liberal" groups demanding Home Rule, but not secession, to left-wing Nationalists who accept the Congress demand for the right to complete independence. As in the case of the Hindus, the British naturally tend to seek support among the right-wing groups; and they are able to do this more successfully in the case of the Moslems because of the devout Moslems' fear of Hindu domination. At the Round Table Conferences much was done to play off the Moslems against the Hindus; but of late the renewal of government by Ordinance in India has driven more of the Moslems over to the Nationalist side, and there is now a pact between the Congress and the most influential of the popular Moslem leaders, and the two groups are again largely working together. It should be added that whereas the political and religious leaders of Hindus and Moslems are apt to fall out, and there are occasional serious cases of communal rioting between fanatics on both sides, in the vast majority of villages where Hindus and Moslems live side by side there appears to be no friction between them, and the whole village works together for the remedying of its common economic and social grievances. The sikhs, concentrated in a part of the Punjab, are another minority which emphatically demands separate representation. Formerly the Sikhs were regarded as the most loyalist of all the Indian peoples to the British rule. But of late they have gone over largely to Nationalism; and they too are at present working in with the National Congress.

THE GOVERNMENT OF INDIA

The present Government of India rests upon the Act of 1919, which arose out of the Montagu-Chelmsford Report, and the British Declaration of August 1917, since reaffirmed by Lord Irwin as Viceroy, with the authority of the British Government, in October 1929. Under the Act of 1919, it is laid down that the object is to provide for "the increasing association of Indians in every branch of the administration and the gradual development of self-governing institutions with a view to the progressive realisation of responsible government in British India as an integral part of the British Empire." The statement of Lord Irwin in 1929 lays down that "it is implicit in the Declaration of 1917 that the natural issue of India's constitutional progress, as there contemplated, is the attainment of Dominion Status." These guarded statements, however, say nothing about the pace at which the advance to self-government is to be achieved.

That India is still a very long way off Dominion Status under the existing Constitution goes without saying. The final constitutional authority is still the British Parliament, acting through the Secretary of State for India. This British Cabinet Minister is advised in England by an appointed Council, which has final control over Indian expenditure. In practice, however, the centre of power has shifted from this Council to the British Cabinet, acting in direct touch with the Viceroy and his Government in India.

The Central Indian Government consists of the Viceroy in Council. There is a Legislature of two Chambers, each with an elected majority; but in the Council of State, or upper Chamber, there are only 33 elected as against 27 nominated members. Moreover, the elected members are chosen on a very restricted property franchise, and include European representatives; so that the Government is practically certain of a majority. The Lower House, or Legislative Assembly, has 104 elected and 41 nominated members. In this case too the electorate is narrow, though the property qualification is not so high as for the Upper Chamber. If Indian Nationalists were ready to work the Constitution, and to act together, they could probably secure a safe majority in the Assembly.

The powers of the Indian Parliament are, however, very limited. The Viceroy can veto any bill he pleases; and in addition to this, he can pass into law any bill that is passed by one Chamber, even if it is rejected by the other. He can even, with the assent of the Imperial Parliament in London, enact any measure which both Chambers have rejected, if he considers it to be essential to security; and in cases of emergency he can do this on his own responsibility, without reference to London. Ordinarily, the Legislative Assembly has to vote the budget; but if it refuses any grant which the Viceroy regards as essential, he has power to override its decision and spend the money against its will. Moreover, money to be spent on the armed forces, on political and religious services, on certain salaries and pensions, on loan charges, and for any charge prescribed by law, is excluded from the Assembly's control; so that in effect the most onerous of Indian financial obligations remain under purely autocratic control. Thus in the last resort every power nominally accorded to the Indian Parliament is reserved by the Viceroy. There is no final concession of responsible government.

The Viceroy actually governs with the aid of an Executive Council of officials, each at the head of a Central Department. There are six "Ministers" of this type, four English and two Indian; but they are all officials, and not representatives. Here again there is still no approach to responsible government.

THE DYARCHY

Under the Central authority are the Provincial Governments, each in charge of one of the Provinces into which India is divided up. The system of Provincial Government now in force is known as the "Dyarchy." It is based on a distinction between two types of function, those "transferred" to responsible Indian Ministers, and those "reserved" under British control. In each Province there is a Governor, aided by an Executive Council of officials, and the Governor-in-Council is solely responsible for the administration of all the "reserved" subjects, which include all matters not specifically transferred, and above all law and police. The "transferred" subjects include health and education, public works and other matters relating to agriculture and industry, and local government within the Provinces —that is, broadly, the social and economic services. These functions are placed in the hands of Ministers drawn from and responsible to Legislative Councils consisting as to at least sixty per cent of elected members. The extent of the franchise on which the elections are based can be judged from the fact that there are about eight million voters, including women as well as men, out of a population in British India of about 250,000,000. The Ministers are chosen by the Governor, who has the power of co-ordinating their activities with those of the official Councillors responsible for the "reserved" departments.

This system of "Dyarchy" now extends over the greater part of British India, though it has not yet been applied in all areas. It involves the existence of a very limited form of responsible government extending only to the social services; and its efficiency is much restricted in practice by three facts. In the first place, the actual execution of any policy that is laid down is necessarily very much under the control of the local "Collectors," or Resident Magistrates. These are Civil Service officials, each of whom presides over one of the 273 districts into which British India is divided. These officers, being directly under Government control, have great power in influencing the actual execution of measures approved by the Provincial Legislatures. Secondly, the reservation of the police power, combined with the authority still vested in the Viceroy to govern by Ordinance without the consent of the Central Legislature, enables the official element in the Provinces to override the representative Ministers whenever a conflict of authority arises, and makes the official influence far more felt in the villages, by way of the local police, than that of the Provincial Legislature. This has been particularly the case since the revival of government by Ordinance during the past two years. Thirdly, the dispute between the Government and the Nationalists, and the pursuance of a policy of non-co-operation by the Congress and other leading Nationalist bodies, have meant that the elected Legislatures and the Ministers chosen from them have been for the most part highly unrepresentative of articulate Indian opinion, since the effect has been to confine the range of choice to relatively small "Responsivist" groups willing to co-operate in working a Constitution to which the main body of Nationalist opinion strongly objects.

THE SIMON REPORT AND AFTER

The Simon Commission of 1928 recognised in its Report the need for an immediate further advance towards Indian self-government, but proposed to make this advance by a further concession of provincial responsibility, without any concession of responsible government at the centre. It speedily became plain that any proposal of this sort was utterly unacceptable not only to the National Congress, but to almost every articulate section of Indian opinion, including the Liberals, who had previously been willing to collaborate in working the "Dyarchy."

We do not propose in this chapter to attempt to discuss either the recommendations of the Simon Commission or the complicated series of proposals and counter-proposals which have since emerged from the two Round Table Conferences of 1930–31 and the Committees subsequently set up by the British Government to prepare schemes for a new Indian Constitution. Nor do we propose to follow the history of the relations between Indian Nationalism and the Government through their successive phases of "non-co-operation" as a protest against the Simon Scheme, truce, in order to allow of negotiations at the Second Round Table Conference, and thereafter renewed rupture of relations, leading up to the system of government by Ordinance which has been in force since 1932. It is enough to say that the Simon Scheme proposed to end the "Dyarchy" in the Provinces, by transferring the "reserved" functions to Indian responsible Ministers, subject to the reservation by the Governor of large powers for the maintenance of order. At the centre, it proposed the replacement of the present Constitution by a Federal system, based on the Provinces, with the object of facilitating the subsequent entry of the Native States into an inclusive All-Indian Federation, and with provision at once for consultation between the new Indian Government and the representatives of the Native States. It did not, however, propose to grant responsible government at the centre, or to take away the vast powers possessed by the Viceroy to override Parliament; while it actually suggested that the control of the Armed Forces in India should be taken away from the Viceroy in Council, and transferred to the Viceroy alone, in order to remove this matter out of the range of the Indian Parliament not merely during a transitional period, but for as long as British forces remain in India at all.

In the course of the subsequent discussions, it became plain that the Government would be unable to secure enough Indian support to work any new Constitution that did not go considerably further than this; and negotiations turned largely round the degree of central responsibility that the British Government would be prepared to concede. The idea of an All-Indian Federation, including the Native States, was brought forward for immediate adoption from the British side, because the British Government hoped to be able to use the Native Princes as a loyalist counterpoise at the centre against the Nationalists. The question of communal electorates also led to much trouble between Hindus, Moslems, Sikhs, representatives of the "Depressed Classes," and other elements; and, although draft schemes now exist covering much of the ground, it is still quite uncertain what the constitutional structure of the new India will be, or whether the proposed new Constitution will ever be adopted at all. Among a section of British Conservatives there is very strong opposition to any further concessions beyond those made in 1919; and while the majority of the Conservative Party has so far supported the National Government over the scheme embodied in the "White Paper," one effect of the opposition has been to stiffen the repression in India, in order to give a firm demonstration of the will to maintain law and order. With the future thus uncertain, it seems best to content ourselves with describing the Constitution as it is, without attempting to evaluate the numerous conflicting projects for its amendment.

At present, Great Britain is holding India by force, against the great mass of articulate Indian opinion, Hindu and Moslem alike. There are groups of "loyalists," including, besides the Indian Princes in the Native States, many of the landowners and other of the richer classes in India, who fear that the Nationalist Movement may develop Socialist or confiscatory tendencies. There is a vast peasant mass of which only a small minority takes any part in political movements of any shade. There are, however, certainly some millions of active Congress supporters in India; and of those Indians who are politically active at all the great majority are behind either the Congress or the Moslem Nationalist organisations. The Liberals and the other Indian parties which stand to the right of the Liberals include important individuals, but no widespread rank and file. Alone among the political movements Congress and the Moslem bodies have successfully touched the villages. Communism has some underground strength among the factory workers, but no considerable organised following of its own, though a good many of the younger Nationalist leaders have been to some extent influenced by Communist ideas. In the Congress organisation, as in the Kuomintang in China, there are many different points of view on social and economic policy. At one extreme are Indian bankers and mill-owners strongly opposed to any form of Socialism; at the other Trade Union leaders and young intellectuals—often the same people, for the Trade Unions are largely led by intellectuals owing to the prevalence of illiteracy among the workers—and these latter are usually at least half-Socialists, and sometimes half-Communists. Jawaharlal Nehru stands as the typical representative of this school. Between these two extremes Gandhi, with his asceticism and his blend of political and religious doctrine, strange to the modern Western mind, still commands a far larger following than any other man in India; but it is doubtful how far he proposes to resume his place as a political leader. Probably Gandhi does not know that himself; for he is a man who obeys his "call" when it comes. For the present at any rate, he is giving all his attention to the campaign on behalf of the untouchables and leaving politics to others. But there are many who believe he will come back at the next crisis, when the British Government begins to apply whatever new Constitution it decides to grant; and it is probable that, if Gandhi wants to come back, he can.

Throughout, the essence of Gandhi's policy has been non-violence. He has stood out against not only any attempt at revolution, but violence in any degree. Peaceful non-co-operation, with "Civil Disobedience" as its extreme instrument, has been the basis of his strategy. How long will he be able to hold Indian Nationalism at this point? More than once, he has called off Civil Disobedience on the ground that it has led to violence. Will he always be able to call it off with success?

It must not be forgotten that, under the British rule, the Indian population, except certain hill tribes near the frontier, is almost completely disarmed—except of course for the British-controlled Indian Army. It is very difficult for an Indian to get a licence even for a sporting gun, much less for other firearms. This is a most serious hardship for the Indian villagers, whom it leaves defenceless against the frequent bands of robbers and dacoits who do manage to possess themselves of weapons, and often sweep down and sack a village before help can come. The Indians want arms; but the Government does not allow them for fear of arming the Nationalist Movement. Therefore, much depends for Great Britain on the loyalism of the Indian Army; and it is hard to say how far Nationalist propaganda has penetrated among the soldiers. The growth of Sikh discontent is in this matter highly important; for Sikhs are of high fighting value, and form an important section of the Army. On the other hand, the Hindu, and especially the Bengali, is not a fighter; and the majority of Indian Nationalists certainly do not want a violent revolution. They would far sooner come to terms with the British Power, whose strength they know, than fight it by violence. But they will come to terms now only if the terms are consistent with national self-respect, and involve at the least the gaining of full self-government, even if it be within the Empire, after a brief agreed period of transition. Will a British Government be found to go at least so far as to meet this claim? If not, India can still be held by force for a time; but any really serious embarrassment of Great Britain in Europe will not improbably involve the loss of the Indian Empire.

Finally, a further question arises. Both British opinion that favours "Indian Reform" and a large part of educated Indian opinion which has got its training under Western influence tend to think of the problem of Indian self-government almost exclusively in European parliamentary terms. But is Western Parliamentarism really the best model for Indian self-government? In face of the widespread illiteracy, there at once arises a difficult problem about the extent of the franchise that is to be granted. Indian Nationalists demand universal suffrage, in order to enfranchise the peasants and workers. British parliamentarians reply that only literate voters can work the ballot, or conduct a parliamentary election in a satisfactory way. The Simon Commission proposed a franchise extending to ten per cent of the total, or about twenty per cent of the adult population, which is more than three times the size of the existing electorate. This by no means satisfied Indian opinion, apart from all the other objections to the Report; and Gandhi, in the course of the discussions, suggested that the solution would be for the villagers to vote, not individually, but collectively through delegates who would cast a group vote on their behalf in the electoral districts. This method, which is of course practically the Soviet method, was strongly objected to by the parliamentarians; but the contention that it would be by far the most effective way of eliciting village opinion is hardly open to dispute. This suggests strongly that, even if India does in due course receive some sort of parliamentary Constitution at British and Anglicised Indian hands, the further course of her political development may diverge very greatly from the path laid down for her in advance by the British advocates of Indian Reform. Ultimately, India will go her own way and work out her own form of government, whatever her leaders may accept for the time as a means of getting power out of alien hands. Certainly, on the face of the matter, Sovietism looks far more suitable than Parliamentarism as a model.

BOOK III

THE POLITICAL MACHINE

1. PARLIAMENTARY SYSTEMS

BETWEEN THE STATES described in Book II of this work there are obviously very wide differences of structure and essential quality. Even if we leave out of account the political systems of the Far East, we are still left with three main types of State—the Parliamentary, the Fascist and the Soviet. Russia stands obviously as the example of the third of these types, and Italy as the example of the second; for the new "Third Reich" of the Nazis is still too inchoate to admit of satisfactory analysis. But when we begin to look for a representative example of the parliamentary State we find ourselves at once in a difficulty. Great Britain, as the pioneer of the parliamentary system, has evidently strong claims to be taken as the type; but the differences between the political systems of Great Britain and the United States are so wide that these two, at any rate, must be taken to a large extent separately. To a smaller extent there are very important differences between the systems of Great Britain and France; and France more than Great Britain seems to have provided the model for the parliamentary institutions of most of the new States constructed in Europe on the morrow of the World War. We shall have, therefore, in discussing the parliamentary type of State, to consider at any rate these three as essential varieties of the type before we can go on to institute a satisfactory comparison between Parliamentarism and the two rival systems.

In the first place Great Britain is in form a constitutional monarchy, whereas France and the United States are both republics. The British Government still consists in constitutional theory of the King's Ministers, appointed by and responsible to the Crown, whereas in the other two countries the Government is in theory a

Government of the people and not that of a ruler set apart from the people. But whereas in the United States the Cabinet is a mere appendage of the President, who has far wider powers than either the French President or the British Monarch, in France the Cabinet is the effective Government and depends, like the Cabinet in Great Britain, for office and authority directly on its power to command the support of a majority in Parliament.

Secondly, whereas in both France and Great Britain the executive power is effectively in the hands of a group depending on parliamentary support, the Constitution of the United States is based on an attempt to make a sharp separation between the legislative and the executive powers. The chief executive in the United States is not the Cabinet, but the President, who is independently chosen by delegates elected for the purpose by the whole body of voting citizens, and is therefore at least co-equal in status with Congress, the elected legislative body. The American President appoints his own Cabinet, requiring only the confirmation of the Senate, and his Ministers are subordinates rather than colleagues, and thus differ greatly from the Cabinet colleagues of the Prime Ministers of Great Britain and France. The American Constitution raises the executive power to a far higher level than it possesses in either of the other States, and it also gives far more scope for the exercise of authority by a powerful and determined individual leader. The American system is only half a parliamentary system, and in its actual working the President, though he possesses no legislative power, is at least as important as the Congress.

Thirdly, the United States is a Federal Republic, whereas both Great Britain and France are unitary States. The Federal Government in the United States is not an all-purposes Government like those of France and Great Britain. It has competence to deal only with certain matters and to levy only certain kinds of taxes, and it is kept continually in check and prevented from exceeding its appointed functions by a written Constitution in which the limitations of its authority are explicitly embodied. This Constitution is hard to alter, and its authority is upheld by a Supreme Court which has absolute power of veto over legislation which the judges hold to be "unconstitutional." In matters of regional and local administration France is highly centralised in comparison with Great Britain, but in both countries Parliament has to deal with all subjects, and possesses exclusive power to enlarge or restrict the functions of local or regional government. In the United States, on the other hand, the separate States of the Union do not derive their powers from the Federal Government. They are in theory independent and original sovereign authorities which have only surrendered under the Constitution of the United States certain definite and limited powers to a central authority. It is true enough that with the growth of population and the advance of economic activity in the United States the powers of the Federal Government have in fact expanded far beyond the intentions of the original framers of the American Constitution, and that the Supreme Court has shown throughout its history some degree of elasticity in reinterpreting the phrases of the original Constitution so as to adjust them to developing needs. It is further true that the sovereignty of the States was decisively restricted by the outcome of the Civil War, which settled once and for all the question of the right of a State to secede from the Federation. But despite these modifications of the original Constitution, the federal character of the American system still remains a matter of the utmost practical importance. It has, for example, stood powerfully in the way of the development of industrial legislation of the type common to all other advanced industrial States. Industrial legislation still remains in America largely within the competence of the separate States of the Union.

Fourthly, while all the three countries we are considering have bicameral systems, and their popular Chambers bear a marked resemblance one to another, there are deep differences between them in the character of their second Chambers. France and the United States both have Senates elected on a representative basis, whereas Great Britain has still a hereditary House of Lords freshly recruited from outside only by the appointment of new peers, which is a matter within the competence of the Government as the adviser of the Crown. All three second Chambers have a reputation for behaving more conservatively than the other Chamber of the national Parliament; and indeed it is largely the appointed function of all three to act as a brake upon the activities of the Government and the popular Chamber. But this conservative tendency exists in very different forms in the three second Chambers, and is by far more marked in the British House of Lords than in either of the two Senates. The House of Lords in Great Britain is in effect a permanent Conservative Chamber with a limited veto upon legislation passed by the House of Commons. It is thus in effect inoperative when a mainly Conservative Government is in office, but perpetually in opposition when any other type of Government is returned to power. There is no such automatic predominance of a single party or interest in either the French or the American Senate. Of these two, the American is the less inclined to lag in opinion behind the other Chamber. The American Senate is chosen by precisely the same body of electors as the House of Representatives, from which it differs mainly in that the representation is very differently weighted, that the age qualification for membership is higher, and that the members are elected for a longer period and retire by rotation and not all at once. In France, too, there is a higher age qualification for Senators and a longer period of office, with the same arrangement for retirement by rotation; but the French Senate is not a popularly elected body in the same sense as the *Chambre des Députés*. It is indirectly chosen by Conventions consisting mainly of the members of local governing authorities, and this indirect method of choice has combined with the other factors to give it a distinctly more conservative character in relation to the lower Chamber, especially in economic matters, than belongs to the American Senate.

PARTY ORGANISATION

Fifthly, party organisation is radically different in the three countries, and it is on the organisation of parties that the working of the parliamentary system fundamentally depends. In Great Britain the tradition of political life strongly favours a system of two parties alternating in power, so that there is always a single Opposition which provides the basis for an alternative Government. This ideal of two parties and two parties only has indeed not been fully realised in practice. Throughout the nineteenth century the Irish were present as an inconvenient third party group, interfering with the smooth working of the two-party system; and before the Irish had been removed from the scene by the concession of Dominion Status to the Irish Free State, the Labour Party had arisen as a new third party influencing the political situation. However, both the Irish Party and the Labour Party up to 1914 were rather groups than parties in the full sense. Like the Radicals, who constituted a half-independent party for some decades after the Reform Act of 1832, the Irish Nationalist Party and the pre-war Labour Party were both able to exert their influence by throwing their force for or against a Government based on one of the main parties, but were not themselves claimants for office. Only after the war did a real three-party situation appear, in the course of that transition which displaced the Liberal Party from its old position of primary importance and caused what remained of it ultimately to change places with the Labour Party and cease to be a serious claimant to office. Great Britain thus reverted in effect to the arrangement of two primary parties; but this had lost its old simplicity, as the Liberal group in the middle might easily be strong enough to prevent either of the main parties from governing without its aid, and was not, like the Irish in the nineteenth century, interested only in a single question and therefore able to stand aside from other phases of the political struggle.

Undoubtedly a two-party system, and even a system in which there are two predominant parties flanked by secondary groups, greatly facilitates the working of parliamentary institutions and leads to the existence of powerful and relatively stable Governments. It is not, however, a situation which can be created at will, as appeared very plainly in the post-war experience of the new parliamentary States. The party position in these countries resembled much more closely that of France, where there exist not so much highly organised parties in the British or American sense, as groups of members, far more numerous and of a far more shifting and unstable character. The existence of this group system means that Governments, which must get a majority behind them, can be based only on coalitions combining a number of groups; and the position is complicated by the fact that the party groupings do not coincide in the two Chambers. There is a smaller number of groups in the Senate than in the Chamber of Deputies, and the Senatorial grouping is the less unstable of the two. Governments, however, are based mainly on the groups which exist in the Chamber of Deputies, and the shifting coalitions among these groups render French Cabinets weak and unstable, so that France changes her Government far more often than Great Britain. This weakness of the Government as a body, and the weakness of the party formations, tend to add to the importance of the individual member, who holds his seat far more on grounds of personality than in countries where the party system is stronger, and is moreover in French politics an important factor locally as well as nationally, because he possesses considerable influence over local appointments.

On the surface the American political system resembles the British far more closely than the French; for in the United States as in Great Britain there have been for a long time two great traditional parties, and these parties have shown themselves in America far more resistant to the emergence of new groupings than in Great Britain. In American politics the Republican and Democratic Parties still hold the field, so that it is exceedingly difficult for anyone to get elected to either House of Congress except under the auspices of one or the other. Nevertheless the American party system is in fact very different indeed from the British. In Great Britain there has always been one party standing broadly for a Conservative policy—that is, for keeping things as much as possible as they are, while making timely concessions to the necessity for change—and another party standing definitely to the left of the Conservatives, and committed to the gradual modification of social conditions by means of progressive legislation. In effect both the great parties, even in Great Britain, have always been conservative in the sense that they have stood together for the maintenance of the established social and economic system. But in Great Britain the advocates of the established order have divided themselves definitely into a right and a left wing, so that, when the Labour Party arose to take the place of the decaying Liberal Party as the Opposition to the Conservatives, it was able easily to inherit the existing progressive tradition.

In the United States, on the other hand, it is quite impossible to label one of the great parties conservative and the other progressive. For in both there exist both conservative and progressive elements, and membership of the one or the other is far more a matter of locality and chance personal association than of deliberate choice on political grounds. There are great families traditionally associated with the two parties, and there are also whole areas which are traditionally either Republican or Democratic. Consequently any new political tendency that emerges in the United States, provided that it is sufficiently consistent with the American tradition to be considered at all through the American established political institutions, will make its way inside both the political parties and will not easily become the policy of one party encountering the united opposition of the other. At present the policy of President Roosevelt, supported by the majority of his own Democratic followers, is also keenly disliked by a minority of Democrats, but enthusiastically supported by a large body of "Progressive Republicans," drawn chiefly from the Western States. To European observers American party conditions seem to be totally unreal; but clearly the function of the party system in America has been in the main not to organise differences of political policy, even within a basis of common agreement about the foundations of the social order, but rather to make workable a parliamentary democratic system that has to be operated over a territory so vast and on behalf of a population so diverse as those of the United States. The American parties are far more pieces of machinery for working the Constitution than the expression of rival political tendencies.

PARLIAMENTARY PROCEDURE

Sixthly, there are great differences in the working of the parliamentary institutions of the three countries in matters of parliamentary procedure. In Great Britain and to a large extent in France almost the whole body of public legislation originates with the Government and embodies a governmental policy which is then presented to Parliament for endorsement or amendment or rejection. In the United States, on the other hand, while the administration—that is to say in effect the President—does to a large extent initiate legislation, there is also a large mass of independent legislation, initiated in Congress itself, and thereafter sent up to the President for his endorsement or veto. Private members do also possess the right of initiating legislation in both Great Britain and France; but in America the right is far more actively exercised, largely because of the fact that there the administration appears before Parliament as an independent power, and not as an executive directly emanating from a parliamentary majority. But whereas in this respect there is a contrast between the United States on the one hand and Great Britain and France on the other, in another respect Great Britain has to be contrasted with both France and the United States. For both the French and the American Parliaments work mainly through a system of Standing Committees on particular branches of public policy; and these Committees, dealing continuously with a special range of questions, come to exercise a very real and important influence on the character of legislation. In France a Government bill is often greatly altered by the appropriate Committee of the Chamber or Senate; and often the two Houses, through their respective Committees, fall out over the details of a particular bill, and the question is fought out over the head of the Government, which has no power to enforce its will. In Great Britain, on the other hand, the power of the Government over legislation is far greater because of the absence of any corresponding Committee system; for even when bills are discussed at a committee stage by a Select Committee rather than by the whole House, these Select Committees are in practice not independent bodies but mere miniature reproductions of the numerical distribution of the parties in the House as a whole and are firmly under the control of the Ministers. The strength of the Government as against the Parliament in the British system has so far made any effective development of Committee work impossible.

PARLIAMENTS AND ELECTIONS

Seventhly, there are important differences between the three countries in the extent of the franchise, the periods for which the members of Parliament are elected and actually sit, and, in practice, in the matter of dissolution. Women have a vote in Great Britain and the United States, but not in France. In the United States the House of Representatives is elected for only two years, and is in recess for a large part of the year, even apart from the fact that it does not actually begin its sessions until a long time after the election has taken place. This greatly diminishes its power in relation to the President, who is elected for a longer term, and can therefore outlast the Congress which is elected with him. But it may also result in confronting the President, during the latter part of his period of office, with a Congress elected after the currents of opinion which brought him to power have changed, and thus with a hostile parliamentary majority. In Great Britain, on the other hand, the House of Commons is elected for five years, and sometimes runs for its full term; but there is a traditional right for the Prime Minister to ask at any time for a dissolution, and the defeat of the Government on any issue regarded as involving the confidence of the House of Commons is usually followed at once by a General Election, save on the rare occasions when the existing House affords a possible basis for an alternative Government. The French system differs profoundly from both the British and the American. The Chamber of

Deputies is elected for four years and is hardly ever dissolved until it has run its full term; for whereas under the British party system there is seldom any possibility of changing the Government without changing the composition of the House of Commons, in France there are always many possibilities open owing to the number of separate party groups, and the fluctuating nature of the relations between them. Often a change of Government in France means no more than a very slight reorientation of policy to either the right or the left, and sometimes not even this. For example, quite recently one Radical leader after another tried his hand at forming a Government, but there was no real shifting either of policy or of parliamentary backing through all the changes of Government.

It would be possible to select for comparison many other features of the three parliamentary systems which have been chosen as typifying the main forms of parliamentary Government, and to complicate the comparison much further by referring to the institutions of other parliamentary States which possess other varieties of political institutions. Nevertheless, in spite of these numerous and far-reaching points of difference, there is among all the various parliamentary systems a great deal in common. They are all based on the assumption that the authority to make the laws in a State ought to rest largely if not exclusively with a number of representatives chosen in some way by the whole body of citizens possessed of voting rights, and that this representative system constitutes at any rate an essential element in the right government of the State. They may differ very greatly both in the powers which they assign to the representative legislative machine as against other elements in the Constitution, and in the power which they confer either explicitly or by implication upon individuals, but they are all attempts to reconcile some sort of "democracy" with the conditions of the large modern States, in which it is quite out of the question for the whole body of citizens to participate directly in the government, as they could in some degree at least in the tiny City States of Ancient Greece. The theory behind modern parliamentary institutions seems to be that, since all the persons whose right to participate in the making of laws is recognised cannot be present in person at their making, they should, instead of this, be given the right of representation—that is, of choosing a smaller number of persons whose votes will be taken as carrying with them the assent of the wider electorate which they represent. It is not, of course, essential that parliamentary institutions should be democratic; for the right to vote for the election of representatives can be either extended to the whole adult population, or restricted to any extent by the exclusion of greater or smaller classes from the suffrage. The fundamental idea of Parliamentarism is that of representation rather than that of democracy, and only by gradual stages have representative assemblies in most countries come to be based even in part on something approaching universal suffrage. It is, as we shall see, this idea that men can be represented along parliamentary lines, as well as the "democratic" character of the representation, that is now being challenged by the rival forms of political organisation with which we shall have to go on to compare the parliamentary system.

2. DICTATORSHIPS

As soon as we turn from a comparison of the various parliamentary systems to a consideration of the political institutions which are broadly grouped together under the name of dictatorships we find ourselves in a different world, to which none of the categories familiar to nineteenth-century political theory can easily be made to apply. This is not because dictatorship is a new thing in the world's history, for there have been in the past many forms of dictatorial government. It is rather because political theorists have in recent times formulated their doctrines almost exclusively in terms of parliamentarism, and have tacitly or explicitly assumed that some form of parliamentary government is the only appropriate or legitimate system for the working of a modern civilised State. All the familiar categories of modern political thought are therefore parliamentary categories; but these by no means fit the institutions which are now being evolved by a number of leading States described in an earlier section of this book.

Dictatorship brings us into a different world—or rather into two different worlds, for there is fundamentally very little in common between the dictatorship of the proletariat as it exists in Russia and the Fascist dictatorships that have been created in Italy and Germany and Austria—the last of these being clerical as well as Fascist, and perhaps at bottom even more clerical than Fascist. There are indeed institutional similarities between Fascist and proletarian dictatorships, and it will be our business to take note of the points at which these rival systems have resorted to similar methods of organisation. But in noting these resemblances we must not for a moment leave out of account that the two systems are in their aims and underlying philosophy utterly distinct and antagonistic, so that the resemblances lie near the surface, covering up far more important features of essential difference.

Between the dictatorship of the proletariat in Russia and the Fascist dictatorships of Italy and Germany and Austria there lie certain other dictatorial systems which cannot be grouped with either extreme. As we have seen, Turkey and China are both in form one-party States, operated through systems of government which rest upon the power of a nationally organised party, backed up to a large extent by military force. Moreover, there are in Europe a number of States which exist under forms of government closely approaching dictatorship but differing from the definitely Fascist States in that their institutions rest not on the authority of a political party preaching a "demagogic" policy, but rather on that of a Crown which still aims at governing by autocratic methods. Yugoslavia and Rumania both belong to this type, and so did Spain up to 1931 under the dictatorship of Primo de Rivera. Hungary is in a somewhat different position, in that she is ruled authoritatively under a Regent instead of a King; and Poland again is different, in that in her case the dictatorial institutions are in the hands of Marshal Pilsudski and his group of Generals, acting within the framework of what is still in form a parliamentary republic.

It will be best for the purpose of the comparison made in this chapter to follow the same course as we adopted in comparing the various parliamentary systems, and to confine our attention to a small number of the outstanding countries. We shall take Russia as the typical representative of proletarian dictatorship, Italy and Germany as the representatives of Fascism—though in this case it will be difficult to speak precisely of Germany at the present inchoate stage of her new constitutional development. Let us begin by considering not the points of difference between these various dictatorships, but their common differences from the parliamentary systems discussed in the last chapter.

PARLIAMENTS UNDER DICTATORSHIP

In the first place, wherever any form of dictatorship is in force, Parliament, even if it continues to exist, becomes an unimportant and uninfluential body. In Russia, which had no strong parliamentary tradition to break down, the Duma was simply swept away with the advent of the Soviets; but in both Italy and Germany the Parliaments are still there, though Germany has now abolished her upper Federal House as no longer necessary in view of the destruction of the autonomous constitutional power of the various States of the Reich. Italy apparently proposes to preserve her Upper Chamber but to destroy the Chamber of Deputies and replace it to some extent by a new Chamber of Corporations, but at present both Houses of the Italian Parliament remain in existence, though the "popular" Chamber is now in effect chosen by the Fascist Grand Council from nominations made by the various "corporative" bodies recognised by the Fascist State. In both Italy and Germany however, Parliament has been reduced to a position of very little real importance in the constitutional system. It survives as a sounding board for occasional pronouncements by the leaders of the State and as a body which is called upon at need to ratify legislation already approved by the effective governing institutions, or to record a vote designed to serve as a symbol of the national will. Despite this continued use which the Fascist dictators find for Parliament it is clear that if Parliament totally disappeared, as it has already disappeared in Austria, the lack of it would make no real difference to the working of the State system. Parliament has become in the Fascist countries the fifth wheel of the coach, and not even the spare wheel of the motor-car. It has no real place in the operative system of government.

PARTY DICTATORSHIP

Secondly, in all the new types of dictatorship party organisation—that is, the organisation of the one dominant party which is allowed to survive—becomes far more important constitutionally than under the most developed parliamentary system. In effect the party becomes the ultimate organ of government and the direct source of public policy. In Italy the Fascist Grand Council, and not Parliament, is now the real legislative body; and in Russia, although the ultimate constitutional authority belongs on paper to the Congress of Soviets, the real work of policy-building and law-making is done mainly in the Conferences and through the machinery of the Communist Party. This is not true to the same extent in Germany, where the party machine, though it was the decisive factor in making the revolution, has as a whole far less influence on policy than in either Italy or Russia. This is partly because Germany, more than Italy and of course infinitely more than Russia, has organised the new State on the principle of personal leadership from above, so that the members of the dominant party are called upon rather to carry out the orders of the party leaders than to take any effective share in the framing of policy; but it is also partly because the Nazi revolution is still in an intermediate phase and has not yet settled down to the working of the new constitutional system which it is engaged in setting up. It seems inevitable that, with the consolidation of the Nazi State, there will come an increased pressure from within the ranks of the party for an effective share in the determination of public policy—to say nothing of the possibility of conflict among the leaders, who appear to hold divergent views about the basis of the State. But even now, despite the institution of personal leadership, there is so much to do in controlling the various agencies which the programme of *Gleichschaltung* brings within the scope of publicly organised activities that reliance has to be placed largely on the initiative of subordinate leaders in carrying through the programme of the new régime. Thus even in Germany the party as a whole counts for a great deal, despite its repudiation of the democratic principle even within its own ranks. The party is autocratically led; but the Nazi dictatorship could not hold the country without a strongly organised party as its instrument.

FREEDOM OF SPEECH AND ORGANISATION

Thirdly, under a dictatorial system the discussion of public issues proceeds in quite a different way from that to which we have grown accustomed under the parliamentary régime. In parliamentary countries the freedom of speech and of organisation and peaceful agitation have been thought of as essential within certain defined limits to the conduct of public business. It is true that no parliamentary country permits complete freedom in these respects. Persons accused of being agitators do get jailed, and the freedom of speech does not mean so much as it purports to mean in face of the domination of the most effective organs of publicity by narrow and powerful vested interests. Nevertheless, discussion within fairly large permitted limits is an essential characteristic of parliamentary organisation, arising naturally out of the confrontation of rival parties, each claiming the right to put its own case in an endeavour to convince public opinion. On the other hand, all the dictatorial systems adopt a quite different attitude to this question of freedom of speech and organisation and propaganda. For it is common to all of them to hold that these freedoms are to be permitted, at any rate during a transitional stage required for the stabilisation of the new régime, only within limits set by the assumptions on which the régime itself rests. Critics who accept the underlying philosophy and policy of the dominant régime can to a great extent speak their minds freely, provided they do this within the framework of the party organisation and are prepared to accept without further question any decision reached collectively by the party, even if it is entirely contrary to their own view. There can be considerable freedom of speech under dictatorships in relation to matters which are regarded as still unsettled. But as soon as the dominant party establishes an orthodoxy in relation to any particular matter the right of criticism is in that respect regarded as at an end, and the critic is in danger of being expelled and perhaps victimised unless he confesses his error and agrees to accept the conclusion reached by the party and base his future actions and utterances upon it. That is to say, under all dictatorships there is held to be an orthodoxy to which, as soon as it has been laid down, all good citizens are under an obligation to conform; and failure to conform to this orthodoxy is regarded as depriving the nonconformist of all right to take part in the government of the State or to endeavour to persuade others to accept his point of view. This is obviously a standpoint characteristic of men who feel themselves to be on the defensive, with a duty of upholding against all forms of attack the essential institutions in which they believe. It is a spirit of dogmatism and self-confident rectitude that has often appeared before in the world's history, but has usually been associated in the past with religious rather than with purely political principles. It reappears to-day as a purely secular Calvinism which has a good deal in common with the rule of the "Saints" under Cromwell and still more with the government of Geneva under Calvin and Beza.

These limitations on the freedom of speech and organisation and agitation do not mean that freedom disappears; for, as we have seen in our discussion of the various dictatorial systems, there has been under some of them, and especially in Russia and Turkey, a great burgeoning of discussion and active controversy on all manner of subjects. The freedom of speech is not totally destroyed; it is rather canalised, compelled to flow through certain forms of thought and doctrine and, at any rate in Russia, caused to flow all the more swiftly by being given a channel along which it is to move. This secondary freedom appears far less under the various Fascist dictatorships; but there are signs of it in Nazi Germany in the intense activity which Nazi writers and artists show in endeavouring to pour all their ideas into the new mould of National Socialist doctrine.

Fourthly, dictatorships weight opinion differently from parliamentary States. Under the parliamentary system the weighting of opinion is done in part by the character of the electoral franchise and by the relative powers accorded to the elective and non-elective elements of the legislative and administrative machine. But to a large extent it is left to work itself out through the economic institutions which lie outside the direct domain of government. This involves that it is in fact weighted very heavily in favour of the possessors of great wealth, for they are able to use the institutions of freedom of speech and organisation far more effectively than those who have less economic resources at their command. Parliamentarism, coexisting with the private ownership of the means of production, thus weights public opinion in favour of plutocracy, even where the franchise is practically universal and the power of the popularly elected House of Parliament very great. On the other hand, dictatorships set out to weight opinion deliberately by the manipulation not of the voting system but directly of all the essential institutions through which it is able to find expression. The opinion that is meant to count is the opinion of loyal party members, and the opinions of persons outside the charmed circle of the party count only as antagonistic forces of which notice has to be taken in determining the limits to which the approved policy of the party can be pushed. Opposition opinion must be measured; but so far from wishing to elicit it in any form in which it can gain strength by becoming organised, dictatorships set out to keep it under by preventing it from gaining the force which is generated by publicity and organisation. That is why dictatorial systems usually need large corps of spies. Having damped down opposition opinion and prevented it from finding open expression, they must find out what it is for fear of coming unexpectedly up against it in the execution of their policy.

GLEICHSCHALTUNG AND REPRESENTATION

Fifthly, under all dictatorial systems the process which the Germans call *Gleichschaltung* is put extensively into force. This process consists essentially in securing that as far as possible every form of social organisation that is capable of influencing the attitude and opinion of the members of the State shall be brought under a leadership which is fully in sympathy with the attitude of the dominant party, and shall thus become a positive agent in the furtherance of its policy. This is the essential idea underlying the conception of the "totalitarian" State. But obviously the same principle is at work in Russia in a different form. It is no less a part of the policy of the Communists than of the Fascists or Nazis to make sure that all the key positions in Society shall be occupied by men who can be guaranteed to use them in furtherance of the aims of the controlling group within the State.

Sixthly, under all systems of dictatorship the question of representation is conceived very differently from the idea of it which underlies parliamentary government. Parliamentarism is essentially individualistic in its basis. It builds up its system of representation on the foundation of the individual voter, who is regarded as choosing someone to represent in the governing body of the State his individual point of view. Dictatorial systems, on the other hand, are never individualistic in this sense; for their aim is never to give the individual citizens the power to make their influence felt in the determination of public policy. In most cases, they tend rather to think of men as divided into groups, which need to be either browbeaten, or cajoled, or enlisted in the service of the State, and to think of these groups as possessing more importance than the individuals who make them up. Communism conceives these groups as being fundamentally economic classes, and thus arrives at a conception of Society as divided horizontally. Its aim is to represent not individuals but the proletariat, and to make the proletariat the ruling class until such time as it has ceased to be a proletariat by merging all other classes with itself into a classless fraternity. Fascism, on the other hand, thinks of men as divided fundamentally not by economic class but by function, and therefore as falling into vertical groups, each possessing a relation to the State defined in terms of the service which it is called upon to perform. This conception underlies the idea of the Corporative State, which is an attempt to organise all the various functional groups within Society in subordination to the political State as the organ endowed with the overriding function of co-ordination and control. Thus neither Communism nor Fascism sets out to represent the individual, or attaches any importance to individual representation as distinct from the representation of groups which are entitled by virtue of their special position in Society to share in the framing of public policy. This difference is fundamental, but we need say no more about it here, as it will be discussed further in subsequent chapters of this book.

CONTRASTING TYPES OF DICTATORSHIP

So much for the features which, despite many differences in the forms in which they find expression, are common to the new dictatorships of the post-war world. These resemblances are striking, but they are, as we saw at the outset, secondary in that they belong to the sphere of organisation and mechanism and not to that of ultimate character and objective. The same instruments are capable of being used in radically different ways. A surgical knife can be used to cure a man or to kill him; strychnine is a tonic as well as a poison. The same motor car can be used to carry you to John o' Groats or to Land's End. Now, then, for the radical differences between the rival forms of dictatorship.

First, there is all the difference in the world between using dictatorship as an instrument for the preservation and for the destruction of class differences. Nor is this a question of ultimate objective alone. For it vitally affects the present working of a dictatorial system. If the object is the elimination of class differences and the establishment of democracy by the institution of a classless Society, it is obviously necessary to begin at once with the building up of the democratic institutions which are necessary to the working of a Society based on equality of citizenship among all the members. The basis of the dictatorship must therefore be as broad as possible, consistently with the need for admitting within its ranks only such elements of the population as will not obstruct too dangerously its democratic aim. For this reason it is essential for the Communist Party in Russia both to be large and steadily to broaden its basis by bringing additional elements within its ranks—e.g. from among the workers in socialised agriculture—and also in its internal working to be as democratic as possible in order to train its members for the responsibilities falling upon them both in the current administration of the State and in the building up of the wider democracy that is in view. On the other hand, a Fascist dictatorship, since it sets out to preserve and not to obliterate class distinctions, has to be on its guard against letting the democratic and proletarian elements in its ranks get the upper hand in the formulation of party policy. It may need to make its party large, in order to get a sufficient basis of support for consolidating the dictatorship; but it will also need to organise the party internally on authoritative rather than democratic lines so as to ensure the predominance in it of those elements which can be relied on to preserve the class character of the "Totalitarian" State. The party has to mirror the social system which it upholds: if the system is to maintain class distinction, so must the party.

This difference leads Fascist dictatorships to place the ultimate emphasis on personal leadership as against corporate control; for, though the aim may be to build up a Corporative State, the Corporative State is held to require a personal leader, a *Duce* or a *Führer,* who is the ultimate fount of authority and party inspiration. On the other hand, proletarian dictatorship, even if in emergency it accords great power to a single individual, has a natural hostility to personal leadership, at any rate by any living man. It may canonise Lenin when Lenin is safely dead, or in China, under Russian influence, canonise Dr. Sun Yat Sen under the same conditions. But it will not canonise Stalin or Chiang Kai-shek, however much power it may in fact accord to these living leaders.

Again there is a vital difference between Fascist and Communist dictatorships in the form and extent of their direct control over the life of Society. The Communist dictatorship, because it aims at abolishing classes and establishing economic equality, is necessarily induced to take under its direct control and management all the essential institutions for the production and distribution of wealth. It must manage these things directly because only if it assumes direct responsibility for them can it acquire effective control over the distribution of incomes. On the other hand, the Fascist State, aiming at inequality, can be well satisfied with an economic system which dispenses unequal rewards in accordance with the "marginal productivity" laws of capitalist political economy. It needs, indeed, to bring the economic agencies within the State under some sort of supervision. Up to a point *Gleichschaltung* must be applied to them in order to keep the workers under due discipline and subjection, and to ensure the compliance of employers with the general policy of the Fascist State. But these ends can be secured without taking the positive conduct of industry into public hands. Fascist dictatorships, therefore, leave industry for the most part in private ownership, and aim simply at ensuring its conduct in harmony with the needs of a State that upholds class difference and economic inequality. This implies that the scope of dictatorship is far wider under Communism than under Fascism; for in fact, as long as the great capitalists remain in possession of the essential means of production, they are bound to constitute a force in Society—a kind of economic dictatorship—which no purely political dictatorship can hope to make thoroughly compliant to its will. No Fascist dictatorship can be purely a political dictatorship; it must either become an economic dictatorship as well, or govern in alliance with the economic dictatorship of Capitalism.

It follows from this difference that Fascist and proletarian dictatorships differ fundamentally in their effects on the general character of living within the Societies in which they are established. Fascism, leaving differences of income between different classes in Society broadly undisturbed, except probably for some worsening in the position of the working class, permits men, outside the range of their political activities, to go on living much as they lived before the dictatorship came into being. Communism, on the other hand, in uprooting class differences and advancing rapidly towards equality of income, compels men to readjust their entire notion of social relationships and values, and also causes many of them to have to alter suddenly their whole standard and way of life. It thus produces much more powerful reactions on the quality and character of personality and private intercourse than Fascism, and these differences react upon the real content of political activity by bringing a far greater part of men's lives within the scope of politics, and unifying far more of their actions and ideas under the conception of an embracing social plan, for which they have a common responsibility. Proletarian dictatorship implies radically new social valuations in a far more fundamental sense than Fascism, because it rests on a far more fundamental economic revolution. For, whereas Fascism aims mainly at preserving old institutions that are threatened, Communism seeks to establish values that are new.

In general, then, while there are certain features of close resemblance between the dictatorial systems which are at present contending for mastery, it is quite a mistake to suppose that they stand in any sense for a common idea. They are all anti-parliamentary, but for directly opposite reasons. Communism is anti-parliamentary because it regards the parliamentary system as incapable of being adapted to serve the purposes of establishing or conducting a classless Society based on economic equality. Fascism, on the other hand, is anti-parliamentary because it regards parliamentarism in its modern democratic forms as incapable of serving any longer as an effective instrument for the preservation of class differences and the nationalist idea. For Communism, though it has found embodiment so far only in the national State, is essentially cosmopolitan, denying not only class privilege but also that national exclusiveness upon which Fascism everywhere insists. It is sheer obscurantism to lump together forms of dictatorship which rest on this sharp antagonism of fundamental ideas. They have certain instruments in common; but they set out to use these instruments both for totally opposite purposes and in radically different ways.

3.   PARTIES AND PARTY SYSTEMS

THE FUNCTION of a political system is to provide a legal and constitutional framework within which the arts of life can find room to grow. Accordingly, the political system must be made in accordance with the requirements of the underlying conditions of life. The relations which it sustains among men must be such as to afford reasonable opportunities for the developing use of men's powers to create for themselves the means of good living. The political institutions of Society must be in harmony with the technical needs of the age. They must be consistent with the full use of the available powers of production, in order that the standard of living may be raised to the highest practicable point. They must take adequate account of the cultural wants which the advance of technique and education has put into men's minds.

It may be argued that to do all these things is the function, not of the political, but of the economic system. But it is quite impossible in reality to keep the two distinct. For the relations among men which the political system sustains are economic as well as political relations. The State, as it exists at any place and time, is based upon a particular system of property rights which the State Courts will sustain. The political constitution embodies implicit, if not explicit, assumptions about the rights of private property and the sanctity of constitutional relationships. It is an instrument for the enforcing of private as well as public rights and claims appropriate to a particular economic order. If this economic order satisfies the above conditions, in that it does give men room to develop the arts of life and to make full use of the available resources of production for enlarging their satisfactions, well and good. If not, the political order, being based on the economic order as an instrument for its defence, will stand powerfully in the way of the economic changes which the development of the powers of production requires, and will have to be swept aside before these changes can be made effective in a new economic system.

But, it will be said, the political system is not rigid, but highly adaptable. It can be modified without being destroyed; and it can be used as an instrument for making necessary modifications in the economic order. Indeed, throughout the past century it has been steadily modified, and used to correct economic maladjustments of many kinds. Extension of the franchise has converted the parliamentary State from an oligarchical into a partly democratic institution, and the converted State has again and again modified the economic system by various measures of social reform. Taxation, for example, has been changed from a mere means of meeting the expenses of government into an agency for the redistribution of incomes. Industrial conditions have been regulated, popular education enforced, public health improved. The State, in one aspect, has been developed gradually from a mere machine of government into an agency for the promotion of popular welfare.

In this, there is, of course, much truth. The State is not rigid, but can be bent by the pressure of forces acting upon it from within. The economic system which it sustains can be modified, so as to meet demands for welfare. Both these things have in fact been done to a very considerable extent. The question, however, is whether the doing of them has not strained the parliamentary system and the economic order on which it is based to the limit of their possible elasticity. Can the State, having reached the concession of universal suffrage, go on becoming more democratic, and yet preserve its parliamentary form? Can it keep going on doling out more doses of welfare, and yet defend the capitalist system of property relationships?

It was thought at one time that universal suffrage was the last word in democracy. But in fact modern States, even where they have made voting rights practically universal, have fallen far short of handing over all power to the electorate. In one way or another, they have held back from the "sovereign people" far more than they have conceded. This is most obvious where there still exists, side by side with the popular Chamber, an oligarchical Second Chamber possessing wide powers, and a Crown or President with large prerogatives belonging either to himself or to his advisers. But it is no less effective where there is a written Constitution, capable of amendment only by a very difficult process, and embodying fundamental principles to which all acts of the popular legislature have to conform. The Supreme Court of the United States, armed with the written Constitution, is quite as powerful an obstacle to political and economic adaptation as even the most strongly entrenched King and aristocratic Upper Chamber can possibly be. No large State has ever tried parliamentary democracy in any full sense of the term; and perhaps none ever will.

These, however, are by no means the only limitations upon the democratic character of parliamentary States. Let it be granted that, if the great majority of the electors strongly and determinedly wanted some particular change in the established system, it would be impossible for the aristocratic elements in a parliamentary State to stand out against them, or for a written Constitution, no matter how difficult the process of amending it might have been made, to be proof against their desires. But in fact things seldom happen in this way. The great majority of the electors never strongly and determinedly want anything that is capable of being expressed in an Act of Parliament or a Constitutional Amendment, though the majority may on occasion so decisively not want something which the politicians desire

to impose upon them as to nullify by their sheer resistance the operation of a duly enacted law. Prohibition in the United States is an
obvious case in point; and the Frenchmen's power of simply refusing
to pay taxes which they consider excessive is another. Positively, the
majority may indeed on occasion passionately want certain things,
such as peace or bread; but the positive wants that rouse a whole
people are not constitutional or legal but severely practical. When it
is a question of passing laws the majority is always—and always will
be—indifferent or lukewarm about any particular law—even the enactment of prohibition. The struggle will be between minorities,
which may be large or small, but will never become majorities. A
majority may vote on one side as against the other; but any such
majority includes a high proportion of lukewarm voters.

Under these conditions, equality of voting rights does not mean
real democracy; for it puts a disproportionate power in the hands of
those who are best placed for getting indifferent electors to the poll.
In the more backward countries, this often means that the party
which controls the Government can rely on winning the election. In
Rumania, for example, every General Election returns the supporters
of the Government with an overwhelming majority, and reduces the
Opposition parties to a tiny handful. But if the King changes the
Government and calls the late Opposition to office, it can be certain
in its turn of the same vast majority as was secured previously by the
other side. This is partly due to Rumania's peculiar electoral system;
but it is by no means wholly so, for in primitive countries the Government has enormous powers of influencing the voters. It can in-
timidate; it can hold out the hope of favours to its friends; and it
can even, in the last resort, miscount the votes.

In some advanced communities, these methods are not open when
the parliamentary system is in effective being, though as we have
seen, they exist in full measure in Nazi Germany. But in "democratic" countries, if the Government has far less power, the moneyed
interests have far more. The indifferent electors are open to the mass-
appeals of a Press owned and controlled by rich men; and money
can be poured out in direct and indirect election propaganda. No less
important is the power possessed by the vested interests to influence
the actual course of economic events. By withdrawing their "confidence" from a Government, they can create depression, and render
it unpopular. They can hamper its activities by rigging the market

against it as a borrower, or by delaying tax payments. They can force it to fight on ground they choose, or to forfeit the confidence of its own supporters by declining battle. Incessantly, they can din into the minds of the people ideas favourable to the promotion of their own interests, and spread about misrepresentations which their opponents, far less well equipped with the means of publicity, will not find it easy to correct.

In fact, real democracy is not, and can never be, consistent with any large degree of economic inequality. If men were wholly rational and politically minded beings, they would be immune from disingenuous propaganda. But in that case the problem would not arise, for a rational and politically minded community would assuredly not tolerate economic inequality on any significant scale. As things are, universal suffrage does not mean democracy, even to the extent to which the constitutions in which it is embodied are, even in form, democratic.

For the "democracy" can act only through representatives, and those representatives can act only through parties and under the conditions set by the parliamentary system. This is generally recognised; and it is admitted that, in the vast majority of cases, electors give their votes for a party and not for the particular person who happens to be the party candidate in their constituency. But when the candidates have been elected, most of them soon find that they are in effect little more than voting machines in their turn, at the call of the party to defend its policy, but not asked to think for themselves. There is a Government, and an Opposition caucus (or perhaps several such caucuses); and it is the business of the private member, especially if he is on the Government side, to support the party leadership without making trouble.

A great deal therefore depends upon the character of the party leadership and its relation to the general body of the party. If parties are reasonably democratic, so that the leaders are in reality expressing the collectively formulated opinion of a large rank and file membership which effectively directs their activities, then the party system does embody an element of real democracy, even if it is working within an undemocratic social framework. A democratic party can exist in an undemocratic Society. But if parties themselves are not democratic, then universal suffrage can be no more than a means of choosing between rival undemocratic parties.

There is, of course, a very great difference between parties in this respect. The tradition of the party system is in most countries, if not in all, thoroughly undemocratic. The great historic parties have not been built up from below, on a basis of mass-membership, and have not got their policies from the expressed will of their members. They have been created from the top, by bodies of politicians with the support of wealthy men or powerful interests; and when they have subsequently acquired a popular membership, they have usually treated their members merely as auxiliaries in the electoral struggle, and have not endowed them with any recognised power over the policy of the party. The leaders—with an eye, of course, on their followers —proclaim the policy: the constituency organisations are only means of getting the necessary support. In Great Britain neither the Conservative nor the Liberal Party has any wide real basis of popular control; nor have the conferences of these parties any recognised power to direct their leaders.

THE WORKING-CLASS PARTIES

The Labour Party, and Socialist Parties elsewhere, are far more democratic than this. But in Great Britain even the Labour Party was built not from the bottom but from the top, by a caucus of Socialist and Trade Union leaders. Only after 1918 did it begin to organise a mass-membership of its own in the constituencies; and even to-day its Conference, which has formal power to frame its policy, is controlled not by its rank and file members but by the "block votes" of the big Trade Unions. This diminishes the influence of local Socialist opinion upon the party machine, and helps to assimilate the Labour Party to the British political tradition, which is that of centrally controlled party machines, leading political opinion from above. The history of the two British Labour Governments of 1924 and 1929 illustrates the consequences of this assimilation, which has lessened the control of the party machine by the Trade Unions themselves, though it rests fundamentally upon their voting power.

In contrast to the British Labour Party, most continental Socialist Parties have been built up from below, on a basis of individual membership. But the exigencies of the parliamentary system have made them continuously eager to escape from the trammels of democratic control by their members, and there have been in their history frequent struggles between their popular Congresses and the elected parliamentary groups. For Socialism, playing the parliamentary game, is under strong inducements to assimilate itself to the undemocratic methods of the older political parties.

The Communist Parties, above all that of Russia, have a different tradition. Compelled to act for the most part illegally and underground, they have had forced on them an exceedingly rigid discipline; for an underground party is lost unless its members act under orders and with a high degree of loyalty. Accordingly, Communist Parties have had to be built up mainly from the centre; but as, unlike other parties, they have needed to call on their rank and file members for a heavy toll of positive service, they have never been in a position to take towards them the half-contemptuous attitude characteristic of other leaderships. The Russian Communist Party still retains large elements of an authoritarian leadership derived from its underground days; but it has become a body through which its rank and file membership expresses itself effectively from below in the building of Socialist policy.

The Russian Communist Party, however, differs fundamentally from parties which exist under a parliamentary system, in that it embodies in itself the power of the Government and does not tolerate the existence of other parties. It is not one of two or more parties contending for political office, but the very foundation on which the instrument of government rests. It is in fact no longer a party in the traditional sense, but the authorised agent of a dictatorship. Therein it is like the Fascist Party in Italy, the Nazi Party in Germany, and the Party of Mustapha Kemal in Turkey, though, unlike the Fascist and Nazi Parties, it has not endowed itself formally with any constitutional privileges. It has not needed such privileges, because it has found in the Soviet system of representative political organisation an appropriate instrument ready to its hand. The Russian Communist Party can govern through the Soviets and through the enormously varied forms of "collectives" which now manage the affairs of the U.S.S.R., because these institutions are, like itself, the direct embodiments of the authority of a class. On the other hand the Fascists and Nazis have been unable to use Parliament for this purpose, though they have so far preserved *pro forma* the outward semblance of the parliamentary system. Parliament has not met their needs because parliamentary institutions have life and meaning only to the extent to which they stage the rivalries and oppositions of parties contending for power, so that there is always a potential constitutional alternative to the rule of the party in power. If a Parliament is deprived of this character, and made a one-party affair, it becomes at once a mere registering machine for the decisions of the ruling party, and loses all life and meaning of its own. It may still be kept in being, as it has been so far in Italy and Germany—though at least in Italy its supersession seems now to be imminent—but nobody takes any notice of it, or regards it as more than a ceremonial survival from an older system. The Party, and not the Parliament, is in Italy and Germany the real instrument of Government.

PARTIES AND DICTATORSHIP

But how far are the parties which have thus usurped the State power themselves internally democratic? Of the Turkish ruling Party we do not know enough to speak with confidence; but something can be said of the others. The new Fascist Parties, which repudiate Parliamentarism, alike stress to the utmost the claims of leadership. The Nazis openly repudiate the idea of democracy, and substitute for it that of "demagogy" in the classical sense of leading the people, rather than being directed by them, as the fundamental political principle. It is necessary to get the people on your side, but to do so by leading and inspiring them, and not by letting them rule. That seems to be the Nazi creed. Mussolini is less given to the avowal of demagogy in this sense; but he too clearly believes in the principle of leadership from above, as applied to the party as well as to the State. The Fascist and Nazi leaderships do not get their policy from the party; they devise and reinforce from above, by all the arts of discipline and propaganda, the policies which the leaders think suitable.

Perhaps Stalin, who without holding any important State office, manipulates the affairs of all Russia from his point of vantage as Secretary of the Communist Party, holds a not dissimilar view of the art of leadership. He seems, at any rate, to have made the U.S.S.R. at the centre far more a personal dictatorship of his own, and far less a party dictatorship of the Communists as a body, than it was before his rise to power—even under the leadership of Lenin. Building on the authoritarian traditions common both to Russia and to the Bolshevik Party, he has been able to enforce his personal control over the evolution of Russian policy in recent years. He has driven out Trotsky and other leaders in the party who have ventured to disagree with him, and has enforced within the party a far more rigid uniformity of doctrine than used to exist. But, great as his authority is, he has to use it within conditions set by the existence of the Soviet system, and to carry with him the men who, in their turn, must carry the local Soviets in favour of his policy. In Italy and Germany, on the other hand, there is in effect no organised popular opinion beyond the party to which the party has to make itself acceptable; and the party itself has been built up far less upon a policy than upon an appeal to mass emotion. Accordingly he who can control the party by satisfying its emotional needs can thereby control the State, as long as the emotion holds, without the need for securing an organised basis of support outside. This makes it possible to push the principle of personal leadership much further in Italy and Germany than it can be pushed in Russia, where the Soviet system imposes limits on the absolutism of party rule. But an emotional appeal does not hold for ever; and Italy seems to be already emerging into the stage at which the leadership must be held by constructive actions as well as by acute psychology.

There is, as we have seen, behind this a far more profound difference. The German and Italian States, under Fascism, retain all the old economic inequalities and class-distinctions, whereas Russia has moved rapidly in the direction of economic equality. Russia is building for democracy, but for a democracy of a sort radically different from parliamentarism and far more real because of its foundation in the idea of equality. Moreover there are already in the "collectives" real organs of democratic self-expression which make the Russian system far less authoritative than it seems at the centre.

The Fascists and Nazis, on the other hand, are building in the name not of equality or democracy, but of the "National Idea." Their theory puts the State, as a collective authority, far above the individuals who are its subjects, and bids the individual find his satisfaction in serving the State. It is his business as a subject to serve, and not to control; and he has no rights against the State—not even a right to a share in the shaping of its policy. There is accordingly in these States no theoretical recognition of the democratic case, and no presumption in favour of equality. The presumptions are all the other way; for the stress is laid on the different relations in which men stand to the State, by virtue of their different functions, and not on their common human needs. This means in practice the continuance of large inequalities of wealth, tolerated and recognised by the dominant party.

But the party, as the protector of this wealth, is always in a position to call upon its owners for support. It therefore controls practically unlimited funds, in addition to the public resources upon which it can draw through its control of the State; and it can use these funds for intensive propaganda and for the rewarding of its members and followers upon a wholesale scale. With these means in its hand, it can at once use to the full the arts of the demagogue in its dealings with the mass of the people, and hope so to debauch its own rank and file party membership as to prevent the growth of any effective spirit of democracy within itself. Only in face of economic collapse do these resources fail it; and even so it can keep round it to the end a large subsidised following.

PARLIAMENTARY PARTIES

Parties under the parliamentary system cannot hope for such resources as accrue where the one-party system is in force. But even parliamentary parties often depend very greatly on their power to dispense rewards among their members. In the less developed countries especially, a change in the Government often means a wholesale shift in the occupancy of public offices, even the most humble; and this "spoils system" has been also prevalent in the United States, where President Roosevelt is at present making some attempt to restrict its operation. The weakness of political parties in France has often been attributed to the fact that their patronage falls for the most part to the share of the individual deputies rather than of the parties or groups in power. Great Britain is relatively free from this "spoils system," owing to the strong tradition which excludes it from the Civil Service; and so was Germany until of late. But it exists everywhere to some extent; and even in Great Britain the party in power can dispense, if not many offices, at any rate an ever-increasing shower of honours and decorations.

The art of political bribery thus occupies an important place in the working of the parliamentary system in most countries, even apart from what is sometimes called the "bribery" of the electorate by the promise of social reform. This so-called "bribery" has undoubtedly had a most important influence in the political evolution of the parliamentary system. Under the conditions of a restricted franchise, such as existed in Great Britain before 1832, it takes the form of an enlarged Civil List of pensions and emoluments, of a granting of sinecure places to influential persons and their favoured dependents, and of other methods of allowing a privileged minority to dip its hands deeply into the public purse. Under a more extended franchise, including the middle classes but still excluding the workers, these earlier "abuses" are restricted, and direct bribery is frowned upon; for, at any rate in Great Britain, the middle classes seek their rewards rather in the adoption of a commercial policy adjusted to their needs than in direct pickings from the State. With the further extension of the franchise to the workers the existing parties, which retain their middle-class character, find themselves under the necessity of bidding against each other for the support of the new class of electors. In Great Britain, there was a tremendous outburst of social legislation in the decade that followed the Reform Act of 1867, which first gave the artisans the vote. The rise of the Labour Party after 1900 caused a fresh crop of concessions to the claims of the poor; and there was a third crop immediately after the War, in the hope of buying off the again enlarged electorate. An extended franchise means, under the parliamentary system, that no party can hope to hold power for long unless it is prepared to spend public money on some sort of social provision.

As long as the capitalist system remains in health, this can be done without difficulty; for the expanding resources of production provide means of giving something to the poor without impoverishing the rich. But when Capitalism ceases to prosper, it becomes necessary to call a halt; and then the tribulations of parliamentarism begin. Commonly, the rival parties, in order to avoid the necessity of out-bidding each other, form some sort of coalition to "save the country," and combine their propaganda machines to convince the electorate of the need for "economy." But this method, though it may be effective for the time, has the serious disadvantage of removing the possibility of an alternative Government that can be relied on to observe the rules of the "party game." It drives what opposition is left outside the coalition to think in unparliamentary terms, and it lowers the prestige of Parliament among the electors. It is, moreover, difficult to resume the party game on the old terms when once it has been abandoned; for a coalition is usually fatal to the weaker partner, and the new opposition that it generates may not be so complaisant as the old. Nevertheless, if Capitalism itself recovers, the parliamentary system is likely to resume something like its old form in the countries in which it survives; for peoples do not as a rule discard a political system as long as it can be made to work. Only if the strain is too intense and prolonged, so that parliamentarism crumbles before Capitalism can revive, are countries which have been used to parliamentary institutions ready to resort to revolution, and to set up a new system in their place.

4. POLITICAL LEADERS

WHEN ORDINARY MEN AND WOMEN think of politics, what sort of a vision do they most readily conjure up in their minds? To a great extent they think first of politicians. For most people find it easier to think in terms of personalities than of ideas. There was a time when most Englishmen would probably have reacted instinctively to the mention of politics with the names of Mr. Gladstone and Disraeli. No one in England has quite the same quality of personifying politics to-day; but assuredly most American citizens at present would be likely to react with the name of President Roosevelt. That these reactions, and many others differing from them only in degree, should occur is a clear sign of the overmastering importance of personal leadership in the ordinary conduct of political affairs.

Next to personalities, most people in parliamentary countries will probably think of political parties. This is true also in those countries in which a single party has come to exercise a monopoly of political power. But even in the countries of party dictatorship the personal reaction will usually come first. An Italian will tend—and will be encouraged—to think of Mussolini before he thinks of the Fascist Party, or a German of Hitler before he thinks of the Nazis. Even in Russia, though the Communist Party may come before Stalin, Lenin certainly comes in many men's minds even before the Communist Party. This may not be the case with the politically minded minority who are used to thinking in terms of political organisations in which or against which they are playing an active part. But it is emphatically the attitude of ordinary people who are political only by necessity or exception based on peculiar circumstances, and not by temperament.

Consequently to fight a political struggle without a presentable personal leader who is able to conjure up powerful emotions in his followers is to fight with one hand tied behind the back. Even the strongest case needs a personal leader to make it acceptable to a sufficient body of supporters; for the bulk of those supporters will need to personify it in order to make it real to their minds. At times of exceptional crisis there may arise mass movements which throw up their own leaders and appear to move on irrespective of the quality of these leaders, and at such times the leaders may change quickly and seem to count for little. Or again, when men are living tranquilly under a settled system of government, personal leadership may be for the time of minor importance and a régime be safe even in incompetent hands. But when anything of major importance has to be done, and above all when the entire future of a social system is in question and popular support is needed for settling the issue, the "cause" that is to be victorious must find a personal leader capable, if not of actually leading, at least of looking the part.

The more politically minded and the more habituated to political activity a people is, the less it usually needs the sense of a personal leader—as long as the chief task is to keep an established system working with tolerable smoothness and efficiency. For as men learn to think politically, the causes which enlist their support become capable of commanding their loyalty without so much need for personal mediation. But even the most rationally minded among us, however active in politics we may be, do not easily dispense altogether with the craving for personifying our aspirations. The religion of humanity has always been a highly select creed: most people continue to require a personal God.

In politics individual leadership can sometimes be satisfactorily replaced by the corporate leadership of a group. But Juntas have for the most part a bad name, especially where they have been called upon to act in periods of crisis. They carry on more easily on the whole in States that are relatively small. They were common, for example, both in the City-States of Ancient Greece and in Medieval Germany or Italy, and they can exist far more easily in a Nation-State small enough for all the people who matter to be fairly well in contact one with another than in a huge or scattered territory. Moreover, Juntas have always needed for their success a basis of aristocracy—the corporate support of a reasonably coherent privileged class.

Even so, their power is rather that of administering a system already in being under conditions of relative stability than of adapting themselves to the necessity of drastic change. In a crisis the corporate leadership of a group is apt to give way to the dominance of a single personality, as Calvin dominated Geneva or Pericles Athens or Pitt England and Napoleon France at the time of the Revolutionary Wars.

These dominations were no doubt of widely differing kinds. Calvin's rule of the "Saints" outlasted its founder, whereas Cromwell's did not. For Cromwell, unlike Calvin, was driven to attempt to base his leadership on a highly personal ascendancy. Pericles dominated Athens, and Pitt England, without demanding any very special constitutional powers, so that, when the men were gone, the group institutions which they had led remained in being to serve as instruments of government without them. Pitt's England lasted on, but the Athenian Empire which Pericles left had only a brief spell of continuity before it. Napoleon, on the other hand, overthrew the republican constitution of France and climbed to power as the personal representative of a popular nationalist sentiment greatly heightened by war; and defeat destroyed his system, though he had made it impossible over a large part of Europe for the victors to put the old institutions back. Pitt and Calvin, and to a much smaller extent Pericles, were the personal leaders of strongly based "systems" capable of governing corporately without them except in a crisis. Cromwell was also the leader of a corporate movement, but of one too weak to rule merely as a group, so that he had to correct its weakness by the force of his own personality. Napoleon rose to power not on the foundation of an organised system capable of doing without him, but on a wave of national feeling essentially devoid of corporate character and organisation. He, even more than Cromwell, had to make his ascendancy personal; and only victory followed by a period of tranquillity and construction under his personal leadership could have availed to make his system lasting.

POST-WAR LEADERS

In recent years six men have in various ways emerged as the personal leaders of great countries—Lloyd George in Great Britain during the latter part of the war, Lenin in Russia in 1917, Mussolini in Italy, Mustapha Kemal in Turkey, Hitler in Germany, and President Roosevelt in the United States. France has never had a personal leader in the same sense, for both Clemenceau and Poincaré, who in turn came fairly near to leadership, failed quite to overcome the essentially group character of government in the French Republic. France is a country of individualists; but this quality, so far from making under her political system for the personal ascendancy of the individual, renders her politicians pronouncedly equalitarian among themselves, so that the rest will never tolerate, if they can help it, the ascendancy of a colleague. They pulled down both Clemenceau and Poincaré as soon as the immediate tasks for which they had been raised up had been fulfilled. After the fall of Bismarck, Germany never had a personal leader till the emergence of Hitler. Wilhelm II was incapable of leadership, and no one else could lead as long as he remained on the throne—or perhaps Germany might have won the war. The Weimar Republic was too much based on a compromise among conflicting forces to generate leadership except by way of its own destruction. Lloyd George did lead Great Britain for a little while, far more than Clemenceau led France or Woodrow Wilson the United States. But as soon as the war was over his ascendancy collapsed, both because he had no clear conception of what he wanted to do, and, more fundamentally, because the corporativeness of British parliamentary life reasserted itself promptly when the fighting was over. In Great Britain as in France the individualism of the politicians made against personal ascendancy. Post-war Britain, like post-war France, was looking not for a personal leader but for a return to the old ways as the means to a quiet life.

There remain five men—Lenin, Mussolini, Kemal, Hitler and Roosevelt. Among these Roosevelt alone had to face a deeply entrenched tradition of corporate control. The American Presidency is indeed an office possessing far larger powers than are accorded to anyone under the French or British systems. Nevertheless, nothing short of overwhelming economic emergency facing the American people could have swept President Roosevelt to the height of power and personal prestige which he has been able to enjoy, and in all probability nothing except a continuance of the emergency will enable him to retain his authority. The American tradition is waiting to reassert itself and ready to discard Roosevelt, even as it discarded Wilson, as soon as his work is done. His position is, however, different from that of Clemenceau or Poincaré or Lloyd George, not only because as President he has wider powers, but also because the strength of the forces that are lying in wait to displace him lies mainly not in but outside politics—in the business world rather than in Congress. It is in these circumstances just possible that he may be able to prolong his ascendancy and to alter permanently the structure of American institutions by creating a new political machine based on the support of a mass of popular opinion that has been hitherto unorganised and uninfluential in political affairs. It is possible that, with this support, he may be strong enough to stand up to the attacks of "Big Business" even when the emergency is over. But this is unlikely, for it would involve the building up behind the President of an essentially new party, and the smashing of the existing machines of both the great traditional parties, since both are so permeated by business influences as to be useless as supports for a new régime. America is far more likely to revert to the old ways and to discard Roosevelt when he has done his work than to make the "new deal" the foundation for a lasting personal leadership.

Lenin, Mussolini, Mustapha Kemal and Hitler have been differently placed, in that there existed no sufficiently strong tradition of corporate government by a group of political leaders to stand in their way. But Lenin's position differed from that of the others. Mussolini, Kemal and Hitler all created their own parties round their own personal leadership, whereas Lenin rose to the undisputed leadership of a party already long in being and possessing a strong corporate sense and a definite policy. Lenin did not need to make a new party or a new policy, but only to adapt an existing party and an existing policy to the circumstances and opportunities of the time. The Bolshevik Party had indeed a very strong tradition of corporate rather than personal leadership. But the crisis made indispensable the emergence of a single dominant leader, and Lenin's qualities plainly marked him out for this pre-eminence. When he died there was for a time an attempt to revert to the corporate leadership of the group of "old Bolsheviks"; but the emergency was still too pressing to admit of this solution in face of deep-seated differences of opinion among the leaders themselves. Russian Communism had to find a new personal leader; and of the two men capable of taking control of the situation Stalin was successful. Trotsky's exile followed almost as a matter of course, for a country in a desperate crisis cannot endure the simultaneous presence of two claimants to personal leadership leading in opposite directions. The alternation of a Gladstone and a Disraeli belongs to tranquil times when the only practical differences of policy are of a secondary sort, and there is a deep-seated agreement on primary issues underlying these differences.

LEADERS AND PARTIES

Mussolini, Kemal and Hitler made their own parties, creating powerful mass organisations out of a previously unorganised body of sentiments and passions. Nationalism was in all three cases the fundamental element in their appeal, though they reinforced it with numerous other elements, and gave it in effect different interpretations to attract different classes. Kemal rallied chiefly the peasants and soldiers of Turkey, sweeping away with their aid the controlling group of "Young Turks" who had led the country to military disaster. The "Young Turks" had been "Westernisers"; but Kemal, having compassed their defeat, went far beyond them in Westernisation when once he had based his power securely on military victory over the Greeks and the recovery of national prestige. Kemal's building of the new Turkey thus illustrates very clearly the point that a leader who has come to power on the basis of intense nationalist feeling can often do things which on the face of the matter are likely to outrage the established national tradition. The "Young Turks" had been innovators before Kemal; but whereas their Westernising tendencies had made them unpopular, his prestige enabled him to carry through far more ambitious measures than they had ever dared even to project. Hitler also had to deal with a people smarting under defeat, but his task differed from Kemal's in that he was confronted by a powerful but sharply divided working-class movement on the one side and a still strongly entrenched reactionary aristocracy working in alliance with an important section of large-scale Capitalism on the other. Between these two opposing forces there existed a condition of stalemate, but it was out of the question to destroy them both at once. Hitler created his movement on a basis of opposition to them both, appealing to nationalist feelings against international Socialism and to working-class sentiment by making large promises of the economic fruits of a Nazi victory. But having built up his movement he allied himself with the reactionaries against the Socialists in order to climb to power. The reactionaries joined him, hoping to subordinate his forces to their own; but they had no effective personal leader to put up against him. President Hindenburg was far too old, and von Papen had manifestly no popular appeal, as his failure during his Chancellorship showed. Hitler's personality was the trump card with which the Nazis took the trick the Nationalists had hoped to make their own. The personality of the leader counted in the crisis for more than all the traditional discipline behind the reactionary forces, which were still hampered in discovering a leader by the ghost of the old failure living on at Doorn.

Mussolini had prepared the way for Hitler by teaching him the art of organising a party on the foundation of personal leadership. Mussolini had, indeed, a harder task than Hitler's, for he could not play to the same extent on the exacerbation of nationalist feelings by military disaster. Nominally Italy had won the war; but actually her people felt, if not that they had lost, at any rate that they had been deprived of their share in the spoils of victory. Economic distress stimulated passions which found an outlet in blaming the weakness of the politicians. Socialism grew strong enough to prevent these weak politicians from governing the country, but did not feel itself powerful or united enough to seize power. It had but a scanty following in the southern part of the country, and elsewhere the Catholics, organised in a widespread party of their own, stood between it and the reactionary parties, paralysing its action. In the Italy of 1921, fully as much as in Germany ten years later, the situation was one of stalemate, and this situation created the opportunity for the emergence of a personal leader. D'Annunzio, too unstable and uncertain of what he wanted, and too little of a diplomatist to become the leader of a nation, showed Mussolini the way by revealing the strength of the passions that were ready to be let loose. Mussolini seized his chance and became "Il Duce."

Mussolini, however, is far more than Hitler, and not much less than Kemal or Lenin, a man of ideas. He not only had the personal ambition to lead and the personal qualities that would induce men to follow him; but he was also able to make in his mind a working model of the new State that he meant to build up. Italian Fascism has embodied itself on the whole in a clearly conceived policy, and the laying down of that policy has been mainly Mussolini's personal achievement. No doubt a great deal of the machinery of the Corporative State still exists rather on paper than in reality; but it has to be conceded to Mussolini that he has shown himself a constructive and not merely an emotional or rhetorical leader. The plan of the Corporative State, though it is drawn partly from Hegelian, partly from Christian Social, and partly even from Guild and Syndicalist sources, is essentially Mussolini's own. German Nazism, while it also proclaims the gospel of the Corporative State, rests on a far more confused body of doctrine. Clarity of a sort may perhaps emerge from it at a later stage, but no one can yet tell what the future structure of Nazi Germany is to be. Nor do such ideas of a constructive sort as have yet emerged from the Nazi triumph seem to have much to do with the policy of the Nazi leader. Hitler enjoys immense prestige and popularity in Germany to-day; but whereas Mussolini undoubtedly leads Italy, the German *Führer* seems rather to be led, now by one counsellor and now by another, without any clear idea of the constructive purposes to which he means to put his power. But Hitler has plainly shown that he is an exceedingly astute tactician. He showed it both in taking power when he did with the help of the Nationalists, and in refusing it earlier when it was offered to him only on terms that would have made it fatal to his personal ascendancy. He is an orator with an immense power of appealing to the popular passion of a nation that has grown neurasthenic in defeat. He leads Germany, but whither does he lead it? Towards an immense concentration of power in the hands of the Nazi Government, no doubt; but for what purposes is this plenitude of power to be employed? If Hitler has no clear vision of his own about the future, beyond the vision of making Germany great again among the nations, he will be driven to choosing in internal policy among the conflicting plans of his immediate lieutenants, between whom it is already no secret that very large differences of outlook exist.

Amongst those who are at present high up in the counsels of the Nazis, there are some who, like Goering, are above all militarist-nationalist with an insatiable passion for power. Such men are sometimes, but not always, monarchists. But whether they want to restore the monarch or not, they believe firmly in a disciplined State controlled tightly from the top and based on the preservation of class differences in pretty much the traditional forms. If Hitler finally allies himself with this group among his followers, how long will his own personal leadership remain effective? Or, even if he remains as the figure-head of the new Germany, can he be more than a prisoner of the old governing classes, in a far deeper sense than that in

which Mr. Ramsay MacDonald is the prisoner of the British Conservatives? If he becomes the figurehead of a Government dominated
by the aristocrats and the plutocrats of the old Germany, how long
will his popularity hold? There are powerful proletarian and petty
bourgeois elements in the National Socialist Party, and they have
both been promised much. In the last resort Hitler appears to have
much more in common with the left wing of his own party than
with the right wing. For he is emphatically not an aristocrat, but a
petit bourgeois, and he has far more sympathy with the peasant and
the small business man than with the great landowner or industrialist
or financier. It would be more in character for him, when he must
choose, to choose the side of Goebbels and Darré and Feder and Frick
than the side of Goering. That after he had been a year in power it
should still have remained doubtful which way he would go says
much for his astuteness as a politician but little for his possession of
the greater qualities of leadership. The recent suppression of the
Storm Troop leaders seems now to have aligned Hitler with the Right
of his party; but it is by no means certain that the second *coup* of
1934 finally settles the question. The neurosis of post-war Germany
made Hitler the national leader, and presented him with an unparalleled opportunity for reasserting Germany's place among the
nations. But, this done, what is he to do next? Can he solve Germany's
internal problems, which are, after all, in the long run far more
fundamental? The people wants a personal leader, and it has found
no one who suits it so well as Hitler. But unless a leader can go on
leading, how long will he continue to satisfy men's needs? Not long,
if there remains a crisis to be faced, as there must in Germany for
a long time to come. Hitler may remain to lead Germany in default
of anyone better. But he appears, by turning upon his own Left
wing, to have decisively abandoned any attempt to redeem the economic promises which were so lavishly made before the conquest of
power. Is not his genius rather that of agitation than adaptable to the
constructive exercise of the power which he has won?

This study of the position of certain outstanding personal leaders
has seemed necessary in order to make intelligible the history of the
past dozen years in Europe. For that history is assuredly inexplicable
unless account is taken of men's desire in extreme emergencies to
find a personal leader round whom they can rally. If in any country
the situation reaches a point at which it becomes intolerable to go on

any longer without far-reaching changes in the political system, men's instinct will be to look for salvation to a personal leader rather than to any group or corporate leadership that cannot get itself identified in the popular mind with a person as well as a cause. Groups and corporate bodies serve well enough for administering a going concern. But it needs a man courageously to initiate drastic change. That, at any rate, seems to be the popular view.

In those countries which have not been driven up against emergencies so extreme as to compel revolutionary change, the need for leadership is felt much less strongly. In Great Britain and in France the parliamentary tradition of group leadership has been strong enough so far to hold its own not only because the parliamentary sense is stronger in the British and French peoples than in the countries of which we have been speaking, but also because neither Great Britain nor France has yet had to face a really fundamental crisis involving its entire political system. Even in these two countries, however, the tendency of lesser crises to put a premium on personal leadership has been sufficiently shown. Poincaré was invested with wide powers and approached for a while the stature of a personal leader when he was called in to stabilise the franc and balance the budget after the great French inflation; and the "National" forces in Great Britain had to dress Mr. MacDonald up to look as like a leader as possible in order to deal with the purely financial crisis of 1931. These, however, are only instances of half-leadership within the limits of an existing situation and of the parliamentary system. They only suggest that if in either Great Britain or France a real crisis does arise, group leadership will be likely even in these countries to give way to the dominance of an individual.

5. REGIONAL AND LOCAL GOVERNMENT

IN THE FOREGOING CHAPTERS of this book, the problems of politics have been discussed chiefly in their national aspect, as they affect the central government of each country as a whole. But every State, except the very smallest, has in one way or another to be broken up into smaller areas for purposes of detailed administration. It is of course possible for this to be done by the central Government simply sending officials of its own to look after the administration of each area, the entire policy that is to be followed locally being dictated from the centre and not left at all to the local inhabitants, save to the extent to which they are able to influence the central Government and its officials. Subject territories, especially if they are inhabited by peoples whom their rulers do not regard as "civilised," are often administered in this way, by purely autocratic government from above; but it is rare to find such a system applied to the local government of territories inhabited by full citizens of the ruling State. Moreover, even where the form of administration appears to be wholly autocratic, the Governor who is set to rule in this way over a subject people often finds himself confronted by a native system and culture which it is impossible for him to ignore. The villages under his jurisdiction have their own strongly established customs in administering justice, regulating marriage and social conduct, and providing for the cultivation of the land and the control of other economic services. There may be chiefs or headmen or councils of elders whom the inhabitants hold in high respect; and it is usually the line of least resistance to recognise these institutions, except where their ideas conflict seriously with the interests of the rulers, and to work through them to some extent, perhaps binding the chief or headman to the interests of the government by giving him special privileges, or even a salary paid by the State. Many of the European Powers have developed this system of utilising and "taming" local institutions for the government of certain of their colonial possessions and dependencies.

At a second stage, the autocracy of the Central Government and the officials whom it appoints is tempered by the establishment of Advisory Councils, with which the local Governor or Commissioner is to consult, without being in any way bound to accept their advice. This system too is made use of extensively in the administration of colonies; but the Advisory Councils may have a very different character according as they represent predominantly the subject population that is being ruled, or a minority of settlers belonging to the ruling nation, and also as their members are chosen by nomination or by election on the basis of a wider or narrower franchise.

Historically, Councils of this advisory type, where they have been chosen wholly or partly on a representative basis, have often developed after a time into Legislative Councils, empowered to pass laws for the government of the area, subject to the right of veto preserved by the Governor on behalf of the Central Government. Often, the powers of such Councils have been restricted to certain types of question, regarded as of chiefly local concern, other questions being "reserved" to be dealt with by the Governor, without the Council having in relation to them more than merely advisory powers at most.

Where, however, legislative power is conceded, it is difficult permanently to restrict its scope. The Self-Governing Dominions of the British Empire have developed the virtually complete independence which they now enjoy largely by passing through the successive stages outlined in the two preceding paragraphs. These, however, are areas occupied mainly (except in the case of South Africa) by peoples of the same stock as the imperial country, or at least standing at the same broad stage of civilisation. The situation is different where the Council either represents only or predominantly a small minority of settlers, or is drawn from peoples regarded as standing at an inferior level of civilisation. There is in these cases far more opposition to the granting to such bodies of any wide legislative power. In the British Empire Australia and Canada enjoy full "Dominion Home Rule": India does not, though certain powers have been transferred to Central and Provincial Assemblies composed chiefly of Indian representatives.

The more a State rests on force, the more authoritative and the less representative its regional and local institutions are likely to be. Thus, where a national minority is held under the government of a predominantly alien State against its will, the Central Government often seeks to break up all forms of local and regional representative organisation, and to govern the recalcitrant areas entirely by means of centrally appointed officials. This has been the situation, for example, in certain parts of Yugoslavia in recent years, where national minorities have been resisting absorption and assimilation by the Serbian dominant group. The same conditions applied largely to the subject territories of pre-war Russia.

Wherever a State is made up of diverse national elements, each largely concentrated in a particular part of the country, the demand for regional self-government comes to be connected with the claims of the various national minorities to cultural as well as political autonomy, if not to absolute independence or right of secession to a neighbour State. Regionalist claims of this sort exist to-day, not only in Yugoslavia, but also in Rumania, Czechoslovakia, Poland, Denmark, Belgium, and several other States. A similar situation exists in Spain, where the Catalans, Basques, and other "nationalist" groups have profited by the advent of the Republic to secure a large measure of regional autonomy. Ireland long presented a similar problem within the United Kingdom; and the dismemberment of the Turkish Empire is a history of nationalist movements claiming first a measure of autonomy, and then full independence. The break-up of Austria-Hungary was the culmination of a similar process.

Where national or religious minorities exist, not in defined geographical areas, but scattered among the rest of the population, the demand for autonomy has to take a different form. It is found in the claim for separate national or cultural electorates, as in the case of the Moslems in India, and in the demand for cultural autonomy through the right to conduct separate schools and churches and to secure recognition of the right to use the minority language in the courts. But this expression of minority claims can only be mentioned here, as it would take us too far afield from the main theme of this chapter.

FEDERAL SYSTEMS

The forms of government which we have been considering so far are mainly those which involve the setting up of what are in effect subordinate or even parallel organs of legislation and administration to those of the central State. They arise in Empires, or in diversified States made up of distinct national elements. But of course the question of subordinate legislatures can arise in countries quite apart from any question of the self-government of colonies or of separate national areas. It exists in all federal States, such as the United States, or Switzerland, or Canada, or Australia—for the technical difference which makes the United States formally federal, and Canada formally a case of "devolution" need not concern us here. In this broad sense, both pre-war Germany and the Weimar Republic were federal States, whereas Nazi Germany is not; for the Nazis have already destroyed the self-governing institutions of Bavaria, Saxony, and the other German "States." In all federal Constitutions, there is a sharing of powers and functions between the Federation and its constituent units; and this may take many different forms. But in all modern federations there is a powerful tendency for more power to pass to the central body, especially in economically developed countries; for it becomes more and more desirable to have a common basis not only for tariff policy and the regulation of trade, but also for industrial and labour conditions, and for such services as education and public health, at any rate in their broader aspects. We have seen how the federal Constitution of the United States has stood in the way of this desirable growth of common standards, and how under stress of the emergency the old constitutional barriers have been partly broken down by the masterful hand of President Roosevelt.

The United States, however, is too large to become a unitary State. It will preserve federalism, even if the powers of the centre are greatly increased. And, in countries made up of geographically distinct national elements, there may well be a movement away from centralisation, despite the economic factors making for its increase. The right solution in these cases, where it can be applied, is to confer upon the Central Government, over a wide field of services, the power to prescribe common minimum standards, while allowing "States," or regional Governments, a large discretion both to improve upon them and to adapt them, within the prescribed minimum, to local and "nationalist" needs. This seems to be the solution which is being steadily applied in the U.S.S.R. to-day.

REGIONS

In countries which are neither so large as the United States, nor made up to any great extent of diverse national elements, the problem of regional government may well arise. Such States are bound to have traditional administrative divisions; and in some of them at least local governing authorities possessing a measure of subordinate authority are certain to exist. At any rate in Western Europe, these subordinate governing authorities are usually strongest, and have the longest tradition behind them, in the cities and towns, many of which gained their rights of self-government under Charters granted in the Middle Ages when the feudal system was at its height. In some countries, such as Germany and Italy, these self-governing cities acquired the full status of independent States; and though they have now been absorbed into the national States which have grown up during the nineteenth century, they have retained a large amount of power, which has been seriously undermined only since the advent of Fascism. Italy, indeed, was "unified" in 1860; but in Germany Hamburg and other "Free Cities" retained the status of equal partners in the Reich with Bavaria and the other German States right up to the coming of the Nazi régime. In most other countries cities never reached this degree of independent authority. In Great Britain, the Crown always asserted its full authority over them, and their powers, akin to those of the feudal lords, were curtailed with the successful centralisation of the English State after the Wars of the Roses. In France the cities had at one time much greater power; but the *ancien régime* had already subjected them to its final control, while allowing them large privileges, before the Revolution came to centralise the French State and abolish in the name of democracy every sort of privileged corporation claiming rights against the Central Government. The French Revolution explains the high degree to which French local government is subject to central administrative control. It also explains why, in France, the Regionalists, who demand the revival of the old historic Provinces as units of provincial government, are usually monarchists, who hate the Republic, and why Regionalism has come in France to be connected in men's minds with reactionary views on national politics. For the modern French *départements,* presided over by the *préfets* as officers of the Central Government, were deliberately created to replace the old Provinces— and created for smaller and quite different areas—in order to destroy the traditional units of administration which the republicans regarded as dangerous because of their historical association with the monarchical régime.

TOWN AND COUNTRY

City Governments may be strongly autonomous, as in the City-States of Germany yesterday and Switzerland to-day. They may have large administrative powers of self-government, under regulations laid down for them by the Central Government, as in Great Britain. Or they may be administrative organs subject to far more detailed central control, as in France. But almost always the administration of cities is based on some sort of representative body, either directly descended from, or created in imitation of, the municipal corporations, or city "Gilds," that grew up during the Middle Ages. Cities have almost everywhere a long and strong tradition of corporate self-government. This tradition is sometimes oligarchical, and more often it became so in the period between the decay of the gild system and the rise of political democracy in the nineteenth century. But it is nearly always a tradition of corporate government; and it was easily transformed, under the influence of nineteenth-century ideas, into a tradition of corporate self-government on the basis of an extended franchise.

It is otherwise with the countryside. In Asia indeed the village has an even longer tradition of self-management than the corporate towns; and the same is true in some degree in many parts of Eastern Europe In China, as we have seen, the long tradition of local self-government in the villages has been the principal force making for the preservation of social order through all the sequence of civil wars and political confusions. The Asiatic town has usually a good deal less self-government than the towns in Western Europe; and even where there is some sort of elected or representative council, or ward official, the chief magistrate is commonly appointed either by the national Government or by a provincial Governor who is its nominee. The village may also have—and in Eastern Europe and the Near East usually has—a public official responsible to the Government set over it; but as his duties commonly cover a number of villages, the purely local and traditional institutions of collective control are often able to assert themselves with effect. In colonial territories in Africa and elsewhere the villages are usually under the jurisdiction of resident magistrates or officials appointed by the ruling Power, most often from among its own nationals. But these officials, who are administrative as well as judicial in their functions, have charge in most cases of a number of villages; and, where the colonial system has been superimposed upon a tribal system of organisation, they often work largely through the local chiefs and headmen, and much of the native method of administration sometimes survives. The village, however, is seen at its most effective and self-governing in China; for in India, where its tradition is no less strong, its powers of self-government have been largely circumscribed or superseded by the centralised administration of the British.

In Western Europe, village organisation has lost much of its strength. This is partly the consequence of the feudal system, which in some countries subjected the village almost completely to the lord and his officers. In England, for example, the villages fell under the control of local lords, who managed them as "manors" with the aid of representative assemblies of the manorial tenants and of manorial courts under the lord's control. The decay of the feudal system brought with it the decline of this local administration, the gradual intrusion of the King's courts into the affairs of the village, and, in the long run, the handing over of control of the village administration to nominees of the Crown. Thus, in England, the county justices of the peace became the local governing authorities for all the areas outside the corporate towns; and, when the powers of the Crown passed over largely to Parliament after the Civil Wars and the Revolution of 1688, this meant the control of the countryside by the country gentlemen, centrally appointed but sure of the complaisance of a Parliament composed of persons like unto themselves.

Not till nearly the end of the nineteenth century did representative government penetrate again into rural England, with the establishment of County Councils in 1888 and of Parish Councils in 1894, though the way had been to some extent prepared by the earlier creation of Boards of Guardians and Rural Sanitary Districts under the Poor Law and Public Health Acts. County and village self-government, thus re-created in imitation of urban representative institutions, have usually remained weak; and the hand of the Central Government has lain on them more heavily than on the corporate towns.

CENTRAL CONTROL

The growth of locally administered services under central regulation has been an important factor in strengthening central control even over the cities. As modern States have found themselves compelled to develop education as a public service and to build up an elaborate organisation for the protection of public health, the relief of distress due to poverty or disability, and the provision of public utilities, it has become impossible for the local bodies to finance these services out of local taxes, and the State has had to come to their assistance with ever-increasing "grants in aid" out of the proceeds of national taxation. For it is very difficult to find independent sources of tax-revenue for local bodies. This problem is serious even in Great Britain or France, where there are only two sets of authorities to be provided for. It is still more difficult in large federal States, which have to find sources of revenue for three sets of authorities, federal, regional and local. It stands awkwardly in the way of projects for splitting up unitary States into a number of partly autonomous regional areas.

Thus in Spain to-day the problem of allocation of revenue between the national Government and Catalonia is still unsettled; and there are many similar problems all over Europe. In the United States, the Federal Government is financed mainly by means of customs duties and income tax, and State and local authorities mainly by taxes on property. In Great Britain local resources come from rates levied on local property; but the recognised unfairness of local rates has led the Central Government to grant large rebates and exemptions, and these have caused a shortage of local revenue which has had to be made good by national grants in aid. The Weimar Republic, in reconstructing the finances of Germany, provided resources for the separate States mainly by grants from the centre.

It is a familiar saying that he who pays the piper calls the tune. As local authorities come to depend more and more on grants made out of national funds, the control of the Central Government over them inevitably increases. Moreover, the areas of the existing local authorities were for the most part delimited at a time when effective distances were far greater than they are to-day and local services could be satisfactorily administered over far smaller areas. Such services as the provision of light, heat and power, the organisation of road transport, and above all housing and town and regional planning now need to be co-ordinated and controlled over much larger areas than those of the great majority of existing local authorities. This results in some services—the control of transport and the generation of electricity, for example—being taken wholly or partly out of the hands of the local authorities, and administered by Commissioners directly responsible to the Central Government. In other fields it holds up or distorts development: for example, it stands powerfully in the way of a rational re-planning of housing and industrial development by the creation of new towns, and encourages instead the amorphous growth of suburbs round the circumferences of the existing cities.

In these circumstances, there are some who contend that, save in the largest States, there is no room for local government in face of the development of modern technology, and that local services are destined to be taken one after another out of the hands of local bodies and transferred to national control. But there are strong reasons against this conclusion. It is very doubtful whether any national democratic system can be effectively built up except on a basis of local self-government, which provides both an invaluable training ground for national responsibility and a necessary means of preventing hopeless congestion at the centre, which is bound to lead to irresponsible bureaucratic control. There is a strong case in all States of considerable size for endeavouring to overcome the serious difficulties which stand in the way of the creation of regional organs of administration, intermediate between the Central Government and the purely local administrations of the various urban and rural areas. The pressure for this regionalist solution is much strongest where it is reinforced by nationalist claims to autonomy; for apart from this regional sentiment it is apt to be weak or non-existent. A man may feel strongly as a citizen of Manchester or Bradford or Bristol: he does not feel any sentiment of loyalty to North-West or South-West England as a unit. On the other hand where traditional divisions do exist, loyalty is felt. A man can be a loyal citizen of Virginia or Massachusetts or California as well as of Richmond, or Boston, or San Francisco, of Wales as well as of Cardiff, of Scotland as well as of Glasgow, of Catalonia as well as of Barcelona, and of the Gironde as well as of Bordeaux. The stimulation of these intermediate loyalties is of value as a safeguard against bureaucracy: nor is there any reason to believe that new loyalties cannot grow up round appropriate areas, provided they are equipped with the necessary organs for united administrative action.

The line of demarcation between national, regional and local powers and functions cannot, however, in the world to-day usually be so drawn as to leave certain matters entirely to the central, other matters to regional, and yet others to purely local authorities. It is bound to be more often a case of the central authority laying down general principles and enforcing a common minimum standard, and then handing over the actual administration of services to regional and local bodies in accordance with the special needs of each area. The work of regional and local authorities must be mainly that of administering nationally planned services so as to go beyond the minimum requirements laid down by national legislation, and so as to diversify the provision in accordance with regional and local differences of need and desire. If this principle is taken as a general guide, there is no reason at all why modern technical developments should undermine local self-government, however much they may call for an adaptation of its methods and areas to modern economic conditions.

Local "patriotism" is not a possession that the world can afford to throw away, above all if it is setting out to combat the excesses of nationalism. For though local patriotism has sometimes been regarded as the enemy of the cosmopolitan spirit, it is capable of becoming its powerful ally against the attempt to make all men the absolute slaves of the all-devouring national State. It is no accident that the Nazis in Germany have set out to uproot local loyalties, or that the Fascists in Italy have destroyed municipal autonomy and placed the cities under *podestàs* completely controlled by the Central Government. Nor is it any accident that the Russians are doing their utmost, within the broad framework of the Federal Soviet Republic, to stimulate the autonomy in cultural and educational matters of the many nationalities that exist within the frontiers of the U.S.S.R. For the recognition of lesser groups within the State, even if they are national groups, is the best way of correcting the excesses of that "totalitarian" Nationalism which Fascism has elevated into an ideal. The more local and regional loyalties flourish within the great States, the less danger is there that aggressive Nationalism will be able to tear the world to pieces.

6. GOVERNMENTS AND FUNCTIONAL GROUPS

EVERY MODERN SOCIETY is a network of associations. Apart from their organisation as citizens into political parties the inhabitants group themselves in countless other ways according to their particular interests, activities and points of view. The associations which they form are of every variety of size, importance, character and relation to the State and one to another. At one extreme they are so loose and evanescent as to be barely distinguishable from quite unorganised temporary groupings of individuals: at the other they are so closely knit and durable as to command powerful, deeply-rooted loyalties from their members and to enter deeply into men's consciousness so as to influence greatly their activities and conceptions of life.

Very often these particular associations are spoken of as if they existed, in some sense, "within the State," and even as if they owed their being to the State's willingness to grant them recognition. It is true enough that they need the State's countenance if they are to function freely, and that States everywhere claim the right in the last resort to suppress inconvenient associations by law. In matters affecting the possession of property, the rights of members in relation to the group, the freedom of meeting and publication, it often greatly concerns an association what attitude the State takes up towards it. For example, in all capitalist countries there have been prolonged controversies over the status to be given to joint-stock companies, Trade Unions, and monopolistic combinations. The development of joint-stock organisation in industry was greatly hampered until the State, partly through legislation and partly through the courts of law, granted it full recognition. Trade Unionists have everywhere been forced to struggle hard for the right to combine and to act in combination without incurring legal penalties. There have been prolonged conflicts over trusts and combines; and different States have taken up widely varying attitudes towards them. Over the whole field of economic life, the growth of Capitalism has brought with it huge changes in the forms of association, and in the relation of economic associations to the State.

There are, however, many kinds of association besides the economic. Churches, for example, are in the modern world essentially associations of persons holding a common religious belief. This associative character has been brought out much more clearly by the disappearance of even formal uniformity of religion. "Dissenting" Churches have had to struggle for recognition in much the same way as Trade Unions; and far more blood has been spilt over the claims of religion than over any other political issue.

Economic and religious associations form, together with political parties, the outstanding types of association commanding wide membership and extensive social influence. But there is in addition a host of other bodies which, individually less important, add up to a large contribution to the social activity of contemporary communities. There are, for instance, the innumerable propagandist associations, each formed to further some particular cause or reform—women's rights, birth control, temperance, land taxation, educational reform, vegetarianism, the abolition of slavery or betting, or any of a thousand other special aspirations. Then there are the countless bodies formed to further the interest of, or express loyalty towards, particular institutions, from societies formed to collect money for hospitals or charities of various kinds, to "Old Boys' Associations," societies of Scotsmen or Cornishmen or what not *in partibus infidelium,* societies and clubs connected with particular Churches or other institutions, and many more. There are professional associations which are only half economic, and half technical or scientific, or merely sociable. There are the countless clubs and societies formed in connection with sports and pastimes, either as voluntary associations of people who wish to play or watch some particular game, or—merging into the economic—as bodies organising sport as an entertainment on a commercial basis.

Moreover, there are, side by side with all these associations enrolling a defined membership, a vast number of groups which, without being formally organised in this way, possess the power to act in association whenever something arises to stimulate their group interest. Thus, in the economic field, the whole body of workmen in a factory, whether they are in a Trade Union or not, have to some extent a group consciousness and a power of group action arising out of their common relation to their place of work. So have the dwellers in a particular street or district, especially if the conditions and social status of an area are fairly uniform; or even all the inhabitants of a town or village. The boys at a school, the undergraduates at a College or University, the attendants at a particular Church or Chapel, the members of a clearly defined profession, whether organised or not, the habitual travellers by a particular railway line, the crowd that regularly frequents Highbury or Stamford Bridge, or the "Old Vic" or the Queen's Hall, or regularly listens in on the wireless to a particular sort of programme, or regularly goes to a particular town on market day—even to a certain extent the regular readers of a newspaper or magazine—all these and many more groups like them are capable of acquiring in some degree a consciousness of relationship to a particular institution and therewith of relationship one to another. Ordinarily, this consciousness does not affect their actions in socially important ways; but it may at any time affect them, calling up a loyalty which will influence their behaviour, and perhaps bring them into group conflict with other groups or associations, or with the State itself.

NATIONAL MINORITIES

In some communities, another sort of grouping plays a large part. Wherever a State is so constituted as to consist of a number of distinct national elements, especially if the different nationalities speak different languages or have widely different cultures and standards of life, national consciousness divides the Society into groups which may easily become mutually antagonistic. This happens most easily where there is in the State as a whole a dominant nationality, largely or exclusively in control of the political machine, and where the minority elements are geographically concentrated in certain areas, which they can feel to be their "national home." But the national sentiment can be aroused even where this geographical concentration does not exist, either against a superimposed governing or wealthy class of alien nationality, as in certain of the Baltic countries, or against a minority which is held to be contaminating the racial purity of the predominant people, as in the feeling against the Jews in Nazi Germany or against negroes in the Southern States of America. Within many of the new States of post-war Europe, and some of the old, there are difficult and intense "minority" problems. Before the war, these difficulties were most acute in Austria-Hungary and in Russia. To-day they are at their worst in Yugoslavia, Rumania, Czechoslovakia, Poland, and Germany; but they are also serious in Belgium, where there is strong feeling between the Flemings and Walloons.

Nationalist feeling within a State often becomes organised, leading to the creation of separate political parties on a nationalist basis— sometimes duplicating for each nationality in the State all the class groupings from right to left—and of special associations for fostering the national culture. Where national coincide with religious differences, Churches too are drawn into the struggle, and become agents for the stimulation of nationalist feeling. But this feeling can exist apart from any special organisation through which it finds expression. In this case, as in so many others, beyond the association lies the group, giving to the association a support that extends far beyond its enrolled membership.

INTERNATIONAL GROUPINGS

We have seen that the problem of groups and associations is often written about as if these existed "within the State." But in fact many groups, and some institutions and associations, extend across State frontiers; and many more, even if they are organised on national lines, have international loyalties and affiliations. The Catholic Church is the outstanding example of a definitely international institution setting up a claim to loyalty that transcends national or State frontiers. But the practice of the Catholic Church does not come up to its theoretical claims. Since the rise of national States the Catholic Church has been compelled to organise itself—as it in fact did to a large extent in medieval Christendom—on a basis of national units within each State; and, while Catholics have sought everywhere to press the political claims arising out of the doctrines of their Church, the policy of Catholicism has in practice been tempered to the political conditions of each country. In Spain, until the coming of the Republic, the hold of Catholicism over the State remained unbroken; but elsewhere it had been compelled to give ground. The experience of the French Revolution, confirming the lessons of the Reformation, taught it to be wary of coming to grips with the secular power; and its policy has been to temporise. The Vatican came to terms with Mussolini and has so far refused to quarrel decisively with Hitler. It could not save Catholic Bavaria from incorporation in the Third Reich, or the German Catholic Centre Party from destruction; and it has clearly bidden its followers in Germany to give ground, rather than force an issue with the Nazis. The Catholic Church understands diplomacy better than the politicians. It knows when it must seek safety in retreat, and when it can afford to risk an advance. It can, moreover, reconcile itself to a variety of social systems; for, while it has declared against Socialism and for private property, it knows how to interpret its doctrines elastically at need. There are many Catholics in the British Labour Party; and, in Great Britain, a Catholic can call himself a Socialist without ecclesiastical rebuke.

Next to the Catholic Church, the greatest "international" is that of Labour. We do not put it first because it is far less sure of its internationalism and less united in its policy. The Third, or Communist, International is indeed, like Marx's First International of 1864, a truly cosmopolitan movement claiming a working-class loyalty completely transcending national boundaries. But the Communist International is dominated by the Russians, and has the allegiance only of minority working-class groups elsewhere. In most countries, the major part of the working-class forces is organised in a national Labour or Socialist Party and in a national Trade Union centre; and while most of these parties belong to the Labour and Socialist International and most of the Trade Union centres to the International Federation of Trade Unions, both these bodies are very loose federal organisations, and the affiliated national associations have by no means resigned the final control of policy into their hands. The Socialist political parties work within the framework of the national constitution of each country, and under conditions set by its parliamentary practice and political situation; and the national Trade Unions are similarly conditioned by the state of industry and the possibilities of collective bargaining within each separate country. Attempts to make either the L.S.I. or the I.F.T.U. into a really strong international authority have failed, and are bound to fail as long as the affiliated bodies are aiming at parliamentary victories and successful collective bargaining in each country. A revolutionary movement, content to work underground and denying the possibility of achieving Socialism by constitutional means, can take up an internationalist attitude. A mere federation of independent bodies working on national lines cannot; for international orders may at any time conflict with the requirements of the national situation. Apart from the Communists, the world's Socialists, while they accept the idea of international working-class solidarity, continue to think mainly in national terms, and there is no means whereby the Labour and Socialist International or the I.F.T.U. can acquire the prestige to enable it to guide the national movements in the sense in which the Vatican guides everywhere the activities of the Catholic Church. Labour's internationalism is federal; and federalism is weak.

Nevertheless, the possession of an international idea, even if it cannot find effective expression in an international institution, does prevent the Labour movement from being completely bottled up within the confines of the separate national States. To a less extent, this is true of many other movements, and especially of the loosely organised world movements for the preservation of peace between nations. Peace movements are usually organised nationally; but they too are rescued from sheer "nationalisation" by a sense of international community. Many professional groups have also some rudimentary sentiment of international solidarity, not strong enough to stand up against any crisis in the affairs of nations, but enough to make them in more tranquil times of some effect in the stimulation of cosmopolitan feeling.

In general, however, only Catholics and Communists can claim any high degree of institutional basis for cosmopolitan feeling. But there is a difference here. Catholicism, being a religious and only incidentally a political movement, can assert its internationalism without denying the claims of the national State to political loyalty, and can permit its adherents to be "good citizens" and patriots of their separate countries. Communism, being a political creed with its hopes fixed on world revolution, can by no means do this. It must lead its followers against the national State, and deny altogether the claims of patriotism. It is cosmopolitan in a far deeper and wider sense than the Catholic Church, which in most countries now openly aims only at preserving its own influence over us sinners, and not at politically re-fashioning the world. Only if the Catholic claim to universal "temporal power" were still alive would Catholicism be comparable with Communism as a cosmopolitan doctrine.

Catholicism, however, has sought to reconcile itself with nationalism as a means to self-preservation; for it recognises that men think and feel most easily in terms of national problems and loyalties. Communism, in attempting to make men think and feel in the mass as citizens of the world, is attempting what is at present impossible for the majority. The Russians themselves, though they found it easy to deny all loyalty to Tsardom, think and feel to-day as Russians and not only as cosmopolitans, though they reconcile the two by thinking of Russia as the guardian of world revolution. The disintegration of Social Democracy, based on a cosmopolitan creed, into a series of predominantly national Socialist movements is no accident: it arises out of the necessities of the case. Mass movements can be made only in terms that square with mass sentiments; and mass sentiment is overwhelmingly national. It can be persuaded to superimpose upon this national sentiment some sense of international solidarity, but not to give up the national sentiment or relegate it to second place. National problems are so much nearer to the ordinary man; and the imagination cannot fly easily over an unknown world.

It is often suggested that, whereas Labour still works and thinks mainly along national lines, Capitalism is becoming rapidly more international in its outlook. This is a sheer mistake. There are international capitalists, chiefly in banking and finance; but their influence is certainly less than it used to be. There are international industrial combines; but these are for the most part treaty organisations between national capitalist groups. They no more make for internationalism than treaties between national States. What is true is that the Capitalisms of the Great Powers have increasingly penetrated and controlled the less developed countries. But this is Imperialism, and not internationalism. It makes for war and rivalry between the nations, and not for unity. Moreover, the reply to Imperialism is Economic Nationalism; and nowadays more than ever, in small countries as well as in great, Capitalism is becoming nationally organised in close association with the national State.

GROUPS IN RELATION TO THE STATE

For the most part, then, groups and associations do work, if not "within the State," at any rate within the frontiers which are those of the State. There arises at once the problem of the relations which ought to exist between the State and the groups and associations which are active within the area of its political control. Of unorganised groups the State need take cognizance only as forces that must affect its policy. It must measure up these groups, estimate their potentialities for recalcitrance or support, decide when to coerce and when to yield or compromise, and so make up a policy designed to hold the State together. Is it to allow national minorities to use their own languages in schools and law courts, and to be eligible for official posts? Is it to allow full freedom of worship, and what part, if any, is it to give to religious bodies in the control of education? Is it to try to enforce Prohibition, or prevent betting? What attitude is it to take up towards Birth Control, or Women's Rights? All these are questions which depend for their answers on the strength and attitude of group sentiment extending far beyond actual organised associations or institutions.

Where the State is confronted with formally organised groups, a further problem arises. Are organisations of any particular kind to be prohibited, tolerated, given full freedom of action, positively encouraged and helped, or actually "institutionalised," so as to be made in effect adjuncts of the State machine? Of course, these questions will be answered very differently for organisations of different types. In Great Britain, there is still an established Church, enjoying large privileges under the State, but accepting in return the head of the State as head of the Church and the claim of the State to appoint bishops and other leading dignitaries. This situation is what is left over of the policy of institutionalising the Church under the State. But since the State has come to grant full toleration to other religious denominations, the tendency has been away from institutionalisation; and there is a party in the Established Church that demands the right to choose its own bishops, and is even prepared to contemplate Disestablishment as the correlative of complete religious self-government. The Nazis, on the other hand, are engaged in a struggle completely to unify and institutionalise the German Protestant Churches, so as to make them mere organs of National Socialist policy in the religious sphere, preaching a strange "Nordic" religion that fits in with Nazi racial doctrines.

Or, again, the divergence of possible attitudes can be illustrated from the position of trusts and combines. American Governments have repeatedly legislated to prohibit such bodies, though now, under President Roosevelt, there seems to be a veering round to a cautious recognition of them. German Governments, long before the Nazis, have positively encouraged combination in the form of producers' cartels, close associations of firms in the same processes for regulating sales, output and prices; and the Nazis now seem bent on institutionalising the cartels as adjuncts to the machinery of State. With this recognition has gone, for a long time past, some amount of State regulation of cartel policy; and this too the Nazis are seeking to extend. Great Britain has steered a third course, neither forbidding nor recognising combinations, but allowing them to function freely as long as they do not appeal to the law to enforce their decisions. This is the true *laissez-faire* attitude, consistent with the rest of British economic policy in the past century. It has been applied to Trade Unions also, since 1871, except that the State has claimed to regulate Trade Union political activities, and has passed special legislation (in 1927) restricting the right to strike, and limiting the rights of combination among public employees. In the United States Trade Unions have shared to a great extent the repression accorded to combinations, and have been involved in a continuous struggle with the law; but here too President Roosevelt seems to have veered round to a cautious policy of encouraging combination.

GROUPS UNDER FASCISM

Fascism in Italy and Nazism in Germany are definite attempts to follow the policy of institutionalising voluntary associations. The "Corporative State" is the State which sets out to recognise or permit only those associations which it can embody in the State machine, or dominate with the aid of the controlling party. It aims at building up a State which, reserving to itself the right to ultimate power, will delegate the execution of social functions to corporate bodies responsible to the State and accepting from it the general policy which they are to follow. In return, these corporate bodies will receive representation upon the organs of State. In Italy, for example, it is proposed to supersede the Chamber of Deputies by a Chamber chosen from the various functional Corporations of the industries and services. But this does not mean that the Corporations are to govern, or determine policy; for these are functions reserved for the Fascist Party, which is, through its *Duce* and its Grand Council, the real controlling power in the State. The Chamber of Corporations will be more like a Parliament in a State still under autocratic government than like the Parliament of Great Britain or France.

Undoubtedly, this institutionalisation works in with certain powerful tendencies in the modern world. As voluntary associations have become strong, it has become more and more necessary for politicians to consult them both over legislation and over the administration of laws already in force. It has become convenient in many cases to organise this sort of consultation by giving the voluntary bodies representation on Committees of Enquiry and on Advisory Councils or Administrative Commissions attached to various branches of the Government service, or even to hand over to the voluntary bodies, wholly or in part, the administration of certain services. These concessions serve to bind the voluntary bodies to the State, and often disarm their opposition. In every parliamentary country numerous voluntary agencies are drawn in to help in one way or another in the administration of the State machine.

This is, of course, a very different matter from the institutionalisation which is practiced by Fascism. In the parliamentary countries the voluntary bodies remain independent, even when they collaborate with the State. They choose their leaders and determine their policy quite apart from the State. The Corporativists will not tolerate this independence. In their view the State must be "totalitarian," inclusive. It must subordinate to itself every vital activity of the citizens, making them all subserve the common policy of the State as a whole. This conception is discussed more fully elsewhere in this book; and there is no need to pursue it further here.

The question must, however, be asked "Where, in this matter, does Communism stand?" The answer is that Communism in Russia, where alone it holds power, is in practice as "totalitarian" as the Fascists are in theory, and probably more so than any Fascist State yet is in practice—for no Fascist State has yet established its power to dictate the policy of large-scale Capitalism. The Communist Party rules Russia, and its authority is used to make every form of association that it allows to exist an organ for the execution of the centrally determined Communist policy. That is why the Communists have had no such furious critics as the Anarchists, who hate above all else this complete centralisation of final authority in the hands of the State. Communism, far more than Fascism, deliberately delegates real authority from political to economic organs of control, but only within the overriding dominion of the disciplined Communist machine.

The root difference between Communism and Fascism on this question is one not of present practice but of aim. Fascism regards the Corporative State under party control as the finally satisfactory form of social organisation. Communism, on the other hand, regards the centralised proletarian State as merely a transitional instrument for carrying through the social revolution, and as destined to "wither away" when the revolution is complete. At that stage, the Communists hold, centralisation of government will give place to a decentralised system of functional administration, in which power will be exercised directly through the economic organs of Society, without the need for a coercive State to impress a common discipline upon them. Communist ideal are those of Anarchism; but Communist practice, for the uncertain duration of the revolutionary transition, is that of dictatorship by a party ruling on behalf of the working class. It is far more democratic than Fascism, because the basis of its power is far wider; but it is hardly less authoritative at present.

Communism and Fascism share with certain other schools of thought—notably Guild Socialism—an insistence on the need for functional delegation of administrative power. They are in this respect all opposed to the parliamentary idea, which is that of government by an "omnicompetent" political authority administering as well as ultimately controlling whatever services have to be brought under directly social management. Fascism shares with Guild Socialism an insistence on giving these functional bodies a formally associative basis, that is, on devolving administrative functions upon bodies organised to "represent" the services which they are to control. In practice, however, the two are utterly different; for the Guild Socialists set out to build up a democratic functional leadership from within the group, whereas the Fascists impose a leadership on the group by the authority of their dominant party. Communism, on the other hand, does not at present insist on this associative basis at all. It creates functional organs, but creates them at present rather as administrative agencies than as representative associations of the group engaged in carrying on the service. Therein it behaves like capitalist States, which in creating bodies such as the Central Electricity Board in Great Britain, constitute them of State nominees, and do not build up any representative authority from the service itself. But it is clearly the intention that bodies created in this way by the Communists shall subsequently develop a representative character, as a result either of pressure from below, or of a deliberate change in State policy. Certainly if the Communist State does "wither away," there will be no possible basis for its functional organs save that of association based on the service itself.

BOOK IV

STATES IN THEORY AND PRACTICE

1. THE STATE

THE OUTSTANDING political institution of modern societies is "the State." Not that "the State" is a new thing; for "States" have existed throughout history among all peoples who have advanced beyond a tribal stage of social organisation. Men who live together in small groups under fairly primitive conditions of life may manage without any institution that it is appropriate to call a "State"; but as soon as human societies get beyond this stage "the State" emerges as an apparently necessary instrument for holding them together. There were "City States" in Ancient Greece and Medieval Italy and Germany; the Ancient Empires of Egypt, Persia and Babylon were based on "States" as much as the British Empire is to-day. There have been "States" at every stage of civilisation except the most rudimentary. But what are "States"? Wherein does the essential character of being a "State" lie?

There have been many attempts to define "the State," and they have been based on widely different principles. At one extreme we have the view that "the State" is the whole community of its members regarded as an organised social unity. At the other extreme it is held that "the State" is simply a piece of governmental machinery existing within a community, but to be distinguished sharply from the community. Between these two extremes there are many intermediate definitions; but there are also other definitions that are based upon quite different principles. For both the extremes so far mentioned and all the views that lie between them assume the existence of a community of men that is to be either identified with or distinguished from "the State." But there is also a school of thought that denies the very existence of this community, and holds that community is an aspiration still needing to be realised among men who are at present divided into economic classes too antagonistic for any real community to exist between them. On this showing "the State" can neither be nor represent the community: it can only stand for the dominance of a particular economic class over other men. Under Capitalism, say the Communists, the workers have no country. "The State" to which they are subject is not *their* "State," but the "State" of those who exploit them, and accordingly it has to be defined not by its relationship to the community but simply as an organ of class domination.

On the basis of this definition the "State" is conceived inevitably in terms of force. It is regarded as a coercive instrument devised and controlled by an exploiting class for the purpose of keeping other classes in subjection. It is accordingly thought of as consisting mainly of those instruments which have most plainly a coercive character. The Law Courts, the police and the armed forces are regarded as the typical embodiments of "State" authority, and even legislation is looked at rather from the standpoint of the sanctions which underlie it than of its administrative or service qualities. "The State" is thought of not as a body which provides common services for the use of its citizens, much less as a body in which the citizens combine in order to provide common services for themselves, but fundamentally as a body which imposes upon all those falling within its territory the discipline that is required in the interests of a dominant economic class. Thus Communists regard the "States" of capitalist countries as embodying the coercive institutions necessary for the maintenance of the capitalist system, and in founding a State of their own on the morrow of the Russian Revolution they created it deliberately as the instrument of the dictatorship of the proletariat, that is to say, the coercive authority of the new ruling class of Soviet Russia. It is true that in the view of the Communists this dictatorship is destined to remain in being only as long as it is required to fight the dangers of counter-revolution from within or capitalist aggression from without, and that as soon as these dangers have been removed, and the last vestiges of the old class system destroyed inside Russia, the dictatorship is intended to disappear as well; for there will be no one left to whom it will be necessary to dictate. At this point, according to the Communist view, the State itself will "wither away" and vanish, and the government of men will give place to the administration of things, for there will be in a community devoid of classes and of class coercion no need for a coercive instrument of government. Organs of public administration will still be needed; but they will be organs of economic and social service, and the Communist stoutly denies that it is reasonable to call such things by the name "State."

Of course even those who accept this view of the nature of "the State" do not deny that the capitalist "States" of the modern world embody, in addition to their essentially coercive character, large service activities. Clearly in the last hundred years, and above all in the last fifty, the States of the industrial countries, whatever the political complexion of their Governments, have taken on, in addition to their coercive functions, large functions which are primarily of the nature of social service. Modern States provide and regulate education; they make some attempt to safeguard public health; they pass Factory Acts, Mines Acts, and a host of other protective measures in the sphere of industrial legislation; they set up schemes for the maintenance of the unemployed, and for the provision of medical assistance and benefits in case of sickness, and both in these ways and in many others they make some effort to redistribute incomes through taxation so as to mitigate the extremer forms of poverty and hardship among their subjects. These service elements exist in very different degrees in different "States," and they existed perhaps least of all in Tsarist Russia—which may help to account for the ease with which the Russians accepted a purely coercive view of the "State's" essential nature. They exist most in the democratic parliamentary countries, but there are exceptions to this rule. The United States, partly on account of constitutional difficulties, but still more on account of the large measure of opportunity which American economic conditions have continued to afford to the individual, has been backward in the development of most social services; and on the other hand, pre-war Germany, under a largely autocratic régime, was a pioneer in nearly every branch of public social service. It is, however, broadly true that the public services, and still more the redistribution of incomes through taxation, have usually advanced furthest in those countries which are governed under parliamentary systems based on a wide franchise and the exercise

of executive authority by a Cabinet responsible to a popularly elected
Chamber.

THE STATE AND DEMOCRACY

Nevertheless, Communists contend that these service activities,
however extensive they may have become in certain of the capitalist
"States," cannot alter the fundamental character of "the State" as
an institution. For they hold that the development of public services
and of the redistribution of incomes through taxation is kept in
these countries firmly within limits compatible with the maintenance
of the capitalist system, and that any attempt to use the State machine for the purpose of a frontal attack on Capitalism or for the
enactment of any reform that is inconsistent with capitalist prosperity is necessarily doomed to failure. In support of this view they
argue that the apparently democratic character that has been given
to a number of modern parliamentary States is in reality to a great
extent illusory, because side by side with the popularly elected Chambers and the Governments responsible to them there exist other
State institutions which can be called into play if any attempt is
made to use the popular elements for a purpose inconsistent with
the maintenance of Capitalism. Great Britain, for example, has in
addition to the House of Commons the still considerable powers of
the hereditary House of Lords to delay legislation passed by the
popular Chamber; and over and above this there still remains the
undefined power of the Crown to veto legislation—a power which,
though it has not been in fact used for a very long time, is still held
by some defenders of the existing order to be capable of being constitutionally invoked against any attempt to change the essential basis
of the social system. Indeed, the corresponding power to that of the
Crown in Great Britain has been invoked by the Governor of New
South Wales to veto legislation brought forward by a Labour Government, and as we write the question of the validity of the Governor's act is actually under consideration.

In other countries the place taken in the British Constitution by
the House of Lords and the Crown is largely taken by the existence
of a written Constitution which can only be amended by a highly
complicated and difficult process. In the United States the Supreme
Court, basing its decisions on the written Constitution, can declare

a law duly passed by Congress and endorsed by the President to be invalid and unconstitutional, and the Supreme Courts of the United States and of the separate States have in fact repeatedly vetoed laws both of the Federal Government and of the constituent States. Wherever a written Constitution exists and requires amendment by a special procedure, its effect is to limit substantially the powers accorded to the popular Chamber and to any Government which holds office as its mandatory. It can also limit the power of a popularly elected President where, as in the United States, the legislative and executive powers are divided. There does not exist on the face of the earth a parliamentary State which is democratic in the sense that its social system can be altered simply by the vote of a single popularly elected body of representatives without the need for any further authority. Moreover, to pass a law is by no means the same thing as to enforce it; and in practice there reside both in the administrative machine of the modern State and in the structure of capitalist Society very large powers to obstruct the enforcement of fundamental changes, even if the difficulties of passing them into law can be successfully overcome.

This, however, is not the only consideration that leads the Communist critics of parliamentary institutions to question the truly democratic character of the parliamentary State. For it is held that universal suffrage is not in itself a truly democratic instrument as long as the right to vote is exercised by citizens differing very greatly in economic condition and social status. Wherever large inequalities of wealth exist in a community, and wherever a large part of the population occupies a status of wage employment and thus depends for the means of living upon an employing class, enormous powers of influencing political opinion necessarily exist in the hands of the richer sections of the community. This applies with especial force in large societies where the institution of universal suffrage involves very extensive electoral areas with very numerous bodies of electors. For the size and populousness of the electoral area inevitably make an effective propagandist appeal a very expensive matter, and those candidates who can go into an election campaign with plenty of money at their back are bound to have an advantage. Moreover, even in the most "democratic" societies the instruments of propaganda are mainly under the control of the richer classes. Newspapers are owned mainly by very rich men, or sometimes by particular capitalist interests. Broadcasting stations are either controlled by the Government and worked by it in the interests of the existing system or hired out to persons who can afford to pay for them, so as to become vehicles of one-sided political propaganda. Theatres, cinemas, churches, indeed every type of institution that either needs large capital for its conduct or depends on large subscriptions, tend to be dominated predominantly though not exclusively by the upholders of the existing social order. Public education also tends to reflect the ideas appropriate to the established social system. In fact, in a social system based on the acceptance of large social inequalities the atmosphere of inequality necessarily pervades almost every type of social institution.

WORKING-CLASS ORGANISATIONS

There exist indeed in such societies, over against the institutions controlled by the richer classes, certain institutions and associations created by the poorer classes themselves. Chief among these stand in most developed countries the Trade Union movement, and after it the Co-operative movement created by the poorer consumers for the purpose of protection against high prices by means of mutual trade. There are also Friendly Societies, which arise among the poorer members of the community, though in fact a good many Friendly Societies have very little democratic sentiment, and are largely devoid of democratic methods of internal government. Even Co-operative Societies tend to be run largely by their officials, because the business of mutual trading is not in its every-day conduct interesting enough to elicit the active participation of the majority of those who trade at the Co-operative Store. The Trade Unions as organs of collective bargaining and industrial struggle do arouse a far greater degree of active loyalty in the minds of their members. Trade Unions are accordingly far more effectively democratic in their methods of government, and have been in the industrial countries the most important focusing points for working-class loyalty. Formally or informally, working-class political movements have been largely based on Trade Unionism; and almost everywhere Labour or Socialist parties and Trade Unions have worked in close alliance.

These democratic associations created by the workers themselves to serve their own purposes act to some extent as a counterpoise to the social institutions which are impregnated with the ideas and attitudes appropriate to the established social system. But working-class institutions themselves are by no means wholly immune from the influence of the system in which they have to exist. Co-operative Societies have to trade under conditions set by the existence of capitalist trading, and Trade Unions have to bargain for the maintenance and improvement of industrial conditions under the capitalist system, and are compelled in pursuit of their members' immediate economic interests to accommodate themselves to the exigencies of that system. In doing this they cannot help imbibing something of a capitalist attitude, for from the standpoint of bargaining success they are far more likely to win concessions when Capitalism is prosperous than when the capitalist can plead depression as a reason for reducing wages or increasing the hours of labour. Trade Unions therefore are often deterred from attacking Capitalism, especially in "bad times," by the fear of causing additional unemployment, and are even impelled, despite their professions of Socialist faith, to work for capitalist revival as a means of preserving industrial standards. In doing this their leaders cannot help sacrificing some of their Socialist fervour; for it is exceedingly difficult, when you have just been negotiating with a capitalist with whom you very much want to come to terms, to go to the street corner and denounce Capitalism with quite the irresponsible fervour of Socialists who have no corresponding obligation to look after the immediate economic interests of a wide body of workers.

The same difficulty confronts Parliamentarians who are returned to Parliament as opponents of the capitalist system. For they find themselves met with the necessity of keeping the capitalist system working until they are able to introduce a new system in its place. If they are in a position swiftly to replace Capitalism by Socialism, well and good; they need not hesitate to do things which will destroy capitalist confidence and undermine capitalist prosperity. But, as we have seen, in no State is the mere conquest even of a clear majority in the popular Chamber of Parliament in itself sufficient to enable a party to transform the social system at a blow; for there will remain all the other elements in the State to be dealt with. Accordingly, Socialist Governments, when they come to office, are apt to find that there is an inconsistency between their desire to advance towards Socialism and the necessity under which they labour of keeping the capitalist system at work. No more than Trade Union leaders can they afford to cause widespread unemployment unless they will be in a position speedily to take effective steps for the reabsorption of the unemployed.

CAN THE STATE BE DEMOCRATISED?

On these grounds Communists argue that the entire project of transforming the basis of society by parliamentary means is founded on sheer illusion. The "State," they say, is so strongly entrenched as the defender of capitalist interests and is so decisively an embodiment of these interests that it is impossible to use it as an instrument for the transformation of Capitalism into a different system. Accordingly, whereas Labour and Social Democratic parties have made their objective the capture of the existing State machine, and its use for the constitutional establishment of Socialism, the Communists argue that the existing State must be not captured but smashed to bits, and a new State based on the dictatorship of the proletariat set up in its place. This was how the Russian Revolution was carried through; and this, it is argued, must be the technique of real revolution in any country.

It has, however, to be borne in mind that, as we have seen, the Tsarist State in Russia was of all the great States of the modern world the most crudely an embodiment of force and the least an instrument of social service. Tsarist Russia was not even a capitalist State; it was rather a feudal or absolutist State in which Capitalism was only at an early stage of development. Such Capitalism as did exist in Tsarist Russia was indeed of a highly advanced technical variety. Such factories as existed were mostly large and highly mechanised, and the workers in them were accordingly congregated into great masses under the dominance of large-scale employers. Moreover, the Russian proletariat, small as it was in total number, was one of the most exploited proletariats in the world. Whereas in the more developed capitalist countries proletarian shades off into *petit bourgeois* through an infinite number of gradations of income and status, in Russia there were no large intermediate groups to soften the harshness of class divisions. Accordingly the Russian proletariat was keenly class-conscious; and it gained thereby a large power of co-ordinated action, whereas the great mass of the Russian people, peasants cultivating the land at an extremely low standard and still subject to an absolutist political régime, had little coherence or consciousness except in matters affecting the immediate life of their own villages. Such middle class as existed was weak and consisted largely of petty officials, servants of the absolutist State. The proletariat, small as it was, was thus the one active and coherent force capable of assuming power when the Tsarist régime crumbled under the enormous pressure of war. The theory of the dictatorship of the proletariat fitted exactly the needs of revolutionary Russia in 1917; but it does not follow that it fits in the same form the needs of countries in which the stratification of economic classes is widely different.

For in these other countries social contrasts are by no means so extreme, nor are classes marked off from each other with the same sharp distinctness. Moreover, wherever the parliamentary system has advanced towards universal suffrage and responsible government, the State has become in reality an instrument of service as well as of coercion, and men's consciousness of the State is very different from the consciousness which existed in Tsarist Russia. In Russia most men did think of the State as essentially coercive and repressive and as very little else; but in the parliamentary countries, even if they do think of it as coercive and repressive, they necessarily regard it also as a service institution from which they receive certain benefits and upon which they are constantly exerting pressure in order to secure fresh concessions. It is therefore far less easy in the parliamentary countries to secure an acceptance of the Communist theory. For superficially it does not appear to square with men's actual experience of the State. This does not necessarily mean that the Communist view is untrue, for it may be perfectly true that the State in these countries too is so deeply impregnated with capitalist prepossessions as to be incapable of being used as an instrument for the overthrow of Capitalism. But even if this is so, men in the parliamentary countries will not readily believe it, or probably for the most part believe it at all until they have tried to use the State machine to serve their ends. For on the face of the matter parliamentary States have been becoming gradually more democratic for a long time past, and it seems natural to think that this process can go on until they become completely democratised. It is therefore unlikely that in the parliamentary countries the Communist view of the State will prevail, unless one of two things happens—unless a Socialist Government actually tries to use the State as an instrument for the establishment of Socialism and has to confess its failure, or unless, in face of a Socialist advance, the parliamentary State is either overthrown by a Fascist revolution or so modified in an anti-democratic direction as to become clearly unusable as an instrument of far-reaching social change.

SOME THEORIES OF THE STATE

This discussion of the Communist theory of the State has taken us far afield from our original attempt at definition. But to that attempt we must now return. Historically, States appear to exist as means of holding men together in more than tribal communities, so as to endow them both with a central organ of government among themselves and with a central agency to stand for them in their collective dealings with other groups. "The State" historically is the central organisation which unites a particular society of men into a corporate body both in their internal and in their external relations, and this character of the State has been well expressed in the name given to it by Thomas Hobbes, who called it "Leviathan." This description, however, tells us what the State does rather than what it is. It is clearly something distinct from the individuals whose unity it somehow expresses. Are we then to regard it as the government established to bind those individuals together? Such a definition only compels us to define another word, for the word "Government," like the word "State," can be used in a number of different senses. When we say "Government," we mean sometimes the body which in fact holds in a society the central executive power—for example in Great Britain and in most parliamentary countries, the Cabinet. But we can also mean by "Government" the entire machinery that exists in the society, not only for carrying through executive acts on behalf of the society as a whole, but also for passing new laws and administering old ones. In that sense "Government" means legislature *plus* executive *plus* judiciary. Clearly, to the extent to which the Government is to be identified with the State, the word must be interpreted widely enough to cover all these.

There has been in the political theories of the past a great deal of discussion about the *origin* of the State. For many centuries the favourite political theory was that of the Social Contract, by which the State was conceived as existing by virtue of some sort of contract or compact involving all its members. It was never very clear whether the Social Contract theory was meant to be an historical account of how the State had actually come into being, or only a philosophical explanation of the underlying nature of the State as something already in existence. Commonly the theory was cast into an historical form, but by some at any rate of its exponents the historical element in it was plainly acknowledged to be fictitious. Rousseau, for example, stated plainly that he was not in the least interested in the question whether the State had historically originated by means of a contract or not, and that the lack of historical foundation for the doctrine would not in his view in any way affect its validity. Essentially the Social Contract theory was not a theory of origin, but an attempt to explain the nature of the State as an existing thing, and to define the character of men's obligations towards it.

The Social Contract theory took different forms in the hands of different writers, and admitted of many different interpretations. In one form the contract was regarded as existing between the people on the one hand and the Government on the other. The people, it was held, agreed to submit themselves to a Government in order to get order and security. But they did this only on the condition that the Government should govern in their interests and not in its own. People and Government had both rights and duties towards each other, and failure to fulfil these duties would involve a breach of the contract. It was implied in this doctrine that the people had the right to expel a Government which failed to govern in its interest, and the contract theory in this form therefore became an argument in favour of revolution whenever an important section of the people found itself at loggerheads with a particular Government. There were, however, naturally defenders of the established order to whom this view of the Social Contract was intolerable. Some of them repudiated the Contract theory altogether, and insisted instead on the "Divine Right of Kings," claiming that Governments, or rather monarchical Governments, which alone they recognised as legitimate, held their power directly from God, so that it was deadly sin to oppose them however ill they governed. This doctrine had, however, its weaknesses; for how was it to be determined which Governments were legitimate and held their authority from God, and which were mere usurpers? Some adherents of the doctrine of the "Divine Right of Kings" were prepared to meet this difficulty by tracing the pedigree of the kings whose rights they wished to uphold back to Adam; but it could be pointed out against them that the king could hardly be a descendant of Adam in any fuller sense than anybody else. In practice the "divine right of kings" became a means of defending the claims of anybody who happened to be king, on the ground that he could not have been king unless God had wished him to be; so that it was in effect a defence of any established Government, provided only that that Government had a monarchical form—for it does not appear to have been considered by anyone that there could be also a divine right of aristocracies or democracies.

In face of the difficulties besetting the "divine right of kings," the adherents of a strong State were driven to look for an alternative justification, and Thomas Hobbes found this in a different form of the Social Contract theory. In Hobbes's doctrine the Social Contract is made not between the people on one side and the Government on the other, but as a compact among all the individuals who are to become subjects of the State. All the individuals agree, according to this theory, to come together into a State and in doing so to renounce all authority into the hands of whatever Government they agree to set up; for in Hobbes's view there can be no State without a Government wielding supreme and universal authority. The people possess the power to establish or not to establish a Government, but when they have once established it and made themselves subject to it, they lose all rights, and the entire power passes from them to the Government which they have agreed to appoint. Hobbes, unlike those who upheld the divine right of kings, does not hold that this Government need be monarchical; it can be anything the people choose to make it—monarchy, or aristocracy, or democracy, or anything else. But once constituted as a Government, it is supreme and unlimited in its power. For Hobbes holds that it is of the essence of sovereignty not to be either limited or divided.

This theory was put forward as reconciling absolutism with an admitted necessity for some form of popular assent in order to make a Government legitimate. But it removed the popular assent well away into an unhistorical past, so that it could never be invoked in justification of present rights or claims. This was, however, manifestly too absurd to be accepted, and the defenders of absolutism almost universally repudiated Hobbes's theory, though it was put forward on their side, because they realised that it was two-edged.

Hobbes's form of the Social Contract theory came in fact to serve the ends of those who held a diametrically opposite view of the State to his. For his successors seized on the admission that a State could be founded only on the consent of those who were to be subject to it, and erected this notion into the doctrine of a continued popular sovereignty which remained in being throughout the life of society. The people, it was said, possessing as Hobbes admitted the ultimate authority to constitute a State, could by no means resign this authority. It must remain with them always, conferring upon them the right not only to establish a State in the first instance, but at any time again to destroy it or modify any of its institutions. This was the form which the Social Contract doctrine took in the writings of John Locke, and more fully in Rousseau's *Du Contrat Social*. It put forward the sovereignty of the people as the only legitimate foundation on which any State could rest; in fact it made the will of the citizens the basis of political obligation.

But while Rousseau and his successors contended that only this basis of popular sovereignty could make a State legitimate, obviously they could not and did not contend that all actual States were expressions of the will of the people. Popular sovereignty was clearly an aspiration and not a present reality embodied to the full in the Constitutions of actual States. Accordingly, Rousseau's doctrine of the Social Contract became a gospel of revolution, profoundly influential in shaping the course of revolutionary opinion in France, and finding expression in the *Déclaration des Droits de l'Homme et du Citoyen,* which was the charter of the French Republic.

The more Rousseau's doctrine became a dynamic of revolution, the less was it able to serve as an explanation of the nature of existing States, much less of their origin. Writers who accepted the notion of the ultimate right of the whole people to have the sort of State it wanted began to repudiate the Social Contract doctrine as altogether unnecessary for the affirmation of this principle. Bentham, for example, repudiated the doctrine of the Social Contract as historically false and logically misleading, and preferred to give social institutions a purely rational basis in his doctrine of Utilitarianism, under which the State was conceived as an instrument for forwarding the greatest happiness of the greatest number. But Bentham would have been of course the last person to apply this notion as an explanation of the nature of existing States.

THE BASIS OF THE STATE

In effect States exist and exercise powers of government over particular areas for a variety of reasons. Of many States it is impossible to trace out the historical origins; for they have developed gradually from one form to another, sometimes by constitutional changes in their structure and sometimes unconstitutionally—that is to say, sometimes by self-adjustment and sometimes by revolution. Conquest, too, has played a large part in bringing territories under the domination of particular States, or in determining the structure of entire States by superimposing a class of conquerors upon an existing population. All States, whatever their origins and subsequent changes, embody at all times mixed elements of coercion and consent. For no State ever yet existed over the whole of its territory on a basis of pure coercion. No State could maintain itself unless there were somewhere consent to its maintenance, at least among a section of the population, and some positive will to sustain it against attack. But the element of positive will behind the State may be stronger or weaker, and may be either concentrated among a quite small section of the inhabitants, or widely diffused among a much larger number. What is called democratisation of States has consisted of a double process—in part of a wider diffusion of the will to maintain the State by the admission of larger elements in the population to a share in its effective control, and in part of a still wider diffusion of voting rights, not necessarily carrying with them real control over its activities. For the control conferred by a vote obviously varies with the powers accorded to the representatives chosen by means of that vote and with the effective freedom given to the voters in choosing their representatives.

The ideal in the minds of modern democrats has been to make the State into an organisation embodying not merely the passive consent of the whole body of citizens, but their positive will—that is, to turn the State into an effective embodiment of the will of the people. But it is by no means clear what the will of the people is, or even how the people is to be defined. Counting heads is the traditional way of determining the popular will, but this counting of heads can be done only within a framework of institutions through which the voting rights are to be exercised, and their results embodied in positive acts of State. A vote for a parliamentary representative in Great Britain is not the same thing or of the same effect as a vote for a Soviet representative in Russia, or as a vote for a Fascist representative in Italy. Moreover, even under parliamentary conditions a great deal depends on the conditions under which the voting is done, and the count made. There are many electoral systems—that of large single-member constituencies as in Great Britain or in France, that of Proportional Representation as in most of the newer European countries, and many variants of both these systems. There is room for many different ways of fixing the boundaries of constituencies, and the term "gerrymandering" indicates that the allocation of electoral boundaries may have a considerable influence on the results of the vote. Again, the size of the constituency materially affects the power of the moneyed interests to influence the result by making election campaigns more or less expensive. There is further the question of the frequency of electoral contests and the presence or absence of any right to recall the representative who has been chosen. There is the question of the qualification of candidates and that of the openness or secrecy of the ballot. In view of these and many other considerations of a similar sort the mere existence of an extensive voting right by no means necessarily connotes full freedom for the individual electors to get representatives who will express their desires, even apart from the fact that many members of the electorate may be by no means clear as to the political desires which they wish to express, and still less so about the means of making these desires effective. Moreover, as we have seen, no actual State ever has left matters purely to the counting of heads; in every State some check exists on the results of a democratic franchise, either in the form of an Upper Chamber or a hereditary monarch, or in that of a written Constitution, or some division of the executive, legislative and judicial powers, or perhaps in more than one of these forms.

Moreover, the conception that democracy can be established simply by making the counting of heads the ultimate method of deciding political issues rests on essentially individualistic assumptions. It assumes that, from the standpoint of "the State" as the central governing authority, the only wills that are to be considered are those of individual citizens, who will be able to express their desires by the recording of their individual votes in favour of a representative. But in fact societies consist not only of isolated individuals, but also of groups which combine these individuals in many different ways;

and men as members of groups and corporations have desires which are of no less account than their desires as isolated individuals. It can be held that in voting as individuals they will also be giving expression to all those desires which they possess as members of the various groups to which they belong, and this is, indeed, the essential theory of individualist democracy. It is not, however, a self-evident notion, and it has been at all times sharply contradicted, not only by opponents of democracy, but also by those who hold that democracy cannot be made effective unless it takes a corporative as well as a purely individual form.

WHAT IS DEMOCRACY?

There have been in fact at all times among those who have upheld the sovereignty of the people differing theories about what "the people" is. According to the theory of individualist democracy, the people consists simply of a number of individuals without regard to their differing qualities, relationships, or functions, or to anything except their common manhood. But when John Milton, or any of the theorists of the British Commonwealth, spoke of "the people," he certainly did not mean this. For Milton, "the people" was essentially a qualitative and not merely a quantitative conception. "The people" that had a right to sovereignty consisted not of all the individuals included within the State, but only of as many of them as could be adjudged worthy of a share in power on account of their personal quality. Milton's "people" consisted of the "elect," the "Saints," those whose views on the nature of religion and morality coincided with his own, those who were fitted to govern the State by virtue of standing in a right relationship to God. He would have nothing to do with popular sovereignty on any other terms than these. And yet he conceived his notion of sovereignty to be essentially popular, because he held that this right relationship to God was within the reach of any man and was therefore not an aristocratic privilege but a thoroughly democratic condition. But obviously this theory has much in common with the views now current in Fascist Italy or Nazi Germany or Communist Russia. Not that the dominant parties in these countries actually limit the vote to the "Saints" of their own particular brand, or that this was actually done under Cromwell, but that the political rights of those who accept the creed of the dominant group are conceived as larger and more valid than the rights of others, and that the ruling group does arrogate to itself the right to use its popular support as a means of excluding from power those whose views contradict the fundamental principles on which it is seeking to base the State. This is the *Gleichschaltung* attitude which is at present being proclaimed in Nazi Germany: the assumption behind it is that popular sovereignty will work as the basis for a political system only within certain limiting conditions, of which the most important is that there must be a foundation of common agreement concerning the nature of the State and of the whole complex of social institutions existing in the community. Many people denounce this theory as undemocratic, and it does clearly contradict the assumptions of individualist democracy. But if it is in one sense "undemocratic," it certainly cannot be brought under any of the categories that are habitually contrasted with democracy; it is not monarchist, or oligarchical, or aristocratic; for though some may regard it as a variant of aristocracy it is in reality completely differentiated from aristocracy in the ordinary sense in that it accepts the condition of granting civic rights to everyone who is prepared to conform to the essential structure for which it stands. We can denounce this theory as "undemocratic" if we like; but when we have done so we have not got very much further, for we shall only have to invent a new category under which we can bring it.

THE NATURE OF REPRESENTATION

Apart from theories which rest on some basis of *Gleichschaltung* there are other doctrines which deny the underlying assumptions of individualist democracy in the name of the democratic idea. These theories assert against the atomistic individualism of the parliamentary democratic theory the claims of the group. Groups and associations are, they claim, just as much natural elements in society as individuals, and society can be built up on sound foundations only if there is within it wide freedom of association and a sharing out of the functions of social administration among a number of co-operating but internally autonomous groups. According to the parliamentary democratic theory a large number of persons enjoy the right to vote in order that they may choose some one person to represent their views. But the democratic critics of Parliamentarism deny that one person can effectively represent a large number of other persons over the whole field of social affairs. For this implies that his

views on a large number of different subjects will by a fortunate accident coincide with the views of those who combine to elect him.
This system, it is contended, leads inevitably to misrepresentation.
Men are compelled to choose one man rather than another as their
representative because they agree with him on some particular issue
that happens to be uppermost at the moment, or because he appears
before them as the standard-bearer of a political party with whose
views on certain subjects they agree. But it is inevitable that the representative so chosen should fail to represent the views of his constituents on a wide range of subjects which do not come uppermost
in the election campaign. Representation is doubtless the only possible democratic method in large communities; but it is urged that
representation would be far more real and effective in expressing the
will of the represented if men were called upon to choose, not a single
person to represent them in all matters, but different representatives
for different purposes, so that there would be not a single representative body claiming "omnicompetence" over the whole field of social
affairs, but a number of functional bodies each in charge of the conduct of some particular branch of the common service. It is held, for
example, that industries should be organised on a basis of functional
self-government, so that the workers actually engaged in them would
democratically choose their own leaders and representatives instead
of receiving them by appointment from outside.

   This view of the true character of representation has been chiefly
associated with the doctrine of Guild Socialism, which has stood
above all else for workers' control and self-government in industry
in opposition to the idea of conducting industries, when they have
been socialised, under a bureaucratic system based on appointment
from above. Guild Socialism enjoyed a wide popularity in the years
during and immediately after the war, but has since declined and
virtually disappeared as a separate movement largely on account of
the weakening of the Trade Unions through industrial depression,
but also because the changes in the political situation have forced
to the front the issue of seizing political power, and have therefore
pushed into the background the question of the forms of organisation to be adopted for the exercise of power when it has been won.
Guild Socialism, however, though it has disappeared as a separate
movement, still remains influential in Labour thought; and it is
certain that if Socialism comes about either by revolutionary or by

parliamentary means there will follow a demand from the workers for an effective share in the actual control of industries passing under socialised ownership. The Guild Socialists may not have found precisely the right forms for the exercise of this control—for indeed forms of social organisation can hardly be predicted in advance of the situations which call them into being—but in one form or another a Socialist Society will clearly have to satisfy the demand for self-government in industry if it is to establish its claim to be truly democratic.

This Guild Socialist view of functional representation and functional self-government is often confused in people's minds with the Fascist idea of the Corporative State. In Italy the Fascists also preach a doctrine of functional organisation, and are seeking to build up within the State representative Corporations for the various industries and services, and even proposing to replace the popular Chamber of Parliament by a House of Corporations, so chosen as to represent not individual voters, but functional groups. Herr Dollfuss, carrying on the Christian Social tradition of corporative organisation, proposed a somewhat similar system for the reconstitution of the Austrian Parliament, and it may well be that similar proposals will in due course be made in Germany. But these Fascist ideas of functional organisation differ fundamentally from the Guild Socialist idea that we have been discussing in two respects. First, and most obviously, they are based not on democratic equality among the members of the various services, but on a class division between employers and workers. The Italian Fascist Corporations are built up by bringing together separate representatives of employers and employees and on giving these separate groups equal representation in the co-ordinating Corporation, so that a small number of employers has equal weight in the Corporation with the much larger number of employed. The Guild doctrine, on the other hand, proposed to get away altogether with the class distinction between employers and employed, and to treat the entire *personnel* of industry as a corporate group possessing collective rights of self-government. In the second place, the Fascists propose that the functional bodies shall be treated not as independent institutions, but as essentially subject to the overriding power of the State, to which the suggested new functional Chambers seem intended to be no more than advisory. The fundamental power is meant to remain in the hands of other institutions, such as the Fascist Grand Council, which do not rest on a basis of function. In fact Fascism is not a variant of Socialism, but a system based on the recognition and State authorisation of class differences; and it is not a system of functionalism in the full sense in that it does not, like the Guild Socialists, throw over the notion of the sovereign State, but rather seeks to include all functional bodies within the "Totalitarian" State that it is seeking to build up. It recognises the need for functional organisation, but like Hegel, it wishes to subordinate functionalism to the totalitarian conception.

The fundamental argument of the Guild Socialists has always been that it is nonsense to talk of democracy as applied only in one sphere of social activity and totally denied in others. They have pointed out that men's everyday lives are affected fully as much by the conditions under which they work as by those under which they spend their leisure, and that the existence of an autocratic or bureaucratic form of control in workshop or factory cannot be without its effect on men's power of active citizenship when they are called upon to play their part in political affairs. The factory, they have urged, forms the necessary training-school for active self-government; and unless democracy can be successfully established in the industrial sphere, it will never work out as real democracy in politics, however widely the franchise may be extended. For the conditions under which men work exert a powerful influence upon their minds and attitudes; and they cannot easily learn to control the wider issues that arise in politics unless they are given the opportunity of controlling the more immediate concerns which affect them in their daily lives. Of course, this doctrine involves not only self-government in industry, but also a widespread system of functional democracy extending over every field of collective activity. It is to be noted that, though the Russians have thrown overboard the notion of democratic management of the factories by managers appointed directly by the workers whom they are to supervise, in practice a large amount of workshop democracy has been established through the collective institutions which are described in the section of this book dealing with the Russian system.

CORPORATIVE DEMOCRACY

At many periods in history the idea of corporative democracy has come into sharp conflict with the claim of the State to universal authority. This was the case, for example, throughout the Middle Ages, which were permeated by the spirit of association, at any rate in the towns. Town government in the Middle Ages began as corporate government emerging among groups of burghers, who claimed the right to direct their own affairs and to be free in internal matters from the interference of the Crown or of the feudal overlord. Gradually towns in most countries acquired charters either from the king or from an intermediate lord; and before long within the towns smaller corporate bodies began to claim corresponding privileges of self-government. There grew up Gilds representing the small masters in the various separate crafts, and gradually these bodies acquired recognition and secured charters, either from the State or from the existing town authority. Sometimes the separate Gilds became themselves powerful enough to control the municipal administration, which then turned in effect into a federation of craft corporations. Sometimes the craft corporations remained subject to a general municipal body; but even so they secured important immunities and jurisdictions of their own. The world in the Middle Ages, to the extent to which it advanced in civilisation, became a world of corporate bodies; but these bodies, in accordance with the conditions of the time, were for the most part essentially local, and being local could not, save here and there, gather strength enough to overcome the monarchical autocracy of the feudal lords. Therefore they often allied themselves with the Crown to make the State powerful enough to keep the lords in order; and in this way they helped greatly in the building up of the sovereign State, which in due course turned upon them and compassed their destruction when changes in economic conditions had made their localism an obstacle to economic development. It is true enough that in the later stages of their life these privileged corporations surviving from the Middle Ages came to deserve many of the strictures passed upon them by the eighteenth-century writers, for example by Adam Smith and Jeremy Bentham in Great Britain. As they ceased to be appropriate to the needs of a rapidly expanding industrial and economic system, which now required above all else a free market on a national scale, they became obstructive and shrank up internally into reactionary oligarchies dominated by their richer members and aiming above all at excluding outsiders from their own monopolistic spheres of activity. They were rightly swept away in revolutionary France and, more painlessly, in capitalistic Great Britain; but the abuses of their decline must not be allowed to blind us to their civilising influence at an earlier stage, or to the merits of corporate forms of organisation as means of expressing the democratic spirit when these forms are rightly adjusted to the economic ends of the age in which they exist. The world gained by sweeping away the old monopolies, but it lost a great deal when it committed itself altogether to the individualistic theory of Society, and proclaimed that all corporations were to be treated as enemies of the people. Gradually during the past century the corporations have been coming back, in forms appropriate to the development of the capitalist system. They have returned as trusts and combines on the one hand and as Trade Unions on the other—to say nothing of a host of lesser forms of voluntary social association. The problem for the age that is coming will be to find means of reconciling the collective control of economic and social life with the demand for functional self-government as an expression of democracy.

INDIVIDUALIST DEMOCRACY

It needs to be emphasised at this point that since the theories of individualistic democracy were framed, in the eighteenth and early nineteenth centuries, the entire conception of the scope and purpose of political activity has undergone a fundamental change. The nineteenth-century theorists who put forward the doctrine of individualistic democracy, to be worked through a parliamentary system, could do so the more forcibly because they conceived the functions of the State as essentially limited to a very few things. The State's business, as they saw it, was to protect the fundamental rights of personal liberty and property—that is, to sustain the existing structure of Society—and to interfere as little as possible with anything else. Industry, for example, was to be left to run itself in accordance with the principles of the free market, as those principles would work out under a system based on individual property rights. Almost no social services were thought of as falling within the province of the State. Such services were to be provided, if at all, as far as possible by voluntary charity; even the obligation under the Poor Law to relieve sheer destitution was regarded as undesirable on the ground that public charity was somehow demoralising to the recipient, whereas private charity was not. The Poor Law in its English form was kept out of Scotland on this ground, and in Scotland Poor Relief remained until after 1834 the function not of the State but of the Church.

For a "do-little" State of the type which Bentham and his followers had in mind a system of individualist democracy was not inappropriate. If the State had but a very few functions it was not out of the question for many men to combine in selecting one man to represent them in respect of these functions. But as the sphere of State action was progressively widened in response to imperative economic and social needs, the conditions for the working of the parliamentary system were radically altered, and the chosen representative of the electorate came to bear an essentially different relation to those who elected him. The widening of the franchise continued to be so much the outstanding question in the minds of democrats that they omitted to notice to what an extent the purposes for which the elections were made were being altered. Of course these two things were by no means unconnected; for the widening of the franchise did to a great extent carry with it the necessity for widening the sphere of State action, as pressure from new sections of the electorate was brought to bear upon Parliament for the redress of different types of grievance and hardship. But while the democratic theorists were fully alive to this fact, most of them remained for a long time blind to its ulterior consequences. They came indeed in process of time to recognise and discuss the serious problem created by parliamentary congestion, and to admit that the legislative functions falling upon modern Parliaments are far too varied and extensive to be properly carried out in a democratic way. Out of this congestion there arose new "problems of democracy." Some theorists denounced the arrival of a "new despotism," because Ministers in Government departments were usurping the powers which were held properly to belong to Parliament. But what was the use of denouncing this "despotism" if it was quite out of the question for Parliament to find time to deal with the matters which Ministers and Departments were taking into their own hands? In many cases the form of parliamentary control was preserved by the provision that Orders and Regulations issued under Acts of Parliament must be "laid on the table of the House" before they could become operative. But this was in most cases no more than a farce, for Parliament had neither the time nor the will to consider the innumerable Orders and Regulations which it was by this method induced to authorise. The congestion grew worse as the problems needing to be dealt with by legislation became not only more numerous but also more complex, so that Acts of Parliament grew longer and longer until resort was had to the device of including in the Acts themselves only general principles and leaving what were regarded as details to be filled out by administrative Orders or decrees. But this method of saving parliamentary time only reinforced the growth of extra-parliamentary authority in the hands of the administration, and caused Orders and Regulations to multiply faster than ever. Nor could anyone really say what was a matter of principle on which Parliament must pronounce, and what a detail that could be safely left to a Minister or some other subordinate authority.

THE MACHINERY OF CONSULTATION

In this difficulty recourse was had more and more to the consultation of outside agencies in the framing both of laws and of Orders and Regulations to be issued under them, and in the administration of the various services. Consultative Committees came increasingly into fashion, and were usually based, formally or informally, on the representation of interests concerned with the particular Departments or laws that were in question. Apart from formal Advisory Committees, the practice developed of constantly consulting outside interests in numerous other ways; and thus voluntary associations came again to play an important part in the practical work of government, and Ministers often had to pay more attention to what was said by outside bodies in criticism of their measures than to the debates in Parliament. The theory of Parliamentarism remained, but the practice was being progressively modified. Nor was there any escape from this process of modification, even if Parliament had been willing to sit day and night to consider the measures put forward for adoption. Vainly was it urged that there was far too much legislation, and that it would be far better to let matters alone; for, apart from the vast mass of new laws that were constantly being carried, there were always countless other projects of laws, some of them exceedingly urgent, that were being crowded out for lack of parliamentary time. The real question was not whether Parliament should continue to be the sole governing authority or not, but into whose hands it should resign those powers which it was clearly unable to exercise itself. There were broadly two alternatives—bureaucracy and functionalism. One way of dealing with the situation was to allow the powers of Ministers to increase, and frankly to accept the "new despotism," knowing that it would be tempered in fact by the necessity under which Ministers would lie of constantly consulting the various interests affected. This is the method which has in practice been mainly followed in the parliamentary countries. The alternative would have been to recognise as unworkable the "omnicompetence" of Parliament, and to resort to the alternative of functional devolution of powers, handing over the authority which was dropping from the hands of Parliament not to Ministers or bureaucrats, but to properly constituted organs of functional self-government. This was in effect what the Guild Socialists proposed; and if Socialism is to come it will be found to be the inevitable solution, at any rate in those countries which have been used to the institutions of parliamentary democracy. In countries which have been more autocratically governed in the past it may be some time before this solution is reached, because there will not be the same high pressure from below for the replacement of parliamentary institutions by some more effective form of representative democracy. In Russia the "collectives" will grow first of all as organs rather of criticism than of administration; but there are already signs of their developing from a critical towards an administrative type of activity.

In the long run the bureaucratic solution which has found favour so far in the parliamentary countries will be realised to be no solution at all; for the bureaucrats will be unable to command a sufficient measure of popular assent to their doings to be able to carry on. A parliamentary system that degenerates into bureaucracy and resigns real power more and more into the hands of an administrative class is already in process of decay, and is certain in the long run to provoke a revolt not only against bureaucracy, but also against the ineffective form of democracy by which the bureaucrats attempt to sustain their power. A good deal of the feeling which rallies behind Fascist movements in the parliamentary countries is in essence anti-bureaucratic feeling. Its revolt against Parliamentarism, though it is often captured by anti-democratic forces, is not really a revolt against democracy, but against the caricature of democracy which arises when Parliaments attempt a multiplicity of tasks that are beyond their strength. For under these conditions the executive government, nominally still responsible to Parliament, and through Parliament to the electorate, is in fact engaged in carrying on a host of activities for which it can have no real mandate either from the general membership of Parliament or from the electorate. It has no real representative authority behind it; and this means that it soon comes to have no authority at all; for the method of choosing leaders through a party commanding a parliamentary majority is no longer an appropriate method of finding real leadership when Parliament has ceased either to get an effective mandate from the electorate or to pass on such a mandate to the Ministers who are in possession of the actual administrative power. Under these conditions there arises a clamour for more effective leadership; but this is unobtainable under the parliamentary system as it is at present understood. It can be found only if one of two remedies is applied. One remedy is the democratic remedy of breaking up parliamentary authority among a number of functional bodies, each capable of securing a democratic mandate within its own sphere. The alternative remedy is that of reducing Parliament to a mere registering machine for decrees worked out under the authority of a dominant party expressing the will not of an undifferentiated electorate of individuals, but of a coherent and organised social or economic interest. This is the method of party dictatorship, most likely to be adopted when Parliamentarism is actually confronted with a critical emergency that has to be faced, but that the parliamentary leaders with their tradition of hovering between bureaucracy and Parliamentarism find themselves quite unable to face in a realistic fashion.

In fact the State is an organisation which admits of unified democratic control only if its functions can be kept narrow and simple. But the State cannot either deal with the problems which confront it in the modern world or become democratic without becoming increasingly involved in a range of activities that is both exceedingly wide and exceedingly complex. Both the pressure of a wide electorate and the existence of an increasingly complex national and international situation will compel it to assume increasingly wide and complex functions if it is to maintain its claim to sovereignty. But the acceptance of these functions will irresistibly drive it first towards a bureaucracy that will arouse widespread hostility and involve serious loss of prestige, and then by way of reaction towards some form of dictatorship as the only means of making effectively possible the conduct of the wide authority which has fallen inevitably into its hands. The only alternative to dictatorship in one form or another is that of functional reorganisation. Unless those responsible for the conduct of the State can be induced to accept in one form or another this functional solution, they will have to accept the dictatorship either of a party or of an individual Cæsar as the only alternative consistent with the condition of reasonable administrative efficiency in the modern State.

2. THE SOVEREIGN STATE AND ITS NEIGHBOURS

STATES as they exist to-day claim complete "sovereign" independence, save to the extent to which some of them have resigned a part of their sovereignty into the hands of larger federal units, as in the case of the constituent parts of the United States or Switzerland. Where such federal organisations exist the attributes commonly associated with "Statehood" usually come to belong rather to the federal bodies than to the so-called "States" of which they are composed. There is no real analogy between a closely knit federation such as the United States, in which all external relations and many of the most vital internal services are managed by the federal body, and a loosely organised association of independent States, such as the League of Nations. Therefore in speaking of States we have in mind those unitary political systems which claim complete sovereign independence and those federal States which put forward a similar claim in respect of their external relations.

This claim to sovereignty on the part of the State is in effect a claim to completely exclusive powers of control within its own territory—save for the complication introduced in certain cases by the existence of federal constitutions—and to complete independence in its dealings with other States. All States that are recognised as civilised are held to possess this complete sovereignty as of right, and to be capable of losing any part of it only with their own consent. It is even a moot point whether they can part with any of it without losing their essential character of being States, for it has been a favourite thesis of political jurists that sovereignty is incapable of being alienated or divided.

There does indeed exist something called International Law which is held to limit the absolute freedom of States to behave exactly as they like without regard to any binding principles of conduct. International Law falls into two parts. Private International Law lays down the principles that should govern the relations between subjects of different States where the legal systems of their respective countries are both involved, and also the relations between any one State and the subjects of other States, for example in such matters as the regulation of passports; whereas Public International Law is concerned with the relations between State and State. Private International Law has, however, to be interpreted in the national courts of the separate States, though since the Hague Conventions of 1896, 1902 and 1905 some part of it is determined by international conventions to which a number of States are parties. These conventions have not been signed by either Great Britain or the United States owing to differences between the concepts underlying their legal systems and those of the countries of Continental Europe, which are derived more largely from Roman Law.

THE LAW OF NATIONS

Public International Law is based on a body of principles of public conduct that is nowhere codified or plainly laid down, but has been expressed chiefly in the treatises of a succession of leading jurists beginning with Grotius, whose famous seventeenth-century treatise first clearly formulated the guiding principles. International Law purports to derive these principles partly from the "laws" of reason and partly from the recognised practice of civilised States. The sources of International Law are to be found partly in custom and partly in the texts of treaties and agreements actually made between different States. Though it is nowhere explicitly laid down what International Law prescribes, all civilised States have at one time or another expressed their consent to be bound by its principles, and its binding character has been repeatedly affirmed in the texts of treaties and international declarations. On the border line of International Law lie further principles of civilised conduct which, without being regarded as binding in the full sense, are held to be part of the "comity" of nations—that is to say, part of a recognised code of international good manners. But what is "law" and what merely "comity" cannot be explicitly laid down in every case.

Some theorists have objected altogether to the name "International Law," on the ground that nothing is "law" unless there exists somewhere a tribunal with power to enforce it. Two tribunals capable of declaring International Law do exist to-day—the Hague Court of Arbitration established in 1899, and the Permanent Court of International Justice set up under the Covenant of the League of Nations after the war. But in the nature of the case these bodies cannot have the same power as national courts of enforcing their decisions. A State cannot be arrested or put in prison, though it can be assessed in damages, and could be fined; and there exists no international force corresponding to the police force of a National State. But it is not clear that the notion of law does in itself connote the existence of an authority capable of coercing the offender, though in any single State there is always such an authority at the back of the national law. It seems to be legitimate to speak of "International Law" if there does in fact exist a body of principles of conduct to which States recognise an obligation to conform—even if it remains open to these States to break the law without any certainty of being brought to book. International Law rests so far on opinion rather than on formal sanctions, but it is none the less a kind of law.

RELATIONS OF "CIVILISED" TO "UNCIVILISED" COUNTRIES

The principles which civilised States usually recognise an obligation to observe in their dealings one with another they do not necessarily recognise as binding upon them in their dealings with States or peoples they do not regard as "civilised." The advanced States have certainly never recognised the "sovereignty" of tribal communities. Nor have they behaved to the more backward States in the same way as to States which they regard as standing at the same stage of civilisation as themselves. Imperialist expansion has ridden roughshod over the rights of "uncivilised" peoples, and even States recognised as States but not admitted fully to the comity of nations have had to accept interference in their affairs in forms definitely inconsistent with their sovereignty. The partition of Africa among the Great Powers was based on disregarding the "sovereignty" of primitive tribal societies, and the penetration of China was accompanied by the enforcement of "extra-territorial" rights for subjects of the more advanced countries. For these countries insisted that they should carry their own "law" into China and that their nationals be kept immune from the jurisdiction of the Chinese courts. Turkey had for a long time to submit to similar claims to extra-territoriality; and the abolition of these special immunities of foreigners within a country is generally regarded as one of the necessary steps towards the full recognition of a State as a member of the comity of nations.

STATE SOVEREIGNTY

While the effect of International Law is to impose certain obligations upon States in their mutual dealings, it is in fact even more an assertion of their individual sovereignty and independence than a means of binding them together within a world system. Indeed, the principles recognised by the international jurists are based mainly upon the attempt to prevent any invasion of national sovereignty. Each State is held to be bound to respect the independence and territorial integrity of every other recognised State; and each State, irrespective of size or power, is held to be the equal of every other recognised State in the sense in which within a State individuals are held to be equal before the law. On these principles are based certain deductions—that no state has any right to interfere in the internal affairs of another State or to invade its territory in time of peace, that each State has jurisdiction over its territorial waters and over the air above its territories, together with a right to free use of the sea outside territorial waters, that States are bound to observe covenants into which they have entered, but cannot be bound without their consent, and that each State has a right to govern itself as it chooses and make what laws it pleases within its own territories, subject only to covenants into which it has entered with other States and to the vaguely defined principles of civilised international behaviour. Some would add a further principle, broadly laid down in the Hague Convention of 1907—that when a dispute arises between States over a question which involves the interpretation of an existing covenant or of a principle of International Law, States are bound to resort to arbitration if they cannot settle their difference by direct negotiation. This, however, has never been accepted as an unqualified obligation, though among States which adhere to the League of Nations or to the Permanent Court of International Justice—all League States and some others—the obligation to accept arbitration in "justiciable" disputes (that is, broadly, disputes turning on the interpretation of existing covenants or principles of law) has been greatly extended since the establishment of the League.

The existence of the League of Nations and of the Permanent Court of International Justice has of course greatly influenced the recent development of International Law. Under the League Covenant the member States entered into large though ill-defined international obligations which have since been filled out by a considerable number of supplementary conventions. Under the "Optional Clause" and the "General Act" numerous States have committed themselves, subject in most cases to extensive and ambiguous reservations, to resort to arbitration in disputes not only of a justiciable kind but also where questions which cannot be settled on purely legal grounds are involved. Apart from the League Covenant and the Conventions made under it, there have been numerous international "pacts" and treaties designed to lessen the danger of war and widen the province of international arbitration. Under the Kellogg Pact of 1928 most States have formally renounced all war save in self-defence against an aggressor; and there have been numerous pacts of non-aggression between particular States, and many promises by one State to respect the territorial integrity of another. Soviet Russia has made many pacts of this sort with her European neighbours, and it is a point of real importance that these Russian pacts include a definition of the "aggressor," the absence of which renders many other pacts, including the Kellogg Pact, largely valueless in practice. Germany too has in 1934 made a pact of non-aggression with Poland to last for ten years.

THE LEAGUE OF NATIONS

It must, however, be realised that all these pacts and treaties, as well as the League Covenant itself, are based on accepting the final sovereignty of each independent State. The States which are banded together in the League have by no means thereby renounced their separate sovereignties in its favour. They have only entered into further mutual obligations of the same order as they were accustomed to impose upon themselves by treaty long before the League came into being. The League of Nations as it exists to-day is not even the beginning of an international sovereign authority, but only a loose association of sovereign States.

This appears plainly in the League's structure. The League Assembly is a gathering of delegations from a number of national Governments; and the general rule governing its activities is that for vital decisions in matters of policy unanimity is required, and that each League State meets every other as an equal. It has indeed been impracticable to preserve either of these principles completely and yet make the League work at all. But all departures from them have been made only in the most hesitant fashion and subject to as many reservations as possible. Take first the question of equality between the States. This principle is recognised in the structure of the League Assembly, which is supposed to be the ultimate governing body. But it would be quite out of the question to carry it into the structure of the League Council, which is in fact far more influential than the Assembly in the determination of League policy. On the Council only a few great States are represented as of right, and the smaller States have to scramble for the remaining seats or to make arrangements for sharing them out in accordance with a regular rotation—which has become the prevailing practice.

The rule of unanimity has also had to be modified in order to make the League machinery work. It is held not to apply to mere questions of procedure, which can be settled by an ordinary vote. But it has also been departed from on more important questions in the working both of the Assembly and of the Council. It has been necessary, for example, to lay down that in certain cases a decision can be made against the vote of a State which is itself directly concerned in the question that is being investigated by the League, as when the Council is considering whether a member State has broken some obligation which under the League Covenant it has undertaken to observe. In the Assembly decisions can be taken on certain issues by a majority vote, provided that all the Great Powers, subject to the above reservation, are in agreement. But all these departures from the rule of unanimity have been made with the greatest reluctance, and there is still nothing in the League Covenant which enables any State to be bound to anything to which it has not explicitly agreed to be bound by Covenants into which it has entered; so that in the eyes of the international jurists the principle of State sovereignty still remains intact. It is true that under the League Covenant "sanctions" can clearly be employed against a State which has been adjudged guilty of an actual breach of its obligations under the Covenant, and there is even an ill-defined obligation upon member States in certain extreme circumstances to employ their forces at the League's order against a defaulting State. But all these provisions are so hedged round with restrictions and so ambiguously worded as to be very difficult to interpret; and no attempt has yet been made to put "sanctions" into force against a defaulter, though threats to do this have been directed against certain of the smaller States. The extreme difficulty of actually invoking "sanctions" against a Great Power was made manifest when the League was attempting to deal with the situation created by the Japanese seizure of Manchuria.

That the League is in no sense at all a super-State appears most plainly in the right preserved by each member State to withdraw from it on giving two years' notice. It is indeed laid down that a State must on withdrawing fulfil all its obligations under the Covenant up to the date of its withdrawal; but it does not appear how this obligation is to be enforced. Japan and Germany have both lately given notice of withdrawal from the League; but does that mean that Japan will be compelled to accept the verdict of the League's report on Manchuria, or that Germany recognises an obligation to respect the League Covenant until her notice has run out?

The plain fact is that the development of any effective organ of supra-national government or control is inconsistent with the retention of State sovereignty in the full sense. Sovereign States can bind themselves by treaties, and have done so for centuries past. But neither through the League nor in any other way have methods yet been devised of compelling States to respect obligations into which they have entered, or to behave in a manner consistent with international amity, unless they are prepared to do these things of their own accord. The essence of State sovereignty is that the State recognises no superior to itself, though it does vaguely acknowledge certain broad principles of international conduct which it reserves the right to interpret in its own way.

NATIONAL AND INTERNATIONAL OPINION

The recent withdrawals of Japan and Germany from the League, as well as the failure of the Economic and Disarmament Conferences, have revealed the extent to which States, in spite of the League Covenant and all the other pacts to which they have become parties, continue to regard their own national self-interest as the supreme law of statecraft. There has no doubt grown up in a few countries a quite large body of internationally-minded opinion, which realises that the civilised world is heading straight for a new war even more desperately destructive than the last unless it can find means of overcoming the national egoisms and lusts for prestige and power of the great sovereign States. But over the world as a whole it is an undoubted fact that nationalistic feeling has been growing faster than the sense of internationalism, and that the exigencies of economic depression have served only to heighten national egoisms by giving them a basis of immediate economic interest. The sovereign State is self-seeking and neglectful of world needs not only because it is often in the grip of imperialistic adventurers and militarists lusting for glory, or even of racialist fanatics afire with a mission, but also because ordinary people can think and feel far more readily in terms of national than of cosmopolitan interests and ideas. In a world of sovereign States dominated by conflicting national egoisms, the State that ventures to act internationally necessarily takes a big risk, for unhappily it takes two to make an agreement but only one to pick a quarrel. Just as tariffs and commercial restrictions imposed in one country compel other countries to adopt retaliatory measures, so political egoism in one State generates defensive counter-egoisms elsewhere. Armaments breed armaments, contempt of internationalism in one country creates in all its neighbours scepticism as to the value of international undertakings to keep the peace. It may be true that in most States the opinion of the majority is pacific in the sense of not wanting war; it is certainly not pacifist to the extent of not desiring its own State to be as well prepared for war as the rest.

Thus if one country goes wild with nationalism, pacific people in every other country are put at a disadvantage. For can even nine States agree to cut down their armaments if a tenth insists on being armed to the teeth, or even, short of this, exalts war into the supreme training ground for national virtue? The nine States cannot disarm unless a sufficient number of them can trust to holding together and are prepared to pool their reduced forces for mutual defence. But in a world of sovereign States it is exceedingly difficult to find such assurances, for there is no certainty that existing alliances will hold good. States in pursuance of their national interests are apt to change sides with bewildering rapidity. The friend of to-day may become the adversary of to-morrow, as national egoism dictates a change of allegiance. Even if States bind themselves together in a pact of mutual defence, it is difficult to have faith that such a pact can hold good under all circumstances that may arise. The easiest conclusion to arrive at is unhappily that the only security lies in being armed at least as heavily as any other State.

States could not take up the purely egoistic national attitudes which they do in fact adopt unless they were largely supported in this by the attitude of their subjects. There are no doubt very few countries, if any, in which a large section of the people actually wants war, but there are several countries in which a very large mass of opinion does regard war at some time in the future as preferable to the continued acceptance of the existing State frontiers. This is true of Hungary and of Bulgaria even more than of Germany. For the Germans, as far as it is possible to judge, are thinking far more in terms of the penetration of German influence into other States by means of a series of national Fascist revolutions than of the extension of the actual territory of the Reich. For the present at least the Germans do not want to annex Austria; they only want Austria to pass under Nazi rule. They do want to get back the Saar, but that they have every hope of doing without resort to war. They do want to recover the Polish Corridor; but even in that case they have been prepared to enter into a pact with the Poles on terms which seem to preclude forcible action for its recovery for ten years to come, because other considerations have overridden in their minds the desire for actual re-annexation of their lost territory. The Germans hope to see Nazi-like Governments installed in a number of European States, and German influence thereby extended over a large part of Europe. If this *Gleichschaltung* can be accomplished, territorial annexation is not for the present at least an overwhelming national necessity in their minds.

Apart from these countries, which are determined in one way or another to reverse the verdict of the Peace Treaties, there is everywhere, no matter how averse from war the main body of opinion may be, a deep distrust of the value of international guarantees and obligations and a growing sentiment that in armaments as well as in economic policy each country must attend to its own security. Hope in the League of Nations is almost at the lowest possible ebb; and in a situation in which even some declared internationalists are turning nationalists in despair it is not surprising if popular feeling is on the side of maintaining the sovereign State as free as possible from international entanglements. For under these conditions even the desire to remain at peace may act on the side of nationalism because, when internationalism seems to mean entering into obligations in which men have no faith, they turn to isolation in the hope of being able to hold aloof from a struggle they see no means of preventing.

THE OUTLOOK FOR INTERNATIONALISM

This situation is beyond measure discouraging for those who understand that the policy of national isolation involves both the impoverishment of the peoples through exaggerated economic nationalism and the abandonment of any constructive attempt to check the most dangerous of the forces that are making for war. If each Great Power plays only for its own hand, and the Great Powers are divided into those that are in aggressive mood and those that are keeping quiet in the hope of not being involved, the outlook is grim indeed for the smaller countries which are not in a position to stand up alone to a powerful aggressor or to hold aloof under arms. To a considerable extent in these circumstances the smaller Powers are induced to enter into pacts among themselves in the hope of making blocs that shall be at least formidable enough to be let alone. But blocs of this sort are not easy to hold together; for the small States suffer from just the same jealousies, antagonisms and conflicting ambitions as the great States, and an aggressive Great Power which sets out to sow dissension among them is likely to have an easy task. The Little Entente has appeared for some time past to be the strongest combination of this type; but the Little Entente is in danger to-day both from the possibility of internal Fascist revolution in Rumania and from the counter-attraction to both Rumania and Yugoslavia of a Balkan pact of security; and this danger will be intensified if Czechoslovakia is partly encircled by the success of a Nazi *coup* in Austria and by a reconciliation between Germany and Poland based on the German Polish Pact of January 1934 and the introduction of a more thoroughly Fascist political system under Pilsudski's influence.

It is indeed fatally easy to conclude, in face of the difficulties confronting internationalism, that the world is not yet ripe for any form of international solidarity beyond the acceptance of a few elementary principles of International Law governing the relations between States, the conclusion of special pacts and treaties which in no way limit the sovereignty of the "high contracting parties," and perhaps the use of a deflated League of Nations as an instrument for the pooling of information and the carrying on of a certain number of useful international social services such as the regulation of the drug traffic and the relief of famine in stricken areas. Plans for the "reform" of the League of Nations on these lines are afoot, and the idea of the reformers who take this view is not to strengthen the League as an agency of international control, but rather by the giving up of a more ambitious conception of its existing functions to save a few useful secondary activities from the wreck. The only suggestions for the "reform" of the League that do appear to contemplate the strengthening of it as an agent of international control are those which involve its reorganisation on a more "realistic" basis, as a League of Great Powers to which the smaller countries will be admitted only if they are prepared to accept a decisive inferiority of status and influence. But even this project is "realistic" only on the assumption that the Great Powers are prepared to work together.

If, however, the Great Powers do really differ in their attitudes, and the differences between them do threaten to lead to war, will any reconstitution of the League machinery to provide for co-operation among them really produce any effect? Under present circumstances the turning of the League into a machine for regular consultation between the Great Powers would be virtually the scrapping of it as a body with any claim to stand for internationalism or to transcend in any degree the absolute claims of the great States. It is better to keep the League as it is than to reorganise it on these terms. For it is something to have secured through it the practice of regular consultation between great and small States on terms of comparative equality. League diplomacy has been better than the secret diplomacy of the foreign offices of the Great Powers.

THE FUTURE OF THE LEAGUE

Yet is it worth while to try and keep the League alive at all? Is it to-day anything more than a pretence, and as a pretence has it not lost its value now that everybody has seen through it? It is, no doubt, difficult to abolish the League, for it has acquired a great many administrative and supervisory functions which it would not be easy to provide for in other ways. For example, if the League were to go, what would happen to the "mandated territories"? These territories, taken from the defeated countries under the terms of the Peace

Treaties, are now administered by one or another of the victorious Powers under a "mandate" from the League, and the terms of the mandate do include provisions of value. A State is responsible for administering its mandated territories in the interests of the inhabitants; and it is compelled to face publicity and to give an account of its stewardship before the Mandates Commission of the League. Moreover in the mandated territories the principle of the "open door" is definitely secured under the Covenant of the League, so that, for example, it is impossible for Great Britain to unify her colonial possessions in Africa with her mandated territories on terms involving preference to British goods or British capital. These principles are worth saving if they can be saved; but can they be saved at all unless the League continues to exist? Will not the disappearance of the League be followed by the simple incorporation of the mandated territories with the colonial Empires of the Powers which hold the various mandates, and will not these Powers then promptly apply to them the principles which they adopt in their own colonial administrations?

Or, again, what is to happen to the territories now under League administration or control, such as Danzig or, at least until 1935, the Saar? Or again, are the numerous pacts and covenants which have been made under League auspices to remain in force or to be abrogated when the League is dissolved? What is to happen to the International Labour Organisation? Or to the Permanent Court of International Justice? Assuredly it is not possible simply to wind up the League without providing by some other form of international agreement for a continuance of a large part of its work. But what pretty quarrels there will be when the League Powers are called upon to decide in the case of each of these services what precisely is to be done, and under what auspices and conditions the work is to be carried on for the future. These are strong reasons for preserving at least the framework of the League if it can be kept in being.

Nevertheless, if the League is in relation to the major issues of world politics merely futile, it can hardly go on as it is—under an obligation to deal with questions which it has not the smallest chance under present conditions of handling with success. For if it is left to carry on as best it can under the existing Covenant, how long will it be before some fresh issue arises to cause yet another Great Power, perhaps Italy, to follow Germany and Japan into secession? But the secession of one more Great Power would make impossible the continued use of the League as the chief recognised organ of international administration; for the secession of Italy would leave only two Great Powers, France and Great Britain, as members of the League, and clearly the other Great Powers would not accept the authority of a body including only these two.

There is indeed the other possibility that the League will be strengthened by the adhesion of the U.S.S.R. But this, in the continued absence of Germany and Japan, might easily turn it from a body claiming to be at least an embryonic organ of world government into an alliance or pact of States banded together against a rival group of States. It may possibly be desirable for such an alliance to be made; but the turning of the League into it would be a clear denial of the principles upon which the League was ostensibly founded.

It is, however, possible that the adhesion of the U.S.S.R. might bring Germany, and even in the long run Japan, back into the League, in order to avert the danger that such an alliance would present. But, if this happened, it would probably involve in effect a watering down of the League's objects to mere consultation, without any attempt to advance towards even the most rudimentary forms of real international control. For, whatever the French, with their ever-present fear of aggression, or the Russians, eager to be let alone to pursue the reconstruction of their economic system, might desire to make of the League, there is little hope that a really inclusive League could go beyond the will to co-operate of its least co-operative members.

The League therefore is in danger of being shorn of most of the functions which have made it on paper an instrument for the handling of major international issues, and of being reduced to a form in which it can be made acceptable to a sufficient number of Great Powers to allow it to continue its secondary activities. This would mean that it would have to be reconstituted on lines which would allow the common membership of Powers which are actually engaged in arming one against another in contemplation of a possible war. Under such conditions it would be only too plain to everyone that the entire task of building up internationalism would have to be begun afresh—if internationalism is to be built up at all. The League method would have definitely failed, and men would either have to accept its failure as meaning that internationalism is impracticable or to try something else.

But what else are they to try? There is nothing else within the limits set by the acceptance of State sovereignty and of absolute national rights. There is nothing else as long as men continue to accept as final forms of political association which hold them apart in a number of separate national States each of which is an independent repository of armed forces and proclaims that it is free to do exactly what it likes within its own frontiers. For as long as some States are free to adopt forms of social organisation and to foster among their subjects attitudes of mind which result in their behaving aggressively towards other States, there can be no real international security and no escape for any country from the necessity of remaining armed in order to resist possible aggression. In effect the notion, at present fundamental to International Law, that each State is perfectly at liberty to do just what it likes within its own frontiers, is plainly inconsistent with any advance towards real internationalism.

POOLED SECURITY

The above argument seems to lead straight to the somewhat depressing conclusion that, as long as there are countries in the world which go wild with nationalism, other countries cannot take any steps to reduce their armaments, and that pacific-minded people in those countries must confine their activities to urging brotherly love upon an unresponsive world, and hoping that history will not repeat itself, and the guns will not go off—that is to say, that we must postpone disarmament or any international co-operation until the Greek Kalends or until the universal arising of Socialist States, whichever be considered to be the less distant date. Faced with this dilemma, however, those who believe that the present state of things is tending to a renewal of war on a world-wide scale and that another war would lead, not to Socialism but to the complete breakdown of civilisation, have made efforts to devise a possible way out of the impasse—a way which finally involves, by one means or another, the creation of an international armed force for the maintenance of peace.

They begin by pointing out the defects of the League of Nations which have already been mentioned—defects which are increased by the fact that the League of Nations, whatever its apologists may say, is at the present time patently not a League of Nations at all, in the sense in which President Wilson intended it to be. A League of Nations which does not and has never included the two largest of the independent States, Russia and the U.S.A., and from which two of the next largest have actually seceded, cannot be called a world federation in any reasonable sense of the word. The League of Nations to-day is essentially an alliance of the constituents of the British Empire and France, with Italy as a lukewarm adherent, and a congeries of smaller States forming the rank and file. It makes no difference, to the inefficacy of the League as a world political force, that some of its ancillary activities, such as the International Labour Office or certain conventions on minor subjects, have extended beyond these States. No agreements on drugs or the prevention of white slave traffic, or even the mandate system, however useful these may be, suffice to create or even to begin the creation of an international political authority; and if some of the more passionate advocates of the League of Nations could recognise this fact, it would at least make for clearer thinking upon international questions.

What the advocates of "pooled security" propose is in effect that those countries which are prepared, in the interests of peace, to accept a real limitation of their separate "sovereignties" in the sphere of armed force should band themselves together into an open alliance— that is, an alliance which would remain open for any State to join. This pact or alliance would involve a series of mutual non-aggression pacts, including a definition of the aggressor, on the lines of the pacts already concluded between Soviet Russia and her neighbours. But they would go beyond this to the extent of embodying mutual guarantees of assistance, so that each signatory State would be bound by treaty to come to the assistance of any other that was attacked, with the whole of the combined military and economic strength of the allied Powers.

From this point it would be possible to advance a stage further still —to an agreement to create a common armed force under the joint control of the States entering the alliance. This proposal has assumed a number of different forms, ranging from the proposal to form "dumps" of weapons defined as aggressive under international control, subject to a pledge to use them only in the common service of the allies against an aggressor, to proposals for actually pooling, wholly or in part, the armed forces of the allied States, so as to form them into an international army, under the control not of the separate States, but of some common political organ established by them all. Moreover, such an "international army" is envisaged sometimes as made up of national units, and sometimes as a common force made up of units drawn from mixed nationalities, and under officers of intermingled nationality.

It seems highly improbable that any proposal of this sort, in its more far-reaching forms, could find acceptance at present among a sufficient number of States to make it practicable. But this does not exclude the possibility of some advance towards it. Clearly, the breaking down of national sovereignty does in the last resort involve the disappearance of national armaments; and the paradoxical first steps towards this may have to include the creation for a time of armed forces under international control. But it seems probable that the only practicable approach to such a system of "pooled security" would be by stages, beginning with the conclusion, between an open group of co-operating States, of mutual pacts of non-aggression and joint guarantee against attack, and only then proceeding to consideration of the expediency and possibility of instituting any system of actually internationalised armaments. It would of course be indispensable to keep such an alliance continually open to all States that were ready to accept its obligations, and to ensure by its terms that it could not in any case be used as a means of helping aggression by any of the signatory States.

Obviously, this proposal bristles with difficulties, both practical and theoretical. It could not be adopted at all unless at any rate a sufficient nucleus of the great States—say, at the least, Great Britain, France and the U.S.S.R.—were prepared to come in, and to abrogate their separate national sovereignties to the extent required. If this could be secured, which is not quite impossible, because nineteenth-century ideas of sovereignty may weaken in face of the horrifying form which they assume in the hands of their twentieth-century exponents, there is the further difficulty that the proposal could not immediately mean any reduction in armaments, if the new grouping were really to defend its members against aggression. Real reduction in armaments could only come about progressively, as more and more States came in.

Some alliance of this sort, possibly leading up to some actual pooling of armaments, appears to be the only survivor worthy of consideration among the countless peace projects that have been discussed during the past few years. But even this project—or indeed any project for any sort of internationalism—is bound to come sharply up against the strength of national sentiment. There can be no solution of this problem unless that sentiment can be either greatly weakened or else given a changed direction. To weaken it by any frontal attack is not possible; for as matters stand no other loyalty is capable of standing up in time of crisis to the sentiment of nationalism in men's minds. The only hope, then, is not to make a frontal attack on nationalism, but to induce national consciousness to operate in a different way.

SOCIALISM AND NATIONALITY

At this point it becomes necessary to take into account the Communist view that the "workers have no country," because they are everywhere an exploited class, and under Capitalism the various countries belong not to them but to those who buy their labour as a means to profit. This doctrine, proclaimed in the *Communist Manifesto* of 1848, sets up against national loyalties the international loyalty and solidarity of the working class as a whole. In some degree Socialist movements in all countries have been built up on a conception of international brotherhood, and Socialists have always been opposed to national military aggressiveness. But except on the extreme left wing of the Socialist movement it has never been quite clear whether the essential doctrine is that of international working-class solidarity or that of the universal brotherhood of mankind. The two doctrines may, however, lead to very different practical conclusions. If the basis of action is to be world-wide class solidarity, it will be necessary to build up a world working-class movement transcending national frontiers, whose lead the workers in all countries will be called upon to follow, even against the claims of their national States, and possibly against the self-interest of their national economies. If, on the other hand, what is proclaimed is the brotherhood of mankind without regard to class differences, the appropriate policy is one of pure pacifism—the refusal to engage in war whether the war is being fought for objects that will further or retard the Socialist cause—or, short of this, a policy of activity within each State to bring about peaceful co-operation by way of the reduction of armaments, the conclusion of pacts of non-aggression, and the building up of constructive economic relationships. The idea of international class solidarity thus leads to that of world revolution, whereas the idea of the brotherhood of man leads rather to the promotion of peaceful co-operation within the existing system of States.

In effect most Socialist parties except the Communists have relied on the appeal to internationalist sentiment mainly in this second form, and have made the brotherhood of mankind rather than the world-wide solidarity of Labour the basis of their policies. They have indeed recognised a special common interest among the workers of all countries, and a special concern of the working class for the preservation of peace. But most of them have by no means gone to the length of proclaiming that the workers have no country, or of disclaiming altogether any special loyalty, if not to their own States, at least to the national groups of which these States stand at present as the representatives.

It will be remembered that in 1914 the majority of the British, French, and German Socialist parties all rallied to the sides of their respective national States. This was not the case in Italy to the same extent, for the majority of the Italian Socialists struggled long to keep Italy out of the war. Nor was it the case in Russia, where Socialism, unable to act as a parliamentary force, could not feel itself bound to any allegiance to the Tsarist régime. But it is significant that, even in Russia, the war issue divided the Social Democrats— even the Bolshevik section. Moreover, in all the belligerent countries, among the factions that refused to support the war a good many took this attitude on pacifist rather than on Socialist grounds—the Independent Labour Party in Great Britain for example. The Bolsheviks—apart from a small group headed by Plekhanov—did altogether refuse to give any kind of support to the "imperialist war" on definitely Socialist grounds. But they stood almost alone.

It is in fact practically impossible for a parliamentary Socialist party in any country working under a parliamentary system to deny altogether the claims of nationalism without committing suicide as a parliamentary force. It is not possible by mere propaganda to expel the nationalist sentiment from men's minds—or from the mind of the working class; and it is futile to suggest in face of the facts that the exploitation of the workers under Capitalism will at present cause their sentiment of international solidarity to prevail against their national consciousness whenever they can be induced to believe that the "nation" is threatened by foreign aggression. In 1914 the German,

French and British working classes all believed in the existence of such a threat, and all supported their respective Governments on the ground that the war was a war of national defence. Nor is there any doubt that the same thing would happen again, even though the number of recusants might now be very much larger than it was in 1914. For as long as capitalist Governments remain in power and in control of the instruments of propaganda, they will not be at a loss for means to make people believe that they are fighting in self-defence. Nor is it likely that in any fresh war the issues will be so plain as to make one side plainly and simply the aggressor and to give the other a monopoly of pacific virtue.

In these circumstances what can be done is to foster the sense of international class loyalty to the point at which it at least becomes a powerful force in men's minds, even if it is not able to win a decisive victory over national sentiment in face of an actual outbreak of war. It is possible to get the workers into a mood in which they will not easily permit "their" State to attack another State—above all a State in which the working class is in power. It is not possible to prevent the majority of the workers from going to the defence of "their" State, however capitalistic it may be, if they believe that it is the victim of an attack—at least this is not possible in any State which is conducted on parliamentary lines, though it may be possible in a State not based upon the parliamentary system, if that State has already accumulated inside its borders a dangerous body of proletarian discontent.

It does not follow from what has been said that a war in which the majority of the workers have begun by rallying to the side of the State may not turn subsequently into a revolution against the State. But it will do so only if nationalist sentiment has been thoroughly alienated from the Government by its methods of conducting the war, or perhaps by the actuality or imminence of defeat, and has thus been brought over to the revolutionary side and become the ally instead of the rival of class sentiment. The revolution will be in that case a national revolution aiming at the substitution of a different national system for that which has become discredited. The revolutionary cause will not triumph unless it can identify itself in men's minds with the true interests of the nation as well as of the "workers of the world"; and the task that will at once confront a successful revolution will be the building up of a new national State.

This means that class consciousness cannot in fact oust nationalism from its position as an underlying motive of political conduct. What is needed is to express class-consciousness in forms that will make it consistent with the requirements of national sentiment. It is of no use for Socialists merely to proclaim that they will not fight for their country in any circumstances. Such a declaration has a pacifist and not a Socialist ring. In fact those who are not absolute pacifists must be prepared to fight in the last resort; and accordingly they would presumably be prepared to fight for Socialism, say to defend an established Socialist economy against attack. What they presumably mean when they say, for example, that they will not fight "for king and country" is that they do not consider that fighting for the national State as it is can be a way of fighting for Socialism, and that in any war between non-Socialist nations they would refuse on Socialist grounds to take a fighting part. But what would happen if there should come a war in which a non-Socialist State joined sides with a Socialist State to resist a combination of far more definitely anti-Socialist States? If, for example, Great Britain and France and Russia found themselves allied against Germany and Italy and other Fascist Powers? Would British Socialists really take the view that it was wrong for them to fight in such a quarrel? They might bitterly regret the necessity of fighting, and do their utmost up to the last moment to preserve the peace; but, when it came to the point, surely, unless they were personally absolute pacifists, they would be prepared to fight?

This, however, is of course a purely hypothetical situation. The point of mentioning it at all is merely that of pointing out that it is unwise for Socialists, unless they are pure pacifists, to make general declarations about their unwillingness to fight in any circumstances. For in doing this they are taking up an attitude which is certain to be misunderstood and to alienate support, and one which it is by no means evident that they have thought out clearly for themselves. Let Socialist propaganda by all means stress the vital importance of preserving peace. Let it press for working out across national frontiers a common policy of international collaboration which the Socialist movements in all countries will be pledged to pursue. Let it urge in every country the reduction of armaments, the conclusion of pacts of non-aggression, and even more the building up of positive forms of economic co-operation between countries over the widest possible field. Let it make plain to everybody the Socialist intention to build up a unified world on a basis of national groups which, while preserving their internal autonomy, recognise a common responsibility one to another. But at their peril will Socialists put their propaganda in a form which implies their hostility to all forms of national sentiment, or their desire simply to override and ignore all national frontiers in building up a unified world-wide Socialist Republic.

It is significant that Soviet Russia has in recent years gone further than any capitalist State in recognising the cultural and political claims of the numerous nationalities which exist within her territory. The old Tsarist Russia was an Empire ruling over many subject peoples; but the U.S.S.R. is in effect a federation of largely autonomous national republics. By recognising nationalism within the embracing federation of the U.S.S.R., the Communists have been able to get nationalist sentiment in Russia to a considerable extent on their side; and it is clear that unless they had succeeded in rallying this sentiment to reinforce class solidarity, their State would hardly have stood firm through all the difficulties of the past sixteen years. We do not suggest that even the U.S.S.R. has entirely solved the problem of national minorities; for in Russia as elsewhere nationalist sentiment is still capable of flaring up against the established régime under the stimulus of economic unrest, as seems to have happened in the Ukraine and certain other areas during the recent period of agricultural collectivisation. Nevertheless, Russia has managed to an astonishing extent to weld together the many different nationalities of the Soviet Union into a harmonious federation based on the recognition of nationalism in all those forms in which it is capable of finding expression without setting race against race or State against State.

Over the world as a whole Socialists, having to work within the framework of the existing capitalist States, can act with success only if they make their objective the conquest for Socialism of their respective national areas. Each Socialist party is under the necessity of framing a policy appropriate to its own national conditions and consistent with the state of national feeling. But its duty as a Socialist party is to make this policy square with the requirements of Socialism as an essentially internationalist creed. It must therefore seek to lead its own country into close economic and political collaboration with any other countries in which Socialism is in power; and it must protest vigorously against all commitments that are hostile to the Socialist cause. It must constantly expose all imperialist or aggressive tendencies on the part of its own national State, and by doing this seek to drive a wedge between legitimate nationalist sentiment and its imperialist perversions. Working on the basis of a national policy framed in its international aspects in agreement with other Socialist parties, it must set to work to build up internationalism without denying legitimate national claims.

In doing these things, it must above all put forward both its nationalism and its internationalism on a definitely Socialist basis. Internationally it must make its main appeal not to the brotherhood of men, save as an ideal that can be realised only under a different social system, but to the brotherhood of Socialists of all countries. It must not content itself with being vaguely humanitarian, but must actively foster the growth of Socialism as a world force and refuse to let its movement be shut up in separate compartments within each national State. But the correlative of this international attitude in national matters is not a denial of nationalism, but an appeal to the working class to take the lead in creating a Socialist nation. Socialists have to point out that the national spirit which exists in men and makes them feel themselves members of a national society, even if that society bases itself on their exploitation, can achieve satisfactory recognition only in a nation which has made an end of the exploitation which divides fellow-nationals into conflicting classes. Socialists have to make men feel that only by Socialism can the claims of nationalism be at once met and reconciled with the claims of cosmopolitan loyalty.

Admittedly it is by no means easy to translate these general ideas into positive programmes. But a Socialist movement which fails so to translate them is in desperate danger of being swept away on the very eve of victory by a wave of nationalist sentiment. For if it fails to get this sentiment on its side, the opponents of Socialism will inevitably enrol nationalism under their own banner for the defence of class privilege, which they will know how to dress up as national regeneration. German Socialism failed in this way. The German Socialist leaders blundered twice—or rather, they were guilty first of a crime and then of a blunder in their attempt to retrieve the situation. Their crime was that of supporting the German State in 1914, though the rulers of Germany were at least as much to blame for the outbreak of war as their adversaries. The German Socialist leaders could not have helped the mass of their followers being swept away by national sentiment. Nevertheless they ought to have opposed the war, as equally ought the Socialists of France and the Socialists of Great Britain. For nothing that we have been saying means that Socialists, however essential it may be for them to bring national sentiment over to their side, have a right to follow national sentiment when they have failed to win its support on Socialist terms. Having committed this crime in 1914, the German Socialists in 1918 followed it up with a blunder. In the German Revolution of 1918, the thwarted national sentiment of the German people was seeking an outlet; but it could find no outlet in the timid compromises of the Weimar Republic. At the moment when national sentiment could have been enlisted as an ally of the Socialist cause, the German Socialist leaders were afraid to appeal to it, though there was only one way of making that spirit work on the side of Socialism, and that was the courageous making of a Socialist revolution. The German Socialists were too nationalist in 1914; but in turning to internationalism later on they became the allies of *bourgeois* pacifism instead of militant Socialism, and alienated from themselves the most powerful forces that might have battled for them on the Socialist side.

Socialist leaders in other countries need to take warning by this example. If their internationalism is merely pacifism, and does not lead them to a courageous attempt to institute a Socialist system in their own country, nationalist sentiment enlisted against them in spite of all appeals to class solidarity will inevitably sweep them away. The only way of breaking down the sovereignty of the national State is to conquer it from within with the aid of the national as well as the class sentiment of its working citizens.

3. THE STATE AS EMPIRE

THE AGE in which we are now living has been called the "Age of Imperialism," or, more explicitly, of "Economic Imperialism." What is meant is that, especially during the past half-century, the advanced States of Europe, followed later by Japan and in some degree by the United States, have reached a stage of capitalist development at which it has become economically necessary for them to find outside their own territories and one another's not only markets for surplus goods, but also outlets for the investment of capital on an ever-increasing scale. This economic pressure has led to an active search for fresh and where possible exclusive markets, for concessions for the development of unexploited areas, for sources of raw materials not obtainable in adequate quantities, if at all, in the older countries, and for the means of employing surplus capital at a good profit, in face of a falling tendency in home profits, by lending it to the needier countries.

In this process of imperial expansion, the Great Powers have during the past half-century parcelled out among themselves whatever native territories were left over from earlier periods of conquest. African independence has practically disappeared; and large additional tracts in Asia have been added to those annexed by European Powers at an earlier period. Inevitably this process has involved large rivalries, and led to constant disagreements between the Powers, which have been in sharp competition to get possession of the most eligible areas. European history for some time before 1914 was punctuated by "incidents"—Fashoda, Agadir, and so on—arising out of these rivalries; and incidents of this sort were the most fruitful sources of war tension between the leading States. It was not regarded as at all out of character when, in 1919, the victorious Powers proceeded to re-distribute among themselves, under the form of "mandated territories," the Colonial Empire of Germany.

Modern capitalism has led to these consequences both because of the continually increasing pressure to find fresh markets and sources of raw materials and because of the change in the character of capitalist production. The capitalists of the first half of the nineteenth century were not imperialistic, because the goods they wanted to sell were mainly finished consumers' goods. Mass production had not yet been applied to the making of instruments of production; nor were the owners of capital under any great difficulty in finding openings for investment within the older countries. But as the pace of capitalist accumulation increased, there was a growing need to invest abroad in order not to glut the home capital market. Foreign investment was made possible by the mass production of capital goods, which made it practicable to sell to the less developed countries, not only textiles and other consumers' goods, but also railways, dock-plant, machinery for mines and factories, and a host of other capital goods.

When this was done it was clearly impossible for the purchasers to pay at once; for the capital could not be repaid until it had done its work in developing the country and adding to its national wealth and income. Accordingly capitalists in the advanced countries became large owners of railways, public utility concerns and industrial plant in the less advanced areas, and also large creditors of the less developed States, which used the money in part for building railways and conducting other services needed to further national economic growth.

Loans of this sort inevitably led to the Governments of the more advanced States "taking an interest" in the government of the less advanced areas, with a view to safeguarding the investments made by their own capitalists. The capital which the "nationals" of a particular State invest abroad is felt to give that State a concern in the affairs of the country in which the capital has been invested, especially if the "debtor country" is economically backward and not regarded as a fully civilised and independent State. In the name of law and order and of settled government, the advanced States intervened more and more to control the rulers of the less advanced areas, sometimes turning them into mere puppets, and sometimes driving them out and annexing their territories. In areas under tribal rather than State organisation, sheer annexation was the usual outcome; but in countries which had more fully constituted State systems, there were many different degrees of imperialist control, from virtual annexation to the acquisition of a recognised "sphere of influence" over a nominally independent State. Each Great Power came to have its "spheres of influence" as well as its annexed or "protected" colonial territories; and more and more of the world was marked out into such spheres of influence or positive control under the conditions created by the ever-expanding process of foreign investment. The United States up to 1914 had largely escaped Economic Imperialism because of the abundant outlets still remaining for the investment of capital at home. But even the Americans had begun to build up an Empire in Hawaii, Cuba, the Philippines, and a few other territories. There was, however, a good deal of hesitation about this development on the part of American political opinion; and the United States remains the one Great Power not definitely committed to a policy of Imperial expansion of territory, but none the less determined on that account to secure the predominance of American influence over the American Continent, and to give to the Monroe doctrine an economic as well as a purely political interpretation in relation to other Powers.

When a Sovereign State becomes the centre of an Empire, new political problems at once arise. Side by side with the question of internal government in the original State there arise the questions of the methods of government to be adopted in the new territories and of the relation of these territories to the original State. Empires can of course arise in very different ways, and the character of the imperial dependencies may differ widely from case to case. No State ever acquired an empire except by conquest; but how empires develop depends greatly on the nature, populousness and type of civilisation of the conquered territories.

PRESENT-DAY EMPIRES

All Empires of to-day, except the British Empire—for Russia and China can no longer be properly regarded as Empires—consist of a civilised State holding dominion over territories occupied mainly by peoples less advanced in civilisation. The French hold a large part of Northern and Central Africa and extensive territories lying between Southern China and India, as well as Madagascar and numerous lesser possessions. The Dutch have the populous East Indian Islands, Java and Sumatra, and other dependencies in Asia and South America. The Belgians have the great Congo territory in Central Africa, now held to be one of the best administered colonial territories. The Italians have Libya, a large but mainly desert tract in Northern Africa, other African possessions on the Red Sea, Rhodes and some smaller Aegean Islands, and some coast towns in Dalmatia. The Spaniards have left a few possessions in North-Western Africa out of all their once great Empire. The Portuguese retain large areas in Southern Africa and a few small possessions elsewhere. Den-

THE CHIEF EMPIRES

		(populations in millions)
THE BRITISH EMPIRE		
United Kingdom		46
Self-Governing Dominions		30
Irish Free State	3	
Canada	10.5	

THE CHIEF EMPIRES—(*Continued*)

THE BRITISH EMPIRE—(*Continued*)

(populations in millions)

Newfoundland	0.3
Australia	6.5
New Zealand	1.5
Union of South Africa:	
White	1.9
Coloured	6.4
India	356
British India	274
Native States	82
Other Possessions	60
In Africa	42
In America	4
In Asia	11.2
In Europe	0.3
In Oceania	0.4
Mandated Territories	9
Of U.K.	7.5
Of Dominions	1.3
Total	501

OTHER EMPIRES

	Home Country	Colonies	Mandates	Total
France	42	59	6	107
Holland	8	62	–	70
Japan	66	28 (+ Manchuria 25)		119
U.S.A.	125	15	–	140
Belgium	8	10	4	22
Portugal	7	8	–	15
Italy	42	2	–	44
Spain	24	1	–	25

mark still has Greenland, and is associated with a now independent Iceland under the same Crown. The United States has Hawaii and, for the present, the Philippines, as well as Alaska and certain small Islands in the Pacific. Finally, Japan has Formosa, Korea, part of Sakhalin, and, to all intents and purposes, Manchuria and Jehol, and is threatening other areas in Mongolia and Northern China. Except

Ireland, which has recently emancipated itself in part from its union with Great Britain, Iceland, which is an independent State, Alaska, which is virtually a detached part of the United States, and the Italian possessions in Europe and the Aegean, every one of these territories is an instance of the dominion of an advanced "civilised" State over a people less civilised according to European notions. There are, nowadays, in theory no subject territories in Europe. Imperial possessions are, almost by definition, possessions outside the continent of Europe, possessions in which, save for Japan, white men's States hold dominion over brown, or black, or yellow men's countries.

THE BRITISH EMPIRE

The British Empire differs from all the others in including, besides vaster subject territories of the ordinary type than any, huge countries now largely inhabited by white men, and governed by white men's States on the British, or at least the European model. Canada, Australia, New Zealand and Newfoundland are white men's countries, in which the original natives who are left have been reduced to a condition of sheer insignificance, and no longer constitute any appreciable fraction of the population. The Union of South Africa is in a different position. It is a white men's State; but in it the whites rule over a large subject population of black men to whom they deny political rights. Some of these white men's States of the British Empire have now subject Empires of their own, in the mandated territories taken from Germany after the War. Australia has a mandate for New Guinea, New Zealand for western Samoa, the Union of South Africa for South-West Africa. Empires within Empires thus add to the confusion.

White men's States cannot be governed in the same way as the territories of peoples who are not regarded as "civilised." Great Britain lost the greater part of her Colonial Empire in the eighteenth century by trying to keep it subject to herself; but she did not repeat her mistake in the nineteenth century. Canada, Australia, New Zealand and South Africa were allowed to climb through representative institutions to responsible self-government; and so was Newfoundland, though she has just slipped back owing to a corruption which has induced her bond-holders to persuade Great Britain to put in a "receiver." The self-governing Dominions, including the Irish

Free State, are virtually independent States united to Great Britain only by a common monarch and a general obligation to act together in their external relations. Except in the case of Ireland, which is still subject to severe economic pressure from Great Britain, the bond between Great Britain and the Dominions is now based in effect on consent and interest, and not on any coercive authority in the hands of the "Mother Country." No one doubts Canada's or Australia's or South Africa's power to secede, though its use may be regarded as unlikely for the present. Armaments are expensive; and at present Great Britain bears most of the cost of imperial "preparedness."

India, far vaster and more populous than any other subject territory in the world, cannot be treated in practice quite like the smaller Dominions inhabited by coloured peoples. Great Britain, or rather the British East India Company, was able to conquer a large part of India in the eighteenth century because of its divisions; but India could not possibly be held in subjection if it were united in the will to escape. The British rulers must therefore compromise with at least some section of Indian opinion, and keep Indians divided in order to govern.

This is the more possible because India is rather a sub-continent than a nation, and includes numerous peoples speaking many different languages and also sharply divided in religion and view of life. Moreover, Great Britain does not directly administer all India. There are many large and small "Native States," mainly autonomous under their own rulers, though always subject in the last resort to British interference. Native rulers, feeling their thrones safer under British rule than in face of a powerful nationalist movement, usually side with the British; and so do sections of the richer classes in British India, and also some of the outcasts under the oppression of the caste system. Moslems also sometimes take part with the British against the Hindus; and Great Britain has been able to maintain so far the loyalty of the native Indian Army under British leadership. Representative institutions, based on a narrow franchise, have been granted, and gradually extended; and many of the internal services have been handed over to Indian administrators subject to Indian Ministers under the so-called "Dyarchy." But the fundamentally British Indian Civil Service remains to keep a tight hold on the administration; and the ultimate control policy, as well as the direct administration of the armed Forces and the Police, still remains in British hands. A united India could not be prevented from exacting any reform it might wish, even to full independence. But a united India is not yet; and many Indian Nationalists do not want a complete British withdrawal, because they fear that India would fall to pieces, and perhaps into disastrous civil war. These Indians want "Dominion Status" within the Empire—that is, complete self-government under a unified Indian Constitution strong enough to hold the country together. But what, in such a scheme, is to be the position of the Native States?

COLONIAL GOVERNMENT

The British Empire, as we have seen, differs from all the rest in that it includes a number of virtually independent States inhabited by peoples of European stock, and further in that India stands on a different footing from any other country under foreign rule. Apart from these very large exceptions, the British Colonies and dependencies are of the same type as the imperial possessions of other States, and are administered in much the same way, under Colonial Governors responsible to the Home Government. In the more advanced areas—the West Indies, for example—there are partly elected and partly nominated Councils of the inhabitants, based on a fairly wide franchise. But in most of the colonies, though Councils exist, they consist mainly of official members, and the elected element represents chiefly or even exclusively the small minority of European settlers. Protectorates remain in most cases under native rulers, with varying degrees of supervision over their activities by officials of the controlling Power. Increasing use has been made in recent years by the imperial Powers of Councils containing at least some elected members in governing their possessions, and this is often spoken of as a step towards colonial self-government. It is, however, often rather a step towards greater freedom for the white settlers to exploit the native inhabitants.

In this matter, a great deal depends on two variable factors—the density of local population, and the suitability of the country for white settlement. Where climatic conditions make an area unsuitable for settlement by citizens of the imperial Power, the white population usually consists of officials, soldiers, merchants, and white supervisors of local industries. This is the case with a great many of the Colonial possessions of the European Powers, which have mostly only small populations of European stock. Under these conditions, economic development has to be based on native labour; and this usually means, save where there are minerals to be exploited, the promotion of native methods of production, especially in countries already populated thickly by native agriculturists. Nigeria furnishes a good example of this type of possession. On the other hand in Kenya, which is sparsely populated and, in part, climatically capable of white settlement, there has been an active movement to alienate lands from native occupation in the interests of British planters. The same thing happened earlier in Malaya, where there was also a large immigration of Chinese and other foreign workmen to the mines and plantations. Dense population sets limits to the practicable alienation of lands to Europeans; but European planters and mine-owners always depend on native labour, and when the natives are unwilling to work under European discipline, coercion is often applied, in forms ranging from a near approach to actual slavery—veiled under the form of forced "contract labour" for long periods under onerous conditions—to indirect compulsion by means of pressure on native chiefs or the imposition of hut taxes which the natives cannot pay without getting wages from a white master. The League of Nations has during the past decade done a little to modify the worst of these conditions in the mandated territories and in certain States not recognised as fully "sovereign," such as Liberia and Abyssinia; but much more remains to be done, for as yet there has been no effective attempt to deal with conditions in the actual possessions of the imperial Powers, as distinct from areas held under mandate from the League, though there has been in recent years some improvement in the administration of a good many colonial possessions and dependencies.

EMPIRE SETTLEMENT

Most of the imperial countries try to encourage settlement by their citizens in their Empires. But the range of territories which are both climatically and economically favourable is not large; and the main streams of European emigration flow to the United States, Canada, South America and other countries already populated largely by European stocks—subject, of course, to the restrictions on immigrants imposed by these countries. In some areas, such as Kenya, there has been settlement by Indians on a considerable scale; and readers will remember the great "coloured labour" controversy over the use of indentured Indian labour in South Africa, which ended the practice and brought Gandhi to fame as a national leader. Countries largely inhabited by Europeans normally offer strong resistance to mass-immigration of workers from countries with a much lower standard of life, especially Asiatics. The United States and Canada severely restrict Asiatic immigration; and for generations Australian politics have been dominated by the determination to preserve a "White Australia," despite the obvious fact that a large part of the Continent is quite unsuitable for European settlers. The Australian workers rightly feel that Asiatic immigration, whatever conditions might be imposed at the start, would inevitably in the long run undermine the high Australian standard of living. Hence the constant fear of Japanese expansion; for the land of Japan is already divided into minute holdings, and the suitability of Manchuria for extensive Japanese settlement is still very doubtful.

IMPERIALIST EXPANSION

The past fifty years have been essentially the age of imperialist expansion on the grand scale. The partition of Africa among the European States took place mainly after 1880, leaving Abyssinia as the sole independent native African kingdom, except Liberia, which was re-settled by negroes from the United States between 1822 and 1847, the date at which the Republic was definitely constituted. Egypt also ranks to-day as an independent State; but after forming part of the Turkish Empire it was for a long time virtually a British Protectorate, and was formally declared one in 1914. It was made nominally independent in 1922, but is still largely under British control, while the Sudan, nominally Anglo-Egyptian, is in effect part of the British Empire. France, expanding from her early settlements in Algeria, is the leading Power in Northern Africa, with nearly 40,000,000 African subjects in all. Great Britain, without the Union of South Africa, has 42,000,000, spread over a large section of the Continent, Belgium 14,000,000, and Portugal 9,000,000, while Italy with under two millions, and Spain with less than one bring up the rear. Africa has been the area in which imperialist expansion has been manifested in its simplest and most outright forms.

Asia has raised more complicated problems. It is not widely realised how greatly the British rule in India has been extended during the last half-century. Between 1884 and 1900 Great Britain annexed Upper Burma, with three million people, and also took over more than half a million in Malaya. France acquired over 13,000,000 subjects in Asia, and Russia over three millions, apart from Manchuria. But Imperialism in Asia had for the rest to stop short of mass-annexation; for China was too big to be swallowed, and, apart from French Indo-China and Manchuria, the imperial Powers had to content themselves with "concessions" and "leased territories" on and near the coast, and with economic penetration. Japan, after her victory over Russia in 1905, secured a predominant influence in Manchuria, and annexed Korea in 1910, having already taken Formosa from China in 1895. Before the War, the European Powers and the United States acted together in a loan arrangement, called a "consortium," in their dealings with China; and this was formally revived in 1920. In 1912 the Chinese Revolution made China a Republic, and after the War she was admitted to the League of Nations as an independent State. But the recent seizure of Manchuria by Japan has shown the League's inability to protect Chinese sovereignty; and her northern provinces are now endangered by the fear of further Japanese aggression. British interests are mainly in the South, by Hongkong, and in the Yangtse valley up from Shanghai, and French interests in the South-West. Russia confronts Japan in the North, where there is a struggle for influence in Mongolia. Communist influence in China has been considerable, and in the South-East and the Central Provinces there are, as we have seen, Chinese Soviet Republics at war with the official Chinese Government of Nanking.

Germany lost her Colonial Empire after the War and it was shared out among the victors, under the form of mandates from the League. Nearly all the annexable territory having been secured by one Power or another, there is not now much left to scramble for, unless one Power can oust another. Germany wants her Empire back, but has no chance of getting it by consent. Italy, with much the smallest and least productive Empire of any of the European Great Powers, is seriously discontented with her position; but there is not much room for her to expand. She would like to get a Protectorate over Abyssinia, and even to take over some of the Colonies belonging to the smaller Powers. France has of late given an increasing attention to the economic development of her large Colonial territories, and to building up economic relations with them by way of trade. But, apart from Algeria, French domestic and Colonial products do not complement each other well as a basis for mutual trade, and there has been no very rapid development of Colonial production. Great Britain has established a general system of Empire trade preferences under the Ottawa Agreement of 1932, without so far changing radically the currents of trade; for British industries need a world market, and the British Dominions and Colonies must sell a large proportion of their foodstuffs and raw materials outside the Empire. Great Britain cannot absorb the Empire supply of wheat or wool or tea or rubber; and the Dominions are determined to give preference to their own industries over those of Great Britain. India normally sends less than a quarter of her exports to Great Britain, and more than ten per cent to both Japan and the United States. Imperial *autarkie* is, even for the British Empire, which is the most varied in needs and products, an unrealisable dream.

Imperialist expansion generates imperial rivalries. Powers scramble for territory, spheres of influence, trading and industrial concessions. They support their traders and their financiers who wish to export capital to the less developed countries in search of higher profits. The other imperial Powers are jealous of Great Britain, which built up its Empire earliest, and annexed the most favourable areas. Another great European war might lead to a wholesale repartition of Colonial territories. If Great Britain were involved in it, India would probably be lost. But the chief imperial aggressor at present is Japan, spurred on by pressure of population and need for expanding markets for her rapidly developing industries. Japan aims at hegemony over all the Far East. Who can say where her ambitions stop? Japanese prestige has risen fast in Asia, while that of the European Powers has fallen, especially since the League's failure over Manchuria. It is significant that when the League censured Japan, the delegate of Siam joined Japan in refusing assent. Australia values the British Empire chiefly as a means of defence against Japan. China hovers between cultivating the support of Europe, accepting the influence of Russia, and coming to terms with the Japanese. Japanese, as well as Russian, influence penetrates into India. Asia begins to throw off respect for the culture of Western Europe, and to ferment towards a collective attitude of its own. Either Japan or Russia seems destined to dominate Asiatic policy; and between these two there is ever-present danger of war. There would be war, were not Japan fearful of the United States.

In the years before 1914, much was heard of "the White Man's burden"—the civilising mission of advanced Europe and America over the rest of the world. Less is heard of it now; for Imperialism, retaining its commercial importance, has lost its romance. Democratic writers used to hold out the hope that the Imperial Powers would gradually extend to their subject peoples the blessings of self-government on the European model. But there is little sign of this outside India, and, perhaps, Algeria. Africa is starved of money for educational and cultural development; for the native has little power to bear taxation, and what can be raised is applied mainly to other uses. The native must pay for being governed; there is no money left to train him to govern himself. Nor do white settlers want to be governed by native majorities, or white traders and industrialists to be subject to native-made laws. African self-government is postponed to the Greek Kalends; in the Union of South Africa it is not favoured even as an aspiration for the millenium, any more than negro rights are so favoured in the Southern States of America. French Imperialism does not object to racial intermarriage; but it has no love for self-government. British Imperialism opposes both, though it is less frank about the second.

India is the exception; for there self-government is, perforce, being seriously discussed. But the nearer we get to working out a half-parliamentary constitution for India, the more sceptical many of us become about its suitability to Indian conditions. May it not turn out that the Soviet form suits both India and China better than the parliamentary? But an Indian Soviet system presupposes an Indian Revolution, and probably also a Russia powerful enough to give effective help. The season for that is not yet. Russia has enough to do at home; and Indian Nationalism falls far short of a united revolutionary force.

African revolt seems still further off; and what could come of it? Unless the European Powers were to tear one another to pieces, the African peoples could not throw them off. A Socialist system in Europe might mean a rapid advance towards African education and African self-government. But is Socialism conquering Europe? That too is not yet.

When the League system was set up, idealists hoped that mandated territories would be actually administered in the interests of their inhabitants, and that from them new rules of civilised conduct would spread to the Colonial possessions of the imperial Powers. Great Britain has indeed given up a mandate—in Iraq—and recognised Iraq as an independent State. But there are more signs of a desire to assimilate mandated Tanganyika to colonial Kenya than Kenya to Tanganyika. The League has enough to do to prevent the worst abuses in the mandated territories: it is too weak to influence imperialist behaviour elsewhere. Till the next war, Empires will go on much as they are, unless India revolts or Japan expands further.

BOOK V

POLITICAL PRINCIPLES

1. THE BASIS OF SOCIETY

ALL HUMAN SOCIETIES rest upon an economic basis. Whatever their qualities of culture or their achievements in the art of living, they depend on their economic opportunities for the means of living at all. Men cannot possess a culture, or create a civilisation, unless they are able to provide themselves with the elementary means of life.

The absolute physical needs of living are indeed not very exacting in relation to the enormous productivity of the immediate civilisation in which we live. If we all set out to do no more than provide ourselves with the barest necessities, and all worked together with that one object in view, there would be in these days no great amount of work for us to do in those parts of the world that have been foremost in developing the powers of production. Even as matters stand to-day, with many millions out of work and many millions more working to produce goods and services that would not be needed for the bare maintenance of physical life, we are more apt to speak of glut than of scarcity of the great basic commodities. But let us not forget that this "glut" is only relative. If all the people of India and China and Africa were given enough to eat, the heaped-up surpluses of the developed countries would be gone in a moment, and there would be shortages everywhere even of the merest necessaries of life. Even to-day, the number of people still living in primary poverty is far greater than the number that the growth of productivity in the advanced countries has raised to a higher level.

There are, however, great communities which have gone far beyond the bare provision of physical necessities. Even in these communities, there remain many who go short of the requirements of healthful living. But this indigence is a result of maldistribution, and not of absolute shortage. If all the products in the more advanced countries were distributed on a basis of equality, there would be, in spite of unemployment and under-use of productive resources, far more than enough to keep everyone alive and in physical health. Moreover, if the sole object of these communities were to increase their output of necessary goods, they could speedily produce much more than they are producing to-day.

In fact, no Society, even the poorest, ever organises its production solely for the purpose of satisfying physical needs. In the least productive Societies, some goods are made and some labour spent with other objects than this. As productivity in any Society increases, a smaller proportion of the total energy is spent in providing for bare physical wants, and a larger proportion in satisfying other desires. The progress of civilisation is from the production of bare necessaries of life to what are called its luxuries and adornments. There are two reasons for this. The first is that men, even before they have got enough to eat and to clothe themselves against the weather, and to meet other needs upon the primary physical plane, begin to feel other desires as more insistent than the desire for more of these elementary goods. They make "sacrifices" to their gods, even of food that they need for themselves; and they want some luxuries and adornments even before their bodily needs have been fully met. Man does not live by bread alone—even when he has not enough bread.

There is, however, a second reason. No human Society, not even the poorest, has ever taken equal account of the wants of all its members. There has never been a Society in which, from the standpoint of wants, "each has counted for one, and none for more than one." In fact, as Societies have risen from primitive indigence to a higher level of productivity, for a long time the margin between their different valuations of different people's wants has tended to grow wider. They have divided themselves more sharply into richer and poorer, differentiating their members into those with greater and smaller claims upon the social product. This differentiation evidently involves a larger preference for things other than the means of meeting merely physical needs. It leads to a more differentiated consumption, which the productive system must be differentiated in order to supply. It adds itself to the first cause in creating a demand for luxuries and amenities in preference to raising the general standard of life by means of a larger provision of elementary goods.

Thus, even in very poor countries, such as China, there are considerable numbers of persons who are individually rich and able to afford a high and diversified standard of consumption; and this tendency is usually increased whenever a poorer civilisation comes into contact with a richer, and so begins to learn new wants based upon its higher standards of living. In undeveloped Societies, this rich class is usually small in relation to the whole number of the people; and there is often a wide gulf between it and the mass, with hardly any developed intermediate class. But this is not always the case. China is a very poor country; but it possesses, in addition to a top layer of very rich individuals, a large intermediate body of persons living a long way above the very low peasant standard of existence. Russia, on the other hand, had before the Revolution a relatively insignificant middle class.

In the more advanced Societies there is usually the greatest diversity of standards, from the outcasts at the very bottom of the social scale to the millionaires at the top. Between these extremes, every possible intermediate grading exists; for, as statisticians are fond of pointing out, the distribution of incomes in capitalist countries tends to follow a normal curve. Naturally, these communities spend a far smaller proportion of their total income on bare necessaries than communities lower down in the scale of productive power.

In the more primitive communities culture, to the extent to which it exists, tends to be an expression of the popular consciousness. It is achieved mainly by the spending on things other than elementary physical needs of persons who have not enough income to meet their needs to the full. Commonly the religious impulse is the chief inducement to this spending. But as the total wealth of Society increases, and the element of income differentiation within it grows larger, spending on cultural objects comes to be more closely associated with the possession of a larger income than the majority of people possess; and culture itself comes to be more the peculiar possession of a superior economic class. As a matter of historical fact the arts, to the extent to which they have become disassociated from the crafts providing objects of everyday use, have been developed chiefly under the patronage and in the hands of a limited class in receipt of higher incomes than the mass of the people. Even the poor artist has been commonly richer than the average craftsman; and the market for his art has been among persons belonging to a superior class.

Only when a high standard of productivity is reached in a Society is this tendency in part reversed. As the general standard of living rises, a larger part of the population reaches a point at which it is able to devote an appreciable part of its income to meeting other than physical needs. As this happens, the arts become again more "popular," in the sense that they begin to reach down towards the wider classes that are becoming able to afford them. There is, however, no return to the primitive condition in which the arts existed as a direct expression of the social consciousness of the entire people. For the supply of culture only filters down gradually to the classes below those for whom it has been previously designed; and the standard of culture continues to be set largely by the character of upper-class demand. In all highly civilised communities, cultural standards include a large element of snobbery.

It remains true that, when the advance of productivity gets past a certain point, cultural demand becomes more diffused, and involves a larger section of the total population. The spread of novel-reading, of the cheap production of books and pictures, and of the cinema and wireless in the richer countries to-day furnishes clear examples of this tendency. But the re-popularisation of culture is greatly retarded by an opposite development. As productivity increases, the standards of physical need do not remain the same. This is not only because conventional notions of what is necessary to life expand as the means of satisfying them become more abundant, though this does of course happen, but also because in advanced Societies living becomes more complicated, so as to enforce a larger expenditure in meeting indispensable wants. The growth of towns and of urban ways of living is a great creator of new minimum needs; and in modern conditions far more has to be spent on transport and other forms of service, as distinct from consumable goods. The mere mechanism of life and work becomes more expensive for the individual as well as for the economic system as a whole. In effect, a large part of the apparent advance in the standard of living is eaten up in providing for new needs which have in themselves no cultural value, and make no net contribution to the satisfaction of the recipients.

Nevertheless, standards of culture and satisfaction, as well as of consumption, do rise; and culture and the sense of cultural satisfaction do become more widely spread. But the culture remains a class-culture, though the growth of popular education, necessitated by the requirements of an advanced economic system, as well as made possible by the increase of productive power, does help to narrow cultural differences between rich and poor, and to facilitate the movement of individuals up and down the social scale. The characteristic of civilisation in the most advanced capitalist countries is—despite the survival in them of hereditary aristocratic elements—relative ease of individual movement from one class-group to the groups above or below it combined with very great, but infinitesimally graded, inequalities of wealth. The class-structure is not rigid but elastic; but it is unmistakably a class-structure all the same.

THE ECONOMIC BASIS

The economic foundation of the type of Society with which we are familiar in Western Europe and in the United States is modern science, in the broadest sense. These advanced Societies are above all else the consequences of a tremendous expansion of human knowledge in mechanics, chemistry, biology, astronomy and a host of other sciences. Sometimes this expansion has come from the work of the pure scientists, labouring for the advance of knowledge itself rather than for the discovery of improved methods of production. Sometimes it has come from practical men who would disclaim all "scientific" knowledge, or from the practitioners of the "applied" arts and sciences. Whatever its source, it has meant a great enlargement of the powers of production, or in other words of men's economic command over nature. It has revolutionised not only men's methods of producing wealth, but also their entire way of living. Adding immensely to their productive power, it has also multiplied their needs, and forced them to adopt new conceptions and standards of existence. For example, it has urbanised communities to a degree hitherto unknown and impossible. It has prolonged life, and especially lowered infant mortality to an astonishing extent. Nor has it left untouched the life of the country-dweller; for, apart from the contributions of mechanics, chemistry and biology to the productivity of agriculture, the improvements in transport and communication have altered profoundly the life of the village, and the diffusion of electrical power bids fair to alter it hardly less notably in the near future.

There is no need to labour the point that modern communities and their characteristic cultures rest fundamentally on scientific and technological foundations. Everyone is aware of this, and no one attempts to deny it. But when this conclusion is broadened out into a generalisation about human history as a whole, or applied directly to the explanation of political and cultural, as well as economic, institutions, there are many who furiously repudiate the doctrine. They will agree that modern culture and the modern State could not be what they are without modern science and modern industrialism; but they appear to hold that there is something positively immoral in seeking to explain these things by referring them to their economic foundations. Culture, they tell us, is of the mind: it transcends the merely material. And the State is a spiritual, or at any rate an ideological, expression of men's social quality, and not a mere reflection of their economic interests.

Well, so is industry itself a thing of the mind—mind acting upon matter. So is industry itself an expression of men's social quality, as expressed in the economic institutions which they constitute for its conduct. The attempt to base the discussion of social questions on a contrast between the respective influences of "mind" and "matter" is entirely fruitless; for there is no such contrast. Throughout the field of social experience, mind is constantly acting upon matter, and matter upon mind. The material things which act upon men's minds to-day are themselves the products of the past activity of minds upon other material things which were in turn the outcome of earlier mental as well as material forces. A machine is a thoroughly material object; but it embodies the discoveries of a succession of inventors and appliers of new ways of shaping the world of inanimate nature to serve the purposes of men.

Let us, then, put out of our minds once and for all the notion that the interpretation of political forces in economic terms involves a view derogatory to the mind of man. Men make their economic as well as their political systems and conditions, by working upon the materials and forces that are available for their use. These materials and forces, as they exist in any epoch and in any Society, are not mere gifts of nature, but the inherited products of past ages of human effort directed to the use of the forces which nature provides. Man's economic heritage is essentially a social heritage.

The "economic" interpretation of history means therefore, not that man is the mere blind instrument of purely automatic natural processes, but rather that men can make their history only by building upon the real resources that are at their command. There is a limit to what each age can do, set by the character of its resources and the limitations of its own strength and creative energy. The extent of its power depends partly on the objective opportunities for growth which its inherited equipment presents, partly on its own individual qualities of will and practical curiosity, and partly on its capacity for co-operative effort. For social action is itself a tremendous creative force. Men can accomplish by acting in organised and co-operating groups far more than by merely individual effort.

SOCIETY AS A WORK-GROUP

Society is, at its basis, a work-group. Its fundamental purpose is to ensure to the members of the group the means of satisfactory living, by the right direction and expenditure of their combined working power. The most primitive Societies plainly reveal this essential economic quality. There are work-groups, with an elaborate differentiation of functions among their members, long before there is any such thing as a State.

It is, however, an error to imagine that any Societies, except perhaps the most primitive of all, are mere work-groups, organising their social labour with no other purpose than the satisfaction of the economic needs of the group. Equally is it an error to suppose that primitive Societies, up to the advent of the State, exist in a condition of social equality among all their members. For there exists in them from a very early stage, if not from the very beginning, a differentiation not only of functions, but also of status, between men and women. This is seen most plainly among the primitive hunters, among whom the work of hunting is the preserve of the men, whereas the women remain at home to carry on the rest of the work. Between these two kinds of activity there is, as far back as we can see, a differentiation of honour. The chase, involving danger and strength and affording opportunity for the display of prowess, is held to be honourable and to confer distinction, whereas the work of the village is looked down upon as menial. Often the man kills the quarry, but it is the woman's business to go out and drag it home; for the hunter cannot demean himself to work in which there is no element of prowess.

As communities of this type develop more settled habits of living, the amount of work to be done in and about the village expands and grows into the differentiated labour of agriculture and primitive industry. But even so, it remains for the most part women's work. Women, rather than men, are the first industrial workers and the first labourers in agriculture. The class-distinction between men and women is probably the earliest class-distinction of all. Only industrial arts closely connected with prowess, such as the making of weapons, are regarded as worthy of men; and it is no accident that so many legends from the childhood of man represent the smith as lame. If he were not lame, he would be, like the rest, not an industrial worker, but a hunter or a warrior.

Economic activity thus begins under a cloud of social disrepute which has never yet been wholly dispelled, even in the most advanced industrial Societies. To look down upon merely economic activities is deeply "natural" to us still, in the sense that it goes back a tremendously long way in the history of mankind. The prejudice many people feel against the economic interpretation of history is based on the contempt of the savage for forms of activity in which he can see no prowess. Even the Russians, who are most determined to destroy anti-industrial prejudice, rank the Red Army on a level with the "shock brigades" of industrial workers. And in capitalist countries, for all their devotion to money-making, the man who leaves the workshop for the trenches is still widely felt to be adopting a nobler vocation.

Communities, however, cannot advance far in civilisation or comfort as long as their members eschew all forms of productive work except the chase. Gradually, the men have to supplement the women's labour in field and work-shop. As a superior class, they begin by pushing the women out of the tasks that are felt to be the least dishonourable, leaving to them the more menial occupations which have most clearly the character of services done for the men. Woman's place begins to be "the home" rather than the village; and she sinks in the social scale as a consequence of the change. But at this point clear differentiations of class emerge among the men. Those who are compelled to take to productive labour in field or village are reckoned the inferiors of those who can still confine their activities to deeds of prowess. The stronger and the more cunning retain the superior functions for themselves, and become a superior class—a leisure class whose ordinary needs are to be satisfied by the labours of others. The long process of changing class-differentiations has begun.

It is no part of our purpose here to follow this process through its many subsequent changes; for that would involve writing a sociological history of mankind. We are concerned only to point out that the growth of social classes is, at bottom, only the reflection of the process of economic development. The emergence of classes which claim that their needs count for more in the organisation of the common resources, that they have a right to monopolise the opportunities for prowess, and that they constitute a socially superior group, is the necessary outcome of the process of economic advance. It has its basis in the changing nature of man's power to use the resources of production that are at his command.

THE LEISURE CLASS

It would not, however, operate as it has done in history if man were, in fact, the "economic man" of the classical economists. For the starting-point of the process of class-differentiation is even more the desire for prowess than the desire for larger consumption. The "leisure class," as Thorstein Veblen has called it, emerges out of the claim of the strongest that the rest shall work for them in order that they may confine their activities to deeds of honour. This sense of the differing honourableness of various kinds of activities lies at the root of the process of social differentiation.

This is important; for the force which we have seen thus working in primitive Societies is still active in the world to-day. It remains active, not only in the honour still paid to warriors and in the prestige given to red-coated huntsmen, champions in the various branches of sport, and every sort of physical prowess that is unproductive of values—note here the passionate desire among gentlemen to preserve "amateurism," lest their prowess should be deemed to possess a commercial value—but also in many other ways. Civilised communities, with narrowed opportunities for the more primitive exercises, have transferred the notion of prowess to many other activities besides the obvious one of sport. Late in the day it has been accorded

THE BASIS OF SOCIETY

to actors and writers, even if they write for a living, to the upper
ranges of the professions—in fact, to almost anything except ordinary
manual labour. Most notable of all is the change which has made it
honourable to be, not a workman but—the phrase itself is highly
significant—a "captain" of industry. "A Nation of Shop-keepers"
has a definitely contemptuous ring; "A Nation of Captains of Industry" sounds very different. The Wesleyans and Evangelicals in
England made it one of their chief missions to overthrow the notion
that there was anything "lowering" about industry and commerce,
and to encourage the new industrial employers to make money "to
the glory of God." And the Americans, getting a fresh start in an
undeveloped country of unparalleled economic wealth, succeeded
for a time in exalting the successful man of business even above the
baseball player, until the contacts of the American rich with the
ideals of the older countries made the dollar millionaire eager to
marry his daughter to a title, and the growth of an idle rich class
in the United States caused a revival, in the interest of its sense of
superiority, of the prestige of unproductiveness.

Our point is that the development of industrial civilisation required imperatively that devotion to the higher branches of industrial
work should become not only a means to additional material satisfaction for those who engage in it, but also a source of prestige. This
was accomplished in two ways; first, by making the possession of
money itself a source of honour, and secondly by according a notion
of prowess to the work of the large-scale *entrepreneur*. The possession of money could become a source of honour because it enabled
the possessor to buy those things which were the symbols of honour
among the existing ennobled class. Hence the avidity of the successful merchants of eighteenth-century England in buying landed
estates. And hence in France and other countries the wide-spread
purchase of patents of nobility; for, whereas in England it was
enough for a man to have an estate, in France he had to produce
his papers of admission to the charmed circle. Money could, in both
countries, buy its way to prestige; and from that the step was not
long to a concession of prestige to mere wealth, apart from its conversion into the familiar symbols of social superiority. From this
again it was not a difficult step to impute prestige to the captain of
industry as a captain of industry, and not exclusively on account of
his wealth.

The more this happened, the more men were able to value successful industrial activity, in its higher branches, not only as the means to making money, but also as a source of prowess and prestige. The prowess and the prestige continued to be measured mainly, not by what a man did—there is very little prestige in being a good employer, and none at all in making something useful rather than something nasty—but by the amount of money he was able to make. But the money became a symbol of success, fully as much as a thing desired for the sake of what it could be used to buy. Indeed, a large fortune can hardly be valued in this latter way, unless it can be so expended as to add still more to its owner's prestige.

Great fortunes can, however, be used as a means to further prestige very easily indeed. This can be done in two ways, by buying the means of ostentation and the means of power. As the primitive hunter showed off before the others, the rich man can show off before those not quite so rich as himself. Much of the expenditure of the rich ministers to satisfaction only in this sense. The only want it satisfies is the want to feel and look superior. But even more important in the world of to-day is the expenditure of money as a means to power, which is itself valued largely for the prestige it brings. A rich man can buy the services of the poor, not only in order to employ them for profit, but also in order to increase his power and honour. A rich man can no longer keep a private army of retainers, though he can of flunkeys; but he can make hordes of poor men fetch, carry, preach and propagand at his will. Happiest of all is the great newspaper-proprietor, whose very spending on propaganda is also a source of profit.

THE POSITION OF WOMEN

Spending for ostentation reacts disastrously on the position of women. For though, when the less strong or less cunning males were driven to agricultural or industrial labour, they were strong enough to push the women down below them into more menial jobs, the advent of men into productive work did lessen sex-inequality. For example, women in the Middle Ages were socially nearer to being men's equals than women in the advanced Societies of the nineteenth century. This was more true of upper-class women and peasant women than of the wives of many types of industrial workers, except under the domestic system; for in domestic industry, as well as on the land, women were recognised breadwinners as well as men. The upper- or middle-class woman was not a breadwinner; but she had a large and diversified household to manage while her husband attended to the landed estate or to the shop, or workshop. Baking, jam-making, spinning and weaving at home kept her hands full, and gave her a responsible work of direction. She had no time to become a doll.

The Industrial Revolution took away a large part of women's work from them—far more than enough to outweigh in social importance the increased employment of women in the factories. The domestic system died out, and with it over a large part of the country went the earnings of the wife. The crushing out of the peasantry drove most of the women out of agriculture; for the new farmers employed chiefly male wage-labour. And the women of the upper and middle classes stopped weaving and, more gradually, baking and cheese-making at home, and bought instead the products of the factory system. Meanwhile their husbands, enriched by the flood of new wealth, wanted pegs on which they could hang out for inspection the symbols of their prowess. Woman became the peg for masculine ostentation; the idler and the more decorated she became, the greater was the glory of her lord.

The Victorian lady was a product, and even more a symbol, of the growth of economic inequality. As the middle classes got richer, the circle of gentility widened, and it became a more and more common ideal to be utterly useless. Even child-bearing acquired a mild stigma of vulgar productivity; and though the middle-class woman had far less else to do, the middle-class birth-rate began to fall. By way of reaction, Victorianism engendered the Woman's Movement, a revolt against the cult of the doll which was strongest among middle-class women, because they had been condemned to the sheerest futility. But the Woman's Movement was caught in the toils of the class system. Revolutionary Russia, sweeping away ostentatious spending, leapt to almost sex-equality at a single bound. Class-equality and sex-equality are inseparably bound up together.

THE GROWTH OF CAPITALISM

Meanwhile among men the structure of Capitalism was being built up. Capitalist enterprise began to develop within the framework of feudal Society, and its first standard-bearer was the merchant. We have seen how, in Great Britain, the wealthy merchants enriched by foreign trade bought their way, by land purchases and intermarriage, into the ranks of the landed aristocracy. This was easier because, in the wars of the seventeenth century, the battle for parliamentarism had already been won. The merchants and the smaller landowners had already proved to the Crown and the great landlords the expediency of ruling on terms which they could accept. Great Britain remained an aristocracy after 1660 and after 1688, but an aristocracy based on a clear recognition of the claims of the commercial class. What remained of feudalism had learnt to accommodate itself. It readily accepted pride of place in a parliamentary system which admitted all wealthy men to a share in power. Thereafter, it set to work to preserve aristocracy by a constant assimilation of the top layer of the *bourgeoisie*.

In France, though men could rise by purchase into the nobility, this assimilation did not happen. Absolute monarchy remained in possession of the political field; and the aristocrats, excluded from political power, clung the more tenaciously to their feudal privileges. Industry developed under royal patronage; and commerce was not strong enough, in a country less active in foreign trade and Colonial enterprise, to force open the door of political recognition. Whereas in England the standard of life rose as commercial expansion brought more wealth, in France feudal exactions kept the peasants in misery, and high military expenditure combined with the extravagance of the Court and the exemption of the nobility from most forms of taxation to impose heavy tax-burdens on the middle classes as well as on the poor. French feudalism did not bend: it broke. The French Revolution came before the revolution in industry had had time to produce its social and political effects. It was not a product of the machine age; it had nothing to do with steam-engines or the factory system. It was the overdue throwing down of an aristocratic and absolutist régime that had been superseded in England long before.

But Revolutions happen very differently according as they happen soon or late. The English Revolution of the seventeenth century, happening soon in relation to the need for it, ended in a compromise, in which the old order was able to preserve much of its power. Its outcome was a partnership of landlords and merchants. But the French Revolution of the eighteenth century came too late

for such a compromise. It had to face a middle class both angrier
and more advanced, and to face it with a privileged class already
weakened and debauched and a State system already in financial
decay. The French revolutionary leaders could not patch up a
partnership with the old order, though some of them tried. They
had to make a brand-new order; and inevitably they made it on
the basis of the forces which they had led to victory. France proclaimed the principle of democracy, of a democracy in which there
was to be no privileged order at all, but only a full recognition of
the political rights of man, among which the right to property un-
burdened by feudal exactions seemed the most self-evident of all.

France, under the duress of war, slipped back into absolutism; but
it was a new kind of "democratic" absolutism, and the French never
forgot their democratic lesson. They re-affirmed their faith in 1830,
in 1848, and again after 1870, when an assembly of monarchists had
perforce to proclaim a parliamentary Republic. By that time there
were new models on which such a Republic could be based. The
American Republic, too young in 1789 to serve as a model, had
grown to full stature; and Great Britain had applied the revolutionary teaching in her own reformist way.

Great Britain was, indeed, the first country consciously to re-make
her political institutions in the light of capitalist needs. The Americans had made their Republic, not for Capitalism, but on the only
lines possible for a country which had hardly any aristocracy and
had cast off its monarch. Political democracy arose there in default
of any possible alternative, though all that could be done to check
it was done by placing the interpretation of a nearly rigid Constitution in the hands of the Courts. This system turned out to suit
admirably the needs of expanding American Capitalism; but it was
not devised with this object, save to the extent to which the constitutional needs of large-scale Capitalism are the same as those of
private enterprise in far more rudimentary forms.

Great Britain, on the other hand, did definitely re-fashion the
Constitution of 1688 in order to bring it into line with industrial
Capitalism. Nor was this done without a struggle. Aristocratic Society, which had been able easily enough to assimilate a limited
number of wealthy merchants, could not use the same methods in
coming to terms with the far larger horde of industrial capitalists—
often uncouth "self-made" men—who were being raised to riches

by the new processes of production. These newcomers had to force their way to social and political recognition, against the resistance of a privileged class wise enough, and already diluted enough by commercial admixture, not to resist to the end. The Reform Act of 1832 gave the industrial capitalists their Charter without a revolution, and therefore with the minimum of stirring up of the classes still left in subjection. For, whereas Revolution brings all the social forces into play, reform does not.

Because the old governing class gave way in time, the Great Britain of 1832 was able to stop short of political democracy, and to maintain the exclusion of the workers from voting rights. It took four more Reform Acts and nearly a hundred years to complete the advance to universal suffrage. But why, it may reasonably be asked, were these further advances made at all? Why did the urban workers get the vote in 1867, the village workers in 1884 and the women in 1918 and 1928? Why did not Capitalism, having won political power, keep the power to itself? Why resort to a system clearly capable of being used against capitalist interests, and certain to intensify the pressure for social services and increased taxation of the rich?

Anyone who maintains that parliamentary democracy is the form of political organisation most appropriate to Capitalism must be prepared to answer these questions.

CAPITALISM AND PARLIAMENT

In relation to British conditions, the answers are not difficult to find. The Reform Act of 1832 did not hand over all power to the industrial capitalists; it only admitted them to share with the older aristocracy. Nor did the capitalists form a homogeneous group; and the more "democratic" small capitalists wanted reinforcement against the tendency of the greater to go over too much to the aristocratic point of view. The Radical capitalists, led by John Bright, hoped to be able to lead the upper artisans against the surviving elements of aristocracy. Hence the parliamentary support for reform which led up to the Act of 1867. True, the reform was granted in the end by Disraeli, supported by Bright, against the more reactionary Whigs; for Disraeli hoped, by giving what was bound to be given, rather than opposing it, to get some of the new voters on his side. The Act of 1884 came from the Liberals, and was the logical complement of that of 1867; for when once the vote had been extended to a large section of the workers, it was natural for the more "democratic" of the capitalist parties to seek to extend it further. Finally, the women got the vote in 1918, nominally as the reward of their War service, but largely because it was hoped that they would prove, as politically uneducated voters, a more conservative force than the men. A similar motive was behind the concession of the so-called "Flapper Vote" in 1928.

Of course, in securing the extension of the vote the pressure from without of the unenfranchised counts as well as the desire of the representatives of the already enfranchised to broaden their basis of support; and reason as well as interest plays a part. If government is once placed on a basis of parliamentary representation, there exists an institution in which the unenfranchised can claim a share without any structural change in Society; and it becomes very difficult for the opponents of democracy to put forward any plausible case against the gradual extension of the vote. This is the more so because capitalist privilege is not the privilege of a class possessing a defined legal status, nor does the capitalist class form, like earlier privileged classes, a clearly delineated group. Accordingly, under pressure from outside, aided by the more democratic elements already within the circle, the suffrage is extended ever more widely; and the attempts to set up bulwarks against democracy come to take the form of limitations not on the grant of voting rights, but on their effectiveness. The power of elected representatives is curtailed or kept in check by insistence on the non-representative elements in the Constitution, or on representative institutions which can be kept aristocratic, or plutocratic, even when a wide franchise has been conceded for the popular Chamber. Consequently, as we have seen in an earlier section, the existence of universal suffrage does not mean democracy, even in a formal sense; and although it does lead to a change in the activities of the State and to an extension in the scope of the social services, it has shown itself to be fully consistent with the maintenance of Capitalism as long as Capitalism remains healthy and progressive in an economic sense.

Representative parliamentary institutions of a quasi-democratic nature were essential to the development of the capitalist system in the nineteenth century; for only by means of them could the capitalists re-shape State policy in accordance with their needs. In Great

Britain, for example, the aristocratic Parliament of landowners which existed up to 1832 could never have been persuaded to repeal the Corn Laws, or to introduce Free Trade. Nor could it have been persuaded to leave industry alone in internal matters, when industrial development appeared to threaten landowners' rights. In France, Capitalism could not grow till it had thrown off the regulative shackles of the *ancien régime*. In Germany, where feudalism retained more strength, the industrialists needed the *Reichstag* to help them drive a tolerable bargain with the Junkers. In Russia, where feudalism remained in control, Capitalism was only able to develop at all in patches, and in face of tremendous obstacles. In the United States, on the other hand, Capitalism, well armed with representative institutions, encountered no obstacles when once the vexed question of slavery, and of the "planter" interest, had been cleared out of the way. Parliamentarism, despite its opening of the gates to the demand for social reform—which was effectively checkmated in America by the Federal Constitution and the powers of the Supreme Court—provided a political machine which nineteenth-century Capitalism found excellently adapted to its needs.

This was even more because parliamentarism kept people out of politics than because it drew them in. The vote was not only a political right, but also a buffer between the Government and the mass of the citizens. If the citizens did not like what the Government was doing, they could always be told that they had their constitutional remedy, and referred to the next General Election or to their local representative, who would have no difficulty in explaining to them his individual impotence. The next General Election, however, would prove in fact a useless instrument for remedying most of the grievances of the electors. It would have to be fought between organised parties, on issues on which these parties agreed to differ; and at most on only a very few out of the many issues interesting to different sections of the electorate. The electors would be able only to choose between parties, and not to press for particular measures; and there would be no means of forcing to the front issues on which the leading parties were at one. Nor could the electors, save rarely, do much to push their particular points of view within the parties; for the parties themselves were not democratic, and got their policies from above rather than from below.

The partial remedy for this situation lay in creating, outside the party machines, voluntary propagandist organisations devoted to the advocacy of some particular measure or to some particular subject. Voluntary Societies of many different kinds have indeed, in the parliamentary countries, gone very much further towards the realisation of democracy in their limited spheres of activity than the more narrowly political institutions. In parliamentary countries, and especially in Great Britain, this type of voluntary organisation was, in the nineteenth century, by far the most effective agent of political pressure from below. The Anti-Corn-Law League is the outstanding example of its success; and the methods of the League have been used again and again for every sort of purpose. But to-day they have lost much of their effect. For they depend for their success on being able to put their demands into a form in which they can be embodied in an Act of Parliament, or some similar legislative measure, and carried by themselves without upsetting the rest of the social structure. When demands become so far-reaching that they cannot be dealt with in this way, they can find expression only in the creation of a party seeking political power, and not of a propagandist society seeking to get its claim satisfied through the existing parties. Moreover, when divisions of opinion become so sharp as to affect the whole structure of Society, even secondary reforms come to be identified in men's minds with primary differences; so that projects inoffensive in themselves are resisted because they are regarded as leading towards larger changes. An outstanding example of this is the changed attitude of the British Parliament towards municipal trading. As long as the Capitalist parties were not seriously afraid of Socialism, it was relatively easy for progressive municipalities to get trading powers; and in some cases Conservative municipalities, such as Birmingham, led the way. But nowadays municipal enterprise is suspect of being "socialistic"; and proposals for its extension are voted down in Parliament, not on their merits, but on this ground.

Consequently, political propaganda comes to be more concentrated in the party machinery, or in societies which are mere auxiliaries of the rival parties; and this further weakens the political influence of the ordinary citizen. Parliament, becoming stiffer and less responsive to outside demands, unless they come up through the machine, loses prestige. It is no longer a case of "men or measures," but a choice between parties standing for rival social systems. But, when that is the case, will men consent to have the issue settled by mere voting, or will they insist on appealing from the vote to some sort of force?

2. ORDER AND LIBERTY

POLITICAL THINKERS have been traditionally divided into two contrasted groups as the apostles of "Order" and "Liberty." Those who uphold the claims of "Order" lay stress on the need for security for the individual citizen and for strength in the body politic as a means of resisting external attack; and they sometimes go further, and proclaim order and discipline imposed upon men as required by the slovenliness and slackness of "human nature." The followers of Hegel advance beyond this point to an assertion that the individual can realise himself only in and through the State, in which his personality finds its highest expression, and that each man should accordingly have his defined place and function within an order imposed by the supreme authority of the State.

Against these doctrines the upholders of "Liberty" proclaim the rights of the individual, both to go his own way as long as what he is doing does not interfere too seriously with the like liberty of others, and to play his part as a citizen in deciding what the policy of Society is to be. The doctrine of political liberty has thus two aspects—personal freedom and collective self-government. But in these two there is a latent antagonism; for the policy upheld by the majority may conflict with the claims of the minority to personal freedom. Libertarians themselves have always been greatly concerned with discussing and delimiting the respective rights of majorities and minorities.

The apostles of "Order," of course, proclaim that their way is the only way of really securing liberty. They urge that only a strong State, able to discipline its individual members, can be in a position to guarantee individual rights. The security of property, the sanctity of contract, the preservation of the "liberty" of the Society itself against the threat of foreign conquest—these are often held up as the benefits to be secured by a powerful State organised above all else for the enforcement of order. The adherents of the doctrine of "Order" are usually pessimists about human nature, or about the natures of most men. They come uppermost at times of acute social disturbance, when the rivalries of factions within Society or the prevalence of war between Societies upsets the established habits of men, and creates a strong demand for an authority powerful enough to enforce obedience upon the factions, and to make the State too formidable to be lightly attacked from without.

Machiavelli's *Prince,* written at a time when men were weary of wars and civil dissensions that seemed to lead to no settled result, is the supreme expression in political theory of the demand for strong government as a means to public security. Hobbes, in his *Leviathan,* makes the same demand for a government proof against the upsets and perils of civil warfare.

LIBERTY AND TOLERATION

"Liberty," on the other hand, waxes popular when men are living under more settled political conditions, and are therefore less afraid. When the general structure of the political and economic system is regarded as fixed, and proof against attack, men turn to the demand for secondary rights within that general structure. They set out not only to make the forms of government more democratic—that is, more responsive to such popular pressure as is consistent with the general character of social relationships—but also to assert a host of special rights for particular sections and interests. Above all, at such times men become more tolerant of differences of practice and opinion; for they do not regard the expression of such differences as menacing the general structure of Society or as involving the danger of civil war.

Tolerance, which is own brother to individual liberty, is the offspring of settled political and social conditions. In England, the eighteenth century was more tolerant than the seventeenth, because the Revolution of 1688 seemed to have settled the general structure of English society for a long time to come. The French Revolution and the great changes in industrial structure brought back political intolerance at the close of the eighteenth century. But after the Reform Act of 1832 and the successful establishment of industrial Capitalism tolerance returned, to be carried much further by John Stuart Mill than it had been by John Locke, and to extend to the legislation of Trade Unions and of Republican agitation as well as to the repeal of the laws discriminating against Dissenters and

Catholics. The gospel of "Liberty" did not advance so far or so fast in most continental countries during the nineteenth century, partly at least because they did not feel the same confidence as Great Britain in the continued security of their established political and economic institutions. Even France, despite the endorsement of "Liberty, Equality and Fraternity," oscillated between tolerance and repression through a succession of revolutions. In Europe, only Great Britain carried personal liberty and political tolerance to the point of permitting wide freedom of discussion and dissent, because only Great Britain felt full confidence that her established institutions were proof against serious attack. The United States, at this stage, carried "freedom" even further than Great Britain; for American institutions seemed even more secure until the emancipation of the slaves in the South and the influx of nationalities in the North roused up the spirit of intolerance and created the psychology of "100 per cent Americanism."

Political tolerance, and consequently the willingness to concede "freedom" to the individual or the group within Society, are always limited within the bounds consistent with the security of the established social system. There is always a point at which those in authority in the State will punish and repress rather than tolerate movements that are felt to endanger the basis of Society as it is. The existence of libertarian institutions developed during a period of security may indeed create a powerful prejudice against repression, and make its use harder when at length a fundamental challenge to the established order does arise. But if the challenge is real, the tolerance will be gradually withdrawn, and freedom will be restricted on the plea of national emergency. Or, if the State machine is too deeply committed to tolerance to be used successfully as an instrument of repression, or too much influenced by the forces which it is desired to repress, the upholders of the order which is challenged will resort to unconstitutional methods of defence, and perhaps make a revolution of their own in order to ward off the danger. In one way or another, intolerance will return; for no established social system is tolerant enough to tolerate its own supersession.

INTOLERANCE AND ORDER

The need for "Order" becomes, at such times, the rallying cry of disorderly movements,—*Camelots du Roi,* Storm Troops, *Heim-*

wehren, Dinasos, Fascisti of every sort and kind. Moreover, in periods of crisis, those who have been proclaiming the gospel of freedom also turn into advocates of authority, whenever they see a chance of assuming power themselves. Tolerance then survives only as the protestant doctrine of those who are conscious of being weak; the democratic revolutionaries may aim at re-establishing it some day, but for the time being they have to let it go, because it endangers the success of the revolution. Lenin said that there is nothing so authoritative as revolution; and Communists proclaim the unlimited rights of free speech only when they are not in power.

There is no hypocrisy in this attitude; for when the institutions against which the Communists are fighting claim merit on the ground of their democratic tolerance, the Communists are fully entitled to hold them to their word. But in fact no régime is ever tolerant without limits; and least of all can tolerance of the extremes of political difference be endorsed by revolutionists who are attempting to change the entire basis of the social system. A change of this magnitude is bound to arouse deep passions and resentments, and to set the adherents of the displaced order plotting against the new régime. To tolerate such plottings is out of the question, when the supreme task is to lay the foundations of the new order. Accordingly victorious Communism suppresses anti-Communist criticism no less thoroughly than triumphant Fascism or counter-revolution suppresses the Socialist Movement.

It is, of course, open to argument that, in certain circumstances, this suppression may be unnecessary. If in a period of stable institutions tolerance and respect for law have become so firmly implanted in the minds of the citizens that they refuse to resort to violence, and that even those who are threatened by a change of system will give up their privileges sooner than fight to retain them, some degree of tolerance can be maintained even during a transition from one social system to another. But this has never happened save when, as in Great Britain in 1832, the rival claims of the chief contestants have been capable of being reconciled within a single system broadly satisfactory to them both. The old governing class in Great Britain did not resist parliamentary reform by force; for it was able to make a satisfactory compromise with the industrialists. The slave-owners of the Southern States did fight, because the very institution of slavery was at stake.

The gospel of "Order," which precludes tolerance, is then the appropriate gospel for an epoch of radical transition, whereas "Liberty" blossoms only within the environment of a settled and secure social system. Within a settled system, what sorts of liberty blossom depends on the character of the system itself; for the formal freedoms allowed under law mean in practice very different things according to the social environment in which they are set. Many of the most loudly acclaimed freedoms of to-day are in fact freedoms available only to those whose incomes are large enough to permit them to be enjoyed; and some nominal freedoms are in fact means whereby the very rich are enabled to use their riches for restricting the freedom of others. Freedom of contract has often been invoked by employers to check the alleged "tyranny" of Trade Unions; freedom of movement means something to those who can afford to move, but little to the very poor. Freedom of speech and writing are valuable privileges; but they are apt to be applied very differently in practice to the cultured and to the uncultured agitator or "blasphemer"; and they become also means to the unrestrained unscrupulousness of the millionaire-owned press. Freedom of speech and writing can be used as instruments for organising a mob to howl down opposing speakers, or to suppress a book of allegedly "immoral" tendencies. In effect, the freedoms that are recognised are mainly those which the controlling elements in Society desire and value; and freedoms which do not fit in with this requirement have to make their way against formidable apathy as well as opposition among those who "count" in political affairs.

KINDS OF FREEDOM

Indeed, the public opinion that is hot in defence of one form of freedom is often unable to recognise another, or to accept it as being freedom at all. Because the Russians suppress anti-Communist criticism, and are brutal in their "liquidation" of the surviving elements of the property-owning classes, many people are quite unable to realise how tremendously the Communist victory has liberated thought and speech in a host of other directions, by throwing upon the innumerable "collectives" the responsibility for making the new Society work, and seeking to enlist every available worker as an active citizen playing his part in building up the new conditions of life. Nor, on the other side, do Socialists sufficiently realise that Fascism and Nazism would never have become successful movements with a wide popular following unless they had liberated at any rate some new freedoms in exchange for those which they took away.

To each type of social system corresponds its own conception of freedom, which it sets out to impress upon the mind of the people. While it is still struggling to establish itself it is more alert to suppress opposing freedoms than to assert its own. But if it wins and settles down to enjoy the fruits of victory, it will soon elaborate a code of freedom corresponding to the needs and values of the new Society.

This, however, does not mean that the conflict between "Order" and "Liberty" is merely one of time and appropriateness. There is also a difference of ideal. Of two contending forces, each ready to go to any length in suppressing the other, one may stand for a conception based mainly on Order, and the other for a conception of Liberty. While the two are struggling for mastery, each will be prepared to act in a dictatorial way; but it may make a great deal of difference to Order and Liberty which side wins.

Except in these times of transition, the democrats usually constitute the party of Freedom, and the opponents of democracy, under whatever banner, the party of Order. For, though a democratic majority can tyrannise over a minority, except at moments of acute and fundamental conflict there is not likely to be a majority that wishes to tyrannise. Within a settled form of Society, opinion divides itself, not between majority and minority, but between minorities; for a majority is seldom interested in the same thing. Each section is keener on getting freedom to push its own point of view than on suppressing other views; and in the multiplicity of opinions and interests there is safety for the heretic and the innovator. Democracies are tyrannous only when they are afraid. Settled democracy is the system that provides the best guarantees of personal and group freedom.

THE MIND OF THE MARTINET

This is precisely what makes democracy intolerable to a certain type of mind—the mind of the martinet. The martinet loves symmetry, and democracy is endlessly asymmetrical. The martinet rejects human nature, because as men are different it causes them to react in different ways. When he says " 'Shun!" he wants everyone to go through one identical motion. He has a passion for the parade-ground, for the factory run on the principles of "Scientific Management," for the school that approximates most nearly to the "monitorial" system of Bell and Lancaster. This type of mind is not frequent enough to run the world; but it becomes the executant of interests which want to keep the lower classes in order. It appears everywhere on the side of aristocracy and of vested interest, which use it to discipline the many-headed monster that they fear. For, save at moments when a democratic revolution is fighting for its life, the party of "Order" is also the party of the vested interests. Order is valuable, and valued, as a means of preventing change; and, valued alike by all at times when they feel their established power threatened, it is a continuous necessity only for those whose power depends on keeping an enslaved class or people in subjection. The party of "Liberty" in Great Britain—as long as there was no serious threat to the established order—was able to be at the same time the party of "Order" in India, where the threat was continuously present. British Liberalism dissolved as soon as there was no longer an almost unquestioned social system within which it could work. Any privileged class that is conscious of the need to defend its privileges ranges itself instantly on the side of "Order."

But, in addition to this, the natural adherents of the party of "Order" gravitate inevitably to the side of privilege. For it is easier to keep "Order" in a stratified than in a democratic Society. Social privilege constitutes a body of leaders, on whom the responsibility for maintaining order naturally devolves. It enables a special caste to be trained for leadership, and equips this caste with the requisite power and authority. In a democracy where socially "one man is as good as another" leadership does not disappear; but it has to create itself, untidily and multifariously, by the emergence of leaders from the body of the people and from the various functional groups which they form. Such democratic leadership cannot be mobilised or indoctrinated with the same ease as a ruling caste; nor will its leadership impress the same uniformity and discipline upon the mass. To the martinets, the leadership of democracy will inevitably seem not to be leadership at all.

At times of social stress and conflict, democratic leadership is compelled to take on certain of the qualities which belong by nature to its opposite. Then arise disciplined dictatorships, imposed by a

Lenin or a Mustapha Kemal, which for a period impress uniformity upon the parties through which they work. But this uniformity is compulsory and not congenial. It will not outlast either secure victory or defeat. Correspondingly, in times of conflict the opponents of democracy have, in order to fight it, to put on something of a "demagogic" character, and to admit into their ranks elements that reject their essential ideas. The struggle that is clearly proceeding already in the German National Socialist Party between the Right and the Left is an instance in point. Of the well-known Nazi leaders, Goering, who may be taken as the representative of the Right, is the martinet, the upholder of the traditional Prussian authority, whereas men like Goebbels are agitators of a type more familiar on the side of radicalism than against it. If Goering gets his way the old Prussianism will be restored; if the Left were to win, might not the Nazi *coup* turn even yet into some sort of radical revolution?

From what has been said certain practical conclusions follow. The question is often asked "To what extent should free speech be permitted?" But the question is unanswerable in that form. Freedom of speech and writing is one of the most valuable privileges of a settled social system based on democratic principles. It is indispensable and also natural to such a system. To settled systems based on incomplete democracy, incomplete freedom of speech and writing are likewise appropriate, conferring those limited freedoms which correspond to the limited form of the prevailing "democracy." To undemocratic systems, on the other hand, even when they are firmly settled, freedom of speech is not appropriate, save as a safety valve for secondary discontents. When it passes beyond this limit, it will be repressed, lest it arouse the democratic consciousness.

But neither to a régime of privilege nor to a régime of democracy is freedom of speech and writing appropriate while the decisive struggle is actually going on. For at such times men's first preoccupation is to succeed; and they cannot tolerate in the present freedoms which prejudice their chances. Either will at such times suppress opposition if it can; and the most that can differentiate them is that suppression, being congenial to the adherents of privilege and uncongenial to the democrats, is likely to be practised more ruthlessly by the former. Suppression will, of course, also be pushed further and applied with less reluctance in those countries which have been used to it, such as Russia or Germany, than it will where there has been, relatively, a tradition of political freedom. This tradition does count, to harden or soften the blow; but it is mere Utopianism to expect freedom and tolerance to survive unimpaired in any country where rival social systems are fighting for supremacy.

3. THE PROBLEM OF EQUALITY

EQUALITY has been proclaimed again and again in history as the necessary foundation of a democratic Society. Yet in most senses no one at all supposes that all men are equal. Men differ obviously and profoundly in almost every respect beyond the mere quality of being human beings. They are radically unlike in strength and physical prowess, in mental ability and creative quality, in both capacity and willingness to serve the community, and perhaps most radically of all in power of imagination. Of course, many of the existing inequalities between men are themselves the outcome of inequality—in early nurture, in educational and cultural opportunity, and in sheer provision for physical needs. Inequality of treatment breeds inequality of powers, according to some men the fullest possible development of their faculties and starving others of the means of making their natural qualities effective.

It would, however, be absurd to contend that all inequality among men arises from these causes. Even if all men had equal opportunities, and were born of equally equipped parents, inequalities would persist, both because men would still be born different, and because from the very moment of birth they would be subject to the influence of differing chances and conditions. There will certainly never be a Society consisting of equals, if this means a Society of men and women who are all equal in capacity to do and to serve.

It follows that the advocates of political and social equality cannot be taken as meaning either that all men are, or that all can become, equal in these respects. Social equality means something essentially different from this. It means in effect that, unequal as men are in every possible respect—and all the more because they are unequal—human Societies ought to be organised on a basis that will both avoid as far as possible adding artificial to natural inequalities and recognise the right of each man to have his happiness and well-being considered equally with those of any other in the framing of social policy, subject only to the right of Society to restrict the rights and claims of the individual for the purpose of promoting the greatest happiness and well-being of the greatest number.

This principle has been invoked repeatedly by democrats of many different schools of thought. Most of all it has been proclaimed as the justification for treating all men as "equal before the law," and for the adoption of forms of government resting on the foundation of "one man, one vote." But in no Society as yet have the democrats, even in these respects, ever had matters all their own way. Only in a quite theoretical sense have all men ever been equal before the law; for, even apart from the fact that judges and magistrates can never be wholly without bias in dealing with men of different kinds, the clever man, or the man rich enough to have a clever advocate, is necessarily at an advantage against the stupid or the poor. And in politics, though there have been in many countries governing assemblies chosen practically by universal suffrage, these "popular" assemblies have never been the only governing bodies in the State, nor does universal suffrage work out to secure the reality of equal political rights if it is set in the framework of a Society based on other forms of social inequality.

ECONOMIC INEQUALITY

The real roots of social inequality are mainly economic. It is simply not possible for men to be socially or politically equal as long as there exist among them differences of wealth and income so great as to divide them into distinct economic classes, with widely differing opportunities in childhood to become healthy, educated, travelled, and used to regard the world as a place made to suit their convenience. The slum child is not so healthy as the child whose parents can afford to give it the privileges of good food and sunlight. In the schools, the children of the poorest classes lag behind those who come from better equipped homes. Secondary education is still a privilege reserved for a minority selected mainly on economic grounds. And there is a wide difference, for the most part, between the few who are taught from childhood the arts of command, and the many whose lessons are intended to inculcate rather the duties of obedience and respect for their "betters."

Moreover, there is bound to exist a vast difference of social attitude between those who go through life in a prevailing atmosphere of comfortable economic security and those whose means of living are continually both scanty and insecure. Some among these last will indeed revolt against their condition, and become leaders of radical or revolutionary opinion; but revolt of this sort demands high qualities of personal courage, and far more of the "bottom dogs" of Society will certainly lack both the courage and the ability to stand up against their difficulties, so as to make themselves the equals in power and effectiveness of those who have no similar troubles to face. The few who have both courage and ability will for the most part not remain at the bottom of the social scale. They will climb up to some sort of security, either as leaders of revolt or perhaps by hewing out for themselves a better position within the existing social system. But the less courageous and able will be left, as a mass of social "inferiors" to be played upon by rival emotional appeals from the groups higher up.

In these appeals, money counts. It counts more than ever, as the instruments of propaganda become more numerous and more expensive. The modern newspaper, relying upon advertisements for its revenue, is far more afraid of offending its advertisers than its readers; for the advertisers have both longer memories and longer purses. It costs money to organise the huge electorate of a modern constituency, so that extension of the franchise may even increase the power of the rich over the poor. Moreover, in a Society based on economic inequality, nearly all the established social institutions are deeply impregnated with the ideas of the richer classes, which provide nearly all the leadership. In socially unequal Societies there is an immense weight of tradition on the side of inequality; and those who challenge this tradition come up against powerful obstacles in the minds even of those on whom the traditions press hard. For man is a conservative animal—conservative not only in his desires but also in his passive acceptance of the ills he knows.

These traditions, standing solidly in the way of real political equality, are closely bound up with the inequalities of wealth. For this inequality is, through its influence in selecting the children of the rich and poor for quite different treatment in the formative years of life, a tremendous force perpetuating social differences. Some Societies do indeed allow of movement from one class to another and from one standard of income to another far more easily than others;

and this movement is usually least difficult in young and rapidly developing communities and hardest in old Societies and above all in those in which landed property is the principal kind of wealth. Capitalism, as against feudalism, is in this respect a leveller of established inequalities; but it levels them only to set up new differences in their stead. Young Capitalism permits easier movement from class to class; but it only makes class-divisions less rigid, without making economic inequalities less extreme, and Capitalism growing old tends again to become ossified into class-divisions arising out of the inheritance of wealth and status. It is no longer true, in settled capitalist countries, that it is but three generations "from clogs to clogs"; and, to a startling extent, the children of skilled workers become skilled workers while the children of unskilled labourers join in their turn the ranks of the unskilled.

If we want a Society of social equals, we can hope to build it only on a foundation of economic equality. This is not to say that it is indispensable for all men and women, or all families, to have absolutely equal incomes, or incomes varying only with the size of the family. This may be desirable, in the long run, as the easiest way of solving the problem of distributing the national wealth; but it is not indispensable as the basis of democracy. It will suffice if there are no differences in wealth or income so large as to divide men into separate economic classes, with sharply contrasting standards of existence and habits of social life. For small differences of income among persons whose broad standards of living are the same will not confer on one great power over another, or interfere with their sufficient social equality in other respects—as voters, or before the law, or in their everyday intercourse one with another. But as soon as economic equality exceeds this limit, good-bye to the chance of real fraternity or of truly democratic institutions. Good-bye in fact to the chance of a Society that will take for its essential aim the greatest happiness and well-being of the greatest number.

Even among the relatively poor, objection is often taken to economic equality, even in this modified form, on the ground that it is inconsistent with the principle of rewarding men according to the quality of their service. It is argued that, if this principle is abandoned or limited, there will be no adequate incentive left to make men give of their best. We are not now raising the question whether or not Society will be able some day to dispense altogether with monetary incentives, by finding alternative incentives powerful enough to get the world's work done. But, quite apart from this, there is no evidence that, even if monetary incentives are required, they need be anything like so large as they are in most of the Societies of to-day. For the more equal incomes are, the smaller are the incentives needed to call out special effort. In an equalitarian Society, an extra penny may be as effective as a pound is now. Economic inequality bids up the price of effort, especially among the well-to-do, precisely because the more pounds a man has already the less an additional pound is worth to him.

EQUALITY AND SOCIALISATION

Economic equality, in advanced industrial Societies, can come about only as an outcome of the social ownership of the resources of production. Private ownership of these resources means inequality; it is the foundation on which the major inequalities rest. Therefore, if we want equality, we must socialise.

We must do this, not only in order to get economic equality, but also in order to get social or political equality in any real sense. The pursuit of the greatest happiness and well-being of the greatest number is quite inconsistent with the treatment of the resources of production as the private property of a limited group of citizens. It implies their use as means of promoting the welfare of all. Political democracy cannot be real democracy unless it carries with it real control of the common means of life. For even if all men have votes, they cannot have an equal chance of using their votes aright unless they are tolerably on a level in standards of living, education and culture. When there are rich men and poor men, no merely political devices can prevent the rich from having more influence, man for man, than the poor. Nor can anything stop the rich, or most of them, from cohering together into a class for the preservation of their exclusive claims—from dominating the professions, the schools, the theatres, the newspapers, and from creating a socially stratified type of Society. Only collective control of the resources of production and of the distribution of incomes can prevent these things, which are the inevitable manifestations of a Society based on the recognition of unequal rights.

It is, of course, perfectly true that in any community some must lead, and others follow, that some must occupy the more responsible positions, and others work under orders at the execution of jobs that are largely matters of routine. Nor is it less true that in any community some will be more cultured, imaginative and appreciative of the quality of living than others. But there is no reason why these necessary differences should divide men into social or economic classes. A clever man and a stupid man, a strong man and a weak man, do not belong to different classes by virtue of inequalities of these kinds. Let the Squire's son be a fool; he is nevertheless the Squire's son, and accounted a gentleman. In a Society based on economic equality there will be wise and foolish, saints and knaves, heroes and "poor fish"; but there will be no classes. Nor will there be any reason why the leader should have a bigger income than the led, unless he has bigger needs, or continues to require a somewhat bigger financial incentive, at any rate for a time.

The idea that doing a more responsible job confers membership of a superior class is the outcome of two forces—the system of private ownership, which causes inequality to run like a thread through the entire texture of Society, and the survival of social concepts left over from an earlier phase, in which class distinctions were based on blood and heredity. Industrial Society puts the axe to the root of the old class differences; and it is able to make new ones in their image only because it recognises the claims of private property in the means of production, and so sanctifies the quest for wealth. In place of the old aristocracy it puts plutocracy. But whereas shreds of the old aristocracy have survived the victory of the plutocrats, because aristocracy has *some* basis in good blood, nothing is left of plutocracy when its wealth is taken away. A Society without classes can emerge naturally and easily out of the process of socialisation.

A classless Society, however, does not mean a Society without leaders. It means rather one in which every citizen becomes for the first time eligible for leadership, if he has the power to lead. It means a Society in which everyone is given, as far as possible, the chance to develop this power, by the widest possible diffusion of educational opportunities in the broadest sense, and by keeping the career wide open to talents of every useful kind. It is often said that a community of equals will not allow itself to be led. But in fact most men are, in most things, very willing to be led, and more in danger of giving their leaders too much than too little authority, especially if they are free to choose them and assured that the leaders cannot exploit them for personal economic advantage. Leadership, so far from disappearing, will come into its own in a truly democratic Society. But it is likely to be a more diffused leadership than we are used to; for a better nurtured people will have more citizens with strong wills and minds of their own, wishful to lead, some in politics, some in industry, and some in the professions and in the arts of life.

This is the idea of a classless Society. Some will reject it as contrary to their interests, some as Utopian and against "human nature." For there are some who deny, in deed if not in word, that the aim of Society should be to promote the greatest happiness and welfare of the greatest number, and others who hold, with pessimistic honesty, that most men must be driven and not led. Only with the pessimists need we be concerned to argue; and with them our difference, at bottom, is incapable of being resolved by argument. We say to them that human history has furnished again and again abundant proofs of the capacity of everyday people to rise to appeals transcending their immediate private interests, though often these appeals have only availed to lead them astray. Even the Nazis have risen to power by playing upon men's willingness to respond to leadership, and have owed part of their success to a specious summoning of their followers to sacrifice and an ideal of brotherhood. The Russians, to better purpose, have mobilised on the side of their vast experiment far less men's greed or hate than their will to strive and to serve. Class-inequality poisons the appeal to service, polluting it with racial hatred and nationalistic passion. Only a classless Society can make the simple appeal to all to join together in the common task of raising the entire standard of human living. To get political equality we must get equality in the economic sphere. To get economic equality we must get socialisation.

4. WORK AND LEISURE

IN ANY SOCIETY, the amount of work that is done embodies a compromise between the desire for goods and the desire for leisure. When Society is divided into classes, the ruling class habitually claims for itself a monopoly of leisure, and tries to make the subject classes work as hard as possible to provide it with the means to a high standard of living. The amount of work which a ruling class is able to exact varies with the climate, with the available opportunities for the employment of labour, and with the habits and traditions established in the Society in question. Equally the amount and kind of work that the ruling class is itself prepared to perform differs greatly from one Society to another. In modern civilisation, the advance of Capitalism has been accompanied by a marked decline in the work done by the women in the superior classes, above all since the factory system has transferred to industry a great deal of work that used to be done in the home. In industrial civilisations the men of the ruling class constitute less than in earlier civilisations a leisure class; for economic administration has at length come to be regarded as a work fit for "gentlemen," who have consented to take out their claim to leisure vicariously in the persons of their wives and daughters. As Thorstein Veblen has pointed out, this vicarious leisure satisfies the desire for superiority, and permits the male to find in business an escape from the boredom of a world in which hunting and warfare can no longer furnish full-time unproductive occupation for a ruling class. But in the most advanced phases of industrialism the women, becoming bored with their leisure, force their way into professional work. The women's movement has been mainly the creation of middle-class women who had too little to do, and wanted an outlet for their abilities, and not of the women workers in industry or of overworked working-class housewives.

Leisure can be defined, negatively, as escape from the necessity of productive labour or, positively, as activity of an economically unproductive kind. The negative definition is evidently the more inclusive; for it is possible to pass time in doing nothing at all. It is even possible to feel a craving for leisure of this sort, either as a relief from past overwork or from sheer vacancy of mind. But the leisure which most people chiefly desire for themselves is the freedom to do something else—something different from the job at which they make their living. This leisure can be enjoyed only if the hours of enforced labour are not so long or so exhausting as to leave the worker mentally or physically fagged out. A minority of persons may find in their jobs so much satisfaction as to desire no leisure for anything else beyond the minimum periods required for rest or recreation. But this applies only to a few—to some artists, and to a minority of business men, professionals and administrators who are completely "wrapped up" in their jobs. It certainly does not apply to the vast majority who, even if they do not dislike their work, as many do, still feel that they have more than enough of it, and could well do with more time to devote to more congenial pursuits.

Under existing economic systems, except in Russia, the amounts of work and leisure are determined by the rival pulls of conflicting interests. The workers, especially where they are organised in Trade Unions, struggle for a shorter working day, both by industrial action and by demanding protective legislation, such as Factory Acts; and there is also a continuous conflict in the workshops between the employers' desire to speed up the pace and increase the intensity of labour and the workers' resistance to over-drive and "scientific management" of the labour process. Where Capitalism invades the less developed countries, the workers are usually too weak to resist a very long working day; but the capitalist has to struggle ceaselessly to overcome the "natural laziness" of the "nigger," and to induce workers unaccustomed to the discipline of industrialism to come up to the pace and regularity of labour in the more advanced countries. For even unorganised workers have a great natural power of resistance to being speeded up. That, incidentally, is one reason why slave labour has usually been found to be inefficient. You can drive a slave to the factory, or the plantation; but you cannot make him work hard, except when the overseer's eye is upon him.

In advanced industrial countries the workers have met with considerable success in limiting the hours of labour; and though a part of what they gain is continually being taken back from them by the intensification of the labour process, especially in times of depression when Trade Unionism is relatively weak, they have on the whole made real and solid gains. These gains have an important effect on men's minds. Success in enlarging the time of leisure creates a demand for the means of employing that leisure, and therefore stimulates the desire for a higher standard of life. The less men labour at producing economic goods and services, the more such goods and services they demand. The expansion of industry has been of late most marked in those branches of production which chiefly satisfy the needs of leisure.

Fortunately, the vast expansion of industrial productivity in recent times makes the demand for additional leisure fully compatible, in the advanced countries, with the demand for a higher standard of living. But clearly these two demands cannot be pressed indefinitely without coming into conflict. They are simultaneously expansible only within a system in which productivity is increasing fast enough to provide for both.

If this were the only limit, it would clearly be possible to satisfy both claims in a very high degree. But a further limit is set by the internationally competitive character of the capitalist system. For if one country outruns others in conceding higher wages and shorter hours, it is unable to compete in the world market, so that its factories stand idle, its workers lose their employment and their wages, and necessary imports have to be restricted because they cannot be paid for with exports. Because of these conditions, the capitalist world is signally failing to take advantage of expanding productivity so as to increase the amplitude of both economic wealth and leisure; and the demand for more leisure does become, within the limits of Capitalism, inconsistent with the demand for a higher standard of life.

If, however, we think in terms not of a capitalist country acting within an internationally competitive system, but of a self-contained community concerned only to strike the right balance between the claims of higher production and leisure, it becomes at once evident that a decision has somehow to be made between these two. Such a community can have more leisure by producing less goods, or more goods by accepting less leisure. If the community in question is really democratic, clearly this question, which affects the entire people, falls to be decided by democratic means. It is for those who are chosen to represent on this point the will of the whole population to make the best reconciliation between the rival claims, according to the relative strength of the demands for more leisure and for a higher standard of life.

If the community in question is not self-contained, but has to export goods in exchange for imports, the question remains the same. Let us suppose it to be, like Russia, a Socialist Society with a public monopoly of foreign trade. Then its problem is to determine up to what point it is proposed to go on working to produce exports in order to get imports in return. But its position differs from that of a capitalist country in that it need not produce its exports under competitive conditions as to cost. It can sell them abroad for what they will fetch, use the proceeds to buy foreign goods, and then price these goods at whatever is necessary to cover the costs of the exports for which they have been exchanged. This sort of trading is often denounced by capitalist traders and Governments as "unfair"—as it has been by Mr. Bennett in the case of Russian timber imports into Great Britain—but it is clearly the appropriate form of trading for a Socialist country. It is "unfair" only in the sense that it is not based on capitalist principles.

In a Socialist community, the problem of work *versus* leisure thus presents itself in a simplified form, as the plain confrontation of the demand for more leisure with that for a higher standard of life. In capitalist countries the problem is obscured because, as there is no social control of the distribution of incomes, there is really no such thing as *the* standard of living. The question is not whether all shall work harder or less hard, and so all enjoy either more goods or more leisure, but also in part how hard one section of the community shall be compelled to work in order to provide both more goods and more leisure for another section, and also in order to stand up to the competition of other capitalist countries and so avoid unemployment. Of course, even in capitalist countries, when the workers work harder they usually get some part of the benefit accruing from larger production; but this depends upon the conditions of international competition, and it usually means that the benefit is less than proportionate to the rise in productivity. Moreover, under competitive Capitalism, increased output by some workers often means unemployment for others.

Under these conditions, the problem of work and leisure cannot possibly be faced in a rational way. It is ludicrous that, in view of the increase in productivity, either a far higher standard of living or a far larger leisure has not been secured in every developed country. But only an economic system that sets the community free to use all its productive resources to the full, up to the limit set by the demand for leisure, can enable the problem to be solved. That is to say, only a Socialist system.

It is no answer to object that in Socialist Russia the workers' standard of living is lower than in most of the advanced countries. Of course it is; for Russia is economically still a backward country, still at the beginning of the "industrial revolution" through which Great Britain began to pass at least two centuries ago. Moreover, the Russians, in an endeavour to speed up the process of development

and thus make possible a far higher standard of living, are deliberately lowering their present standards of consumption in order to
secure a rapid accumulation of capital—a fact which, incidentally,
answers those who have been accustomed to dismiss Socialism on the
ground that a Socialist community would never agree to "save."
Russia is still poor to-day; but she is the only country that can rest
assured that there will be no lack of consuming power, however fast
her productivity may advance.

In Russia to-day the need for more goods is so pressing as for the
time to push the demand for leisure into the background. But the
demand for leisure will recur, as fast as the more urgent demands for
goods are satisfied. With it will come another problem—that of the
quality, as well as of the amount, of labour. Much of the work that
men are called upon to do is terribly monotonous, and a good deal
positively unpleasant. The irksomeness of these types of labour grows
greater as men become better educated and more fastidious about the
quality of life. In any democratic community this question of the
character of the labour-process is bound to become important. Men
will insist more and more that machinery shall be used, not only so
as to increase the output of goods, but also so as to lighten and make
less irksome the process of making them. Clearly if as much attention
were paid to this use of machinery as has been paid to it as a means
of reducing costs, it would be possible to lighten immensely the burden of labour, quite apart from any reduction of the working hours.

To a certain extent, however, men will have to choose between
processes which are productive but monotonous, and others which
are less irksome but also less productive. But if hours of labour can
be greatly reduced and far more holidays be afforded—and there is
no reason why a Society able to use all its productive resources without stint (save of human overwork) should not afford them both—
the monotony of certain forms of labour will become far less important. For some workers mind monotony far less than others; and
enough will choose monotonous jobs if these carry with them larger
claims to leisure.

So far leisure has been spoken of as if it would be wholly unproductive of economic goods. But there is no reason why this should
be the case. When once a Society has solved the general problem of
poverty and also made leisure more abundant for all, far more persons than now will devote a part of their leisure to the making of

things which it gives them positive pleasure to make, or positive pleasure to use when they have made them. To-day, many people spend their leisure in gardening, partly because they like gardening, and partly because they like flowers and fruit and fresh vegetables. Many paint or write, or make wireless sets or tinker with machinery for pleasure; and every diminution of the hours of compulsory labour extends the range of these "spare-time" occupations. A democratic Society which has got past the problem of poverty may be relied upon to devote itself to a far greater extent to spare-time production, which will be likely, as its scope expands, to impinge more and more upon the factory, substituting the products of individual choice and enjoyment for mass-produced goods over all that field in which the individual product does really possess a satisfying superiority. The spread of cheap electrical power will help on this development, making it easier for the "hobby" to result in a workmanlike product appreciated by the user as well as by the maker.

Meanwhile, despite the ever-increasing power to produce every class of commodities, from the raw products of agriculture to the most highly finished industrial goods, our Societies continue to condemn the majority of their citizens either to continuous and irksome employment which leaves them with scant capacity for the use of leisure, or to soul-destroying unemployment that is the very antithesis of leisure, because it denies them the means to use the idle time. For, on the conditions involved in competitive Capitalism, the problem is insoluble. It demands for its solution a democratic community collaborating to make the best use of the opportunities for wealth and leisure which its expanding productive powers afford.

BOOK VI

THE FUTURE

1. POLITICAL BEHAVIOUR

MEN's political behaviour needs to be studied in two aspects—their attitude to the Government and other kinds of social machinery, and their participation in these things. Naturally, how men behave in both these ways depends very greatly on the political system under which they live. The citizen of a parliamentary country, unless he is an active politician, thinks of his participation in politics first and foremost as the exercise of a right to vote, either for one representative assembly or for several, and only in a much less immediate way as a power to bring pressure to bear upon the Government by means of voluntary organisation and agitation. The politically minded citizen, on the other hand, probably thinks first of all of the voluntary organisations in which he plays a part, of his party and other bodies to which he belongs, and of his own activities in political discussion and propaganda. If he is not merely an active politician, but an elected person or public official, he thinks first of all of the body he works in, and its place in the life of the community.

But when men think of politics they think not only of their participation, great or small, but also of the political machine as something apart from themselves and their personal or group activities. In parliamentary countries they have a picture in their minds of the Government as the executive of the country, carrying out its decisions through the Civil Service, and initiating policy before the Parliament, and, in a less immediate sense of Town and County Councils and their officials, of the Law Courts and the Police. In monarchies or republics dominated by a powerful figure, they have also an active sense of the head of the State, either as a ceremonial figure clothed with immense social prestige and claiming loyalty, or, with less of this kind of prestige, as a positive leader and director of policy.

When unwilling national or social minorities are subject to a State to which they feel no sense of loyalty or kinship, this vision of the political machine appears as a vision of a hostile power, an embodiment of oppressive force, even if it is also in some degree a dispenser of services. The same attitude may exist among men whose hostility to the State is not that of a subject race, but rather of an oppressed class repudiating entirely the moral claims of the prevailing social system to their allegiance. The Russian proletariat had learnt to feel that way about Tsardom. It had not lost its sense of being Russian; but it did not connect its national sentiment with the Tsarist State.

NATIONALISM AND WAR

In time of war, most men's political consciousness undergoes an important change. Except the groups that stand out against the war, on political or religious grounds, they come to think of the State far more as a Society coincident with the nation, and as far less external to themselves. In varying degrees, war upsets their normal ways of living, and brings home to them the idea of national unity. It does not greatly matter from this point of view whether the cause of their Government is good or bad, or whether the constitution of the State is democratic or not, provided that it has not so estranged their sympathies as to destroy in them all sense of loyalty towards it. Most men have hitherto rallied in time of war even to States to whose Governments they have been antagonistic in time of peace. This was seen very clearly in the behaviour of the various Socialist Parties in 1914. National sentiment proved, even among most Socialists, too strong for international class-solidarity to stand out against it; and opposition within the various countries revived only gradually, as the war dragged on, and weariness and disillusionment began to encroach on the original sense of national solidarity.

The sentiment of nationalism is very strong in the minds of most unpolitically minded people; but it attaches itself to the State machine only at times when men feel that the nation is in danger. That it can be raised against elements within the nation, especially if they can be accused of internationalism, as well as against foreign countries, the experience of Italy and Germany has plainly shown; and, in a far less degree, the British General Strike of 1926 acted upon a section of the British people in the same way. But, except when a sense of threat to the nation can be instilled into men's minds, the unpolitical part of Society does not habitually identify the nation with the State machine. It tends to think of the State as "them" rather than "us," though even in times of peace it tends largely to identify the national foreign policy with the whole people. For the foreigners are always "they"; and, in relation to foreign Governments, the home Government turns into "we."

ORDINARY MEN'S POLITICS

It is easiest to leave over for separate consideration the psychology of war-time, and to discuss first of all the political attitude of the ordinary citizen in normal times. The first thing to observe about him is that he gives very little thought or attention to political affairs. He may read about them in the paper, and discuss them to a certain extent with his friends and acquaintances; but he has not been used to taking them very seriously as a matter closely concerning himself, in which he is under any necessity to take a continuous interest. Politics is for most people something rather remote, uninteresting in most of its incidents and in its mechanisms, and not a matter of continuous concern even during an election, though then political interest of a diluted sort does spread over a larger proportion of the citizens than at other times. Of course, there is always a politically-minded minority; but of them we are not speaking now.

This normal political indifference exists among all classes. Naturally, some sections of the population are led by their circumstances to pay a closer attention to politics than others, especially when the nature of their occupations, or lack of these, brings them into constant contact with the activities of the Government. But, even so, the interest displayed is often narrowly sectional. It is difficult for an unemployed man, if he has been long out of work, not to take an interest in the "Means Test"; but it by no means follows that he will be in other respects a keen politician. A publican may take a deep interest in the Licensing Laws, or a bookie in the laws about betting, and yet have little further political interest. Burglars, though their profession brings them into constant relation to the State, are a highly unpolitical body of men. Nor are the gaols peopled by ardent law reformers, but rather by persons whose views on politics are sketchy and conventional.

It is tempting to say that the working class is more politically minded than other classes, because it alone has succeeded in building up political parties on a broad basis of popular membership. But, while it is true that the working class has, in most advanced countries, a larger and more active politically-minded minority than other classes, this does not mean that the majority is conscious of any sustained political interest. It has a sense of class-solidarity, but that sense is largely instinctive rather than fully conscious and rationalised; and for this reason it does not lead to a continuous political consciousness. In other classes too it takes a crisis to turn instinctive class-solidarity into organised political activity. But the wealthier classes, being smaller in number and more highly educated, are easier to rally when the occasion occurs. Their class-solidarity under attack, in defence of their vested interests, is even more marked than that of the workers. Moreover, it is harder to rally men to attack than to defence; and normally the workers are, in modern capitalist society, the attacking party.

This lack of continuous political interest among the main body of the citizens lies at the root of the operation of political systems. These systems, to the extent to which they profess to be democratic, have been built for the most part on the assumption that man is a political animal, who will be prepared to take his politics seriously. Actually, parliamentary systems, like other more autocratic systems of government, work as they do because this assumption is unreal. Under parliamentary conditions, the influence of the politically minded minority is continually kept in check by the power of leaders to appeal over its head to the unpolitical majority, which is affected far more by slogans than by arguments, and can often be successfully stampeded by skilful propaganda. The minority has, man for man, far more influence than the majority; but between differing elements in the minority comes the political leader, with his power of appeal to the rest of the population. Minorities eager to fight out a dispute to a decisive issue are often checkmated by politicians who would much prefer to shelve an awkward question. Where most of the leaders agree in wishing to shelve a question they can usually succeed, as long as they can keep the social machine running efficiently enough to feed the people. But when the social machine breaks down, the unpolitical majority is largely compelled to line up behind one element or another of the minority. For, as we have seen, nothing so quickly turns the mass of people into political animals as the denial of the means of life.

ACTIVE MINORITIES

In parliamentary countries, the rival political minorities are always trying to catch the attention and support of the non-political majority, and to get it at least passively on their side. Each minority wants votes, and wants to prevent votes being given to its opponents. It uses rational political arguments, as well as irrational appeals, in its propaganda; and in both it tries to appeal to sentiment as well as intelligence. In practice, the more rational appeals are usually successful rather in enlarging the minority, and so making the propaganda more persuasive, than in convincing the majority; and more votes are won by irrational than by rational methods. But perhaps that is more true of Great Britain and America than of France, which has a more widely diffused political education. It is, however, plainly true of Germany, despite the high level of German education; for the Germans are politically a sentimental people.

The art of the political propagandist is thus only half a rational art. Indeed, political propaganda has two objects and two methods, though they are often not kept distinct, and of course cannot be completely distinguished. The enlargement of the conscious minority and the impregnation of the apathetic majority demand widely different techniques; but both are essential to the success of a political party. For the party needs both missionaries and a widely diffused support; and it has to angle for the two in largely different ways.

It is improbable that any political system will ever succeed in turning the majority of men for long into politically-minded persons. The wide diffusion of political activity is essentially a phenomenon of social conflict and transition. As soon as men feel certain that any régime has come to stay, a large number of them will cease to take any continuous interest in its working. Of course, some systems will tend to produce much larger politically-minded minorities than others; and those who really believe in democracy hold that the political system ought to be so devised as to elicit the largest possible amount of active interest and co-operation. But even the most democratic system will not, if once it has settled down, get more than a minority of its citizens to take a continuous political interest. Most of them will have other fish to fry; and it takes all sorts to make a democratic world, fully as much as any other.

The parliamentary system, despite its apparently democratic nature, has not been so designed as to stimulate continuous political interest over a wide section of the population. Rousseau said that the English people were free but once every seven years; and a man who has to wait even five years between moments of freedom cannot be expected to be well equipped to use his freedom when the time arrives. The Russian Soviet system appears to go much further than parliamentarism in endeavouring to stimulate continuous political activity, both because it puts a continuous weight of necessary political work upon all the members of a huge organised party and because the Soviets themselves and the other public organs of the Soviet system are being constantly renewed by fresh elections and are constantly engaged in collective debate on public affairs, in which a vastly larger number of persons has the chance to join in than in any parliamentary country. This ceaseless buzzing of the Soviet system is, of course, partly due to the fact that it is still in the ferment of a great social transition; and its activity may tend to atrophy when the régime has been got securely on its feet. But the Russians, in multiplying collective institutions exercising some element of public authority, are in part deliberately creating the machinery for eliciting the greatest possible total of active attention to political affairs. That is what is meant when it is said that Russia, under dictatorship, is the most democratically organised social community in the world.

POLITICS IN RUSSIA

Of course, this all-pervasive activity of the "collective" is the outcome, not merely of a change in political machinery, but essentially of a change in social system. The Russian State, being Socialist, has far more to do than any other State, and needs far more institutions for the carrying on of its work. In Russia, politics has a far wider range than in any other country. Moreover, the disappearance of class-distinctions, except the surviving distinction between the peasantry and the urban population, which the Communists are trying to abolish as fast as they can, removes an enormous obstacle in the way of collective action and discussion. Where every man is a partner in Society, and everything that can be so organised is organised as a branch of the public service, there is the maximum of opportunity for eliciting widespread and continuous political activity.

POLITICS AND THE SOCIAL SYSTEM

The idea which men have of politics is to a great extent a product of the social system under which they live. Other things being equal, the narrower the functions of government are, the less reason is there why most people should take much interest in them. Of course, this does not apply when men have a particular reason for taking an interest, as when they are being specially oppressed, or very heavily taxed, as may happen equally whether the functions of the State are broad or narrow. Apart from this factor, the broadening of State functions obviously tends to stimulate public interest in politics; for each extension of State activity turns into political what were previously private concerns, and thus attracts to public affairs some interest that was previously outside the political range. This does not mean that the same amount of interest as was aroused before will now take a political form; for the State, in taking over an activity, sometimes makes its operation largely automatic, so that interest in it is no longer much required or easily aroused. It is one of the functions of "socialisation" thus to render automatic those necessary services which can be done efficiently by routine, and to save ordinary people from bothering their heads about them. It will be a blessed day when most of the elementary aspects of providing for our economic needs have been so "rationalised" that we no longer need normally to think about them at all, and are free to devote our energies to other aspects of the art of living.

But this process of "rationalisation" is bound to be gradual, though the advance of productivity is bringing it constantly more within our reach. In general, the functions assumed by the State, or carried on under public control, will be services in which there is room for differences of policy and for active interest by others besides the persons actually engaged in their performance. Consequently, the widening of public activity will usually tend to increase political interest.

This is true above all when the operation of vital services becomes directly a public affair. The large extension of municipal activities in housing has been a very important factor in increasing the public interest in local government; and the growth of nationally administered social services has similarly made a larger section of the people interested in national politics.

There is, however, a further factor. The growth of interest depends not only on the extent and character of the services taken under public control, but also on the way in which they are administered. There is a tendency nowadays, whenever a new service is taken over, to entrust the management to some sort of "non-political" corporation or board, in order to remove it as far as possible from the "danger" of political interference with its work. But, while it is doubtless desirable to check political interference with details of management, the political interest of the ordinary man cannot be aroused unless he is given a chance of making his voice heard in relation to the conduct of public services. To desire to exclude this interference is to seek to prevent democratic control, and to damp down political interest. It may be true that the traditional method of question and occasional debate in Parliament is not a satisfactory method of enabling the ordinary citizen to influence policy—an object for which these methods are in fact mainly ineffective. But the remedy, if we want democracy, is not to abandon the right of interference, but to change its form.

REAL DEMOCRACY

This can be done, to some extent, by providing in connection with each socialised service effective machinery through which both those interested as consumers and still more the main body of the workers engaged in it can constantly influence and criticise managerial policy. But it depends not only on machinery, but far more on diffusing through the entire range of public services a spirit of co-operative activity and constructive criticism, so that every worker or group of workers will feel that their work counts and that the responsibility for improving the quality of the service rests upon them, as a personal and group responsibility. Observers of Russian economic conditions notice more than anything else the extent to which the spirit of constructive criticism, made possible by social equality, pervades every branch of Russian industry under the new conditions.

The existence of this spirit is important not only for the well-being of industry, but also for the quality of the entire political system. For men who are encouraged to develop and criticise their own branch of the public service will also be most likely to take an active interest in the working of other branches, and in politics generally as the sum-total of these services.

Socialism, which turns all vital services into public services, is therefore calculated to rouse the collective political consciousness of the community more than any other system, especially if it is in effect a democratic Socialism which sets out deliberately to diffuse responsibility in the widest possible way, and to enlist as many as possible of the citizens in the positive work of government. This involves not merely democratic political institutions, which may come to be the least part of the matter, but the establishment of democratic machinery and a democratic spirit in every branch of social and economic service. The insistence on this need was above all else the strength of Guild Socialism.

For democracy is a quality, not of some particular aspect of social organisation, but of all. A democratic system cannot be made merely by creating a democratic parliamentary machine—though even that is a thing no parliamentary country has ever really done—but only by making democracy permeate every aspect of social life. Obviously this is impossible under Capitalism; for the very relation between capitalist and workman is a denial of democratic equality. Nor can it be done under a State Socialist régime, which centralises authority in the hands of the Government and its executive servants. It can be done only in a classless Society that sets out deliberately to diffuse responsibility as widely as possible, and therefore both allows the widest scope for "functional" self-government and encourages criticism from below in every sphere. There is no real freedom or democracy in any society in which a man cannot, even in obeying those in charge of his work, fearlessly tell them when they are making fools of themselves, and make suggestions as a social equal for the improvement of the service in which he is engaged.

If our object is to get democracy, this is the type of Society we must set up. We shall not, even under these conditions, cause all men to become politically-minded; nor need we even wish to make them so. We shall, however, succeed in widening enormously both the range and the depth of political interest in the community. We shall get more people actually caring about politics and trying to understand them; and we shall ensure that anyone who does want to take an interest will be encouraged to play his part, instead of being deterred by a political machine which regards his interference as an evil, and wants to restrict his opportunities as narrowly as can be. Of course, if we do not want real democracy, we shall not try to set up this sort of Society; but anyone who calls himself a democrat, and does not aim at a Society of this kind, is either an idiot or a hypocrite.

We can now come back to the original point of this chapter. The extent to which men are interested in politics, and actively participate in them, depends on a complex series of factors. Other things being equal, political interest is greater when social conditions are unstable than when they are relatively settled. Other things being equal, political interest tends to increase with every widening of the sphere of public activity and enterprise. Other things being equal, economic equality makes for a widening and deepening of political interest. Finally, political interest is largely a conditioned response to stimuli which the social system can be designed to maximise or to minimise; and it will tend to be greatest where the greatest efforts are made to call it out, not merely through a single political machine, but in every sphere of social activity. On all these grounds, Socialism is in its potentialities the most democratic of systems.

It remains to consider the special problem of political consciousness in war-time, or under the threat of war. As we have seen, war stimulates certain sorts of political consciousness, both because it causes a great increase in governmental interference with private lives, and, still more, because it evokes in men the primitive sense of national unity against "foreigners." These two stimuli act in different ways. The first easily becomes a factor leading to unrest and revolt, and tends to grow stronger as war conditions are prolonged. The second works on the side of the Government against anyone who is not prepared to make the "National Cause" his own. It is highly intolerant and emotional, and correspondingly irrational and uncritical. It confers a remarkable power of believing lies that satisfy its cravings; and it is regularly played on by propaganda designed to exaggerate its effects. It is, however, in need of constant re-stimulation if it is not to flag; and in long wars the resources of propaganda are apt to become exhausted, so that the rival stimulus gets its chance. Long wars are dangerous to States because the irrational impulses tend to wane, and the forces of rational criticism, based on war's discomforts, to wax with their prolongation. Nevertheless, the irrational forces of foreigner-hatred and herd-protection are very strong in most peoples.

War being fundamentally idiotic, Governments at war, or preparing for it, always fear the voice of reason, and do their best to stifle it. Criticism is suppressed, and dangerous rationalists are put out of the way. Moreover, war conditions force Governments to act swiftly and decisively under dictatorial powers, and to suspend or emasculate normal methods of procedure. This narrows the opportunities of the politically-minded who, unless they can be put into the firing-line or side-tracked into the Propaganda Department, are apt to feel unhappy under their enforced silence, and to break out into criticism whenever a chance arises. Nor is the method of sending agitators to the trenches always safe. Both the Germans and the Russians tried it during the World War; and in both cases it was an important factor in undermining the "loyalty" of the Army. Some Governments shoot the agitators; and perhaps that is the least dangerous course if discontent is not too widespread. But it too has its perils; for only the Tsar's Government resorted to mass-shootings; and it did not pay.

War, as it unites the Nationalists and gives them a heightened consciousness of national unity, also solidifies the Opposition. The opponents of the war, in each country, conscious of being a hated and pariah group, are driven in upon one another; and their capacity for co-operation is thus greatly heightened. That is one reason why war is apt not only to create the conditions which make revolution possible, but also to bring into existence a coherent revolutionary leadership. In normal times, the "Lefts" are free to quarrel one with another; war unites them against the State.

Political consciousness is, then, a very complex thing. But unless we understand something about its phases and forms, we can never even begin to understand the real working of actual political systems. For the machinery of State has its meaning only in relation to the attitude of those who work it, or are controlled by it. That is why transplanted institutions so often fail to work in the countries that adopt them in at all the same ways as in their countries of origin. A Constituent Assembly can endow any country with a Parliament, or a revolution with a Soviet régime. But whether these things will work depends on whether the men who have to live under them are in a mood and mind capable of working them.

2. THE PROBLEM FOR DEMOCRACY

WE HAVE MORE THAN ONCE, in the course of this book, had occasion to observe that the scope of politics, in the modern world, is widening with almost inconceivable rapidity, partly as a result of the growing complexity of modern life. Civilisation, particularly industrial civilisation, involves as a condition of its continued existence the coordinated inter-working of a host of institutions of many kinds; and while few States have gone as far as Communist Russia in bringing all these institutions directly within the ambit of the political system, it may be definitely assumed that the days in which their functioning was left entirely to the beneficent direction of Providence or private interest are gone, if not for ever, at any rate for a very long time. Politics is becoming, and is going to become, daily a wider and more complex subject; and it is a growing recognition of this fact among the thinking population which causes books like this book to find their market.

This wideness and complexity has certain special problems for democratic thinkers, which may roughly be summarised as the problems of expertise and of human laziness. A truly democratic polity should be one in which, if not the whole, at any rate the majority of the citizens play an active as well as a passive part in society, not merely paying their taxes and obeying the law, voting at intervals and grumbling at the Government between elections, but actively co-operating in society's business; but such active citizenship demands on the one hand energy and interest, and on the other an increasing amount of expert knowledge on a large variety of subjects. It has been pointed out in preceding chapters that in most countries the majority of people are politically inert and uninterested in the running of their political institutions; one might go further and say that the majority of people are uninterested in the running of any institution at all. Democracy, it would appear, has a distinct tendency to be lazy, or at the best spasmodic in its interest; and this results too often in the effective transfer of power to busybodies or to permanent officials or to pure demagogues. All of these results are generally undesirable: the busybody is apt to turn any institution into a Society for the Improvement of the Poor creating the maximum amount of fuss and ill-bred interference, the permanent official to officer a Circumlocution Office which breaks the hearts and destroys the patience of all with whom it deals, and the demagogue to become, by easy stages, something suspiciously resembling a dictator. Even if none of these extremes occurs, there is something faintly nauseating, to most people, in the sight of a "professional politician" spending his life doing something which the democracy ought to be doing for itself, and wasting a great deal of time, and much insincere verbiage, in assuring the members of that democracy that by voting for him they are in fact governing themselves. Nor is the professional politician confined to politics properly so called; every organisation of any size knows his kind well.

It is true that in societies such as our own, which preserve great differences of wealth and education between persons who are nominally political equals, these phenomena are exaggerated. The busybody, the official, and the demagogue come to their own far more easily in a community many of whose members are too poor or too ignorant to question their competence, to see through their clap-trap, or to kick them for their insolence. No doubt, a high general level of political education would do something to check the power of the crudest type of demagogue. But if inequalities of wealth and class-distinctions are to persist, no educational system will help matters much. It cannot be said of the educated Englishman, still less of the educated American, that he is particularly proof against idiotic emotional appeals; and we have recently seen a whole nation, whose system of public education stands deservedly high, deliver itself over to mass-produced sentiments of the most staggering kind.

Even, moreover, if class-distinctions were to be abolished or much weakened, the problem would not cease to exist. There is too large an irrational element in human nature for us to hope to be able to persuade it to administer its own concerns and to shove society along without a very strong assistance of cajolery and moral and intellectual, if not physical, bullying. The simple view of Jeremy Bentham, that every man acts according to a rational calculation of his own advantage, is most patently not true; in fact, a study of the political events of recent years would suggest that idealistic motives, particularly if they lead to obviously impossible ends by obviously revolting means, have far more power than rational considerations of personal advantage to influence men's actions. This may be, and probably is, too pessimistic a conclusion; but the problem of motives, of how to persuade or induce men to take their political affairs seriously in hand, remains to be solved.

It must be solved; and no solution will be found if it is sought too much on rationalist lines. For hundreds of generations Europe, as a whole, found its political motive power in the forces of religion, which are *ex hypothesi* non-rational. Most people are aware of the essentially religious nature of medieval social institutions; most know that the development of the sixteenth and seventeenth centuries was immensely helped by the religious strength of the Reformation; but comparatively few realise how large a part was played in the making of industrial England and industrial America by the driving forces of Evangelical Christianity and Wesleyan Methodism. By the end of the last century, however, that force had largely spent itself. Religion was becoming a back number; such religious feeling as remained was dissipating itself among a number of small and nugatory cults; and in the early twentieth century there were many who confidently prophesied its utter disappearance.

It has not disappeared, though its strength is far less than in any previous epoch since the rise of the Christian Church. It is still strong enough to make the organised churches the only force that has so far resisted Nazism. But in so far as it has waned, its place has been taken by a sentiment just as irrational, the sentiment of exaggerated and authoritarian nationalism. The really ardent Fascist or Nazi is no more open to argument than the ardent Calvinist; and if Swinburne were writing to-day, he would curse the apostles of nationalism as bitterly as ever he cursed the Catholic Church. It is true that Hitler has not as yet burnt anybody at the stake; but this is more because the traditions of humanitarianism which have been growing up for some centuries take a long time to uproot than because Hitler has any real objection to inflicting painful death on his enemies. Fascism has rushed in, like the seven devils, to fill the place vacated by religion; it may be questioned whether it is a much more pleasing alternative.

The Western democrat, nevertheless, must endeavour to find some motive which will be strong enough to make men bestir themselves for the common good. So far, the Russian Communists are the only group which has succeeded in inspiring a people with an ideal which is neither religious nor nationalist; and no one can deny that in pursuance of that ideal the Russians, perhaps inevitably, have made great use of irrational and even obscurantist appeals. It is true that the Russian Marxist creed has a considerably larger intellectual content than the creed of Mussolini, and one enormously higher than that of the Nazis, and on that ground should command much greater respect; but the danger of its hardening into a dogma and a ritual cannot be ignored.

It seems to follow, then, that democrats who believe in equality must find for their cause an emotional appeal which is not religious or authoritarian, but will yet be strong enough to secure the steady and continuous effort, and the power to rise above repeated disappointments, which are necessary for the working of an equalitarian Society as well as for its establishment. Such an appeal is not by any means easy to find. The older Socialists, like the early Utilitarians, failed to find it partly because they were both too rationalist and too materialist; they assumed that men were actuated by a rational calculation of advantages, and that the prospect of increasing material comfort was the chief advantage which they desired. This is simply not true. Undoubtedly, men prefer, on the whole, material comfort to material discomfort, and most would agree that below a certain level material squalor and poverty are so brutalising and degrading in their effects as to make a rise in the standard of living essential for the growth of civilisation; but men do not passionately sacrifice themselves for economic advantages *per se*. At least, the majority do not; and the few who do are generally regarded by their fellow-citizens as slightly mad.

Yet is not the desire for freedom and equality capable of arousing a devotion passionate enough to serve our purpose? If it is not, there is indeed little hope for humanity; and there have been enough examples, in the world's history, to give one good hope that it is. It must not, however, try to be too rationalist, or become impatient with those many of its followers who need colour and movement, songs and marchings and even "sob-stuff" to keep a cutting edge on their enthusiasm. It is true that ritual and rhetoric are weapons of double value—though certainly not more so than ideas—and therefore that there are certain dangers in their use; but there is no real reason why the devil should have all the best speeches and the finest processions, any more than that he should have all the best tunes. Those who would empty all colour and all emotion out of the democratic movement, in fear lest they should encourage men to put on black shirts and to use rubber truncheons, are in great danger of emptying the heart out of it as well, and leaving behind only the minutes of a committee meeting. The *Red Flag* may not be a good song; but the red flag itself is assuredly more inspiring than a banner of slate-colour.

To combine emotional strength with a constant reference of one's emotions to the bar of reason, however, is one of the hardest tasks which upholders of democratic equality have to face; and this is what must be achieved if the emotional appeal is not to run to waste or to be turned to the devil's purposes. Democratic equality does of its nature mean hearing what the other fellow has to say and being prepared to revise or to modify one's own proposals; and if, in the course of changing over to a system of democratic equality, it proves necessary drastically to curtail the right of discussion and opposition, it must not be forgotten that this is an unpleasing and dangerous necessity, and should be abandoned at the earliest possible opportunity. Not that it can ever be wholly abandoned, at least in any Society which we can foresee; for the purpose of political discussion is to lead to action, and not to cause enthusiasm to empty itself in the sand of endless committee meetings; and any Society, however democratic, must put limits to the scope of pure obstruction. But, on the whole, the inclination of men is not to obstruct leadership, but to accept it too readily. Democracy is of its nature slower in action than a dictator; but this is not necessarily a bad thing at all times.

The second problem, that of expertise, is of rather a different character. No one will question that the complexity of modern civilisation has made the business of government far more elaborate, and brought within the sphere of politics a host of questions which need both expert knowledge and considerable experience to solve. To a certain extent, of course, modern society has to find answers to these questions by employing the service of specially trained and qualified experts, whose advice, if they are not too tactless and intractable in their way of giving it, will normally be accepted by those whom they are advising; but to say this is only to remove the problem by one stage. For the expert, as almost all Societies have discovered, is a good servant but a bad master; he is competent to advise on the matter on which he is an expert, but he is often quite incapable either of apprehending the wider consequences of the course which he recommends or of evaluating his particular province in relation to that of others.

The democracy, or the representatives of the democracy, therefore, however they are selected, must not merely choose their experts but must also choose between the courses they recommend, that is to say, they must have themselves enough knowledge and experience (the experience being often as important as the knowledge) to judge between the rival claims. The result of this, in modern Societies, particularly quasi-democratic Societies, is to put a quite unfortunate premium upon age. Experience is a quality which can only be gained by years—this is not to imply that all men gain experience by years, for there are many whose minds seem essentially unexperiencing, and more who seem early to lose all capability of receiving experience in any useful manner; and knowledge, even of the unspecialised kind referred to, simply cannot be acquired in a brief space of time, even were our system of education less divorced from the problems of the present day than it is. Many people must have felt from time to time that, if a change of fortune suddenly called them to take charge of the State, they would make a failure of it through sheer ignorance of either the location of some of the States in the post-war world or the meaning of the Gold Standard or some other quite elementary but important fact, and that they would require at least ten years' education before they could venture upon it. The days are past when Pitt could confidently become Prime Minister at the age of twenty-four, and this not because the present-day young man of twenty-four is innately stupider than his eighteenth-century prototype, but because the problems with which Pitt had to deal were so much fewer and simpler.

The result is that government tends more and more to get into the hands of the aged or ageing, and this tendency is exaggerated in democratic Societies, because democracy is inclined, particularly in settled times, both to keep a man waiting for a long time until he has proved his worth and to be very tender about displacing him afterwards. It is not wholly an accident that the two Labour Cabinets which have held office in this country had a very high average age-level. This tendency must be combated; for it is apt to produce a hesitating and hidebound policy and to alienate the enthusiasm of youth. It is not contended that all old men are stupid or stupidly conservative, for there are shining examples to the contrary; nor that youth is always right, for the tragedy is that youth is often wrong, and governments composed, as revolutionary governments are, mainly of younger men, have frequently made the most colossal and disastrous mistakes. But it is better to make mistakes than to make nothing at all; and it cannot be denied either that the general tendency of the elderly is against experimentation, both because habits are strong and because they stand inevitably to lose more if the experiments fail, or that a system which keeps its younger members in virtual leading-strings or positions without responsibility long after they have in reality grown up is heading for stagnation and disillusionment.

The remedy, like most remedies for real problems, is not simple. As has been suggested, it consists partly in the proper subordination of the expert and the knowledgeable man to those for whose benefit they are tendering their advice. A good deal might also be done, and could be done in a Society of equals, by improving both the quality and content of general education, so that it should aim at turning out free men rather than factory slaves, and should give instruction in subjects rather less remotely connected with the lives which its citizens are going to lead. The present wide-spread demand for books of information upon scientific, political and economic subjects reflects the consciousness of many people that educational courses lasting from six or seven years at the least to twenty years at the most have singularly failed to teach them what they now find they need to know.

But, in the last resort, the problem can be solved only by a wide diffusion of responsibility for different parts of the social system. Men can only learn to govern, either themselves or anyone else, by governing; and the best hope for democracy is that, by diffusing responsibility among a vast number of self-governing institutions, whether these be industries, or towns, or schools and colleges, or many others which one might name, it may succeed in training up in action those who will best serve it. In this respect democracy, as it has been hitherto understood in the West, has some practical lessons to learn from Fascism and still more from Russian Communism; for these systems, being unable, from the circumstances of their establishment, to await the ripening into respectable experienced antiquity of their supporters, have been forced to educate in action local and functional captains and subalterns of the State. No one who has been to Russia can fail to be impressed by the way in which young persons, even persons whom we should call children, have been given responsible parts to play in the building of Society; and in Russia in particular, this procedure has been extended to both sexes alike. The Communist system believes in, and utilises, the social and political potentialities of women, whereas Fascism denies them and Western "democracy" leaves them half-unused. To this, as to other problems, the detailed answer will no doubt vary from State to State. But it is on the lines of creating self-respecting and responsible jobs for all those who desire to have them that democracy will in the end solve its problem—if the problem is soluble at all.

3. PARLIAMENTARISM AND SELF-GOVERNMENT

IN THE COURSE of the nineteenth century there grew up in men's minds what was almost an identification of two very different things —parliamentarism and democracy. This happened because the growth of democracy during that century took place in the more advanced countries mainly within the framework of an existing parliamentary system, and the less advanced countries mainly copied the institutions of the more advanced. "Parliamentarism = representative government = democracy" epitomises in a phrase the predominant creed of the liberalism of the last century. But in fact no two of these things can be identified. Parliaments are not necessarily democratic, nor are they always institutions of government. Representative government need not be either parliamentary or democratic. That depends on the character and "weighting" of the representative system. Democracy need not take a parliamentary form, or even base itself upon representative institutions in the ordinary sense of that term. In the nineteenth century the horizon of politics seemed to have been narrowed, leaving only parliamentarism above it. But to-day the facile identification of the three things is no longer possible.

Parliaments began, not as institutions of government, but as organs of criticism. The King governed; and the Ministers were, in fact as well as theory, the King's Ministers. Parliaments existed in order that the King might have means of consulting his subjects, especially in matters of taxation, and if possible securing their assent. As all the people could not be summoned—not even all the people whose opinion was held to count—only the very important people were summoned individually, and the device of representation was hit on for consulting the rest. They came to hear what the King proposed, and to go back and report to those whom they were held to represent. The King recognised no claim of the Parliament to legislate, or even to veto what he proposed. Consultation was a method of smoothing the path of government, not a recognition of the right of the subjects to share in it.

Or rather, no such right was recognised as belonging to the representatives who attended to hear the King's will. When the King did recognise limitations upon his power, he recognised the right rather of the great feudal lords in "Council" than of the Lords and Commons in Parliament. The autocracy of the Crown in England was tempered with feudal aristocracy, not with representation. But the practice of consultation can easily grow into a right, especially when Kings cannot live "of their own," but must raise taxes, and when the power of the subjects to help or hamper the tax-gatherer is very great. Besides, it may suit the King to play off his faithful Commons against the overweening claims of the great feudal lords; but he cannot do this without magnifying the "right" of the Commons to be consulted in affairs of State.

In both these ways, the power of the elected representatives of the "people" grows, especially as the strength of the feudal lords wanes with the passing of the Middle Ages and the development of national spirit, national organisation, and a national market. The right to be consulted about the taxes turns into a right to grant or refuse supplies; and on this right is gradually built up the claim to be the sole source of legislation. Kings use the Commons to help them defeat the feudal lords; but in doing this they raise up a fresh challenge to their autocracy. Gradually the King's Ministers come to be responsible to Parliament as well as to the King; later on, far more to Parliament than to the King. Parliament gradually turns not only into the law-making body, destroying the King's right to govern by "Order," or by special Councils, such as the Star Chamber, not responsible to the "people," but also into a body which can veto the appointment of Ministers, and finally into a body from which the Ministry must directly emerge. This is Parliamentarism, in the fullest sense, as it exists in Great Britain and in France. But Parliamentarism, in this form, has never existed in the United States; nor did it exist in Germany before 1918.

BRITISH PARLIAMENTARISM

The Parliament which gained these powers in England—the English Parliament is known as the "Mother of Parliaments"—was never a democratic body. It consisted—and consists—of two Chambers, one of which is almost wholly hereditary.[1] Gradually, however, the elected "Lower" House established its superiority, by asserting its monopoly of the "power of the purse," that is, the right to grant or refuse taxes. But this Lower House was not itself democratic. It was meant, until quite lately, to represent only those whose social importance was high enough to give them a right to be consulted vicariously, in view of the impossibility of consulting them individually. The members of the House of Commons represented, not the whole population, but the knights of the shire and the free burgesses of the corporate towns—in other words, the substantial taxpayers below the level of feudal lords. Their right to be consulted was not a democratic right, but a property right based on their "stake in the country." It is true that the English Parliament became in the seventeenth and eighteenth centuries grossly misrepresentative even of these elements, partly because the basis of representation was not altered to meet changes in the distribution of the property-owners, and partly because it was deliberately falsified at the beginning of this period by the creation of "rotten boroughs" (i.e. boroughs with hardly any electors or real claim to representation) in order to extend the Crown's influence. But the system that existed before the Reform Act of 1832 was not accused of "rottenness" by most of its critics on the ground that it was not democratic; for that it was never intended to be. The charge meant that it did not fairly represent the property-owning interests.

Even the Reform Act of 1832, which swept away the "rotten boroughs" and widened the franchise, was in no sense a democratic measure. It only brought parliamentary representation, in the "Lower" House, into line with the changed distribution of wealth resulting from the development of Capitalism. Parliament after 1832 remained essentially a Parliament of property-owners.

Not till 1867 was the first reform that implied a recognition of

---

[1] Apart from such Bishops and "Law Lords" as have seats; and of these the Bishops are regarded as "Peers Spiritual," having a heredity of office, though not of blood.

democratic claims introduced in Great Britain. The Reform Act of 1867 widened the electorate far more than that of 1832. It gave the vote to the urban workers who paid rates. But the workers in the agricultural and mining districts, and a substantial body of town workers who were not householders, as well as all women, were still denied the vote. The principle was still that of representing important taxpayers, not human beings.

In effect, however, the Act of 1867 did mean the beginning of democratic representation. For the newly enfranchised class was not sharply enough marked off from the unenfranchised to be absorbed under the old principle of representing property. It was impossible to stop at the point reached in 1867. In 1884 the agricultural districts got an extended franchise, and more urban workers were also admitted. But manhood suffrage was not granted till 1918; and then women got the vote as well as men, though full sex-equality was not established till 1928.

The point is this. Parliament came first, and developed into an institution of representative government, long before it came to have anything approaching a democratic character. The democratic movement of the nineteenth century poured itself into the parliamentary mould, because parliamentarism was there to receive it. Democratic Parliamentarism is not one thing, but two—the imposition of a democratic franchise upon a preceding parliamentary system.

THE UNITED STATES

This is the British evolution, significant because Great Britain has been regarded as the model parliamentary State. The course of evolution was not the same in other countries. The United States, for example, have developed their political institutions in quite a different way. They began with colonial "Parliaments" based on a narrow franchise as advisory bodies to the Crown, represented by the Colonial Governor, then acquired some degree of responsible government for these "Parliaments," and then, having broken away from the Crown, found themselves under the necessity of developing a federal form of government for their new State. The franchise on which the representatives who framed the American Constitution were chosen was narrow—only about 150,000 voters out of a population of 4,000,000—and thereafter the right to vote was extended gradually, as it was in Great Britain, but separately in each State of the Union, till virtual adult suffrage was arrived at. But the American evolution did not create an executive responsible to the Parliament—Congress—but independent of it, on the principle of the "separation of powers": so that parliamentarism never came in the United States to be regarded as *the* democratic instrument, or the only possible form of representation. Under the American Constitution one man, the President, stands as much as the representative of the people as the collective membership of Congress—if not even more; and accordingly the United States has never been a parliamentary country in the full sense of the term.

FRANCE AND GERMANY

France, again, went through many choppings and changings of constitution before settling down to manhood suffrage in 1875; and this absence of continuity in institutional development profoundly affected the character of the French State, destroying both the political influence of the older governing classes and the influence of local governing institutions. This made the French State far more centralised than the British; and it also made parliamentary democracy appear, not as the accepted product of a long continuous evolution, but as a revolutionary force, leaving unresolved elements of opposition still alive among the population. In one sense, this made French Parliamentarism more democratic than British, which still retained large aristocratic elements as a legacy from the past. But it also prevented the complete identification of parliamentarism with democracy that was characteristic of British thought. There remained, and remains, a potential Bonapartism in the French political mind—a potential appeal from the representative assembly to the plebiscitary leader; and this has always checked the growth of the prestige of the French Parliament in the minds of all classes.

Germany, up to the war, stood on yet another footing. The *Reichstag* was based on manhood suffrage, but it was not in any full sense the fount of legislative power. It was checked by the *Bundesrat,* the Federal Council of the German States, dominated by Prussia with its still largely feudal constitution, and based on State Governments of an essentially unrepresentative and undemocratic sort; and it had also to deal with a Chancellor appointed by the Emperor who was in no sense its servant or nominee. Germany in 1914 was scarcely past the "advisory" stage of parliamentary institutions. It had got universal, or rather manhood, suffrage before Parliamentarism, whereas Great Britain got Parliamentarism long before universal suffrage.

REPRESENTATIVE GOVERNMENT AND DEMOCRACY

Nevertheless British political theorists, basing their views on British political conditions, did steadily identify parliamentarism both with representative government and with democracy, as can be seen in the writings of John Stuart Mill; and it was the British influence, reinforced by that of France, that imposed itself on the constitutions of the new States of Europe after 1918. Meanwhile, however, a quite different model of government, also claiming to point the way towards democracy, was being developed in Russia; and the rulers of Russia poured scorn on the claims of the parliamentary States to be the only democracies, or even to be really democratic at all.

DEMOCRACY AND THE SOVIETS

It is true that the new rulers of Russia did not claim that their system was democratic. They announced it as a dictatorship—the dictatorship of a class. But they urged that, even as a dictatorship, which they regarded as purely a characteristic of transition, their Soviet system had more in it of democracy than all the Parliamentarism and universal suffrage of the capitalist States. They held this, not mainly because their franchise was in practice as wide as that of any capitalist country and far wider than that of any country which denied women the right to vote, but rather because they held the Soviets to be far more truly representative than any Parliament in a capitalist country could possibly be. Representation, they urged, is not merely a matter of counting votes, but of enlisting the active co-operation of the citizens, and enabling them to choose representatives, not as isolated individuals voting for the nominee of a party in a geographical area, but as active groups of men engaged in a common service to the community. The Soviets, they said, had emerged directly from the people, as organs of mass action for the expression of felt grievances and the articulation of a policy based directly on these grievances; and accordingly the Soviets represented Russia in a sense in which Zemstvos and the other organs of administration that existed under Tsardom never could.

Now, the essence of the Soviet is not that it is elected by industrial instead of geographical constituencies; for to a great extent it is not.

The Soviet system has created no central organ based on industrial representation for the control of industry. It is rather that the Soviet comes into being as the expression of the needs and desires of an active social group, and is therefore able to represent the group in a way that is impossible under parliamentary conditions. The Soviet system is built up on the representation of groups rather than individuals; and accordingly the larger units are built up by indirect instead of direct election. It is charged against the system that it facilitates domination by the Communist Party, which can "manage" elections of this sort far more easily than it could the electoral ballots of the parliamentary system. This is true enough, though the Southern States of the U.S.A. and recent electoral experience in Europe have shown that parliamentary elections can also be "managed" in case of need; but it fails to meet the point, which is that representative institutions should express the point of view of organised groups, rather than of individual citizens. The experience of other countries—Rumania, for example, or Germany to-day—has shown that there is a type of parliamentary election which is simply designed to yield an unfailing majority to the party in power; and there is evidence in the working of parliamentarism in Eastern Europe to show that the Soviet form of election fits better the needs and political capacities of the less advanced peoples, whatever may be its suitability to the government of developed and educated countries in times of political "settledness." It may turn out that the Soviet, or something like it, is the necessary form of political organisation for the institution of a new social system. And it may be that out of the Soviet form, through transformations and adaptations which it is impossible yet to foresee, mankind will develop new types of political organisation going far beyond parliamentarism towards the achievement of real democracy.

THE ESSENTIALS OF SELF-GOVERNMENT

For democracy, if it is ever to become real, demands a far more flexible form of organisation than the parliamentary system affords. Parliamentarism, falling heir to the government of the sovereign State, has taken over from it its centralising tendency, and its tradition that final responsibility and power should all be gathered up at a single point. Democracy, however, is hostile to centralisation; for it is a spirit which wants freedom to manifest itself immediately and on the spot, wherever the need for the expression of a collective will arises. To canalise it, so as to make it all flow into a single central channel, is to destroy its spontaneity, and to make it unreal. Besides, it results in growing congestion of business, and also in serious waste of time. The politicians, supposed to represent everybody, are in danger of representing nobody but themselves. The citizens defeat the centralisation of power by withdrawing their interest and support, and managing their own affairs so as to evade as far as possible the intervention of the State. The French especially have carried this evasion to a fine art, and have thus greatly weakened the real hold of the State power, despite the large concentration of authority in its hands. They shrug their shoulders and go about their business, ignoring the State.

This method may do well enough, among a people who are artists enough to practise it, as long as nothing happens to shake the foundations of the social system. But it makes the State weak, without supplying any alternative forms of social organisation to reinforce or replace it in case of need. The French Republic has been a sort of democracy; but it has been largely a social, rather than a political democracy, and it is ill-armed to resist attack from within, as we have seen clearly of late.

If ever a Society does set out to be really democratic, it will become so by creating within itself a great variety of flexible and easy-acting institutions, each expressing the collective attitude of some group of citizens engaged in a common service or possessing a common interest. It will be possible for the same citizen to belong to many such groups—as many as he has interests and activities in which he feels the need for association with his fellows. It is not necessary that these "collectives" should be in all cases the bodies responsible for the actual management of the services in question. They may be so in some cases, perhaps in many. But others will be organs of constructive criticism rather than of positive control. A factory, for example, may be managed by an individual manager; but there will arise in it factory committees concerned not merely or mainly to bargain collectively on Trade Union lines, but to express on a host of questions the point of view of the employees, to collaborate constructively with the management in the doing of the common job, and to make articulate the views of the factory workers in matters where the life of the factory impinges on the outer world. There will arise "neighbourhood" groups, not only as organs of municipal government, or perhaps "cells" for the choice of municipal councillors, but as bodies concerned with every sort of common problem that arises out of living together in a particular district or village or housing estate. There will arise far more than to-day like-minded groups of people interested in various sports, arts, sciences, social concerns; and in a democracy all these groups will be regarded not as standing quite apart from "government," but as recognised and important contributors to the work of democratic administration. The work of the "collectives" in Russia is a foretaste of this type of Society, which will be able by these means to satisfy the needs which Guild Socialists set out to emphasise in their attacks upon the parliamentary State; and it is significant that both Italy and Germany have been compelled, in their attempts to establish the "totalitarian" State, to establish over a wide field a bastard type of "collective." It is a bastard type because instead of being created freely from below by the wills of men who are acting together, it is imposed on men from above, as adults sometimes impose on children undesired forms of play, or an unmannerly hostess insists on organising down to the last minute the "pleasures" of a house-party.

Spontaneity in organisation is the hall-mark of real democracy. But this spontaneity can exist only within a framework of essential institutions. Without such a framework, spontaneity means anarchy, and involves the disruption of Society. Men cannot collaborate for their common purposes in spontaneous groups, without constant quarrels between group and group, unless there is a common agreement about their general way of living. They must therefore decide what the essential institutions of Society are to be before they can settle down to live together in a democratic way. The forms of property-holding, the broad methods of distributing incomes, of accumulating capital, and of carrying on the essential services and industries, must be so determined as to provide a framework of institutions within which men's spontaneous collaboration can have room to grow. Moreover, if spontaneity is to exist without leading to fundamental disagreements, these essential institutions must be such as to satisfy the collective idea of social justice. Not every individual's idea, for in any Society there will be some who have a grievance; but a collective idea generally enough accepted to ensure for the essential institutions a strong enough basis of consent.

In developed industrial Societies, we do not believe that this condition can be realised except on a basis of public ownership, at least of all the essential industries and services. For in such Societies, the private ownership of the means of production inevitably divides men into contending economic groups, which scramble for a share of the common supply. Even if these class-divisions are not the only divisions that exist in a Society, even if they are often crossed and sometimes for a time transcended by other divisions, their existence is nevertheless bound to set up a *malaise* which will prevent spontaneity in social organisation from working out to serve the common end, and will turn it instead into an instrument of conflict paralysing the social organism. Democratic *enclaves* may exist within a Society organised on such a basis, as they have existed for a long time past in the parliamentary countries. Democracy, in any full sense, cannot exist; for democracy is essentially a spirit that arises out of economic and social, and not merely electoral, equality. There can be no true democracy of Society as a whole except in a Society that has got rid of class; and class cannot be got rid of except by getting rid of the private ownership of the essential means of production.

It is true that, for less developed Societies, the problem of democracy has often presented itself rather as that of diffusing than of restricting private ownership. It did so in the French Revolution; and in peasant countries the approach to democracy has always to be made first of all by giving the peasants effective possession of the land. Nothing else squares with the prevailing sense of social justice; and no institutions will work out in a democratic way unless they do seem just to those who will have to work them. But in industrial Societies the giving of the land to the agricultural workers is no solution, both because it leaves the problem of industry unsolved, and because in practice the "emancipated" peasants will only fall into the hands of capitalist merchants and financiers, who control the market and the sources of indispensable credit. In such countries, even if the land is left for the most part to individual peasants or farmers, the marketing of produce and the supply of credit must be taken under collective control, if the agriculturist is to enjoy any real freedom. It is a moot point whether the Russians were right to press on, as fast as they have done, with the "socialisation" of agriculture. But let us not forget that the soil of Russia has been handed over for the most part not to State farming organisations, but to peasant "collectives" based upon the idea of group-management by the peasants themselves. "Socialised" agriculture in Russia is not State but co-operative agriculture: it substitutes for the individual peasant not the State but predominantly the peasant group.

The idea of the distributivists, that social evils should be remedied by the diffusion of private property and not by its socialisation, is inapplicable to the conduct of the major services in the industrial countries. It may be right—in some form it undoubtedly is right—to give every citizen a "social dividend," that is, a share in the total productivity of the economic system; but this can be done only on a basis of social ownership. In industrial Societies it is income, and not productive property, that needs to be diffused. This does not mean that private property ought to be abolished, except in the means of production. On the contrary, in a democratic Socialist Society, where the means of production are publicly owned, private property will be far more widely diffused than it is to-day. In capitalist Societies the great majority of the population has only the most insignificant amount of private possessions for personal use. The aim of a democratic Society will be fully as much to extend and diffuse private property in personal possessions as to restrict it in the sphere of industrial ownership.

Democratic Societies of the sort we have in mind may perhaps preserve some shadow of a parliamentary system, in those countries in which parliamentary institutions have become an ingrained habit. But assuredly their Parliaments will bear very little resemblance to the Parliaments of to-day. A large part of their work—perhaps nearly all—will have passed from them to other collective institutions, entrusted with this or that special task of social or economic organisation. They will be far less centralised, and far more flexible, with new institutions continually springing up to meet new needs, and old ones constantly withering away as the need for them disappears. Above all else, they will be far less afraid of spontaneous movements among their citizens, and far readier to entrust social functions to any sort of body that springs up of itself and seems likely to be able to do the job in hand. Their governmental structure will be far less tidy, and far harder to summarise in a constitutional textbook; for tidiness and democratic spontaneity do not go well together. Their aim will be to get as many as possible of their citizens helping actively wherever help is needed; and they will have regard far less to the form and far more to the spirit of democratic association.

The day of these free Societies is not yet; and mankind has a hard task to reach them. For they cannot be reached until men have set up a framework of social institutions that does satisfy the collective sense of justice; and the struggle to establish those institutions still lies mainly before us. But if that is the sort of Society we want—that is, if we really believe in democracy at all—we must be prepared to face that struggle, and to battle with all our might against those bastard claimants who set up against the spontaneity of democracy the disciplined autocracy of the Corporative State. For democracy does not drive men: it helps them to find their own leaders; and those of us who are democrats have the task of making a social framework within which the impulses and desires of ordinary people can find abundant play.

BIBLIOGRAPHY

We do not propose to include in this book any extensive bibliography, partly because the ground covered is so wide that it is quite out of the question to indicate all the sources upon which we have drawn, and partly because the face of politics has been changing so rapidly of late that most of the descriptive and critical studies of modern political institutions are already behind the times. We shall therefore content ourselves with little more than a short list of the books we have found most useful in studying the political institutions of the countries with which we have dealt, followed by a brief list of works dealing with various aspects of political theory and opinion.

BOOK I. BOOKS ON GENERAL POST-WAR HISTORY AND POLITICAL CONDITIONS

C. DELISLE BURNS A Short History of the World, 1918–1928 *1928*

R. L. BUELL Europe, a History of Ten Years *1929*

R. L. BUELL (ed.) New Governments in Europe *1934*

I. BOWMAN The New World *revised edition 1930*

A. J. TOYNBEE (ed) Survey of International Relations *annual*

S. D. SCHMALHAUSEN (ed.) Recovery through Revolution *1933*

R. D. CHARQUES and A. H. EWEN Profits and Politics in the Post-war World *1934*

LEAGUE OF NATIONS Ten Years of International Co-operation *1930*

A. HEADLAM-MORLEY The New Democratic Constitutions of Europe *1929*

THE STATESMAN'S YEAR BOOK

THE EUROPA SERVICE

Current History (New York, monthly)

Foreign Affairs (New York, quarterly)

BOOK II. POLITICAL SYSTEMS

GENERAL

H. Finer   Theory and Practice of Modern Government, 2 vols.
    1932

R. M. Maciver   The Modern State   *1926*

H. J. Laski   A Grammar of Politics   *1925*

H. J. Laski   Liberty in the Modern State   *1930*

H. J. Laski   Democracy in Crisis   *1933*

G. Montagu Harris   Local Government in Many Lands   *1926*

E. S. Griffith   The Modern Development of City Government
    (G.B. and U.S.A.) 2 vols. *1927*

W. B. Munro   Government of European Cities   *1927*

GREAT BRITAIN

A. Siegfried   Post-War Britain   *1923*

A. Siegfried   England's Crisis

W. Dibelius   England   *1930*

P. Cohen-Portheim   England, the Unknown Isle   *1931*

F. A. Ogg   English Government and Politics   *1929*

H. Finer   English Local Government   *1933*

J. P. R. Maud   Local Government (Home University Library)
    1932

W. Bagehot   The English Constitution   *1872*

FRANCE

A. Siegfried   France, a Study in Nationality   *1930*

A. Siegfried   Tableau des Partis en France   *1930*

W. L. Middleton   The French Political System   *1932*

H. Morrison   The French Constitution   *1930*

J. Barthelemy   The Government of France   *1919 and various
    editions*

M. Dendias   Le Gouvernement Local   *1930*

GERMANY

W. H. Dawson   The Evolution of Modern Germany   *1908*

H. Stroebel   The German Revolution and After   *n.d.* (? 1920)

H. G. Daniels   The Rise of the German Republic   *1927*

C. B. Hoover   Germany Enters the Third Reich   *1933*

H. Kraus   The Crisis of German Democracy   *1933*

K. Heiden   A History of National Socialism   *1934*

ITALY

BOLTON KING   History of Italian Unity   *1899*
BOLTON KING and T. OKEY   Italy To-day   *revised edition*   *1909*
G. B. McCLELLAN   Modern Italy   *1933*
F. L. FERRARI   Le Régime Fasciste Italien   *1928*
B. MUSSOLINI   Le Fascisme   *1933*
F. PITIGLIANI   The Italian Corporative State   *1933*
ROSENSTOCK-FRANCK   L'Economie corporative fasciste en doctrine
   et en fait   *1934*

U. S. A.

R. V. HARLOW   The Growth of the United States   *1926*
D. W. BROGAN   The American Political System   *1933*
J. BRYCE   The American Commonwealth, 2 vols.   *various editions*
C. A. and M. R. BEARD   The Rise of American Civilisation, 2
   vols.   *1927*
A. SIEGFRIED   America Comes of Age   *1927*
E. K. LINDLEY   The Roosevelt Revolution   *1934*

U.S.S.R.

M. N. POKROWSKY   Brief History of Russia, 2 vols.   *1933*
M. HINDUS   Humanity Uprooted   *1929*
A. ROTHSTEIN (ed.)   The Soviet Constitution   *various editions*
C. B. HOOVER   The Economic Life of Soviet Russia   *1931*
MARGARET COLE (ed.)   Twelve Studies in Soviet Russia   *1933*
W. H. CHAMBERLIN   Soviet Russia   *1930*
B. MAXWELL   The Soviet State   *1934*

JAPAN

G. B. SANSOM   Japan, a Short Cultural History   *1931*
N. KITAZAWA   The Government of Japan   *1929*
W. M. McGOVERN   Modern Japan   *1920*
S. UYEHARA   The Industry and Trade of Japan   *1926*
P. T. ETHERTON and H. H. TILTMAN   Japan, Mistress of the
   Pacific?   *1933*
INTERNATIONAL LABOUR OFFICE   Industrial Labour in Japan
   1933

CHINA

G. E. SOKOLSKY   The Tinder Box of Asia   *1933*
K. S. LATOURETH   The Development of China   *1929*

T. F. Millard　China: where it is to-day and why　*1928*
R. H. Tawney　Land and Labour in China　*1932*
Sun Yat Sen　Memoirs of a Chinese Revolutionary　*n.d.*

INDIA

Indian Statutory Commission　Report　Vol. I, Survey; Vol. II, Recommendations　*1930*
Stationery Office　Proposals for Indian Constitutional Reform　*1933*
India League　Report on the Condition of India　*1933*
C. F. Andrews (ed.)　Mahatma Gandhi: his own story　*1930*
V. Anstey　Economic Development of India　*1929*
F. M. and B. P. L. Bedi (ed.)　India Analysed, 4 vols.　*1933-4*
D. Graham Pole　India in Transition　*1932*

TURKEY

W. Miller　The Ottoman Empire 1801-1913　*1913*
A. J. Toynbee　The Western Question in Greece and Turkey　*1922*
A. J. Toynbee and K. P. Kirkwood　Turkey　*1926*

BOOKS IV-VI. POLITICAL THEORY

(*a*) SMALL ELEMENTARY BOOKS—HISTORICAL

C. Delisle Burns　Political Ideals　*1915*
Phyllis Doyle　History of Political Thought　*1933*
G. D. H. Cole　Politics and Literature　*1929*
G. D. H. Cole　Modern Theories and Forms of Political Organisation　(reprinted from The Outline of Knowledge)　*1932*
H. J. Laski　Political Thought from Locke to Bentham　*1920*
E. Barker　Political Thought from Herbert Spencer to the Present Day　*1915*

(*b*) SMALL ELEMENTARY BOOKS—THEORETICAL

H. J. Laski　Introduction to Politics　*1931*
C. E. M. Joad　Modern Political Theory　*1924*
G. D. H. Cole　Social Theory　*1920*

(*c*) LARGER BOOKS—GENERAL

Graham Wallas　Human Nature in Politics　*1908*
Graham Wallas　The Great Society　*1914*

R. H. Tawney   The Acquisitive Society   *1920*
R. H. Tawney   Equality   *1931*
H. N. Brailsford   Property or Peace   *1934*
R. M. MacIver   Community   *1917*
H. Krabbe   The Modern Idea of the State   *1922*
L. T. Hobhouse   The Metaphysical Theory of the State   *1918*
H. G. Wells   The Shape of Things to Come   *1933*
L. S. Woolf   After the Deluge   Vol. I   *1931*
R. Michels   Political Parties   *1915*

(d) SOCIOLOGICAL STUDIES

A. Lichtenberger   The Development of Social Theory   *1924*
F. Oppenheimer   The State   *1914*
Thorstein Veblen   The Theory of the Leisure Class   *1899*
W. Bagehot   Physics and Politics   *various editions*
H. S. Maine   Ancient Law   *various editions*

(e) HISTORICAL

A. E. Zimmern   The Greek Commonwealth   *1911*
B. Jarrett   Social Theories of the Middle Ages   *1926*
E. Halevy   The Growth of Philosophic Radicalism   *1928*
D. G. Ritchie   National Rights   *1903*
W. A. Dunning   A History of Political Theories, 3 vols.   *1905*
G. P. Gooch   English Democratic Ideas in the Seventeenth Century   *2nd edition*   *1927*

(f) MARXISM AND SOCIALISM

H. W. Laidler   A History of Socialist Thought   *1927*
G. D. H. Cole   What Marx Really Meant   *1934*
M. Beer   The Life and Teaching of Karl Marx   *1921*
S. Hook   Towards the Understanding of Karl Marx   *1933*
K. Marx and F. Engels   The Communist Manifesto   *various editions*
N. Lenin   The State and Revolution   *various editions*
H. J. Laski   Communism   *1927*
J. Strachey   The Coming Struggle for Power   *1932*
E. Burns   Capitalism, Communism, and the Transition   *1933*

(g) FASCISM (*see also under Italy and Germany*)

J. S. Barnes   The Universal Aspects of Fascism   *1927*
J. Strachey   The Menace of Fascism   *1933*

INTERNATIONAL RELATIONS

NORMAN ANGELL   The Unseen Assassins   *1932*

R. L. BUELL   International Relations   *1929*

LEAGUE OF NATIONS   Ten Years of International Co-operation *1930*

F. MORLEY   The Society of Nations   *1932*

L. S. WOOLF (ed.)   The Intelligent Man's Way to Prevent War *1933*

P. B. POTTER   A Manual Digest of Common International Law *1932*

A GUIDE TO
MODERN POLITICS

INDEX

A NOTE ON THE TYPE
IN WHICH THIS BOOK IS SET

This book is set in Granjon, a type named in compliment to ROBERT GRANJON, *but neither a copy of a classic face nor an entirely original creation. George W. Jones drew the basic design for this type from classic sources, but deviated from his model to profit by the intervening centuries of experience and progress. This type is based primarily upon the type used by Claude Garamond (1510–61) in his beautiful French books, and more closely resembles Garamond's own than do any of the various modern types that bear his name.*

Of Robert Granjon nothing is known before 1545, except that he had begun his career as type-cutter in 1523. The boldest and most original designer of his time, he was one of the first to practise the trade of type-founder apart from that of printer. Between 1549 and 1551 he printed a number of books in Paris, also continuing as type-cutter. By 1557 he was settled in Lyons and had married Antoinette Salamon, whose father, Bernard, was an artist associated with Jean de Tournes. Between 1557 and 1562 Granjon printed about twenty books in types designed by himself, following, after the fashion of the day, the cursive handwriting of the time. These types, usually known as "caractères de civilité," he himself called "lettres françaises," as especially appropriate to his own country. He was granted a monopoly of these types for ten years, but they were soon copied. Granjon appears to have lived in Antwerp for a time, but was at Lyons in 1575 and 1577, and for the next decade at Rome, working for the Vatican and Medici presses, his work consisting largely in cutting exotic types. Towards the end of his life he may have returned to live in Paris, where he died in 1590.

This book was composed, printed, and bound by The Haddon Craftsmen, Camden, N. J. The paper was manufactured by S. D. Warren Co., Boston, Mass.

Date Due

NOV 9'67			
MAY 16 '68			

Demco 293-5